# Fascination and Misgivings

## The United States in French Opinion, 1870–1914

Through the views of French travelers and diverse French studies about the United States, this book shows that the United States held a pivotal place in the French consciousness during the second half of the nineteenth century. The American landscape, skyscrapers, and the presence of Native and African Americans were puzzling and exotic to the French. At the same time, towns and industry gave the proof of an emerging economic power also present on the international scene. Meanwhile, the French people found attractive models of social engineering in American society: schools and universities, the changing role of women, the birth of the middle class. Even before World War I, the United States found its place in French opinion, following trends that were to continue throughout the twentieth century: fascination and misgivings, attraction and repulsion.

Jacques Portes is Professor of American History at the University of Paris VIII. He won the first Organization of American Historians (OAH) Foreign-Language Book Prize, as well as a prize from the French Academy of Belles Lettres, for the French-language version of this book. He has also written, in French, a book about the Vietnam War and the American people, and another about the birth of mass culture in the United States. He has traveled extensively in the United States and has presented papers at OAH and American Historical Association conferences, as well as in Europe.

# Fascination and Misgivings

## The United States in
## French Opinion, 1870–1914

JACQUES PORTES

*Translated by Elborg Forster*

CAMBRIDGE
UNIVERSITY PRESS

PUBLISHED BY THE PRESS SYNDICATE OF THE UNIVERSITY OF CAMBRIDGE
The Pitt Building, Trumpington Street, Cambridge, United Kingdom

CAMBRIDGE UNIVERSITY PRESS
The Edinburgh Building, Cambridge CB2 2RU, UK      http://www.cup.cam.ac.uk
40 West 20th Street, New York, NY 10011-4211, USA     http://www.cup.org
10 Stamford Road, Oakleigh, Melbourne 3166, Australia
Ruiz de Alarcón 13, 28014 Madrid, Spain

First published 2000

Printed in the United States of America

*Typeface* Times New Roman 10/12 pt.     *System* QuarkXPress [BTS]

*A catalog record for this book is available from the British Library.*

*Library of Congress Cataloging in Publication Data*

Portes, Jacques.
    [Fascination réticente. English]
    Fascination and misgivings : the United States in French opinion, 1870–1914 /
Jacques Portes; translated by Elborg Forster.
        p.   cm.
    Includes bibliographical references and index.
    ISBN 0-521-65323-1
    1. United States – Foreign public opinion, French.   2. Public
opinion – France – History – 19th century.   3. Public opinion – France – History –
20th century.   I. Title.
    E183.8.F8 P6713   2000
    973 – dc21                                                            00-020753

ISBN   0 521 65323 1   hardback

# Contents

## Part III
### The United States as Power

# *Preface*

The title of Jacques Portes's book, *Fascination and Misgivings*, immediately reveals its twofold purpose and the two poles between which it constantly oscillates. On the one hand, the United States continues to exert an undeniable fascination on French opinion; it is a fascination in which certain myths (and illusions) of earlier decades are still present. On the other hand – and this is the novel aspect of this study – this same opinion is beginning to show signs of misgivings and hesitation, even criticism and objections to what was until now considered, rightly or wrongly, the American model. This more apparent than real contradiction constitutes the originality of this study, the result of long digging in the rich loam of both literature and journalism, travel accounts and the treatises of economists, work that was rewarded with a doctorate. The present version is a less academic adaptation of that thesis.

The most symbolic example of that duality is the famous Statue of Liberty. The idea of commemorating the centenary of the United States' independence and the Franco-American alliance with the gift of a colossal statue was the brainchild of a liberal French jurist, professor at the Collège de France, Edouard de Laboulaye, at the end of the Second Empire. At the time, the gesture made a political point, which was to consecrate the United States as the land of liberty at a moment when liberty was still under threat in France. It took twenty years to carry out this project, in part because of the change of regimes in France in 1871, but also because of the Americans' lack of interest in this symbolic gift. For to the great indignation of the French, they were not even eager to contribute to the building of a pedestal, without which Bartholdi's work, the generous gift of individuals, associations, and collectives, could not be placed in its assigned location on Bedloe's Island, where it would greet new immigrants as they approached their new country at the entrance of New York harbor. When the famous statue was finally inaugurated in 1886, the anniversaries that would have been appropriate had all passed:

1876 (Declaration of Independence), 1878 (French alliance), and 1883 (recognition of American independence). But who cared? Nobody did, because in the end nothing is more artificial than to cling to historical memories when they are overtaken by realities for which the living are not ready.

These are the realities Jacques Portes has endeavored to capture with the historian's tools, in other words, by keeping close to the documents he assembled in a long and varied pursuit.

The period under study (1870–1914) corresponds to the only liberal phase in French history, a period that seems fairly baffling to the outside observer. During the earlier authoritarian regimes, whether it be the Empire (First or Second) or the monarchy (Bourbon or Orleanist), America had always served as reference, for it was a country where the fundamental liberties, those that were proclaimed in the Declaration of Independence, in the Bill of Rights, or in the Declaration of the Rights of Man and the Citizen, were always respected and honored, whereas in France they were openly flouted. Hence the popularity of Lafayette's flights of lyricism, the sorrow felt at Lincoln's assassination, and the success of the letters Clemenceau published in *Le Temps*. Hence also the role of refuge played by the United States for those who had been banished by the successive French regimes, people as diverse as Chateaubriand, Volney, Talleyrand, Hyde de Neuville, Joseph Bonaparte, and later Cabet and Victor Considerant. After 1871, once France had regained its liberty, the United States ceased to play the role of beacon it had represented for the enlightened segments of French opinion. Witness the famous American Constitution of 1787, so often invoked previously, but barely mentioned by the framers of the French so-called Constitution of 1875. Why continue referring to the United States, now that liberty had been firmly established in the French hexagon?

As the political aura of the United States began to weaken, its perception by the French underwent a radical change. Until late in the nineteenth century, they continued to consider it a simple, even patriarchal nation, committed to the virtues of landownership; in short, a colonial country, if not in its political organization then at least in its activities and its mores. To the average French person, the Americans were the major purveyors of cotton, which had been sorely missed during the Civil War, and the representatives of a society that evoked a certain nostalgia for the French sugar islands. Slavery, to be sure, had just been abolished, but the consequences of this fact were as yet difficult to grasp. What the French discovered in the last decades of the nineteenth century was a new face of the United States, a country in the throes of both industrialization and expansion.

Industry and expansion had hitherto been the monopoly of the old continent. This traditional order of things was first upset by the appearance in everyday life of a whole series of mechanical inventions from across the sea: the Singer sewing machine, the McCormick harvester, the Remington typewriter, canned meats from Swift or Armour, incandescent lightbulbs and Edison's phonograph, Morse's telegraph and Bell's telephone. It was a far cry from the pioneers conquering the Great Plains or the California Gold Rush to the great factories where standardized products that transformed daily life were manufactured even before Henry Ford's methods led to the spread of automobiles for everyone. How had this come about? This was the question economists attempted to answer in works like Levasseur's *L'ouvrier américain*. New forms of work had appeared, and they constituted a challenge to the employers and workers of old Europe.

Crossing another threshold and stepping into a domain that was hitherto the preserve of the traditional great powers, the United States also began to engage in expansion, in what some qualified as imperialism. Not satisfied with dominating the North American continent after driving out the Russians, it decided to move into the Pacific Basin, where it took over Guam, Samoa, the Hawaiian Islands, and the Philippines, and into the Caribbean, where it annexed Cuba and Puerto Rico. And the connection between these two spheres of expansion was to be safeguarded by the takeover of Panama, where the United States bought the French company that was building the Panama Canal. Where would all this ambition stop? And here was President Theodore Roosevelt, offering to help the Emperor of Japan and the Tsar settle the conflict that pitted their two countries against each other and playing the role of mediator between France and Germany in their quarrel over Morocco.

The French certainly did not recognize their America, the America of Fenimore Cooper, Emerson, Mark Twain, or Edgar Allan Poe, in the power that burst onto the stage of material life and international politics in this manner. It had lost what some called its virginity, and what others characterized as its exceptionalism. This was a decisive shift that often baffled those who had little or no information. People had no inkling that one day the French would appeal to the Americans – as a last resort and on two occasions – to help them regain their liberty when it was threatened once again, not by yet another revolution but by the invasion of their closest neighbor.

Between 1870 and 1914 the French thus witnessed a fundamental transformation of their relations of thought, production, and power with America. Jacques Portes has shown great originality when he chose to carry out a global and total analysis of this phenomenon, and to evoke the different forms in which it expressed itself during these decisive years. The fact that such an analysis had never before been attempted is sufficient to underscore the interest and the freshness of this work. In the wake of changes in the traditional perceptions, old stereotypes lost some of their force, while new representations were not easily accepted, and this was true in many different areas. What, in the end, was left of the famous "American Mirage," so well described by Durand Echeverria? Almost nothing.

These are the realities Jacques Portes has captured well. His way of going about it will astonish and even shock certain readers, for it overthrows many received ideas. And yet it has the merit of providing a faithful account of an evolution that was until now poorly understood or altogether misinterpreted. The author is to be congratulated and thanked, and may he be rewarded by the success this book deserves!

Claude Fohlen
Professor emeritus
Sorbonne, Paris

# Introduction

The 1976 Bicentennial of the United States produced many events and publications in most of the industrialized countries, and not just in the land of George Washington. In the same manner, the last American presidential elections could be followed "live" in all French households that were interested in them, just as they were in many other countries.

These examples show, if it needs to be shown, the influence exerted by the United States on what by general agreement is called public opinion in many countries throughout the world. This rash of interest, an almost daily phenomenon, can be explained in many different ways: by economic power, strategic hegemony, or mass-produced culture, all of which came into being in the recent past. Yet the United States played an important role in European opinion, particularly in France, in earlier times, even in the absence of the reasons advanced today. This being the case, it can be asserted that the opinions expressed today about that great country are fed by all the data of the past, which constitute a kind of substratum without which such opinions would remain quite superficial.

Ever since its birth, the United States has played a determining role in French opinion. It has been relentlessly observed by writers from François-Jean de Chastellux right after gaining its independence,[1] René de Chateaubriand a few years later, the still pertinent Alexis de Tocqueville, the young Georges Clemenceau, the social lion Paul Bourget,[2] and the hostile Georges Duhamel to, more recently, Simone de Beauvoir and a great many more or less famous others. In this manner a certain vision of America, made up of exoticism, modernism, and a "get-rich-quick" mentality, was transmitted from generation to gener-

---

1. F.-J. de Chastellux, *Voyages dans l'Amérique septentrionale dans les années 1780, 1781 et 1782* (Paris: Taillandier, 1980). This is the first reprint since 1788.
2. P. Bourget, *Outremer, notes sur l'Amérique*, 2 vols. (Paris: Lemerre, 1895).

I

ation. Thus the employees of the French postal service referred to over-
time as *Californies*; surely this term came directly from the California
Gold Rush of 1848, even if it later took on a derisive meaning. Also
perpetuated was another, darker image, this one of violence and fury:
Chicago still evokes the notion of gangsterism, despite the perfectly com-
mendable results of that city's long-standing anticrime campaign.

Within that lineage of opinions and perceptions, it is important to pay
special attention to a significant period that permits us to grasp in its full
complexity what the French have thought of the United States, since
much of it is certainly still present in their collective mentality.

Thanks to a number of thorough and very rich studies, French opinions of the United States are particularly well known for the period from
the American Independence to the end of the Civil War,[3] and then again
from 1914, when the two countries again fought side by side as they had
done during the War of Independence,[4] until the Second World War.[5]
And finally we have, for the contemporary period, an ever-growing
number of opinion polls, which lay out in detail everything the French
can possibly know and think about the United States.[6]

By contrast, the period between 1870 and 1914 seems to have been
almost totally neglected.[7] Moreover, in reading about the subject, one
frequently encounters titles that refer to notions of indifference or
superficial knowledge,[8] as if these forty years were a "slack" between

3. G. Chinard, "Le mirage américain," in *Les refugiés huguenots en Amérique* (Paris: 1925);
   D. Echeverria, *Mirage in the West: A History of the French Image of American Society
   to 1815* (Princeton, N.J: Princeton University Press, 1956); R. Rémond, *Les Etats-Unis
   devant l'opinion française, 1815–1852* (Paris: Colin, 1962); S. Copans, "French Opinion
   of American Democracy, 1852–1860," Ph.D. thesis, Brown University, 1942; T.A. Sancton,
   "America in the Eyes of the French Left, 1848–1871," D. Phil. thesis, Oxford University,
   1978.
4. Y.-H. Nouailhat, *France et Etats-Unis, août 1914-avril 1917* (Paris: Publications de la
   Sorbonne, 1979); A. Kaspi, *Le temps des Américains, 1917–1918* (Paris: Publications
   de la Sorbonne, 1976).
5. D. Artaud, *La question des dettes interalliées et la reconstruction de l'Europe* (Lille:
   A.R.T., 1978); D. Allen, "Modern American History," in *French Views of America in the
   1930s* (New York: Garland, 1979); D. Strauss, *Menace in the West: The Rise of French
   Anti-Americanism in Modern Times* (New York: Greenwood Press, 1978); K. Huvos,
   *Cinq mirages américaines: Les Etats-Unis dans l'oeuvre de G. Duhamel, J. Romains, A.
   Maurois, J. Maritain et S. de Beauvoir* (Paris: Didier, 1972).
6. J. Rupnick and M. Humbertjean, "Images des Etats-Unis dans l'opinion française," in
   *L'Amérique dans les têtes* (Paris: Fayard, 1986).
7. With the notable exception of the book by S. Jeune, *De F.T. Graindorge à A.O.
   Barnabooth, les types américains dans le roman et le théâtre français (1867–1917)*
   (Paris: Didier, 1963).
8. P. Albert, *La France, les Etats-Unis et leurs presses, 1632–1976* (Paris: Centre Pompidoux,
   1977). The chapter treating the period 1880–1914 is entitled "A Time of Indifference."
   J.-B. Duroselle, *La France et les Etats-Unis des origines à nos jours* (Paris: Seuil, 1976),
   also evokes "a century of distant relations, 1815–1914."

cataclysms, the Civil War and the Franco-Prussian War on the one hand, and the merciless War of 1914 on the other.

To be sure, relations between the United States and France were particularly peaceful during these years. There was nothing analogous to the alliance of 1778 followed by a quasiwar, or to the tensions that arose during the presidency of Andrew Jackson or the reign of Napoleon III. These were moments when the two countries approached but also confronted each other, although their relations never attained the intensity they were to have in the turbulent years of the twentieth century. Between the dates 1870 and 1914, which were more significant for France than for the United States, both on the grand stage of international relations and on the smaller stage of the relations between the two countries, there were few major crises, few outpourings of feelings.

Nonetheless, the scenery of Franco-American relations was not static, and some of the activity that took place upon it was bound to affect French opinion. Thus, the first years of the Third Republic were marked by a certain coolness. The Americans had been frightened by the Commune, and the French, even those who were Republicans, did not appreciate the compliments President Grant bestowed on the newly minted Emperor of Germany as early as 7 February 1871.[9] Victor Hugo, the bard of the Republic, swept the public along in his anger, which recaptured the passionate tones of the *Châtiments*:

> So now, people proud of prodigious endeavors,
> Land of Fulton and Franklin and Penn,
> Living dawn of a world, Oh Great Republic,
> Your name now stands for a step to the dark!
> Treason! to let Paris be struck by Berlin!
> To invoke splendid daylight to foster the night!
> How can you betray your tradition of freedom!
> Lafayette came to aid you, joined by brave Rochambeau,
> Now darkness threatens, yet you smother the torch!
> How can you say: force is all that is true, the sword
> Must dazzle all eyes when it strikes.
> So bow down; twenty centuries of struggle are vain,
> Progress, a vile snake, must writhe in the dust,
> And selfish acts are a people's ideal.
> Nothing is forever, nothing stays absolute.
> The master commands; he is justice and truth.
> So let everything die: rule of law, duty, freedom,
> The future before us, reason to guide our steps,
> Divine wisdom as well as the wisdom of men,

9. Cf. T. Stanton, "Le Général Grant et la France," *Revue de Paris* (1 Nov. 1894): 192.

Dogma and the book, Voltaire and Jesus too –
Nothing counts under a German boot.

You whose gibbet casts a shadow immense
On a world in its youth as on one near its end,
John Brown, you who showed to the eyes of all nations
A new Golgotha under different skies,
Exalted and just one, untie the knot round your neck,
Come and whip now that man with your venerable rope!
For his is the fault that history in sorrow will speak:
– France came to the aid of America, drew
The sword and gave freely her all to deliver a friend,
And then, Nations, America stabbed generous France! –

That the savage, given to skulking and creeping,
That the Huron, proud of his sharp scalping knife,
Pays respect to that great bloodstained chief who rules Prussia,
That the Redskin admires the cruel Borussian,
'Tis no wonder, for he sees him poised for plunder and pillage,
Untamed and ferocious; his wood understands that forest afar.
But that the man who for Europe embodies rule of law,
The man bathed in bright rays of Columbian splendor,
The man who stirs memories of a heroic world –
That this man should now crawl on his belly before
The hideous iron scepter bequeathed by a dread past,
That he casts you, o Paris, into darkness and gloom,
That he delivers to the emperor that proud country he leads,
Entangling it with tyrants, with murder, with horror,
And submerging it in that awful triumph of wrong,
That he places this virgin into that bed of shame,
That he shows the whole world his America, kissing
The heel of Caesar on his foul chariot of triumph,
Oh! that shakes the walls of all the great tombs!
That, deep in their catacombs, rouses the pallid remains
Of proud victors and the valiant who suffered defeat!
Kosciusko, quivering with rage, rouses Spartacus;
Madison wakens and Jefferson rises;
Jackson holds up both hands to be spared this nightmare;
Dishonor! cries Adams; but a stunned Lincoln
Bleeds; the assassin has struck him today.

Be outraged, great people. O nation supreme,
I love you with tender and filial heart.
America, I weep. Oh! the sorrow I feel at this dreadful affront!
Her brow was still crowned with a halo of glory,
Her star-spangled banner made history proud.

As Washington urged on his swift steed of glory,
Sparks adhered to the folds of the standard fair,
Witness to duty fulfilled,
And then, to dispel any lingering shadow,
He filled it superbly with the stars of the sky.
This illustrious banner is deprived of its luster, alas!
And I weep . . . Ah! cursed be the wretch who has made us to see
On this proud flag as it waves in the heavenly breeze
Drops of light stained with mud![10]

The effect of such a cry was devastating and made itself felt until the 1880s. The very bad climate between the two countries explains why the genesis of the Statue of Liberty was so slow. Conceived under the Empire, when the United States offered the very model of the Republic, the project was launched by a national subscription only in 1876, and great efforts on the part of the promoters, Edouard Laboulaye and Auguste Bartholdi, were needed to reach its goal four years later. Meanwhile the statue, which should have marked the first centennial of the United States, became a French Republican symbol at a time when the Third Republic finally found its bearings. Strangely enough, once the colossal work was completed, handed over to the Americans on 4 July 1884, and inaugurated two years later on 28 October 1886, the statue that became an essential symbol of the Great American Republic preserved practically no trace of its French origin. Thus "Miss Liberty," who had started out as a pure Frenchwoman, very soon became a hundred-percent American. In this manner, the extraordinary success of this gift given by France to the United States was diverted from its original meaning, and as a result contributed little to the warming of Franco-American relations.

Little wonder that the centenary of Yorktown in 1881 was the occasion of a few sour notes,[11] and that throughout the 1880s Franco-American relations were dominated by the paltry quarrel over the French prohibition of imported American pork. At this point, the two countries truly treated each other as "porcelain pigs"; they may not have had any serious dispute, but neither did they have any particular reason to mend fences.

It was not until the end of the decade that exchanges became more frequent, and that the American colony in Paris grew large enough to warrant the launching of a Paris edition of the *New York Herald* by James

10. Victor Hugo, "L'Année terrible," Poésie XII, *Oeuvres complètes*, pp. 101–104.
11. The descendants of the few German officers who had aided the Americans during the War of Independence were treated with the same honors as the French, to the great indignation of the latter.

Gordon Bennet in 1887. At the official level, the upgrading to the rank of embassies of the American diplomatic missions in 1893, accompanied by the required reciprocal measures, contributed to facilitating Franco-American relations. That same year the Chicago World's Fair was a major attraction for many Europeans.

Strangely enough, it was the Spanish-American War of 1898 that brought about a real rapprochement between France and the United States. Initially this event no doubt caused considerable concern, but it soon became clear that the Great Republic's ambitions were strictly regional. On the other hand, that Republic now attained the rank of a genuine great power, which made it easier for a country like France to deal with it.[12]

A good diplomatic understanding developed eventually, marked by the conclusion of a treaty of arbitration and by the United States' support of France at the Algésiras Conference. This entente owed a great deal to the accession to the presidency of Theodore Roosevelt following the assassination of President William McKinley. Roosevelt was a francophile, and the French liked him for his dynamism and his outspokenness. Beginning in 1900, the Franco-American rapprochement was celebrated whenever the occasion presented itself: Inaugurations of statues and busts, exchanges of professors, travel and official missions became increasingly frequent. A veritable Franco-American lobby brought together the descendants of the great French families who had played a role in the American Independence movement, people like the Lafayettes and the Rochambeaus, and writers or civil servants who had become accustomed to exchanges between the two countries.

Yet in fact the bases of the cordial Franco-American relations in the *Belle Epoque* were no more firm than the coolness of 1870–80 had been. The two countries maintained solid commercial ties, which remained fairly constant,[13] but the number of French people who emigrated to America, barely a few thousand, was as small as ever.

In short, Franco-American relations were still quite superficial and carried little weight in an opinion absorbed by Fashoda [the colonial conflict with Great Britain in Africa], by the Dreyfus affair, and by the issue of separation of Church and State; however, their positive evolution was bound to be well received.

Thus, a "stock of images, stereotypes, and cultural references" could form over almost forty years, undisturbed by any sudden crisis but

---

12. J. Portes, "Un impérialisme circonscrit," in J. Rouget, *L'Expansionnisme et le débat sur l'impérialisme aux Etats-Unis, 1885–1909* (Paris: Presses de l'Université Paris-Sorbonne, 1988), pp. 21–46.
13. A. Rowley, *Evolution économique de la France du milieu du XIXe siècle à 1914* (Paris: CEDES-CDU, 1982), p. 405.

enriched and continually renewed, at least in part, by new developments in both countries, that of the observed and that of the observers.

To be sure, this period did not bring a major event that would have challenged French opinion as a whole, which did not seem to be interested, but one cannot help thinking of what was to come a few years later. Before too long the French, both in the intellectual milieu and in government circles – and even in the secret chambers of the decision makers – would have to enter into direct and intense relations with the Americans. Some experienced these relations in negotiations, others in their contacts with the troops from overseas, but in both cases, they had to call on their accumulated memories, "the presuppositions, the simplistic clichés, the distorted images," or on the most serious information available at the time. The immediate nature of the events might well profoundly alter this body of data, but it could not disappear overnight. After all, those who had to decide or act both during the First World War and in the interwar period had all been trained and educated in the preceding period, and we know that the years of early training furnish the basis of a person's knowledge and the framework of his or her thinking. When these people came to deal with the Americans, most were initially unable to base their attitude on anything but the data accumulated during the prewar years.

> Practically all of the decision-makers . . . had been born before the century, had lived in the pre-1914 Europe, and were part of a mentality and a set of attitudes that are completely outdated today. . . .[14]

This statement shows the great importance of the period 1870–1914 for the formation of French opinion on many subjects, and particularly on the United States.

The calm relations between the two countries went hand in hand with political stability in both of them – a striking contrast with the preceding period.

In the United States, the nation's unity was no longer contested and the automatic functioning of its institutions had resumed its more or less stately course. In France, despite some major jolts, the Third Republic had acquired a hitherto unknown permanence and, thanks to the victory of the Republicans and the rallying of the Catholics, was no longer seriously challenged.

The studies of René Rémond, Sim Copans, and Thomas A. Sancton have shown that the political position of French observers was of great importance in shaping their opinion about the United States, which acted as a kind of litmus test: "The American experience introduced an

---

14. J. Chelini, *L'Eglise sous Pie XII, "la tourmente, 1939–1945,"* (Paris: Fayard, 1983), p. 9.

element of passion that was liable to upset the equanimity of the most objective minds."[15] This went so far that one author has formulated a rule stating that in the nineteenth century a change of regime in France furnished the key to a change in French opinion about the United States.[16] It seems clear that after 1870 this explanation no longer holds, since the long-lived Third Republic was bound to shape French attitudes toward the American democracy in a lasting manner.

Yet this relative political quiescence by no means diminishes the richness of the period under study here, during which both France and the United States underwent profound changes that modified their respective positions in the world.

In many respects, the United States changed much more rapidly and profoundly than did France. One might liken them to two sailing ships of the same category taking off together at the starting gun and finding themselves at the end of the regatta, one still among the half-tonners and the other among the great ocean-going catamarans. Both countries had about forty million inhabitants in 1870, a figure that had remained almost unchanged for France in 1914, whereas it had more than doubled for the United States. If the French production of raw steel rose from 0.11 to 4.69 million tons between 1870 and 1914, that of the United States increased from 0.04 to 31.80 million tons. If Parisian buildings topped out at five stories, those of New York, a tall city already, joyfully reached forty by the eve of the war.

One could adduce many more statistics and comparisons for other areas, and the results would be similar. Although this comparison is interesting in itself, there is no need to push it very far, for the two countries were endowed very differently by history and by nature. But it is important to recall just how wide the distance between France and the United States became. Not that France remained immobile – far from it – but the pace of change in the United States was much more accelerated, so that its situation at the end of the period was completely different from what it had been at the beginning.

The rapid development of the United States during these years is so well known that a detailed discussion of it would be of little use; however, it has now become clear that by the 1890s, thanks to this development, that country was able to put into place the characteristics it was to retain for most of the twentieth century. A heterogeneous population, powerful economic development driven by very large companies, the diffusion

15. Rémond, *Les Etats-Unis dans l'opinion française*, p. 417.
16. D. Echeverria, "L'Amérique devant l'opinion française," *Revue d'Histoire Moderne et Contemporaine* (Jan.–March 1962): 59.

of machine technology, a way of life marked by an emphasis on convenience, and an increasingly frequent presence on the international stage – these features can be observed almost unchanged from the first Roosevelt to the second.

How would the French react to profound change? The American example seemed rather difficult to follow; France could make every effort to modernize economically and to diversify socially, but it simply could not do it at the same pace. The notion of two sister-Republics did not hold up under scrutiny.

Yet the prodigious development of the United States also contributed to making the two countries more similar, despite the disparity of the results. Before the Civil War, the Great American Republic was an essentially agricultural country, marked by the shameful archaism of slavery, that played no more than an extremely minor role in international affairs. This made it very different from a France that had already entered the era of industrial development and was still very visible in world affairs. By the beginning of the twentieth century, the two countries certainly had different sail areas and tonnages, yet they sailed the same waters and were no longer ships of different categories.

The French would have to become used to this changed balance. To this end they were subjected to the prejudices René Rémond has brought to light in his book *Les Etats-Unis devant l'opinion française, 1815–1852*; however, these prejudices did not allow them to come to grips with the new realities. Shaping French opinion became a new field of endeavor; it might focus on the daily life of the Americans and their food habits as well as on social conflicts or the development of American imperialism. The French had something to say on a great many subjects, and it was necessary to take this into consideration and to extend the study of French opinion to hitherto neglected areas for which the United States furnished the most telling examples.

Thanks to this inevitable renewal of the very bases of observation, the United States should have become more and more intelligible. But once the French became accustomed to scrutinizing the mysteries of the future in America, would they discover them where we know them to have been, that is to say, far away from the traditional examples to which they had usually looked in the past? Would they allow themselves to be carried away by their prejudices, or, rather, by the lure of the turning crystal ball whose thousand iridescent facets reflected American reality of the moment?

These are the questions that must be answered in order to reconstitute the "global opinion" of the French concerning the United States between

1870 and 1914. In this period of long-term maturation, French opinion
was fed by a variety of channels. On the one hand, there was the regular
flood of prejudices left over from the past in areas where they could still
apply, along with new questions raised by the situation within France
itself. In the latter category were the place of the Catholic Church and
the problem of free and universal primary education, to mention only
two particularly striking examples. On the other hand, certain specifically
American events and forms of development claimed the attention of the
French, gave rise to judgments, and contributed to shaping their opinions. Among these were the War of 1898 against Spain and the development of "monopolistic industries" at the turn of the twentieth century.

There was continuous interaction between these two sources of information and reflection, and one must try to determine the share of each
in order to gain a better understanding of the alchemy at work in the
formation and evolution of French opinion. Establishing these boundaries is particularly important because things American became increasingly ubiquitous in the course of this period. American businesses,
particularly insurance companies, established themselves in Europe,
including, of course, France. As was only normal, advertisements rou-
tinely appeared in the press, giving even greater visibility to the American presence. Similarly, beginning in the 1890s, articles about the United
States from press services were featured more and more frequently in
the Parisian dailies, often without additional commentary.[17] Modern
means of communication and transportation brought about a spectacular rise in personal exchanges by mail, mutual visits, and the development of international congresses. A large number of Americans, about
10,000 of them around 1900, were living more or less permanently in
Paris and had daily contacts of all kinds with French people. In fact, the
echo of great marriages between penniless aristocrats and daughters of
magnates of industry or banking – Boni de Castellane and Anna Gould
– is heard to this day.

Aside from the great difficulty of reviewing them in a satisfactory
manner, it should be pointed out that these kinds of multiple contacts
represent a particular aspect of the study of opinion.[18] While the French
no doubt did form an idea of the Americans through these contacts, the
fact that these took place in France itself, within an accustomed framework and the familiarity this implies, was not conducive to shaping
French opinion about the United States as a whole.

17. M.B. Palmer, *Des petits journaux aux grandes agences* (Paris: Aubier, 1984).
18. H. Blumenthal, *American and French Culture, 1800–1900: Interchanges in Art, Science,
    Literature and Society* (Baton Rouge: Louisiana State University Press, 1965).

Devising a poll to probe the hearts and minds of the French in order to find out what they might have thought about the United States between 1870 and 1914 is an unrealistic enterprise. Yet historians of the late twentieth century have become so accustomed to opinion polls that they find it difficult to accept that they do not exist for the last century. Under these circumstances it becomes necessary to establish the precise boundaries of the opinions that can take the place of polls.

When it is the object of a great deal of attention, opinion is not grasped easily. One wishes that the "average French person" of the late nineteenth century had revealed what the United States meant to him or her. But one must accept the obvious fact that these French people are hard to find: They rarely wrote and hardly published anything, and furthermore French researchers do not have the masses of emigrant letters that are so useful to their German, English, or Italian colleagues.

The popular press might fill the gap, for while white-collar workers, manual laborers, and farmers did not express themselves in its pages, their tastes and their aspirations were reflected there. But then, daily papers are by their very nature unsuitable for studying a period of forty-five years, since they are not concerned with the *longue durée* and focus on events.[19] Moreover, the United States, being very far away, was not likely to be treated. The French newspapers did not have permanent correspondents on the other side of the Atlantic and for the most part depended on British press agencies. The great American events were of course covered, especially after the Spanish-American War of 1898, but interest always faded very quickly.

In the end, significant opinion about the United States – and this would be quite different for Germany or England, which appeared more often in current events – is best expressed in books and magazines, since these were not subject to everyday pressures. Here we are dealing with enlightened opinion, the kind that chooses to express itself. This literature consists, on the one hand, of fictional, and on the other, of documentary material. The fiction, which has been studied in some depth by Simon Jeune in *De F.T. Graindorge à A.O. Barnabooth*,[20] provides a superficial, though perhaps lasting image of the United States, but takes most of the information it conveys from the documentary literature. French writers could not, of course, write about the United States as easily as they wrote

19. The methods of content analysis could not be used here, since they are designed to deal with events, not long-term developments, the "longue durée."
20. S. Jeune clearly shows that the authors of novels and plays took their information from nonfiction articles and books.

about their own country; imagination alone could not carry them there. The fact is that no best-selling novel, no major stage play features any Americans other than shallow caricatures. It is true that Jules Verne presented American heroes, but they were only symbols, just like those who appeared in some places in *La famille Fenouillard*: The peerless engineer, the cheeky girl, the unscrupulous billionaire, the shady politician, these were the usual stock characters. While one cannot doubt the popularity of this literature, it is clear that they could not capture the full complexity of the America the French discovered at the end of the nineteenth century.

By contrast, how could French opinion fail to reveal itself through some 500 works, ranging from textbooks to political essays by way of travel accounts, which represent about half of the total; through more than 600 articles published in the most prominent magazines of the era; through a rigorously selected set of articles from the daily press; and through a number of bundles from the archives of the Ministry of Foreign Affairs.

This abundant and diverse documentary material allows us to measure the French people's interest in the United States. It represents roughly 1 percent of what was published, both in books and in magazine articles.[21] This may seem paltry, but a comparison with other countries puts this judgment into perspective: The fact is that the French were not particularly interested in foreign countries, and in this context the United States made a good showing.

It should be added, however, that these books and articles were not distributed evenly throughout the period. A rather lively interest at its beginning, kindled by the attraction of the Philadelphia World's Fair of 1876, receded in the following decade, only to be strengthened considerably until the end of the nineteenth century, and reaching its highest point on the occasion of the 1893 Columbian World's Fair in Chicago. A slight decline took place after 1905, as if the approach of the World War turned the French away from a country they had gotten to know better.

The books and their authors belonged to very diverse categories. Many provide rich material, even though they treated only limited subjects and their authors used the United States only as one example among others. Thus, a colonel of a fire brigade wrote about *Le feu à Paris et en Amérique*, and Marquis de Barral-Montferrat published *De Monroë à*

---

21. This approximation is based on the tables of content of periodicals and an estimate using the *Bibliographie française*.

*Roosevelt.*[22] The place of the United States in textbooks, encyclopedias, and dictionaries was proportionate to the country's role in world affairs, which was still quite limited.

By contrast, travel accounts proliferated in this period, when steam power made travel easier, both by sea and on land. Often repetitive and superficial, they nonetheless reflect a direct vision and physical contact, which are essential for getting to know a country well. Among almost 200 titles featuring such terms as "Voyage," "Promenade," "Travels Through," or "Impressions," there are some that stand out. Fresh and new were *Dans les Montagnes Rocheuses* (In the Rocky Mountains) or *Chez l'Oncle Sam* (at Uncle Sam's) by Baron Edmond de Mandat-Grancey or the *Impressions d'une Parisienne sur la côte du Pacifique*[23] (Impressions of a Parisian Woman on the Shores of the Pacific). Some achieved a great reputation, overrated in the case of *Outremer* (Overseas) by Paul Bourget and justified for *Les grandes idées d'un grand peuple* (The Great Ideas of a Great People) by the industrialist Lazare Weiller, while others were particularly rich, among them *La vie américaine* (American Life) by Paul de Rousiers, *Universités transatlantiques* (Transatlantic Universities) by Pierre de Coubertin, and *Le peuple du XXe siècle* (The People of the Twentieth Century) by Urbain Gohier.[24]

One also finds more ambitious works, "essays" on the United States that inevitably invoked the great precursor, Alexis de Tocqueville. Despite their aspirations, none of the master's followers succeeded in eclipsing him. Yet Claudio Jannet, the Duc de Noailles, and Paul Estournelles de Constant, to cite only a few, wrote important,[25] thoughtful, and complete books which, without altogether revolutionizing the existing knowledge about the United States, nonetheless opened new vistas. Unfortunately for these authors, the only work that could be compared to *Democracy in America*, even if it did not have the same scope, was

22. G.-E. Paris, *Le feu à Paris et en Amérique* (Paris: Gerner-Baillère, 1881); Marquis de Barral de Montferrat, *De Monroë à Roosevelt (1823–1905)* (Paris: Plon, 1905).
23. E. de Mandat-Grancey, *Dans les Montagnes Rocheuses* (Paris: Plon, 1884); Mandat-Grancey, *Chez l'Oncle Sam* (Paris: Plon, 1886); Thérèse, *Impressions d'une Parisienne sur la côte du Pacifique* (Paris: Juven, 1902). This dynamic young women, who ran her own commerical office in Seattle, does not give her last name.
24. L. Weiller, *Les grandes idées d'un grand peuple* (Paris: Juven, 1903); P. de Rousiers, *La vie américaine* (Paris: Firmin Didot, 1892); P. de Coubertin, *Les universités transatlantiques* (Paris: Hachette, 1890); U. Gohier, *Le peuple du XXe siècle. Cinq mois aux Etats-Unis* (Paris: Fasquelle, 1903).
25. C. Jannet, *Les Etats-Unis contemporains* (Paris: Plon, 1876), many new editions; P. de Noailles, *Cent un ans de république aux Etats-Unis*, 2 vols. (Paris: Calman-Lévy, 1886, 1889); P. Estournelles de Constant, *Les Etats-Unis d'Amérique* (Paris: Colin, 1913).

British. It was *American Commonwealth*[26] by James Bryce, which was very influential in France.

French opinion also found expression in magazines, whose continuity and regularity make it possible to follow its evolution in some detail. The *Revue des Deux Mondes* was unquestionably the most important of these publications, due to its coverage of foreign countries and the influence it wielded in intellectual circles. For these reasons, and also because of its moderate political orientation, it can be likened to the prestigious daily *Le Temps*, whose index reveals the frequency with which American news appeared. Representing the liberal Catholic milieu, *Le Correspondant* presented the point of view of an important segment of French society throughout the period. The *Revue de Paris* and the *Nouvelle Revue* did purvey a fresh new vision, but they cover only the end of the period. As the organ of the liberal economists, the *Journal des Economistes* was bound to take an interest in the United States; in fact, it was the only major magazine to employ a regular correspondent on the other side of the Atlantic, in the person of Georges N. Tricoche. The *Revue Socialiste*, finally, was the only publication generated by an increasingly important current of thought.

While these reviews reflect a relatively narrow choice, they do furnish a complete overview of the main currents of thought that affected the French elites of the *Belle Epoque*.

By these means I have been able to identify some 500 persons who wrote about the United States. Such a group cannot, of course, be considered representative of French society; yet the major fault lines that ran through it do provide a better understanding of the ways in which French opinion related to the United States.

A first surprise is the absence of very great names. The fact is that none of the great writers wrote about the United States – instead of Chateaubriand we have Paul Bourget. No great statesman expressed his views on the Republic on the other side of the Atlantic – even Clemenceau, who had lived there right after the Civil War, seems to have lost interest. No intellectual "superstar" had anything sustained to say about it. And yet the authors who did write about the United States were members of the privileged classes, men of letters, journalists, academics, and civil servants, but they tended to play minor roles. Nonetheless, some of them were public figures of considerable importance, such as Emile Boutmy, founder of the Ecole libre des sciences politiques; Emile Le-

---

26. This work, published in Great Britain in 1888, was translated into French twelve years later as *La République américaine*, 4 vols. (Paris: Giard et Brière, 1900–1902).

vasseur of the Institut; Jules Huret, a famous journalist with *Figaro*; and the writer Paul Adam, even if they were not of the very first rank. This phenomenon can be explained by the as yet marginal place the United States occupied in the formation of French culture, by the absence of very close ties between the two countries, and also by the late emergence of American power.

Amidst the occasional writers on the United States, one can make out one group of specialists who constituted a kind of lobby within the French elite. The same names appeared on the covers of many books and under numerous articles, and current American events were also discussed by members of this group. For the period as a whole, this group consisted of approximately thirty persons, but due to old age or the death of some of them, about twenty were active at any given time. Among the academics there were, in addition to Boutmy and Levasseur, André Chevrillon, Auguste Moireau, Achille Viallate, and abbé Félix Klein; among the journalists were Thérèse Bentzon, Auguste Laugel, Edouard Masseras, Mathilde Shaw, Athanase Cucheval-Clarigny, as well as Huret and Tricoche; and among the economists, Louis Simonin, Pierre Leroy-Beaulieu, Gustave de Molinari, Georges Lévy, and Paul de Rousiers. To these well-defined categories, one must add men of leisure such as Paul Bourget, Paul Estournelles de Constant, Pierre de Coubertin, even Claudio Jannet and the Duc de Noailles. These personalities were not all equally influential; some of them, though active enough, remained in the background, but all of them contributed to the shaping of French opinion. Most of them had spent time in the United States and knew it very well, even if they did not devote all their activities to that country. In this group, incidentally, one discerns the influence of certain schools: that of Frédéric Le Play's School of Social Economics on Claudio Jannet and Paul de Rousiers and that of the Ecole libre des sciences politiques on Boutmy, Lévy, Leroy-Beaulieu, and Viallate. By and large, these authors were moderates and did not come from monarchist or the most left-wing Socialist backgrounds. The authors of travel accounts showed similar traits. Most of them did not write in a sustained fashion, even though they had deliberately crossed the Atlantic in order to discover America, following in the footsteps of so many others.

The French who expressed an opinion on the United States, then, were for the most part well-educated individuals from well-to-do backgrounds – workers traveling to a World's Fair as part of a delegation being one of the very rare exceptions – unaffected by strong political commitments.

In the course of the years, as more and more books and articles accumulated, they came to constitute a considerable mass of information that bears witness to the existence of an autonomous opinion concerning the

United States among the French; British mediation was no longer as necessary as it had been in the first half of the nineteenth century. In this respect, the political rapprochement between the two countries in the early twentieth century had a lasting effect, for it was accompanied by a true deepening of French knowledge of the United States, and, unquestionably, a more positive attitude toward that country.[27]

Composed of various strands, this opinion reveals what the best-informed French observers would have thought about the United States in this crucial period for both countries. The inflexibility of French thinking and certain influences from overseas came together to renew what had existed ever since the first decades of the nineteenth century. Different aspects of French opinion crystallized around three themes that illustrate the major change that occurred over the span of half a century.

Exoticism remained consubstantial with America as seen by the Europeans, but henceforth this exoticism was that of modernism and of daily life rather than of the Indian or Niagara Falls. The United States had always furnished models to the Europeans, but now it was the educational model or the social model that was featured, rather than a thoroughly devalued political model. And finally, the United States had now, after 1898, become the country that had power, a fact that was demonstrated with unprecedented vigor in the economic realm, by the size of its immigrant population, and also by its victory over Spain.

By the eve of the war, this new United States had gained a permanent place in French opinion.

---

27. An informal sampling of the travel accounts, which form a fairly homogeneous set of data, shows a clear-cut rise in favorable opinions in the early twentieth century and the almost complete disappearance of hostile assessments.

# Part 1

# THE UNITED STATES AS EXOTICISM

The charm of the United States (and this charm is undeniable) is its exoticism. . . . This is truly a new world, which no longer has more than a remote kinship with the old.

> André Siegfried, *Deux mois en Amérique du Nord à la veille de la guerre* (Paris: Colin, 1916), p. 1

. . . what astonishes and indeed shocks us in the mentality, the manners, institutions, and ideals of America is no doubt that all of this is a premature and troubling unveiling of what will be, in many respects, the Europe of the future.

> Georges N. Tricoche, *Trente années aux Etats-Unis* (Paris: Editions de la *Revue Mondiale*, 1927), p. 298

# 1

# *The Journey*

Travel is the only way to appreciate a country's true exoticism, to discover, as one turns a corner, the scene that speaks volumes about the life of the locals. To be sure, travelers who reached the United States at the end of their voyage, on their way back from Asia, felt that "the picturesque part of the trip was over," but all the others were thrilled to venture into this strange and exciting world, where they found every proof of true exoticism.

All the travelers did not achieve this aim, for some had not properly prepared their itineraries or made do with very superficial views: They would speak about the blacks without having gone to the South, of the Indians when they had only seen them at the Chicago World's Fair, and expatiated on American society on the basis of conversations in a hotel lobby. Others, by contrast, used great ingenuity to ferret out the most hidden facets of the American reality, carefully studying their itineraries and making every effort to meet representative persons.

That is why one must find out how these trips were set up, how one could get from the dock at Le Havre to San Francisco, from New York to the Black Hills of Dakota, and under what conditions they took place.

## DEPARTURE ... RETURN

Boarding a steamer bound for New York was an attraction in itself. For most passengers this was the first time, and they marveled at everything, from the bearing of the crew to the power of the engine, and the looks of the other passengers.

The crossing was a time for reflection and personal exchanges that primed the traveler for the stay itself. It is quite possible that the deplorable circumstances of Georges Duhamel's crossing in 1927 had something to do with the pessimism of his *Scènes de la vie future.*[1]

## Embarkation

Almost three quarters of the travelers boarded a ship of the Compagnie Générale Transatlantique, where they could be sure of their comfort and the quality of the food. Others preferred the Cunard or Allen line, which sometimes landed first in Quebec; but in that case one had to sail from Liverpool or join the steamer at Queenstown. A few people wanted to test the efficiency of German or Dutch lines, but more chose American boats in order to receive the full range of sensations and a first dose of local color, as was done by Marie Dugard, Paul Bourget, or Thérèse.[2]

All these travelers, with the exception of the worker-delegates to the World's Fair of 1876, who deeply resented their experience, made the crossing in first class. They were therefore enraptured by the luxurious appointments – perhaps a bit gaudy on the American boats – by the abundant meals, except on the ships of the Cunard Line, where they were often "detestable": When all was said and done, one was better off on the *Touraine* or the *Bretagne.*

These general conditions remained unchanged from 1870 to 1914, but important technical innovations brought considerable changes to the rhythm of the crossing. In fact, by the end of the period the travelers were no longer given to marveling, for the transatlantic voyage had become almost commonplace, and so short. In the 1870s, the average time was about twelve days; in the twenty subsequent years it declined to about nine days and then to seven by the beginning of the twentieth century. In 1910 the *Lusitania*, famous for her beauty, her speed, and her size, took Georges Fromage across in five and a half days.[3] Under these circumstances, travelers had fewer stories to tell and had full confidence in the safety and the regularity of the crossings. To be sure, René Bazin was very worried about sailing on the *France* in the immediate aftermath of the *Titanic* disaster, but was reassured by the thought that contact with land was maintained by wireless radio.[4] This was not even comparable

1. Duhamel was ill and bothered by the chatter of dull American women; moreover, he was traveling on a banana boat without any amenities, bound for Havana. Cf. K. Huvos, *Cinq mirages américains* (Paris: Didier, 1872), pp. 97–98.
2. These choices were made deliberately, by way of thorough preparation for the journey, usually by those travelers who were looking for a deeper understanding.
3. G. Fromage, *Notes sur un rapide et court voyage aux Etats-Unis* (Rouen: Imprimerie du *Journal de Rouen*, 1910), p. 3.
4. R. Bazin, *Nord-Sud* (Paris: Calman-Lévy, 1913), p. 5; the author was a member of the Champlain Mission.

to the crossings of the 1870s, when 4,000-ton steamers had to struggle through the great storms of the North Atlantic, unless they sank, as in the series of disasters that struck the French Line, the Compagnie Générale Transatlantique.

Of course, most travelers took ship in the spring or summer, when weather conditions are most favorable. But this did not preclude banks of fog around Newfoundland, with the lugubrious tooting of the foghorn and the haunting fear of icebergs – Louise Bourbonnaud saw one 300 meters high! Moreover, the sea could be quite rough and seasickness was not rare, turning people "into rubber." All travelers did not express this as simply as did Abbé Polydore: "I am not feeling very well . . . I think I will be preserved though, for I am all impregnated with salt."[5]

Many travelers who returned to Europe in the fall or even winter must surely have experienced even harsher conditions, but since they were now more seasoned, they almost never spoke about them. The return voyage did not bring the same excitement of discovery, but, rather, the comfortable relief of going home. Only a rational mind like Gustave de Molinari was able to realize as early as 1876 what the growth in maritime traffic would mean: "The day will come when in the interest of public safety it will be necessary to trace on the moving waves one lane for one direction and another for the opposite."[6]

### On Board

Once they were installed in their cabin and had found the gangways, decks, and restaurants, the travelers were set for a stay of a week or two, which could be boring and sometimes downright disagreeable.

Many of them took advantage of this enforced rest to read books about the United States, often travel accounts by previous travelers, and to participate in shipboard activities. In the 1890s, the passengers of the French Line praised the good humor and the qualities of the purser Commetant, son of Oscar Commetant, whose fanciful books about American subjects had enjoyed a certain success around 1860. Beyond the thrills of the crossing, such as encountering another vessel or the fleeting view of a wreck, a veritable ritual was enacted just before the landing, when nerves tended to become frayed.

Among the first-class passengers bets as to the exact number of miles

---

5. Abbé Polydore, *Voyages en France, en Belgique et en Amérique* (Périgueux: Cassard Frères, 1884), pp. 70, 74. The author traveled in 1874, shortly after the shipwreck of the *Ville du Havre*.
6. G. de Molinari, *Lettre sur les Etats-Unis et le Canada* (Paris: Hachette, 1876), p. 2.

traveled were made with the help of little flags that simulated the ship's advance; the correct answer and the winner were not announced before the ship had reached the tip of Long Island. Bets were also made about the number or the letter on the pilot's sail. The arrival of the pilot was, of course, a small event that broke the monotony of the crossing. One or two days before the landing in New York he came aboard and took command of the ship until it had reached the harbor. The boldness of these men who ventured out into the sea in a frail craft – a sailboat until 1901 – and cruised in search of ships and the jobs they provided amazed the travelers in their cozy staterooms. They tried from afar to find the sails of such a nutshell, often mistaking a sea gull for it, and then marveled at the contrast – "a pygmy climbing onto a monster" – between these rough men and the sophisticated ship. The pilot, who brought recent newspapers with him, was a signal that the voyage was about to end; frequently all that was left was one more night in the stateroom when the ship had arrived too late to allow the landing formalities to proceed before the next morning.

The time on board also provided the opportunity to meet Americans, who always constituted a large segment of the first-class passengers. Many were rich businessmen, but they could also be returning American ambassadors, such as Morton or McLane, or even Andrew Carnegie himself, who took the *Deutschland* in 1910, not to mention young ladies traveling by themselves. The travelers were eager to observe the first specimens of this new humanity, although they did not always succeed in establishing warm relations. The businessmen seemed to be perpetually preoccupied, except when they broke into roars of laughter; their wives were retiring, and their children a true nuisance. Only the young ladies found favor in the eyes of even the most querulous observer, and some had their first taste of the "will-o'-the-wisp of the American flirt." Marie Dugard, for her part, said of some Americans who were the only ones to stay on deck in heavy storms that they were "truly the sons of that strong Anglo-Saxon race that has been seasoned by intemperate conditions and takes a raw pleasure in them," while Paul Adam was amazed by the typical American pursuing his goal with "mechanical, formidable, and stubborn" determination. The little shipboard society thus did not yet produce the shock of America, since everyone still reacted according to his or her preconceived notions.

The presence on the ship, often in large numbers, of emigrants sometimes attracted the travelers' attention. Their songs at night gave rise to sober remarks about the sadness of the expatriate or, if the songs were Italian, about their striking melodic quality. If, as might happen, one of these emigrants, sometimes a child, died during the crossing, the sea burial provided another occasion for "reveries on the social microcosm." In the years before the great waves of emigration to the United States, travelers sometimes sought out French emigrants: Among them were two men from Franche-Comté who in 1877 went to America for no particular reason; a family with six children fleeing French unemployment in 1893; some Parisian "street urchins," their faces "marked by vice and brutishness"; and a Parisian woman from the Faubourg Saint Antoine, full of jeering and truculence, who did not hide her hatred of the United States, where she would join a husband who was making a good living. Until the 1880s they might also find some Alsatians fleeing German occupation. In short, it was a group of ordinary people, tossed about by events, for whom their more fortunate compatriots felt sorry, deploring their need to go into exile.

The few days spent aboard a steamer, with their ritual and their brief encounters, constituted a time apart, during which the travelers drifted along, preparing for the shock of the United States; their openness permeates the pages they devoted to the crossing, even if they were written down weeks later.

As the ship advanced into the bay of New York, the passengers' eyes opened wider and wider, like the lens of a camera; no one wanted to miss the least detail of the spectacle that slowly passed by. The United States ceased being something to read about in books and struck the visitor with the full power of first impressions that were in stark contrast with the sluggishness, not unmixed with anxiety, of the days at sea. For every traveler, even those who have not left an account, this was a true initiatory experience.

### *Good Feet, Good Eyes*

Going to the United States was not an adventure requiring exceptional qualities but at most a little extra time and some means. Those who took this trip were not the very young, but rather persons of mature age; the average age of the traveler at the time of visiting America was forty-one years.[7] A man of forty – there are too few women to distinguish individual cases – had usually established a career and a certain social standing and also worked out his own understanding of the world. Even if on arriving in New York he had the most open and impartial mind-set, he would still reason from his experience as a man in the prime of life. And

7. The data that have allowed me to establish the ages of this sample of travelers come from the biographical sketches in the thesis of H. Trocmé, "La ville américaine vue par les voyageurs français à la fin du XIXe siècle," 3e cycle, Université de Paris I, 1975, pp. 255–85.

of course, members of official delegations or wealthy tourists were not usually young people.

Nonetheless, there was the Marquis de Compiègne, the future great explorer and eminent geographer, who was only twenty-two years old when he landed in New York on 25 December 1869 and from there went hunting in Florida.[8] Young as well were Christophe Allard, who was twenty-seven, and Gaëtan Desaché, whom his parents sent to America for a year in 1877. Similarly, the Roulleaux-Dugage brothers were on a trip around the world that brought them to San Francisco shortly after the earthquake of April 1906.[9] But for the most part these travelers were getting a bit long in the tooth and some of them first ventured onto American soil around the age of sixty. Their dean was Pierre Leroy-Beaulieu at sixty-one, Charles de Varigny was only a year younger, and Gustave de Molinari was fifty-seven at the time of his first voyage in 1876.

Many people felt that the trip would be more enjoyable if they traveled in a group. Members of official delegations in particular went on veritable organized trips. Thus the Vicomte d'Haussonville attended the centennial celebration of the Battle of Yorktown in 1881, Charles Bigot went to the inauguration of the Statue of Liberty five years later, and René Bazin was a member of the Champlain Mission in 1912. In such cases the traveler did not have to worry about any material details, was sure to meet interesting people, and did not have to deal with the pitfalls of the English language by himself.

Other travelers setting out for prolonged travel liked to stay in touch with friends or collaborators. Jacques Offenbach arrived in New York with his musicians and his agent, as did Sarah Bernhardt. The grandson of Louis-Philippe traveled with his son as well as with a servant; this was a unique case and caused him a few problems when the servant, given American customs, had to eat at the same table with him.[10] Lazare Weiller, on a study tour, traveled with a secretary, and Father Baudot, returning to his mission in the Rockies, was accompanied by the superior of the Jesuits for America.

8. Marquis de Compiègne, "Un début dans la vie d'explorateur," *Le Correspondant* (July–Sept. 1876): 302–31 and 479–96. Returning penniless to Florida, he went to New York to ask for help from his family.

9. G. Desaché, *Souvenirs de mon voyage aux Etats-Unis et au Canada* (Tours: Imprimerie Bouserez, 1878). The author had gone to the United States and Canada for a year in order to learn English. G. Roulleaux-Dugage, *Paysages et silhouettes* (Paris: Plon, 1908); he was twenty-five years old at the time.

10. Anon., *Journal d'une promenade autour du monde* (Paris: Fayard, 1900), p. 35. The author was probably the Duc de Chartres (1840–1910), son of the Duc d'Orléans and father of the Comte de Paris.

For the most part, people traveled in the company of friends who had participated in the planning of the trip or, in only three cases, of wives, in which case the account was written by women.[11]

Traveling as a group had many advantages but sometimes also tended to isolate the travelers somewhat, since they were not as eager to meet strangers. But in fact the vast majority of travelers went out into the streets and onto the roads of America by themselves.

One problem arose very soon for solitary travelers, and even for couples, namely, understanding the language of Jefferson and Lincoln. Confidences on this subject are rare, for only a few people admitted their ignorance, and the frankness of Urbain Gohier was quite unusual:

> When I landed in New York, I had never left Europe and never spoken a word of English. After a few weeks, I was beginning to think in English, and the American expression sometimes came to me before the French word. . . .[12]

Not many of the travelers had studied in Oxford, like Lazare Weiller, or learned English before they left, like Pastor Charles Wagner, or traveled with a British friend, as did the small industrialist, Georges Fromage. Except for professionally English-speaking authors – Marie Dugard, professor of English at the lycée Molière; Thérèse Bentzon and André Chevrillon, specialists of American literature; or abbé Félix Klein, translator of American books – or those who had an American wife, like Charles Bigot or Paul Estournelles de Constant, the knowledge of English of most of the travelers was mediocre. One senses this in reading their reactions to restaurant menus or to announcements in railroad stations, and one notices it by their mistakes in writing English terms. This weakness did not allow for much more than a visual impression.

### *Length of Stay*

The length of the crossing entailed by any voyage to the United States – and crossing the Pacific took even longer than the transatlantic voyage – justified a relatively long stay in the country. Moreover, almost a third of the visitors used the opportunity to visit Canada as well, thus further prolonging the trip.

11. The husband of Mme. Grandin, Léon, worked as an engineer in Chicago in the year before the World's Fair, and the husband of Jeanne Goussard de Mayolle had come to visit the mines in which he owned shares. By contrast, Georges Aubert, who traveled with his wife and a friend, wrote his *Nouvelles Amériques* himself.
12. U. Gohier, *Le peuple du XXe siècle* (Paris: Fasquelle, 1903), p. 1.

The average traveler spent about two and a half months in the United States, enough time to see a good bit of the country. However, beyond this average, there were notable variations depending on the period. Thus, in the first fifteen years, between 1870 and 1885, most visitors stayed almost three months; later, after 1890, this length of time stabilized at a little over two months. New and easier ways of traveling and the greater prevalence of voyages for a specific purpose, such as a fair or a mission, account for this evolution.

The shortest trip was undoubtedly that of Abbé Polydore, who came to America to raise funds for the reconstruction of his church near Périgueux and spent only five days in the United States, the time it took to travel from New York to Montreal. The delegates who came for the inauguration of the Statue of Liberty stayed only for about two weeks, and the workers' delegation to Chicago's World's Fair of 1893, barely three weeks. Such journeys, which could be intense, did not provide as varied an experience as the longer ones, but at times the acute observation of these visitors made up for this shortcoming. Some travelers simply crossed the United States on their way from Asia to Europe or from Canada to Mexico.

Logging fourteen months in 1875–76, Count Louis de Turenne was the champion of long journeys, methodically visiting most areas of North America.[13] For his part, Gaëtan Desaché spent more than a year, taking side trips from Toronto, where he resided. As for Madame Léon Grandin, she stayed nine months in Chicago with her husband, who was working at the World's Fair. Paul Bourget's stay of eight months was among the longest, but even so Mark Twain found *Outremer* rather superficial. In general, periods above six months were not exceptional; this allowed enough time for a speaking tour, as in the case of Thérèse Vianzone, and for professional activity, as it did for Thérèse in Seattle.

Despite many similar activities, the travelers used their time each in his or her own way. Some chose to deepen their knowledge by staying in one place for a long time, others crisscrossed the American territory as completely as they could; and while most spent only the summer in America, some gained a different impression thanks to a winter visit.

During these few weeks spent on American soil, these men and a few women too could discuss serious subjects without revealing their true personal feelings. By contrast, the purely material conditions of their journeys turned them from observers into participants when they had to deal with the mechanisms of sleeping cars, with the comforts of hotel

---

13. L. de Turenne, *Quatorze mois dans l'Amérique du Nord (1876–77)* (Paris: Quantin, 1879), pp. 390, 396.

rooms, and with incomprehensible menus. This is an exoticism inherent in any journey, but it did provide a first inkling of the surprising character of American society.

## ALL ABOARD!

Immediately after landing on the docks of New York, a traveler had to deal with the urban transportation system, if only to reach a hotel; those who wished to leave the city to go to Niagara Falls or Salt Lake City had to figure out the competing railroad companies. It was only normal that the means of transportation, the very symbol of American activity, should be one of the permanent concerns of French visitors to the United States.

### *Urban Transportation*

The period between 1870 and 1914 was marked by considerable changes in this area. In New York, as in Paris, the trams drawn by two horses gave way to electric vehicles, and steam also gradually yielded to the magic of electricity. By the beginning of the twentieth century, subway systems made their appearance in the large capital cities. This may be the reason why the French, most of them Parisians, did not feel particularly perplexed by the transportation systems of American cities. Yet there were always surprises.

The first thing the arriving traveler wanted to do, if he had not listened to the advice of those who had come before him, was to take a hackney coach or a carriage to the hotel, as he would do in Paris. He would soon realize his mistake; such private coaches were scarce and very expensive, since the drivers charged exorbitant prices:

> I must admit that, however much one believes in liberty, one does pay mental homage . . . to the paternalistic administration that has set the price of a carriage ride within Paris at thirty and thirty-six *sous*.[14]

Other travelers were able to beat the odds, but upon their arrival they too had the same reaction of persons unaccustomed to public transportation and were somewhat disoriented by having to comply with this egalitarian obligation.

In fact, the travelers were surprised, especially in the very first days that leave such an impression on the mind, to see the Americans crowding,

14. Ch. de Limousin, "Une excursion aux Etats-Unis à l'occasion de l'Exposition de Philadelphie," *Journal des Economistes* (Feb. 1877): 253.

even storming into the tramways and other elevated trains. The streetcars always seemed overcrowded, even though they were running frequently, and these distinguished visitors were not too pleased at having to elbow their way in and pushing in order to get a seat. They were nonplussed to note that "riding in a public conveyance seems to be an innate need of the American," as if that were an explanation for the usual overcrowding.

They were also surprised at the abundance of available means of transportation. Around 1875, antique omnibuses painted in vivid colors rolled side by side with low-slung black horse-drawn cars, while a small steam locomotive pulled three carriages on a narrow rail above one's head. In the 1890s, one had to put up, as Paul Vidal de la Blache put it, with the "strident screams" of the electric tramway, whose cars arrived once a minute with breakneck speed, while on the overhead rails the little locomotive, now driven by electricity, continued to buzz by. All these vehicles followed each other in unbroken succession, especially along Broadway, and Paul Bourget felt that "it is the street that walks, that runs"; all of this added up to a giddy sense of movement that seemed unlike anything experienced in Paris. This speed struck the French as typically American – admirable but excessive.

They had similar feelings about the elevated trains, the first of which began running in 1869. All observers noted the extraordinarily practical character of this mode of transportation, whose speed, relative comfort, and accessibility had no equivalent in France. Those who took it, and many did, were impressed by the reliability of the equipment and the security measures set up for its use. All in all, there was complete unanimity in praising the utility of the El as well as in denouncing its ugliness. The rails passed so close to buildings that one could look inside, and the streets were darkened by this strange contraption. Not many French visitors envisaged the adoption of such a system in Paris, even though it was less costly than the planned Métro; it was enough to admire its efficiency in New York. What was good for the Americans was not necessarily good for the French.

However, the French were struck by the simplicity and the meticulous efficiency with which these means of transportation were run. Paying the fare, for instance, was simplified, since the passenger deposited what he owed in a small glass tray next to the driver, who was not distracted by this; if change was needed, it was given by an ingenious system of preprepared envelopes.[15] Reducing the number of employees to a minimum

---

15. This system of the antitheft glass box is still used on the buses of North American cities. One puts in either a ticket or exact change.

made for less trouble between passengers and employees, which so often happened in France.

Simply by using urban public transportation, the French felt that they perceived some of the original features of American life. There were always more vehicles, and they always seemed to go faster than their French counterparts; the passengers were certainly more closely squeezed together, but always calm and respectful toward women. In the same vein, the travelers were moved by the gentleness with which the draft animals were treated, for there were still many horses before 1900. Care was taken to protect them from intense summer heat by a little linen headdress, and they were not brutally beaten when they were out of breath and could not go on. These frequently seen remarks contrast with the charges many Americans leveled against the unspeakable brutality of the coachmen in their cities. This was no doubt a matter of degree; the French, accustomed to greater violence, were touched by what upset the Americans.

The exoticism of American urban transportation thus had less to do with its nature, since trams and railroads also existed in France, than with the manner in which it was used by the Americans. In 1912, this system showed the same characteristics it had shown in 1870, and this was even noted by a visiting worker who, unlike his bourgeois counterpart, cannot be suspected of judging by comparison with the gentle trot of his French hackney coach.

> This coming and going of the inhabitants is done with the greatest speed; railroads, horse-drawn tramways, funicular tramways, electric tramways, etc. are all called upon. The last two types often travel at the rate of 30 km/hour, a speed unknown in France for these kinds of vehicles.[16]

However, this difference in the speed of public means of transportation became attenuated in the immediate prewar years. After all, the Métro, a new thing first seen on the banks of the Seine, did not look very special on the banks of the Hudson. As for individual carriages, they were neither more nor better used in the United States than in France; Jules Huret even noted the success of French carriages in the streets of New York. After 1910, French visitors used the automobile and the subway with much greater ease than they had used the streetcars of the preceding period. The fact is that the Americans had not yet been able to find a truly original way to accommodate French travelers.

16. I. Finance, *Rapport de la délégation ouvrière à l'Exposition Universelle de Chicago* (Paris, 1894), p. 30.

### The Train

Similarly, there should not have been anything exotic or surprising about the train for French visitors, accustomed as they were to a well-tested and tight-meshed railroad network. Yet the American train exerted a kind of fascination for the travelers, who associated it with the settling of the whole country and extraordinary success stories. All travelers were aware of the great reputation of the American railroads, and experiences related to train rides were among the themes that flowed from their pens again and again, unconcerned about repetition.

If all travelers took the train, all did not take the same train. In fact, some of them enjoyed very special conditions. Thus the participants in major Franco-American missions, such as the celebration of the centenary of the victory at Yorktown, the inauguration of the Statue of Liberty, or the Champlain Mission were transported by special trains that were placed at their disposal free of charge by the directors of particularly francophile companies, men like Chauncey Depew, who even served as tour guide to his guests.[17] These privileged travelers experienced neither the fear of missing departure announcements nor the inevitable mixed company of ordinary railroad cars; their often short journeys took place in the greatest luxury, complete with sleeping cars, swivel chairs to get the best view of the landscape, and free refreshments at all times. These trains rushed through all the stations, whistles blowing with all their might, which made the trip even more exciting.

By contrast, travelers who were the first to venture onto the trains of the Southern or the Northern Pacific Railroad had to put up with rather more upsetting incidents. The rails, which had been put down only recently, were laid on a thin layer of ballast, the wooden bridges were quite fragile, and the climate of these regions created clouds of dust that permeated everything. Moreover, these trains were particularly slow and not very clean:

> The tracks are laid in an amazingly primitive manner. Half of the ties are partly cantilevered; the rails are loosely screwed to the top, and the tunnels are nothing but holes bored into the loose mass of earth shored up at long intervals by timbers.[18]

17. C. Bigot, *De Paris au Niagara, journal de voyage d'une délégation* (Paris: Dupret, 1887), p. 150. The following year T. Visinet traveled in analogous circumstances on the occasion of the inauguration of an offical mail service between France and the United States; later, Paul Passy and René Bazin were also members of official delegations.
18. J. d'Albrey, *Du Tonkin au Havre* (Paris: Plon, 1898), p. 203; he was one of the adventurous travelers on his way home from Asia. In the 1880s, Lee Childe evoked the dangers to which railway passengers were exposed by the famous James brothers.

Most of the time, to be sure, traveling conditions were more normal. The American train, about which Abbé Vigneron daydreamed before he ever left France, was characterized first of all by its freedom. Travelers were totally free to choose the railroad company they wished to use and could board the train without being constrained or checked; their tickets were valid for at least ten days. On the other hand, they had to be very careful to watch for departure times, which no one pointed out to them.

Neither at departure nor at arrival is there any obstacle, any difficulty, any barrier. The station is accessible to everyone without distinction. . . . No one is confined, no one is locked in. Tickets are sold until the last minute; friends and relations seeing the traveler off can follow him all the way to his coach. . . . Railroad tickets can be bought in all the hotels, in the city offices of the railroad companies, and from certain private shipping companies. One can even take one's luggage there and they will ship it. Thus one arrives at the station unencumbered, with nothing to worry about.[19]

This was strikingly different from the trains to which French travelers were accustomed. This freedom of access was intoxicating to them, as were the rides impeded "neither by watchmen nor by barriers," or an arrival in Chicago punctuated by the jingling chorus of bells produced by the countless trains entering or leaving that great city. The traveler might worry about this "naive simplicity," but also see it as a typical example of the sense of responsibility characterizing American customs. To be sure, the freedom to choose among railroad companies was not an unmixed blessing; one had to find information in advertising brochures that were more likely to praise the virtues of a company than to furnish schedules and indicate indispensable connections.

These minor inconveniences were noted by many travelers, who were used to more attention to the customer. Things got even worse when the train ventured onto shaky, open-work bridges, unprotected by railings, and sometimes built right above the water, as was the case on Lake Pontchartrain. The freedom of the railroad companies seemed to ignore common sense. Accidents, in fact, seemed almost normal in such an environment, but it is impossible to separate out those who considered American trains as safe as European ones from those who found them much inferior.[20]

19. L. Simonin, *Le monde américain* (Paris: Hachette, 1877), p. 373. This engineer devoted a substantial chapter to the American railroads, which he studied in all of their aspects. So did other authors, among them E. Malézieux in 1870, I. Eggermont in 1876, Léo Clarétie in 1893, and J. Huret in 1901.
20. This was a recurring debate in the *Journal des Economistes*, which, generally favorable to the United States, endeavored to arrive at more detailed comparisons.

Whatever the effects of this freedom, it did permit the development of a network of railroads over the entire continent, doing it better, many observers felt, than the state could have done by arbitrating among a number of super-powerful companies, as in France. Excesses were frequent, and frenetic competition led to unnecessary lines and the duplication of existing networks, all of which may account for the recession of 1907. But then, most travelers were unlikely to concern themselves with such matters, full of admiration as they were for a system that seemed to function beautifully, although they kept wondering whether it would do as well in France.

For the French traveler the American train was also characterized by its comfort, and the reality seemed to outstrip even the dream instilled by reading *Around the World in Eighty Days*. As soon as a French visitor saw the coach, as soon as he boarded it, he was struck by its size, much greater than those he was used to; by the absence of compartments, which gave the impression of spaciousness; by the easy circulation that ensued from this configuration; by the large swivel chairs; by the presence of lavatories and heaters at each end of the coaches. When he had taken his seat, he was astonished to see a young vendor come by with playing cards, oranges, combs, and a whole array of other objects, as well as newspapers and magazines. Truly, nothing was lacking, and the travelers enjoyed the luxury that surrounded them, even if it was a bit gaudy at times.

This first impression was conveyed by the basic railroad coach, but many travelers were soon less than pleased with the rather mixed company in the one-class coach, on which everyone commented, and with the noise and confusion that often reigned there. They learned that a slight surcharge – only $1.50 or $2.00 – would give them access to the famous Pullman car, where they would find even better accommodations. Actually, all the travelers, including the worker-delegates, had the run of these salon cars, whether they were authentic Pullman or other Silver or Wagner cars. Here, instead of wicker chairs, they found richly ornamented velvet seats along with well-waxed woodwork and gleaming copper. A black attendant in a white vest – and the contrast of colors was always striking – took care of one's every need. Moreover, these sumptuous conveyances could be turned into sleeping cars with the flick of a wrist. At night, the black attendant on duty untied a few straps, turned a variety of handles, and the upper bunks came down from the ceiling while the seats became the lower bunks; curtains covered the windows, and heavy curtains protected the traveler's privacy: "This is marvelous! . . . Not one bit of space is wasted; it is designed like the backstage in a theater and runs as smoothly as the inside of a watch."[21] As a special advantage, these "vestibule cars" had at each end a platform, where one could smoke while admiring the often spectacular landscape.

These arrangements were altogether extraordinary, and every traveler was pleased to discover them in turn. What a difference from the French coaches, which were so much smaller and lacked all of these remarkable amenities.

Yet they did raise a few questions, particularly about the one-class coach. Was it not touted as a prime example of American egalitarianism, even though the Pullman, however accessible, was in fact the equivalent of a first-class coach and off-limits to black passengers? Many of the travelers asked themselves whether there were not three classes after all, just as there were in France, namely, the ordinary coaches, the Pullman, and a third one reserved for the "Negroes." From this perspective, the difference with France was no longer as great as it had looked at first sight, and the proclaimed equality looked rather like hypocrisy.

Moreover, despite the screen furnished by the palatial coaches, the French travelers found the mixed company hard to take. During the day they had to put up with the more or less civil manners of their American fellow-travelers – and in the West the spittoon was particularly feared – but they also enjoyed the company of young misses, to whom they were glad to give a few French lessons. Meanwhile, a steady stream of passengers, conductors, and vendors came through the center aisle.

In the evening, they had to face the challenge of undressing, since persons of different sex were separated only by a curtain. These dormitories sometimes seemed "more comical than comfortable," since passengers had to go through all kinds of contortions to hoist themselves onto their bunk. In the morning, men and women in slight attire lined up in front of the lavatories, which often consisted of one small hanging bucket. The vast majority of the travelers found these conditions picturesque rather than bothersome; the contacts between the sexes were easy and natural, and no madonna seems to have haunted these sleeping cars. To be sure, the morning wash was brief, but it was certainly better than the complete absence of facilities on French trains. To be sure, the stove could be dangerous, but it was preferable to railroad cars without any heat at all. To be sure, the black attendant was not always very refined, especially in the West, but he knew how to do a very thorough dusting job with his horsehair broom, and he might even hand you a fresh rose at dinnertime.

21. G. Sauvin, *Autour de Chicago* (Paris: Plon, 1893), p. 191.

I must confess that this flower, given to me by a very black man in the middle of winter deep in the snow-covered American steppe, as my dining car speeded along at sixty miles an hour, absolutely amazed me.[22]

The services offered by the different companies varied and some of the travelers did not experience this "opulent luxury"; they remembered slow, dirty, and rather uncomfortable trains everywhere but in the East. Others, the chronic complainers, found the reputation of the Pullmans exaggerated, the bunks too big or too hard, and the lack of privacy altogether unbearable.[23] Yet, all in all, the French were delighted with the American trains.

This fairly widespread enthusiasm did not mean, however, that they would have liked to see these large coaches with a central aisle and these mixed bunks adopted in France. The French, feeling a need for more distinctions, were not made for this "mixing of classes," even on a relatively small scale. Being able to drink and eat – badly – on the train was no compensation. By contrast, they felt that the elementary comforts, such as lavatories and heating, could easily be adapted to French trains, although individual compartments should under no circumstances be abandoned, and the substructures should be built with unchanged care. Enviable though they were, the American railroad cars remained exotic; and in this they matched the famous eight-wheeled locomotive with its formidable cow-catcher – often compared to a plowshare – and topped by its flared smokestack to which a big rectangular lantern was attached. But even this machine provided a little room for comfort: The engineer's booth was completely glassed in and not exposed to the elements as in France.

In any case, many excessive features – "no precautions against catastrophes . . . in this independent-minded country where everyone looks out for his own safety"[24] – made the French reluctant to pursue all too servile an imitation of the American ways of running a railroad. It should be added that it was only very recently that the French railroad adopted the center-aisle car, free access to platforms, and flexibility in the sale and validity of tickets, as well as vendors selling drinks, food, and small trinkets. Travelers of the late nineteenth century had every reason to find this type of setup convenient and efficient, but nonetheless exotic.

---

22. C. Berie-Mariott, *Un Parisien au Mexique* (Paris: Dentu, 1886), pp. 366–67.
23. P. Saunière, *A travers l'Amérique* (Paris: Dentu, 1884). This snobbish author, who had come by private boat, criticized just about everything. E. d'Eichtal, "Quelques notes d'un voyage aux Etats-Unis," *Annales de Sciences Politiques* 24 (1906): 206; as president of a French railroad company, he could not possibly be impartial.
24. M. Dugard, *La société américaine* (Paris: Hachette, 1896), p. 117.

## AT THE TABLE

French travelers who crossed the Atlantic did not do so for reasons of gastronomy, any more than they do now; it was a foregone conclusion that the food was bad in Anglo-Saxon countries and that the Americans could not possibly do better than the English.[25] Yet the length of their stays and the keen interest of French people for everything connected with food inevitably caused many of them to devote part of their account to the food they willy-nilly had to swallow. Their stomachs still shuddered at the memory, *horresco referens*.

### Altogether Negative Judgments

After the splendid feasts on shipboard, the shock of the first American meals was particularly harsh. Sometimes it took a little while before the traveler could even evoke the experience:

> At the very thought of telling about my gastric misfortunes or praising the talents of some French Vatel established in America, the shade of Brillat Savarin rose up before this modest traveler: I knew that our renowned gourmet had lived in the United States and spent three years in New York. But I owe to the few French-trained chefs I had occasion to appreciate over there the grateful testimony of a Parisian stomach that was repeatedly saved from shipwreck by them.[26]

Throughout the period, and coming from every milieu, opinions about American cuisine were disastrous. Actually the Baedeker guide had already given warning in its 1905 edition: "Nor will American cuisine be to the taste of the newcomer." To be sure, the members of the workers' delegation were sometimes struck by the copiousness and the quality of the food served to their American counterparts in certain factories, but they had reservations about the way it was prepared. In this area, one can speak of a true French consensus all along the social scale.

This convergence of opinions was in part brought about by the nature of the contacts with American cuisine. These took place essentially within the framework of restaurants. The establishments varied greatly, ranging from the famous Delmonico's or Hoffman's House in New York, not to forget the Hotel Martin where one could celebrate a reunion with French

---

25. This section is essentially taken from my article "Huitres frites, ice-cream et eau glacée," *Revue Française d'Etudes Américaines* 27/28 (Feb. 1986): 16–36.
26. M. Baudouin, *La médecine transatlantique* (Paris: Imprimerie Nationale, 1894), pp. 114–15.

cuisine before taking the ship home, to the greasy spoons of the West. The fact is that except in some major cities all that was available were very ordinary restaurants, with the railroad stations in the West inspiring particular fear and trembling – "Coffee, pork chops, French fries" – and it could get even worse.

### Strange Ways and Customs

Before one could even begin to eat, one had to face certain strange ways of doing things. The hungry traveler had to deal with the "American plan." The hotel business was run in one of two ways, at least in big cites; either on the "European plan" or the "American plan." In the first case, the guest paid only for the room and could eat wherever he liked; in the second and more frequent case, he paid a set price for the room plus three meals a day – breakfast, dinner, and supper – to be taken at a fixed time. The price, $2.00 to $6.00, for this full board was attractive, but there was no reduction if one of the meals was not taken at the hotel; and if due to unforeseen circumstances a hapless traveler arrived outside the fixed mealtime and was not served, he was bound to curse these American ways and customs. Worse and more of it, the menu could list as many as fifty dishes in a terminology that baffled the French traveler whose English was rudimentary. Yet in most towns there was no choice, and the traveler had to put up with all these bizarre practices.

Everywhere, in the East as in the West, the service also nonplussed the French traveler. The serving staff was often much too small, and perhaps this was the reason why all the meals were served at the same time under the American plan, but above all it was most unusual. For in the Eastern cities one was practically always served by blacks, and in the West, by girls! Black waiters were a surprising sight, especially because they were often the first blacks with whom the French came in contact – and that at their very first American meals; and French servant girls were rarely seen carrying a tray, except perhaps in the roughest country inns.

Some of the travelers felt that all the black waiters looked alike, with their shiny skin and their rolling eyes; they were described as casual and even insolent, but ever so picturesque. Others, writing both in 1876 and in 1905, felt ". . . a certain embarrassment in seeing a black man deciding to do what a white man would not wish to do at any price," or even had to "overcome a certain repugnance at being served by them."[27]

---

27. J. Leclercq, *Un été en Amérique: de l'Atlantique aux Montagnes Rocheuses* (Paris: Plon, 1877), p. 35. This is a curious comment to make, considering that in France all waiters were white; see also d'Eichtal, "Quelques notes."

The girls who waited tables in the small towns of the West also distracted the travelers from what was on their plates. While some found the fresh and pink complexion of these girls touching, most noted sadly: "A usually homely girl stands before you looking severe." These poor girls were described as austere and disagreeable, completely lacking the charm of the pretty servant girls in popular novels. Pierre de Coubertin, who can hardly be suspected of a basically anti-American attitude, summarized a general opinion as follows:

> At the hotel, we are served at table by . . . "duchesses," except that nowhere in the world would one find such haughty, rude, and perfectly insufferable duchesses. Their brusque tone, their disgusted demeanor, their insolent glances, and their constant mocking make these American waitresses a veritable nightmare for the traveler who leaves the big cities and ventures out into the sticks.[28]

Observing the American customers was also worrisome:

> These people ate as if they were doing a job, with a kind of compunction and in purposeful silence; they assumed a solemn air and cast hostile looks at their neighbors. There is a vast gulf between our appetite and theirs. We only appreciate a good meal in the company of a certain number of chosen and agreeable fellow diners, but the Americans do not like to talk during the meal and therefore eat all the more.[29]

In fact, one finds quite a few remarks about the huge appetites, not to say gluttony, of the Americans. They ate too much, and too fast, and the clever Baron de Mandat-Grancey found that the eagle had a great deal in common with the people of the country whose symbol it was. Like the people, he said, "it feeds constantly yet never gets fat."[30] The speed with which the Americans ate was without question one of the things that most shocked the French, for it went against their very notion of what a meal should be. How could a man make do with a sandwich wolfed down standing up or with some "awful ready-made meal"?

### *But One Has to Eat*

If the reception was not very reassuring, neither was the food, starting first thing in the morning. For as in England, the sacrosanct breakfast was a full meal, and it certainly baffled the French:

---

28. P. de Coubertin, *Universités transatlantiques* (Paris: Hachette, 1890), p. 120.
29. D. Bonnaud, *D'océan à océan* (Paris: Ollendorf, 1897), pp. 38–39.
30. E. de Mandat-Grancey, *Dans les Montagnes Rocheuses* (Paris: Plon, 1884), p. 146. This remark documents an evolution: The Americans still eat fast, but they have not stayed thin.

Oh! for a French stomach, right after arriving in America, the *breakfast* is
not always easy to digest. Getting up and having to swallow eggs, a good
beefsteak and potatoes, with or without oatmeal or hot rolls, is not an easy
job if all the help you get is water that is always ice cold. Many can't take
it.[31]

This reticence had to do with the copiousness of these morning menus,
and especially with the oatmeal and the hot rolls, the omnipresent butter,
and the ice water. Hard to digest and of doubtful taste, these ingredients
were basic to the American breakfast. Pierre de Coubertin claimed that
oatmeal porridge was actually one of the ingredients that made the true
American. Nonetheless, breakfast did bring some nice discoveries, such as
buckwheat pancakes and maple syrup, which delighted the palates of the
most attentive observers and improved their morale for starting the day.

With this heavy ballast, the traveler could face the other meals of the
day. The noonday lunch was considered a simple snack taken on the run:
different kinds of sandwiches washed down with some dubious beverage
or the eternal ice water, and occasionally something original:

The favorite dish seems to be soft-boiled eggs, but I have never seen anything more repulsive than the way they eat them. The waiter brings them
already broken up in a glass. Then one adds salt, pepper, cayenne and condiments of all kinds, and swallows that dreadful mélange.[32]

The French traveler thus continually had to face "indigestible
amalgams" or the invariably tough and overdone grilled meat of the railroad stations. The most savvy knew how to avoid these shoals and sub-
stituted fruit, which on the whole they found delicious and healthful:
". . . at every snack bar and in every dining car, the freshness of the lightly
browned baked apple with its rich, crackled skin is a boon to the tired
traveler."[33]

Finally, it was at dinnertime that the travelers became acquainted with
all the resources and all the tricks of American cooking. One of the first
trials was to see all the dishes of the American-plan dinner arrive at the
table at the same time; often this was an undefinable piece of meat,
served in a large portion and accompanied by many small dishes con-
taining a variety of other ingredients. Referred to by some as "doll
plates," by others as "bird baths," these dishes were filled with a veritable

31. Boudoin, *La médecine transatlantique*.
32. E. de Mandat-Grancey, *En visite chez l'Oncle Sam* (Paris: Plon, 1885), p. 50.
33. P. Estournelles de Constant, *Les Etats-Unis d'Amérique* (Paris: Colin, 1913), p. 120.
    Most of the French travelers admired the abundance and variety of American fruits,
    and only a few complained that they were beautiful but tasteless.

mosaic of foods, including corn, tomatoes, melons, and "small piles" of potatoes. The desserts were brought in at the same time, so that sweet and savory, hot and cold were mixed; there was no real bread, and it was a miracle if a knife cut properly. Aside from ice water, all there was to drink was coffee and milk. One can well believe that all of this frightened the hungry French traveler, but watching a respectable American neighbor in order to find out how to handle things was no help:

> He had begun by taking a slice of bacon, which he carefully cut into small pieces; to this he added a little cream, some asparagus tips, a poached egg, raw tomatoes, the juice of a stewed peach, and a great deal of pepper and salt. Then he poured on black molasses and ate the whole thing with an air of lively satisfaction. It was a dreadful sight.[34]

Matters became even more complicated when the traveler found on the bottom of one of these little dishes products that were unusual, to say the least, but typically American. One of these was Indian corn, which was found everywhere in various forms, either grilled or boiled; slathered with butter, it was delicious, of course; but what kind of gastronomy was it to "nibble like a squirrel," sometimes right in the street? More surprising still was what one could see around 1900 in Seattle, a food cart consisting of "a gas burner in a glass case formed like a reliquary, where kernels of corn dusted with sugar are being roasted." A Frenchwoman had just discovered what later came to be called "popcorn."

Seafood was not specifically American, but the manner in which it was consumed did not appeal. Abbé Vigneron remembered an "awful clam soup," whereas Louis Philippe's grandson loved a dish of "huge oysters in milk soup"; but the most astonishing thing was to find oysters at every street corner, in bars, on small carts, stored in ice and even in their shells in barrels from which they were taken to be served in the most bizarre ways, fried, creamed, in sandwiches, or as a *cocktail*!

Even more novel was the Californian "grape nut," which so pleased Thérèse, before Jules Huret called it by its correct name of "grapefruit."

Equally strange to French habits was the Americans' immoderate taste for sweets; pastry shops and ice cream parlors were not frequented only by young girls:

> If at home we saw a workman go into a pastry shop to have a coffee éclair, he would be ridiculed; in Frisco this happens all the time. It is true that a coffee éclair is better for him than a glass of absinthe.[35]

34. Mandat-Grancey, *Dans les Montagnes*, pp. 8–9.
35. D'Albrey, *Du Tonkin au Havre*, p. 182.

Georges N. Tricoche, who lived in the States, could not get over the quantities of sweets and desserts to be found in the worker's lunch bucket.

For their part, the travelers also came to consume sweet desserts at every meal: creams, pies, and especially the inevitable cake and ice cream. Many people were tired of apple pie, "that unavoidable cinnamon-flavored dessert"; by contrast, ice cream was an absolute discovery. The stalwart Abbé Polydore longingly looked at this frozen delight one Fourth of July but did not give in to this temptation, sharpened though it was by the fearful summer heat. Urbain Gohier or Paul Adam were more audacious when, after many other visitors, they discovered this "national delicacy, which looks like a slice of multicolored soap but tastes delicious and is cold in the mouth."[36] This was one of the few American products that found grace in French eyes, and especially mouths, even though some grouchy folks felt that the resemblance to soap was not only visual.

More generally, all the travelers were astounded by the Americans' constant use of ice: "From pure water to the famous ice cream, everything is frozen and ice cold on the other side of the Atlantic," a situation that seemed enviable to a dentist, who would have liked to see this in France.

By contrast, French travelers were in desperate shape when it came to choosing a beverage for their meal. Recriminations against the everlasting ice water were heard from all sides; it was sometimes dirty and often considered bad for one's health and teeth, but what really bothered the visitors was its inexorable character. By the end of the trip, the gesture of the waiter who placed a glass dripping with condensation on the table even before the customer had ordered provoked one traveler's unrestrained irritation. This reaction was particularly strong because the other available beverages were equally unattractive. There was coffee, a vague liquid made from "some ground-up grains," there was tea, and there was milk. All of this was brought with the meal and inevitably cold by the time the diner felt like drinking it. Actually, the presence of milk was noted with both surprise and indignation: "Men drinking milk!"

At the beginning of the journey, many visitors rebelled against this regime and tried to find wine to give some class to these lugubrious meals. In New York and in a few large cities a bottle of French wine was sometimes available; it would be very expensive and the French diner

36. Gohier, *Le peuple du XXe siècle*, p. 5, associates ice-cream with the English tongue, but this formulation is Paul Adam's *Vues d'Amérique* (Paris: Ollendorf, 1906), p. 99.

was rarely allowed to consume it in the hotel dining room. If he was, he had to brave the indignant astonishment of the other guests. Most trains and many states were altogether "dry." Not until one reached California could one finally taste local wine. The few opinions that were expressed were divided; even though it was not comparable to French wine, the wine of California was nonetheless appreciated.

All in all, the Americans' attitude toward alcohol was judged to be thoroughly hypocritical. To be sure, they did not drink with their meals, but what were they doing in bars at noon, other than taking their disgusting sandwiches and their overly spiced meat with cocktails, "horrible mixtures...made with gin, bitters, and seltzer water." However critical the French travelers were of this cant and of the mediocre quality of the local whiskey, it is intriguing to note that many of them went to these bars and tried these drinks. If the Americans had been as virtuous as they claimed to be, it would have been almost impossible to survive in their country without any alcoholic beverages at all.

### Gastronomic Adventures

Certain adventuresome personalities were able to avoid the culinary *via dolorosa* of the ordinary restaurant. This was the case of those, about half a dozen, who went to the Far West, living among the cowboys. These travelers were unanimous in denouncing the absolute reign of canned goods in the food of these regions. Flour, canned beans, and cans of pork from the slaughterhouses of Chicago were the basic food; nothing there to please the palate. Moreover, empty cans were strewn along the approaches to every house. Whenever a hunter brought back some "antelope" or deer, it was immediately dressed with lard from Chicago.

Thus Baron de Mandat-Grancey, who spent time in the Black Hills of Dakota in 1883, was pursued from house to house by the "infernal smell" of bacon and the potatoes fried in it. He asked about it and learned that there was no local butcher shop, and therefore no fresh meat; increasingly worried, he also realized that around these farms there were neither vegetable gardens nor poultry yards. Totally discouraged, he was one day attracted by a delicious aroma that took him to a ranch where, wonder of wonders, he was served a sumptuously prepared ragout. Sure that he had found a French cook, he inquired, but she was German. He did not mind, and indeed forgot his patriotic hatreds, suddenly feeling fiercely European![37]

Such individual testimonies are evidence for the utter simplicity of the

37. Mandat-Grancey, *Dans les Montagnes*, pp. 43–111.

food eaten in the West, but above all they indicate that the French just could not get used to farms that did not raise their own food.

Other travelers had the good fortune to be invited by families in the East, and in this case the picture was much less grim. Food was much cheaper than in France, and this accounts for the abundance that struck all the witnesses. The workers' delegation could not get over the fact that their American colleagues had meat on the table every day. Moreover, the day-to-day food seemed very healthy and well balanced: Grilled or roast meat accompanied by vegetables boiled in water were something that astonished Emile Levasseur, who was used to the ragouts and sauce-covered dishes eaten by French working-class families.[38]

This favorable impression was confirmed by the privileged few who partook of meals in middle-class families. In late autumn, they discovered the Thanksgiving turkey, the "huge turkey" served with pickles that delighted Pastor Wagner. And Mathilde Shaw had some high-quality and extremely refined meals, even if she did not always like them.[39]

The most audacious were those who left the American plan and ventured into Chinese restaurants. This was a totally new experience for all but a few connoisseurs who had lived in the Far East, among them Edmond de Mandat-Grancey or Camille Saint-Saëns, and except for these two nobody enjoyed it very much. In the windows of restaurants in the Chinatowns of New York and San Francisco dubious meat was hung up to dry and gave off worrisome smells. Once one had gone in, one had to learn how to handle the chopsticks, and then face the dishes. "Execrable" and "disgusting" food, composed of "weird and dirty comestibles," said Paul Bourget, "chopped stuff wrapped in leaves of bizarre *crudités*" – and one could give many more examples and line up many more adjectives: The condemnation was unanimous. The French were simply not ready for culinary adventures; newness and strangeness immediately put them off, and it would take them many years to become familiar with an Asian cuisine that they had discovered, to their stupefaction, in the United States.

### An Unhealthy Diet

The Rabelaisian abundance of the menus, the excessive quantities of meat, and the insufficient amount of bread were the most frequently

---

38. Mme. L. Grandin, *Impressions d'une Parisienne à Chicago* (Paris: Flammarion, 1894). Her opinion is significant, since she did her own shopping. Above all, see E. Levasseur, *L'ouvrier américain* (Paris: Larose, 1898), vol. 2, which precisely investigates this question.
39. M. Shaw, "A travers la Nouvelle Angleterre," *Nouvelle Revue* (March–April 1895): 345–46.

expressed grievances, along with the abuse of sweets. This diet seemed to be marked by perpetual waste, for the American women, even in the working class, did not seem to know how to deal with leftovers and preferred to buy things that were expensive and quick to prepare.

Such snap judgments were often made, but they did not take into account the meals of more humble people, whose garbage cans were not always filled with food. Nonetheless these comments do support others that spoke of the enormous portions served and the phenomenally large but rather tasteless fruits found in the early twentieth century. At that time, France was still a relatively restrictive society, and what its travelers discovered here, suddenly and to their undeniable discomfort, was a society of abundance.

These abuses, they felt, should be punished, and so they noted with a certain satisfaction that many Americans were suffering from stomach troubles. Dyspepsia was seen as a typically American ailment that affected the entire society; after all, advertisements for pills against stomach troubles were found everywhere.

The reasons for this scourge seemed evident to our observers. On the one hand, the Americans ate too much without paying attention to preparations, and on the other hand, what they ate was particularly harmful: "dispepsia [*sic*] [is] an ailment very common among the Yankees who consume great quantities of ice water and hot rolls." These two items were blamed most often, for they were the very ones that were particularly hard on the French visitors, who were accustomed to wine and "real" bread. And finally, American stomachs were impaired by the speed with which drinks and barely chewed food were swallowed. Dyspepsia was thus bound to be "constitutional" in the United States.

In addition to stomach troubles, the Americans had bad teeth. Ice water and eating ice cream were said to account for the number of mouths sporting great amounts of gold, as well as for the prosperity of American dentists. Although French dentists did their best to refute this argumentation, it was heard again and again. Dental work was, to be sure, more common and more visible in the United States than in France, but there was no reason to incriminate the use of ice. However, ice was so contrary to French dietary habits that it was simply suspect.

The third scourge of American diet was alcohol, which was not good for either the stomach or the teeth. The French observers felt that hypocrisy in this area only served to hide an alcoholism that was spreading through all social classes, in particular among the workers. As Emile Levasseur put it:

The *saloon* is truly pernicious. It is a small shop whose dirty windows make for secrecy, but whose open-work door that only has to be pushed invites one to enter. . . . Behind the counter of shiny zinc stand the bartenders, and behind them are rows of bottles, barrels, and spigots ready to dispense the drinks. The customer stands in front of the counter; he doesn't talk much or not at all; he drinks, and he drinks fast.[40]

For the French, this was heresy: a bar where one drank standing up and often alone, as was done not only by laborers but also by white-collar workers in large cities, whereas in French cafes one sat down to have a convivial drink. Women too were at risk, since in drugstores they washed down their ice cream with "tonics" that were not harmless either. Abbé Vigneron was sorry that wine, a much healthier drink, was not consumed instead of these mixed alcoholic beverages, and a few years later Stéphane Josselin went a step further when he wished that wine were given to American children when they were very young in order to avoid the later ravages of strong drink.[41]

The speed with which Americans ate had always struck the French, but this speed increased even more in the first years of the twentieth century. According to Saint André de Lignereux, more than half of the population made do with "ready meals," and this was confirmed by the correspondent of the *Journal des Economistes*, who described one of these establishments in 1903. ". . . a nice little restaurant . . . looking like a thousand country inns . . . where they serve a quick dinner, a super-rapid dinner, or an express supper. Time is money."[42] A year later, incidentally, the hot dog was introduced, although most French visitors did not encounter it. This was the beginning of the "quick lunch," but not quite yet of "fast food."

### A Hopeless Situation

Speedy dietary habits were predicated on a growing industrialization of food, and this the French could not accept. But above all, this evolution revealed the very minor role food preparation played in the lives of most Americans. "It is very odd that for all their inventiveness and their progress in so many areas the Americans should be satisfied with such

40. Levasseur, *L'ouvrier américain*, p. 25.
41. L. Vigneron, *De Montréal à Washington* (Paris: Plon, 1887), p. 54. The abbé's name [Vigneron = vintner] predestined him for this remark.
42. Laborer, "Esquisses de la vie américaine," *Journal des Economistes* (July 1903): 92. The author was the review's American correspondent for several years.

poor cooking."[43] Perhaps this had to do with the absence of cooking classes in the otherwise fine schooling of American girls; the introduction of home economics at the end of the nineteenth century did not fill the gap. This shortcoming greatly displeased the French observers, many of whom complained that they found women who read a lot but did not know how to cook, who could calculate logarithms but knew nothing beyond oatmeal and pork chops.

If girls were not given cooking classes, it was of course because this was not considered important. But could one respect a country that neglects cooking, could one consider it completely civilized? Listening only to their stomachs, many of these travelers undoubtedly replied that one could not.

At the end of this experience, the French returned home convinced of the irreplaceable value of French cooking; yes, American comforts were enviable in many areas, but never would one see a young Frenchman eating standing up, leaning against a shiny counter while munching on a hot and dripping sandwich and sipping some sweet drink or a glass of flavored milk.

## AT THE HOTEL AMERICA

### A Caravanserai

Located in the heart of nineteenth-century American cities, the great hotels were undoubtedly among the most extraordinary landmarks, both in terms of their architecture and for their interior design. French travelers for the most part frequented only the most prestigious establishments, those that offered the latest advances, and it is therefore not surprising that they were stunned: "Hotels are as important to them as cathedrals, monuments, ruins, old chateaux, lakes, mountains and all the beauties nature can offer man are to us."[44]

These remarks are not altogether unfounded. If a certain number of French visitors resided in the most luxurious establishments – Hoffman's, and later the Waldorf Astoria in New York, the Auditorium or Palmer's in Chicago, or the Palace in San Francisco – others, who stayed in more modest hotels, made a special effort to visit the great hotels. One went to the Waldorf as one would go to the Louvre or the Arc de Triomphe,

43. D'Eichtal, "Quelques notes," 213.
44. M. O'Rell, *Jonathan et son continent* (Paris: Calman-Lévy, 1889), p. 349.

one enjoyed walking about in the foyer, taking a close look at the draperies, the thickness of the carpeting, or those utterly delightful places, the "palatial water-closets." In the bar of Hoffman's House one could admire the canvases of William Bouguereau, his "satyrs and nymphs" – quite a contrast with the customers leaning against the bar. Some of the visitors made fun of this bogus luxury, but they would come back to see it, year after year, if they could not afford to stay there. Although most of the hotels throughout the United States were well kept and offered comforts unknown in France, only those of the largest cities exerted this kind of fascination.

The interest in hotels was as much a matter of their comfort as of their organization. Immediately upon landing at the docks of New York, and also on the train toward another destination, the traveler could make use of the system of the "baggage check" – a small copper chip with a number on it – which without further formalities sent all bags and suitcases directly to the hotel he had chosen. The travelers were so pleased that they hoped for the adoption of this system in France.

But they really marveled when they entered the vast lobbies of these hotels. Their immense size, the constant movement, and the variety of services offered captured their attention:

> All the luxuries and all the comforts imaginable are found there: the tele-graph, the telephone, bathrooms, huge marble water-closets, beauty parlors, newspaper stands, currency exchange, public secretary with a typewriter, elevators, etc.; all of this we found extremely convenient.[45]

All this coming and going in the well-lit lobbies and the quality of the boutiques found there almost made one forget that this was just a hotel; it was more like a small town, or rather a caravanserai, an oasis of light, luxury, and sensuous pleasure that one reached after a long day of traveling. These monumental spaces, sometimes crowned by an immense glass roof like the one at the Auditorium Hotel in Chicago, brought the traveler into a world totally different from that of a European hotel. Sometimes such a stay was like being in a kind of air lock before actually plunging into the astonishing American life.

### Discovering Comfort

In the nineteenth century, the great hotels were the first places where certain innovations that subsequently came to improve the daily lives of Americans were applied. It is therefore quite understandable that

---

45. Finance, *Rapports de la délégation*, p. 30.

the French visitors were amazed by what they discovered. The speed of the elevators that took one to one's room, for instance, was related to an early use of electricity and was one of the first things to marvel at. These machines were much faster than the rare ones that existed in France. Similarly, in the 1880s, the hotel was the place where many travelers could experience, for the very first time, large rooms entirely lit by electricity. Year by year, gas lighting was thus phased out, to the admiration of the travelers, until this advance became commonplace after 1900.

The hotel room brought more surprises, which startled the visitor in 1875 as much as in 1910. The traveler almost always had at his disposal a bathroom where a sink provided as much hot and cold water as desired, and which also had a bathtub, although there was no bidet.

> . . . the washstand is a mechanical piece of furniture that brings in water by means of a spigot above that immobile bowl set in marble, which is emptied by pushing a simple button or pulling a simple metal stopper attached to a chain. It is therefore impossible to move this bowl, so that in certain cases . . . one must use the bathtub.[46]

Running water loomed very large in the fascination of the French; it was a convenience to which it was particularly easy to become accustomed and which, exceptionally, no one criticized.

Another amenity offered by the hotel, for those who traveled in autumn or winter, was central heating.

> In one corner of the suite stands a set of ten to twelve hollow tubes which, about one meter high and of a diameter of about ten centimeters, look somewhat like organ pipes. All you have to do is turn one key and they will fill with hot air.[47]

Félix de Biancourt's discovery of the radiator in 1887 was not akin to the naiveté of Flaubert's *Bouvard et Pécuchet*; it had to do with becoming aware of the profound difference that existed between France and the United States in these areas. So unused were the French to central heating that they often complained about the excessive temperature in American dwellings.

The telephone was another discovery. Within the hotel it could be used to order a drink or to summon a member of the staff, but it also permitted rapid communication with the outside. The first contacts with this instrument were not always smooth sailing, and the painter Charles Huard could not get used to it at all:

46. Saunière, *A travers l'Atlantique*, p. 181.
47. F. de Biancour, *Quatre mille lieues aux Etats-Unis* (Paris: Ollendorf, 1888), p. 34.

I was just going to sleep when suddenly a fiendish ringing . . . made me jump to my feet, all upset: I had forgotten the telephone, one of the worst advantages of American life. Eleven times at least in two hours I was surprised in equally horrendous fashion. . . . My nerves shot to pieces, I rushed down to the office to demand a room without telephone. . . . What I was asking for did not exist, and so I went back to my room and spent some time demolishing the apparatus. . . . But by the next day it was repaired. . . .[48]

While such reactions of complete rejection were rare, one sometimes does perceive a certain fatigue with the latest conveniences in these hotels. "Their quest for comfort and luxury is excessive," thought even Marie Dugard, who certainly had nothing against modernism. The hotel and progress were so closely associated in people's minds that Ferdinand Brunetière was disappointed in 1897 when he found himself in an establishment that was comfortable enough but lacking in "mechanical excesses" and particular sophistication.

Travelers had the tendency to generalize on the basis of their experiences in the hotel and to endow all American homes with these multiple and unending improvements; the example of the only homes they visited, often located on Fifth Avenue, seemed to confirm this assumption. Of course, the average dwelling was by no means in the same situation; but then, only the rich are visible.

### Service: The Other Side of the Coin

The marvels of modern technology did not make the French travelers overlook what they considered the gross insufficiencies of service as they understood it. They often complained about plates not changed after every course, about napkins that were too small, rooms that were not properly cleaned and boots that were not shined. And indeed, for all the well-organized and highly adequate service in the lobby – even if one sometimes had to grease the manager's paw to be assigned a good room – things deteriorated when it came to obtaining a personal service.

Throughout the period, the French travelers insisted on putting their shoes outside their doors, to no avail; eventually they discovered the shoe shine boy in the street. Still, they continued to grouse about it, as they groused about the surly and incompetent chambermaids. The consequences were not as annoying as in the restaurant, but they too gave rise to criticism of an overly mechanized and industrialized way of life, and the comfort of good hotels, however pleasant, could not altogether make up for this lack of personalized service.

48. C. Huard, *New York comme je l'ai vue* (Paris: Rey, 1906), p. 140.

The problem of service greatly preoccupied the French travelers; they noted its rather widespread mediocrity and at the same time the quasi-permanent presence of large numbers of American families in hotels. They concluded that this strange situation was caused by the lack of domestic servants and worried about the problems such practices seemed to reveal. That women and children should live for long periods of time in these sumptuous establishments cast a curious light on American life. On the basis of often caricatural examples, travelers began to wonder about the functioning of American society. A great deal of mobility, few domestic servants, and increasing familiarity with modern comforts: All of this was new and unusual to them.

Life in the hotel America thus amounted to a first immersion, albeit in a distorting medium, in American life itself. On the whole, the resulting judgment was very favorable, and the comparison with the French hotel business was not flattering.

These multifaceted travel experiences gave the French observers a first perception of some of the essential mechanisms of the activities and the social organization of the Americans. Their next assignment was to gain a deeper understanding of what their first impressions had so forcefully revealed by discovering the real United States through its smaller towns and its countryside.

# 2

# *At First Sight*

When we meet a new person, first impressions, fallacious though they can be, count for a great deal. The same is true when we travel to a place we have not known before. A first glance perceives differences and scans landscapes and people for the signs of exoticism that will justify the journey. These first impressions often leave the strongest marks, those that one remembers most clearly when it comes to writing down one's memories and reflections.

The French travelers who arrived in the United States were no exception to this rule, and the strength of these first images is evident in their accounts: New York and its bay, Chicago and its sprawling size, monumental Washington, the hum of San Francisco by the Golden Gate, or the power of the Grand Canyon. A marvel of nature, an evening's special light, or the physiognomies of passers-by thus anchored down the first impressions. Pierre de Coubertin was particularly enthusiastic about natural sites:

> ... the banks of the Hudson, the mass of the Niagara tumbling down, the panoramic views of Quebec or Montreal, the Potomac seen from Washington's Capitol, and the sparkling sunsets of Florida are forever present in my memory.[1]

The marquis de Chanteloup-Laubat for his part emphasized the urban landscape:

> No description can give us an exact idea of the American city, built in a checkerboard pattern, covered by an immense network of metal wires, cut by numbered streets, congested with vehicles of all kinds, and crisscrossed by elevated trains that clatter overhead on high steel scaffolds.[2]

1. P. de Coubertin, *Universités transatlantiques* (Paris: Hachette, 1890), p. 62.
2. A. de Chasseloup-Laubat, "Voyage en Amérique et principalement à Chicago," offprint from the *Mémoires de la Société des ingénieurs civils de France* (Paris: Cité de Rougemont, 1893), p. 64.

Just as travelers remembered only some of the facets of the American landscape, those that interested them, so their itineraries led them more often to conventional sites than into true adventures.

## ITINERARIES

### *Ports of Entry*

New York was the grand entrance gate to the United States, considering that 80 percent of the itineraries examined here began in the Empire City; a similar number ended there.

Some of the many travelers who included a detour to Canada in their visit preferred to begin or end their journey in the British Dominion; ten of them arrived from Canada, and twelve left the United States to go to Canada. The most frequented route was via Niagara Falls, which everyone wanted to see. Those who had arrived by the Saint Lawrence River then took the train, which brought them to New York by way of Buffalo and Albany, or else they headed directly for Chicago without leaving the Canadian territory. Another route went along Lake Champlain and Lake George and also led to Albany via Saratoga. All these trips were made easy by the tight network of railroads, and memories of Fenimore Cooper's *Leatherstocking* were increasingly wrapped in clouds of smoke from the wide smokestacks of locomotives. These access routes allowed the French to make the pilgrimage to New France and be amused by the accent of their cousins in Quebec Province.[3]

Shunning this well-traveled Canadian path, a few rare travelers chose more unusual routes. When Thérèse left Seattle in 1910, she went by Transcanadian Railroad from Vancouver to Toronto, and from there to Buffalo; Dr. O. M. Lannelongue landed at Vancouver at the end of his tour around the world in 1909, going from there to Winnipeg and leaving the Canadian territory for Duluth and Minnesota. These peripheral trips took place late in our period and reflect the development of the Canadian West; recall that the Canadian Transcontinental Railroad was not finished until 1885, and that the Western Provinces did not come into being until the early years of the twentieth century. Certain tourists were therefore bound to feel that they had to see Saskatchewan and Alberta.

San Francisco was the only other port of entry of any importance. Eight of the travelers considered here arrived by the Golden Gate.

3. S. Simard, *Mythe et reflet de la France, l'image du Canada en France, 1850–1914* (Ottawa: Presses de l'Université d'Ottawa, 1987), pp. 93–97.

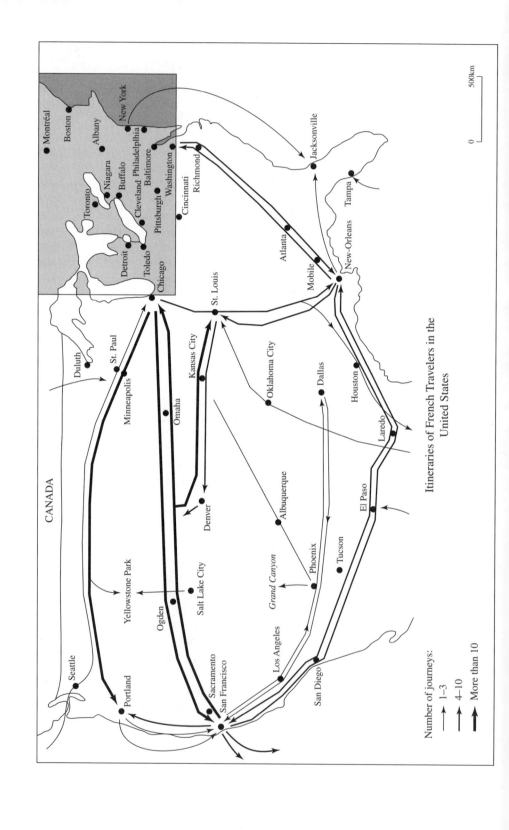

Number of journeys:

→ 1–3

➜ 4–10

➤ More than 10

Itineraries of French Travelers in the
United States

CANADA

Montréal

Boston

Albany

New York

Niagara

Buffalo

Toronto

Cleveland Philadelphia

Detroit

Toledo

Chicago

Baltimore

Pittsburgh

Washington

Cincinnati

Richmond

Jacksonville

Tampa

Atlanta

New-Orleans

Mobile

Duluth

St. Paul

St. Louis

Minneapolis

Kansas City

Oklahoma City

Dallas

Houston

Omaha

Denver

Albuquerque

Laredo

Yellowstone Park

Salt Lake City

Grand Canyon

Phoenix

Tucson

El Paso

Seattle

Ogden

Portland

Sacramento

San Francisco

Los Angeles

San Diego

0          500km

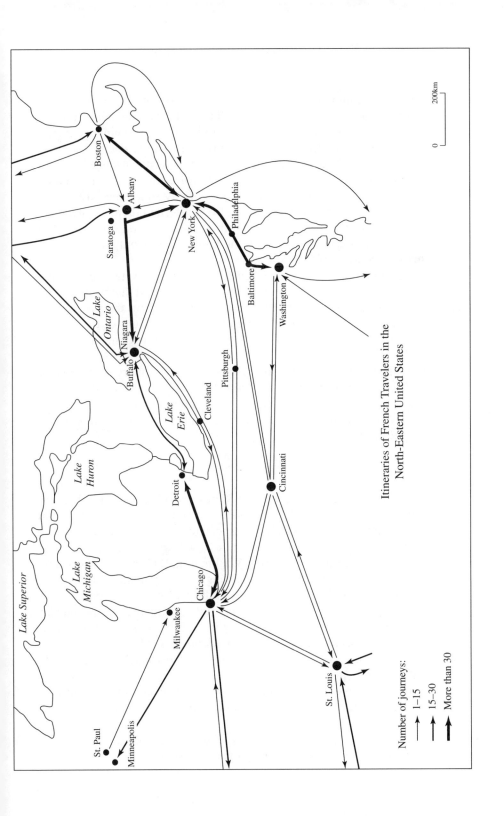

Itineraries of French Travelers in the
North-Eastern United States

Number of journeys:
→ 1–15
→ 15–30
→ More than 30

0 ____ 200km

Before 1869, Edmond Leuba had to take a ship from New York to cross the Isthmus of Panama by the Aspinwall railroad and then board another ship for California; during the later period, travelers coming from Asia were able to return to Europe by using the new Union Pacific Railroad. To them North America was the last stage of a much longer journey rather than its main objective. These few world travelers were anxious to reach the East Coast and stopped only briefly, sometimes at Chicago or at Niagara Falls, pleased that the railroad afforded them a convenient means of returning to their native soil. These travelers were not interested in exploring strange sights in the United States, only in the conveniences made available to them.

The same attitude prevailed when going in the opposite direction, but no more than half a dozen French globetrotters started their tour around the world with America, leaving it at San Francisco on the way toward Asia. Yet these few persons did spend a certain amount of time in the United States, for the first stage of a journey is always more leisurely than the last.

The other entrance or exit gates played only a very marginal role, since only three of our travelers came from Mexico and entered the United States at Laredo or El Paso, among them the journalist Bertie-Marriot in 1884. Another three travelers left the country via New Orleans, and one went out from Boston.

### Typical Journeys

Like any other country, the United States provided certain obligatory stopovers for its visitors. When all is said and done, the traveler's freedom of movement was fairly restricted, especially within a short time span. After all, one had to stay a few days in New York, take a good look at Niagara Falls, and go to Chicago or Washington, D.C., if, back home, one did not want to be accused of not having seen anything. Besides, there were convenient railroad connections to these places, and at particularly attractive prices too, whereas setting out to discover a spectacular lookout in the Dakotas or a small town in Vermont required efforts that did not always seem warranted. The guidebooks of the time, the *Guide franco-américain* and especially the famous *Baedeker*,[4] were perfectly explicit on these points.

Almost 40 percent of our travelers were satisfied with a circuit that one might call the "Eastern Loop," which took them through the cities

---

4. The first *Baedeker*, published in New York by L. Weiss in 1889, did not have the lasting success of the second, which I have used here in the 1905 edition.

along the Eastern seaboard, as well as to Niagara Falls. Many also went to Chicago and Saint Louis, since they wished to see the Columbian World's Fair of 1893 in one case and the Saint Louis World's Fair of 1904 in the other.

This was the minimum program, the basic journey to the United States, which in fact all other trips also incorporated more or less completely. Saint Louis, where for a long time the trains to the West stopped before taking off for the Great Plains, was a kind of hub; frequently it was in this town that travelers decided whether to head West or down the Mississippi to the South.

Quite a few travelers, about 40 percent throughout the period, made their way to Salt Lake City or San Francisco; by the beginning of the twentieth century, their number increased slightly due to the development of the West and the growing number of railroad lines that now reached the most remote areas. In 1883, for instance, the lines of the Southern Pacific, the famous Achison, Topeka and Santa Fe, and the more northerly Northern Pacific went into operation. On these trains the visitor experienced spectacular landscapes, the deserts and the sculpted terrains of Arizona and Colorado, or the forests and mountains of the Northwest.

By contrast, very few of the French travelers, once they had accomplished the traditional Eastern tour, chose to visit the South. That region did not attract them; at most it was part of a larger circuit, but in itself it was not considered worth a special trip. Only four of our travelers undertook this adventure; in the 1870s they were Gaëtan Desaché and Gustave de Molinari, later Paul Bourget, and in the early years of the twentieth century Paul Adam. The last three spent some time in the South; two of them were the greatest French writers to have traveled in the United States, and neither of them, incidentally, went West. One might consider this as evidence of greater sensitivity to human problems at a time when others were looking for the more facile picturesqueness of the West.

This disinterest in the South becomes less stark if one looks at the group of travelers who in addition to the Eastern cities also wanted to see not only the Western plains and mountains but also the Mississippi and the Deep South. These were the ambitious travelers, the ones who sought to discover everything. There were twenty of them in the course of the period, and most visited the United States toward its end. The "Grand Tour," which around 1880 had amounted to little more than an excursion to New Orleans, became more and more sophisticated as the years went by and new railroad lines went into operation. Generally, the later travelers reached California by the Union Pacific but returned by the northern or southern route, using a variety of itineraries and stopovers. Some members of this adventuresome group, Pierre de Coubertin, Jules Huret, and Estournelles de Constant, made their mark by the interesting books they wrote about this experience.

The reasons for choosing the various itineraries are not hard to find. The "Eastern Loop" seemed the most obvious choice, given the many points of interest that attracted almost all of the travelers. New York, Niagara Falls, and Chicago were the most visited places, closely followed by Washington, D.C. The fascination with the West and with Indians, the novelty of the transcontinental railways, and the marvels of nature explain why many travelers heeded the famous call "Go West, young man!" To go South – except to New Orleans, which always attracted the French – required a firmer resolve. The heat was trying and the racial tensions had a "very special character" in this part of the country. To this must be added a propensity for giving priority to universally admired sites, as well as the advice of Americans who confirmed the travelers' prejudices.

The French traveler thus seems to have been fairly unadventurous, rarely straying from the beaten path. However, this assessment should not be allowed to obscure the variations from this pattern that made some of these journeys extremely rich experiences. Thus, in 1880, a young graduate of the Ecole polytechnique, Aimé Jay, was the only one to stop in the young city of Houston or the obscure Nashville, and one of the few to make a detour to Springfield to pay homage to Lincoln.[5] Baron de Mandat-Grancey, for his part, did not hesitate to wander about in the authentic Wild West, at a time when this was a true adventure. Pierre de Coubertin, who traveled in the United States in 1889 and again in 1893, undertook some extremely varied complementary circuits.[6]

One could cite many more individual examples to show the great importance of travel accounts in the formation of French opinion. Often repetitive, but sometimes of great interest due to the places described and the acuity of observation, these reports of first impressions served to open the public's eyes.

---

5. A. Jay, *A travers les Etats-Unis d'Amérique*, published posthumously by G. Chabiraud (Niort, 1884).
6. The aristocratic authors were sometimes adventurous, as for instance E. de Mandat-Grancey, Baron de Woelmont, or the picturesque Duc d'Auzias-Turenne, who ran his "Fleur de lys Ranch" in Montana before going out to Seattle and ending his career in Montreal. P. de Coubertin's second book, *Souvenirs d'Amérique et de Grèce* (Paris: Hachette, 1897), came out of his trip to the Columbian World's Fair.

## NEW YORK, NEW YORK

New York! It is London, Liverpool, and Glasgow, all rolled into one, without any of the characteristic traits of these cities, but with a friendlier climate and the vast ocean in front of it. New York! with no history, it is not Paris, nor Vienna, nor Naples. New York! The Empire city . . . New York! . . . with its population of a million and a half souls milling about at noontime feverishly pursuing their business! This is New York, the queen of the seaboard.[7]

This hymn to the city reflects the fascination it exerted on most of the visitors.

### *Upper New York Bay and Its Panorama*

The travelers were still on shipboard when they first saw the lush banks, covered with many houses, of Long Island, followed by the hustle and bustle of wharves. Only later did they get a first glimpse of Manhattan "whose elongated shape fairly closely resembles that of a monstrous shark."

The judgments elicited by this spectacle are strikingly similar from one end of the period to the other: Everyone mentions the many different kinds of ships and a great deal of noise and excitement. Descriptions like this one by André Chevrillon abound:

> All around one sees great steam ferries, loaded with people and a jumble of vehicles and carts, their huge outriggers strangely flapping up and down against the sky; entire trains, pulled by their locomotive, are carried off on floating platforms, while 10,000-ton steamers sail up and down the estuary. Everything is filled with movement, haste, and confusion amidst an uproar of whistling and bellowing under gigantic and shapeless silhouettes lining a sordid pier filled with carts, where the world's biggest steamships, lined up like hackney cabs in the street, seem very small.[8]

The ferries, both in New York and in San Francisco, were among the main attractions. Their archaic appearance was incongruous in that it contrasted with American modernism, yet at the same time they were huge and terribly efficient, as they ought to be in that country.

Unchanging as well were the visitors' reactions to the skyline of the Empire City. Between 1870 and 1914 the number of stories of the highest

---

7. A. Ronna, *Le blé aux Etats-Unis* (Paris: Berger-Levrault, 1880), p. 213.
8. A. Chevrillon, *Nouvelles études anglaises* (Paris: Hachette, 1910), p. 136.

buildings increased from eight to about thirty, as classic structures gave way to "skyscrapers" and other "cloud busters." Despite this major change, the French visitors always reacted in the same manner to the height of the buildings in New York. From the very beginning they noted that the steeples of the churches disappeared amidst these buildings; later they could not be seen at all, but the shock remained almost the same.

This unchanging perception had to do with the evolution of French cities, especially Paris. In the course of these forty years, Parisian buildings had in fact not gone beyond the ritual limit of five stories set by the famous city planner Baron Haussmann. Thus the height of the roofs of New York had always astonished French visitors, and its progressive increase only confirmed the impression of earlier travelers. They all had said that the skyline was very high, and subsequent observers could only confirm that judgment, which was still correct.

After 1886, one inevitably saw in the panorama of the Upper Bay – "a lake enclosed in green hills" – the outline of the Statue of Liberty. When Abbé Polydore wrote his book in 1884, he was sure that the statue would stand on the little island he had been shown ten years earlier; the Duc de Chartres, grandson of Louis-Philippe, who was no doubt rather uninterested in this republican symbol, indicated that it was given by France in 1878. Other travelers were less ignorant and more precise.

With the exception of two intrepid visitors who took the trouble of visiting Bartholdi's work – and they found the interior without elevator and electricity unworthy of the reputation of the United States – the travelers saw it only from a distance, either from the deck of a ship or from the pier. The statue therefore seemed small to them, almost crushed by the immense size of the bay, nor did it shed much light in darkness. To quite a few French visitors it was a disappointment, "black and menacing," "heavy, earth-bound, and without nobility"; nonetheless, most comments were admiring, and their writers were impressed by the colossal aspect of the work and by its patina. Some wondered whether they should consider it a "colossal objet d'art" or an "enormous knickknack," but beyond every observer's personal taste, what counted was its meaning.

In the first years, the exalted and proud personification of Liberty was still linked to its French origin. "A Marseillaise in bronze," said Napoléon Ney, a member of the French delegation at the inauguration in October 1886. "I don't know whether this represents Liberty, but surely it does represent the enthusiastic, ardent, generous, and sometimes a bit disheveled genius of our beloved country,"[9] was how Pierre de Coubertin felt about it. Others wondered, as some French diplomats did at the time

9. Coubertin, *Universités transatlantiques*, p. 62.

of the protracted haggling over the building of the pedestal, why France had felt it necessary to be generous to such a selfish country.

But as the years passed, resentments and memories faded and the statue became increasingly identified with America: "France, sensing American taste, had the subtlety to give this gift" to the Great Republic. Besides, was not the colossus the very image of that "young and frightening America" which could crush other civilizations or imperiously show them the way to the Liberty it symbolized? The work's Americanness, whether admired or feared, was undeniable; Paul Vidal de la Blache, an incisive observer, confirmed it: ". . . if one wants a symbol, what better place to find it than in this massive colossus that greets those who arrive from Europe."[10] The statue had indeed become the sister who welcomes newcomers at the convent door.

The meaning of Bartholdi's work, which was immediately claimed as their own by the Americans, was clearly perceived by the French, even though some of them deplored that it was so dominated by commercial buildings that some of its powerful impact was lost. Within a few years, "Miss Liberty" had become an integral part of the Upper New York Bay, to the point that if it was hidden by fog, the traveler would come back to see it another time. She, along with the gothic towers of the Brooklyn Bridge and the high buildings of Manhattan, let him know that he really and truly was in New York.

### Seeing the City

The exaltation produced by the Upper New York Bay and its hustle and bustle calmed down as soon as the traveler had landed on the pavement of New York. For now the passengers had to deal with the annoyance of the Customs Service, which everyone knew to be corrupt. Should one slip a few dollars to the customs official to avoid a thorough search of one's luggage and a very long wait, or should one give him one's calling card with the name of the hotel where he could later pick up the reward for his tolerance? These questions were asked by well-to-do travelers who, for the most part, watched with pity and disdain as immigrants were subjected to much more stringent formalities, at least before the facilities at Ellis Island opened in 1896 and put an end to such mixing of classes. For all their frequent complaints, travelers did not have to wait too long in a huge and terribly drafty hall.

---

10. P. Vidal de la Blache, "A travers l'Amérique du Nord," *Revue de Paris* (March–April 1905): 525. This article is particularly rich for the acuity of its perceptions and the originality of its observations.

Once they had left the port buildings, the new arrivals looked around themselves with a certain anxiety. The sight was not encouraging: broken pavement, foundries, peeling façades, shouting coachmen.

> The first impression felt by a European, particularly a Frenchman, upon arriving in America is one of revulsion. In fact, he initially feels like a prey being devoured by a hungry beast.[11]

The brutality of the city thus became apparent from the very first day, yet on the way back, the shock was no longer as rude; the traveler had become inured.

The first ride in the city, by hackney coach or by "car," was quite an experience. Everyone was struck by the hustle and bustle in the streets produced by all kinds of different vehicles, all kinds of people, and by the rumble of sounds that accompanied all this commotion, especially the strident noise of the trams and the whistling of steam: "American noise is somehow sharper, more metallic, and more choppy than the steady hum or rolling, mixed with human voices, that rises up over our cities."[12]

These pulsating streets made an even greater impression because they were often narrow and lined with huge buildings. The skyscraper fascinated rather than pleased the French travelers at first sight: To be sure, these immense structures were functional, and remarkably well equipped – electricity, elevators, central heat – but most of all they were incurably ugly. They did not allow any sun to come in, and their Greek or Asian decorations in particular attracted a great deal of sarcasm. The best that could be said about these "skyscrapers" was that they had a utilitarian function that might justify building them. Given the concentration of things and people, they probably did save time and money, a combination that constituted the secret of the Americans. Above all, these buildings were the result of the Americans' overweening pride, but they "should rest easy, we will not borrow this kind of architecture from them."

Beyond the tip of Manhattan, where most of these prodigious buildings were concentrated, the visitors discovered other surprising vistas, streets lined with red or "chocolate-colored" houses, the famous redstones or brownstones with their traditional fire escapes. Traffic was always intense, especially on Broadway or Fifth Avenue, where one could admire the town houses of millionaires. Central Park attracted a few

---

11. C. de Limousin, "Une excursion aux Etats-Unis à l'occasion de l'Exposition de Philadelphie," *Journal des Economistes* (Feb. 1877): 251–52.
12. Vidal de la Blache, "A travers l'Amérique," p. 522.

adventuresome walkers, but going to the Brooklyn Bridge was a veritable pilgrimage.

What were the feelings produced by such a tour, sometimes supplemented by excursions to such slums as the Bowery or Chinatown? The initial revulsion often gave way to admiration for the city as a whole. The Empire City was indeed a capital, its vigor was comparable to that of Paris, and even more, London, but its most striking feature was energy, not beauty: "What a city, what streets, what movement, what luxury! It is Paris two thousand leagues away from Paris!" Such reactions are found again and again, almost unchanged, throughout the period. New York was always depicted as more active, more lively, and more noisy, as if during the same period Paris had evolved as little as the height of its buildings.

Impressive constructions and high noise levels were only a decor, and the French travelers were equally affected by the "human Niagara" that swirled around them, especially in midtown, where most people lived. Like every crowd, this one at first seemed uniform, and it was difficult to distinguish individual faces, although some distinctions gradually emerged. Yet in the end the impression of uniformity persisted; all the people seemed to be dressed in the same manner, and no one was wearing a livery indicating an occupation. Disturbances and scuffles did not cause irritation or impatience. Streets were crossed on marked crosswalks, and policemen often helped women get across safely, despite hectic traffic:

> These pedestrians, whether short-skirted, wearing jackets or vests, stovepipe hats or some unlikely headgear, whether black, yellow, or white-skinned, beardless, mustachioed, or just sporting a little goatee under the chin – all of them are always running, always running. . . .[13]

New York's crowds thus struck the French as very unusual: No workers' caps or smocks; in the summer men simply wore a shirt under a light jacket; and women went out, by themselves, in light-colored dresses, twirling their parasols without attracting attention. They were even more amazed when they realized that among these pedestrians were no soldiers and very few dogs.

This was indeed a different world, one in which there was no army and no immediately recognizable distinction between employers and workers, masters and servants.

This relative uniformity did not make New York a homogeneous and egalitarian city, for contrasts could easily be seen, more so even than in

---

13. L. Vigneron, *De Montréal à Washington* (Paris: Plon, 1887), pp. 47–48.

other big cities. There were violent contrasts between neighborhoods, the lugubrious tenements of Lower Manhattan and the sumptuous dwellings of Fifth Avenue, the superb, aggressive, and marvelously equipped sky-scraper and the crumbling tenement house. There were also contrasts between the efficiency and the speed of the transportation system[14] and the lamentable state of the roadways: Throughout the city inadequate sewers were constantly overflowing, cesspools were never cleaned out, pavement was broken or missing altogether. And the contrast was stark, from the 1890s on, between the "blind violence" of electric lights and peeling façades and black smoke.

It seemed obvious that these sharp opposites in the urban landscape were related to major social differences that the apparent uniformity of the crowds could not mask. New York, like other big cities, had slums that some of our travelers did not hesitate to visit. The Bowery, located fairly close to the center, was thus the objective of certain expeditions, which were undertaken in the company of a detective to make them more exotic. "A populace made up of the dregs of all society, Irishmen, Jews, Chinese, Italians, a filthy rabble in a disgusting cloaca."[15]

This first overview of the city hardly allowed the travelers to analyze the reasons for this situation, and so they stayed with the stereotypical views of poverty and misery, which added to the picturesqueness of their visit.

In walking the streets – commenting on their system of numbering, their almost perfect grid pattern, as well as the number of rough-hewn poles carrying wads of electric wires – the traveler thought that he was beginning to understand how this great city functioned, seeing that it "conveyed everywhere an impression of power, rigor, misery, and disor-der." The initial revulsion in the face of seeming anarchy and the bru-tality of people and things thus becomes more comprehensible, as does the fascination generated by the bold construction projects and the "self-propelled activity" of the crowd.

### Things to Do in New York

"The most brilliant and most industrious" of cities was not beautiful – everyone agreed on that – nor did it have any real monuments, but there was certainly no lack of things to see.

Brooklyn Bridge, to be sure, was akin to a "European" monument; it was considered a major attraction and everyone really ought to see it,

---

14. See Chapter 1.
15. M. O'Rell, *Jonathan et son continent* (Paris: Calman-Lévy, 1889), p. 43.

even cross it. Comments about it were remarkably unanimous; this was one of the rare occasions on their visit to New York, and indeed the country as a whole, that caused the French to praise the Americans for making a utilitarian work so beautiful. Everyone agreed that the Americans were gifted builders, though not particularly interested in esthetic refinements. The sweep of the cables, the gothic aspect of the towers, the bold span of the construction, all of this contributed to the elegance of the famous bridge. Visiting engineers regretted that France had given up building suspension bridges, romantics went there to see the lights go on in the city, and others felt slightly dizzy as they contemplated the intense traffic. No one but the Americans could have conceived and executed such a "marvel of brilliance and boldness."

Central Park was also a much frequented place, especially on a summer Sunday, when Anglo-Saxon traditions left little else to do. Here opinions were more divided; many thought that this was a chunk of raw nature transported to the middle of the city, while others realized that its creation had entailed a major planning operation. But going to Central Park was above all a chance to discover a population that was different from what one saw in the streets. Here one saw beautiful carriages, all kinds of vehicles drawn by magnificent horses, and dashing young women driving fast buggies. In short, this was a different pace, a display of wealth, even luxury. This reassured the traveler who had gained an unfortunate impression from the roughness of his first contacts with the city, and he almost felt he was back in the Bois de Boulogne. New York, then, was also a well-policed city, the home of distinguished people and the luxurious shops of Fifth Avenue; the American millionaires one saw in French theater pieces actually existed. Most visitors were not as lucky as Paul Bourget and Lazare Weiller, who immediately upon their arrival were invited into the homes of the fanciest families, the famous "Four Hundred," but a walk in Central Park at least allowed them to form an idea of the differences, and the view that all Americans were alike did not stand up to closer examination.

> Strange shops: the pharmacist who along with his drugs sells postage stamps and refreshments; the hairdresser who makes you lie down on a reclining chair and subjects your head to complex mechanical operations; . . . laundry shops run by Chinese . . . And for the dregs of society, the opium addicts by the port, ill-famed dens of vice. . . .[16]

The spectacle of shopping streets was one of the favorite tourist attractions; the shops were really different from shops at home, and New

16. A. Lutaud, *Les Etats-Unis en 1900* (Paris: Editions Scientifiques, 1896), p. 98.

York offered a greater variety than most other cities. It was certainly unusual to see statues of Indians indicate cigar stores, and to be surrounded by the omnipresent advertisements that transformed Broadway into a gigantic address book.[17] Shop-window displays, however, were mediocre, and the merchandise shown there seemed to be piled up haphazardly.

One could adduce many more scenes that precipitated the traveler into a different world. One person might be particularly interested in a coffin factory, another in the fact that shop windows remained lit by electricity all night. All these fragmentary impressions made for a richer stay in New York and afforded the traveler an inkling of the complexity of American society.

Not all of the French travelers, of course, were satisfied to take such a superficial look, and some wanted to find out more. A good third of them decided to see a play in a theater; from Henri Kowalski in 1870 to Lazare Weiller more than thirty years later, they had similar reactions. The actors were lively, but the plays were mediocre, often the result of vulgar plagiarism. One may wonder whether these demanding travelers knew English well enough to appreciate the show properly, or whether they only grasped the most spectacular aspects and used them to formulate definitive judgments about American culture.[18] Some chose to visit the offices of the great daily newspapers, the *World* and especially the *New York Herald* of the francophile James G. Bennet. They marveled at the powerful rotary presses and the reliability of telegraphic communications, unaware that in these areas the great popular newspapers of Paris had no cause to envy their American counterparts.[19]

By contrast, visiting a fire station – not only in New York but in other cities as well – demonstrated the visitors' desire to look for specifically American picturesqueness in the realm of technical efficiency. They watched in amazement as a crew of firemen was ready in record time to rush off to a fire; the bell that sounded the alarm automatically dropped the harnesses onto the waiting horses, the men slipped into their boots before they slid down a long greased pole and jumped onto the already steaming pumper. The speed of the operation astounded the observers: Some spoke of a minute or two, others of thirty or eight seconds. This was one of the occasions when the visitors tended to ascribe to the Amer-

17. Abbé Polydore, *Voyage en France, en Belgique et en Amérique* (Périgueux: Cassard Frères, 1884), p. 102.
18. L. Weiller, *Les grandes idées d'un grand peuple* (Paris: Juven, 1904), p. 329.
19. See below, Chapter 5.

icans even greater feats than they could perform; it was a way to enhance the exotic character of their own journey.

The last item in the more usual sightseeing program was visiting the city's reform institutions. While the old Tombs prison attracted only a few visitors who wanted to walk in Tocqueville's rather large shoes, the mental hospital and the penal colony on Blackwell and Ward Islands exerted an undeniable attraction on some of them, such as Louis Simonin, Paul Bourget, and Jules Huret. Interest in finding out how New York solved the problem of protecting itself from dangerous individuals, the romantic attraction of marginality, or the need to prove that American society, like all others, engendered its own form of deviance – all of these were reasons for the attention these establishments received. This usually led to technical comparisons with analogous French institutions, often in favor of New York, and to philosophical musings about human nature and the losers in a merciless society.

These excursions in town, to which some travelers added the Wall Street Stock Exchange or some peaceful cemeteries, completed the stay in New York. The city now appeared in its full complexity, outstanding for its social contrasts, its misery, and its technical prowess; it looked very American and very unlike home, despite certain analogies with European metropolises. This first immersion in American life left indelible traces, made up of street noises, swirling crowds, and the impression of temporariness and efficiency. It was time to find out whether visits to other cities would confirm these very first impressions.

## ANOTHER CITY OR THE SAME ONE?

... Everywhere you will find, for example, a Washington Street and a Lafayette Street crossing, at right angles, other avenues that bear numbers instead of names. All the houses and all the public buildings look alike ... so that if, having left one city and spent the night in a Pullman sleeper, you wake up in a different town, you will have some trouble convincing yourself that you have not traveled in place as in the *Voyage à Dieppe*.[20]

There were indeed many shared aspects that struck most French travelers as much as they struck Gustave de Molinari, even if minor differences existed between small and large cities, and especially between East and West.

20. G. de Molinari, *Lettres sur les Etats-Unis et le Canada* (Paris: Hachette, 1876), p. 280.

## Some Eastern Cities

Some of these were granted particular attention, either because of their
relative ordinariness, as in the case of Philadelphia, Saint Louis, or even
Boston, or, on the contrary, because of their exceptional character, as in
the case of Washington, Pittsburgh, or New Orleans.

Philadelphia, the second most-visited city after New York, attracted
large numbers of French visitors at the time of the 1876 World's Fair but
elicited only rather bland judgments. Yes, the city had its charm, thanks
to its detached red-brick houses; and while it evoked memories of
the War of Independence for the most educated of the visitors, it was
somehow lackluster. Only a very few bold travelers ventured out to
Cherry Hill, retracing de Tocqueville's steps there too. Some also visited
Girard College, which was famous for educating poor children on a
strictly nonreligious basis; the French visitors liked to stress the founder's
French origin. Fairmount Park, the site of the World's Fair, was appreciated in the summer for its coolness and its beauty.

Saint Louis, site of the 1904 World's Fair, did not seem very special to
travelers who necessarily had already seen other cities such as New York
or Chicago. Its French origin, which they sometimes evoked with a
certain nostalgia, had left no traces, and Sundays there were no more
lively than elsewhere. The sprawling city looked dirty, and on rainy days
the roads turned into truly shocking sewers. One of the city's special features was the presence of a large German minority, whose pubs attracted
the French visitors because of their European atmosphere, which proved
stronger than ancestral hatreds. The other asset of Saint Louis was its
location on the banks of the Mississippi. Often it was in this city that
French travelers first saw the Father of All Waters, as reminiscences of
Chateaubriand flooded their memory, especially in the first years of our
period; however, the reality was actually fairly disappointing. It is true
that the mass of water was impressive, but silt made its color unattractive, and the river carried a great deal of debris. One needed a good bit
of imagination and determination to be swept up by romantic reverie.
The main attraction of Saint Louis was in fact the bridge that crossed
the famous river and struck the travelers as a true technical feat.

Other cities, such as Baltimore or Cleveland, were often only stopovers
where the visitor barely got off the train, and about which he had nothing
to say beyond comments on electric lighting and some other
conveniences.

Boston attracted educated people. They lost no time before going to
Harvard University and – not counting the typically American aspect of

the Commons, another chunk of nature right in the city – were particularly struck by the very British character of the city as a whole. The residential pattern evoked London in a quieter way than in New York, and Boston's population seemed to be less frantic and more refined. There was no hustle and bustle along the banks of the Charles River, and everything made this a true "New" England, which was a comforting impression in the midst of a whirlwind tour.

The federal capital elicited a more sustained attention. To be sure, it had the same features as other large cities, and its street numbering was even more esoteric; yet Washington was without question the country's only monumental city, and that was bound to be important to French travelers.

Despite its French origin, Major L'Enfant's design elicited little enthusiasm; it seemed confused, and its spaces were too large for a city that would not be able to fill them and which indeed did not seem intended to be filled. And finally, the contrasts were particularly stark: "a huge village, a strange scattering of ostentatious monuments and generally very simple houses."

The city's calm and its many parks scattered among the principal buildings were greatly appreciated. And one could even find a hackney coach here! Besides, under its American surface, the city had a certain European cachet; pedestrians were not in a great hurry, although the number of blacks to be seen did add a touch of the unfamiliar. In themselves, the buildings of the capital were nothing special, but in this setting they were impressive indeed. One of the French visitors, a Catholic, thought that it looked like "a Pantheon flanked by two Madeleines," while a more republican-minded observer called it a "Pantheon flanked by two Palais-Bourbon." From the top of the Washington Monument, which few visitors liked, one at least had a beautiful view. As for the White House, it certainly did not look like much and was not worthy of a President of the Republic, especially since one could simply walk in without encountering a doorman or any formality. Some of our travelers took advantage of this situation to say hello to the master of the house – a move that would have been unthinkable in Europe. Beginning in the 1880s, the visitors were delighted with the museums, such as the Smithsonian, and with the Library of Congress which, even then, made them marvel.

The general impression of the federal capital depended on the season in which the visit took place. Its cosmopolitan character, due to the presence of foreign diplomats, was only appreciated when it was not summer; summer travelers, exhausted by the heat, found Washington listless and boring, and its peaceful atmosphere did little to make up for this shortcoming. Between 1870 and 1914, despite the city's considerable size,

French visitors regularly compared it to Versailles. This no doubt had to do with the broad avenues and the parks that afforded a glimpse of large white buildings, but also with the fact that in its remoteness from the great modern centers this capital delighted some of the nostalgic admirers of Versailles.

The French liked Washington because it shared few of the characteristics of other American cities. But Marie Dugard, arriving there from the West, was somewhat put off by the spurious European airs that some of her compatriots had enjoyed.

When compared with the cleanness of the federal capital, Pittsburgh, which many travelers visited just before or just after Washington, presented a very different face. "Imagine a city that looks like a huge factory!" exclaimed Comte Zannini[21] when he arrived in the iron city. The reputation of Carnegie's steel mills certainly warranted a stopover, and Pittsburgh's concentration of industrial power was so great that it created a kind of beauty: ". . . where industry becomes picturesque by dint of its very size, where landscapes dotted with factories take on a special beauty, and where the New World can be seen in its true form . . . ."[22] This kind of appreciation could be applied to any major industrial establishment, yet the impression conveyed by this city of noise and smoke was striking, not only to the middle-class traveler who had never seen a factory and would certainly never go to see one in France but also to the worker:

> . . . I asked myself in some dread, and I still ask myself, how one could live amidst such roar of machinery and such smoke, and how one could breathe such air; my nerves were completely shot. . . .[23]

When visiting Pittsburgh, unlike in other, more ordinary industrial cities, the French visitor had to examine his own attitudes toward American industry and toward the fate of the workers, many of whom were very recent immigrants. The picturesque sight of flares illuminating the night could not cover up the contrast between the luxurious villas of the upper city and the miserable Russian or Italian slums in the lower sections.

New Orleans, a city outside the American norm to begin with, was bound to interest the rare French travelers who visited it. What they observed there over the years was the crumbling of the French veneer

21. A. Zannini, *De l'Atlantique au Mississippi* (Paris: Renoult, 1884), p. 173.
22. E. Rod, *Reflets d'Amérique* (Paris: Sansot, 1905), p. 12.
23. J. Malbranque, "Rapport des délégués . . . ," *Exposition universelle de Saint-Louis, 1904* (Paris: Cornély, 1907), p. 257. The author was a railroad worker.

covering the old town and the advances of an inexorable Americanization. The grand avenues filled with speeding trams and lit by powerful
electric lights made the façades of the Vieux Carré look dirty and
disreputable. It is true that the vegetable market was still colorful and
reminded the visitor of Marseilles, as did the traffic jams in the center of
town and the physiognomies of certain passers-by; still, the decline of the
French Creole seemed irrevocable. Some of our travelers were received
with incontestable nostalgia by members of the French community, and
even heard expressions of regret about the sale of Louisiana, whose discovery Louise Bourbonnaud ascribed to Jacques Cartier.[24]

Nonetheless, experiencing the climate of New Orleans after the wintry
North, the exuberance of nature, the verandas of the houses, all of this
contributed to the exotic character of this detour through the Mississippi
delta: "This is a less austere Spain, a just as voluptuous but less nervous
Italy, a land for skipping school, where one is astonished to see the activity of the inhabitants."[25]

Once one had reached the Western cities, there was no more nostalgia, no more dreaming; here one experienced the full shock of the American city.

### Chicago, the "American City par Excellence"

The reputation of the city of lakes had long been established. Travelers
knew what to expect, whether they approached it from the West, in which
case it was the largest city they had yet seen, or from New York, in which
case it was bound to give rise to comparisons and definitive judgments.

One of the main reasons for this renown was the resurrection of the
city after the great fire of 1871. Until then, it had been just another
Western city that had undergone remarkable growth; and while its
wealth could not be compared to that of Paris or London, it had been
driven by a concern for appearances that had facilitated the spreading
of the fire because even the most sumptuous buildings were poorly constructed. The scope of the disaster did not discourage the inhabitants;
rebuilding began immediately and Chicago soon became the "living and
gigantic emblem of the Phenix." What struck the few French witnesses
as extraordinary was the immediacy of the response and the total lack
of despondency.[26]

---

24. L. Bourbonnaud, *Les Amériques* (Paris: Vannier, 1898), p. 93.
25. J. Huret, *En Amérique* (Paris: Fasquelle, 1904), vol. 1, p. 332.
26. Fortunio in *Le Nord* of 22 Oct. 1871 and Marquis de Chambrun, "Chicago et l'exposition colombienne," *Le Correspondant* (10 Aug. 1893): 435.

The French who visited the city after 1876 were amazed. There was almost no trace of the catastrophe – at a time when in Paris the ruins of the Tuileries still reared their blackened gables skyward. Chicago's new sidewalks were of stone, as were the buildings of the center; tunnels made it possible to cross the Chicago River, whose course had been reversed; grain elevators proudly stood along the banks of Lake Michigan; and new buildings were sprouting like mushrooms.

On the occasion of the Columbian Fair, the French discovered sky-scrapers higher than in New York, noisier and more unsightly elevated trains, even faster trams, and a restlessness that made them say that work was the city's only religion. As the years went by, these characteristics seemed to become accentuated; Chicago became one big superlative, and it is not surprising that the mayor, Carter H. Harrison, felt free to present his city as the greatest in the country, itself the greatest in the world, so that Chicago became the greatest city in the world!

One arrived in this city by a tangled network of railway tracks, and one had the impression of an "iron city with locomotives smoking in the streets." The French visitors found the development totally anar-chic, with the result that, more than elsewhere, handsome buildings stood side by side with wooden shacks, and the streets were in even worse shape than in New York. If the latter city often seemed ugly, the only esthetic asset of the Queen of the Lakes was her site on the shores of Lake Michigan, for she presented all the shortcomings of an American city. References to Europe were no longer made at all; at most, the visitors granted a certain beauty to the functional structures, which they found more appropriate here than on the banks of the Hudson. All in all, the French considered the crowd even less attractive than in the East when they noticed some typically Western individuals who stood out by their outfits and their manners. This was the case, for example, at the Fair, which had brought in large crowds of visitors from all over the country.

Amidst this unanimous criticism, a few dissenting voices could nonetheless be heard. Pierre de Coubertin, Thérèse, or Félix Klein had been so prejudiced against Chicago that they were pleasantly surprised when they arrived there. They discovered fine homes, peaceful and well-designed avenues beyond the usually visited business district; and the admirable development of the university was proof that the citizens cared about more than just their material well-being. However, such opinions remained exceptional, and throughout our period the image of Chicago was very bad, and for certain observers became even worse in the wake of the social unrest that unfolded there in 1886 or 1894: "The revolver often speaks there still. . . . Socialism is out of control; dynamite and arsenic often teach the bosses their lessons."[27]

During their few days in Chicago, the French travelers set out to discover the city. Their activities were very similar to those of New York, and indeed interchangeable: firehouses, newspapers, theaters, skyscrapers, Jane Addams's Hull House instead of the institutions on Blackwells Island. Chicago also offered a few unique sights, among them of course the Columbian World's Fair, as well as Pullman City; visiting them took the traveler beyond first impressions and gave rise to more thorough analyses of American society.[28]

The high point of the stay in Chicago was without doubt the visit to its famous slaughterhouses. In 1875, in response to the Eastern markets' growing demand for fresh meat, the two firms of Swift and Armour simultaneously and in competition founded two enterprises that developed efficient methods for the cutting and shipping of pork and beef. For more than eighty years, these extraordinary "packing houses" would contribute to the reputation of Chicago, to the point that as late as 1965, European visitors would go to that city hoping to visit the slaughterhouses, only to find out that they were gone.

Year after year, then, practically all of the French visitors who had come to Chicago visited the domain of the "Attila of pigs" and oxen. Some of them no doubt refused to repeat what so many others had already said, but not many were able to preserve that laudable restraint.

All the visitors felt torn between horror and fascination in the presence of these "stinking and prodigious emporia," which they first had to describe:

> The fat death-row convicts are first hoisted by elevator to the top floor of a many-storied building; at each floor an executioner with well-defined functions is stationed; the pig is brought down from its Mount Calvary and stopped at several painful stations. The first executioner bleeds it, the second eviscerates it, and I don't know what the third does. Owing to this division of labor, the elevators hoist up a screaming and fully alive animal and brings down some hams.[29]

Very soon, the number of slaughtered animals and the enormous size of the facilities through which one was led by a guide inspired the visitors to philosophize about this "massacre of the innocents," this "hell for

27. Comte des Etangs, *L'Amérique laborieuse et l'Amérique croyante*, lecture given at the church of Gros Caillou, 22 Dec. 1899, p. 6.
28. See below, Chapter 11.
29. L. and G. Verbrugghe, *Promenades et chasses dans l'Amérique du Nord* (Paris: Calman-Lévy, 1879), p. 32.

oxen and pigs," and to compare these hecatombs with the holocausts of pagan antiquity, all the while admiring the ingenuity of the carnage. Nonetheless the description does not stay detached for long, and horror takes over when the visitor breathes a smell of blood, looks at bloody mud, and, above all, notices the professional air of the butchers:

> Seen at night, in the light of lanterns that give a silver sheen to the white reflection of steel knives, with these half-naked men splattered with black blood, with the sound of the wind mixed with the puffing of machines, with the stale and nauseating smells of flowing blood, melting grease, and setting lard. . . .[30]

These men were very well paid and did not seem at all affected by the work they were doing, with either the rifle or the club for the bovines and with the knife for the pigs. The last part of the visit, which led through the different scalding, cutting, and drying facilities, brought more surprises:

> Here we see, through billows of disgusting steam, big vats or barrels of lard boiling on bright fires and big rooms where twenty thousand hams are being smoked. A little further on, we walk through an avenue along which several thousand heads hung from hooks look at us with their half-opened eyes under their wrinkled eyelids.[31]

Most of the visitors could not take these sights. They complained of nausea, felt hemmed in by "salamis, andouilettes, blood puddings, and patés," and Henri de Régnier, troubled by the power of this repulsive carnage, actually passed out! It did not help much that the guide explained that all byproducts were used to make glue, brushes, or, in the case of the grease, margarine. Many visitors did not eat any butter for a few days or even became vegetarians for a week.

The problem of hygiene was not only a matter of individual sensitivity; many witnesses evoked myriads of flies, animals that had died before being slaughtered, and the pervasive nauseating smell – all of this before 1906, before Upton Sinclair in his *The Jungle* uncovered all the turpitudes of the Chicago slaughterhouses. The horror the traveler experienced was not conducive to unbiased judgments. Yet even those who visited Swift and Armour after the scandal broke, at the time when every effort – including gifts and medals to the animals – was made to restore the image of the brands, and when legislation ensuring compliance with the rules of cleanliness had been passed, were still seized by nausea and

30. Jay, *A travers les Etats-Unis*, p. 55.
31. E. de Mandat-Grancey, *Chez l'Oncle Sam* (Paris: Plon, 1885), p. 186.

evoked visions of cannibalism whenever they saw a black butcher. In view of the new regulations, Abbé Klein asked a judicious question when he wondered whether the hygiene of artisanal slaughterhouses, like those found in France, was really superior to that of Chicago.

The fact is that the slaughterhouses were certainly not impeccable, neither before nor after 1906, but what the French visitors objected to was not so much a matter of cleanliness as of the industrialization of food preparation. What upset them was "the expeditious factory, the monstrous organization of a universal butcher-shop." This rejection was clearly articulated by Dr. Lannelongue in 1910:

> This trade is not handled differently in Chicago than in any of our small villages in Gascony. The worthy butcher Labérenne of the hamlet of Pouchon, a well-known character in my region, sees his work habits imitated exactly by the 7,000 butchers at Armour's, and I can guarantee that no sausage made in Chicago would rival one of Labérenne's. It's just that instead of two pigs, Chicago massacres 7,500 per day, that is the essential difference.[32]

The French visitors' reaction to the slaughterhouses was caused as much by a real and understandable feeling of horror as by the refusal to accept an evolution that had a direct bearing on their most intimate conception of the ideal way of life and on their deeply rooted habits.

As they left these lugubrious extermination centers and their stench, our travelers were struck by the messy surroundings of these places: railroad tracks, cowboys, runaway animals, children rooting through scraps for the family's supper. All they longed for now was vast horizons and pure air, but before they left the infernal city, they could stop in at Marshall Field's, the department store whose organization would make the managers of the Bon Marché or the Louvre pale with envy, to buy themselves some perfume.

### Western Cities

Chicago provided the example of an incomparable urban dynamism and of a typically Western uncouthness, and yet by dint of its luxury and the beginnings of refinement, it was still an Eastern city. The French visitors set out for the adventure of Western cities anticipating the noisy confusion of sudden and stunning development, their heads filled with images of pioneering populations and the summary justice of the citizenry.

---

32. O. M. Lannelongue, *Un tour du monde* (Paris: Larousse, 1910), p. 294. On this subject, see also Chapter 1.

Yet the reality was somewhat disappointing. All the cities and small towns of the Great Plains, the Rocky Mountains, and the Pacific Coast had become modernized and changed their character with astounding speed. Take the tiny town of Livingston, Montana, which was visited by Léo Clarétie: ". . . a small town, dating back six years at most, already has electric lighting; it also has factories, unpaved streets, and all the dwellings are log cabins. . . ."[33]

Other testimonies evoke the fabulous development of these recent towns; Omaha, a mere railroad junction in the 1870s, had a university when Abbé Klein visited thirty years later, but the city that attracted the greatest attention was Denver. Around 1870, it had held the record for banditry and lynchings; some twelve years later, trappers pranced through streets lined with banks and schools and traveled by trams, and a few years later still, the last of the log houses had been replaced by luxury hotels and fine shops. This made Marie Dugard wonder:

> . . . I could not help thinking of our provincial towns, so drab and so immobilized by their past. Yes! Our own world truly is the "old world." Never have I more keenly felt the difference between the two countries and the young vitality of the American race.[34]

These towns were indeed "mushrooming," and this movement was spreading all the way to the Pacific.

Thus, when the globetrotter Gaston Stiegler came through Seattle in 1900, he found a "hole" in an extraordinary site, but already crisscrossed by trams rushing by at breakneck speed. A year later, Thérèse was able to open a commercial office for the French sugar manufacturer Lebaudy in a very comfortable house, even though many sidewalks were still made of wood. When Félix Klein went there in 1908 – he had read about Seattle in Mandat-Grancey and Urbain Gohier's books – he discovered a city filled with feverish activity, with skyscrapers under construction and as many automobiles on the street as in Chicago. By the eve of the war, the boom had not slowed down at this "outer edge of Western Civilization," as André Siegfried called it. Such rapid development, which was also found at Tacoma and elsewhere, stunned the French visitors, who claimed that work-related accidents were more frequent there than elsewhere, that the population was too masculine, that everything moved too fast. Almost intoxicated, these travelers reacted by backing off from such a riot of energy, which seemed out of control to them.

33. L. Clarétie, *Feuilles de route aux Etats-Unis* (Paris: Dentu, 1895), p. 181.
34. M. Dugard, *La société américaine* (Paris: Hachette, 1896), p. 54.

The Californian cities confirmed, even sharpened these impressions, and the appeal of San Francisco was as great as ever. The splendor of nature seen as the traveler emerged from the Rockies was only a prelude to seeing the Golden Gate.

In the 1870s, the French travelers were struck by the incoherent aspect of the city, by its air of encampment where blacks, Chinese, and Americans rubbed shoulders, and by the wooden houses dispersed on a checkerboard pattern running up the hills. This urban decor, which did not match the admirable site, prompted the travelers to recall the early years, when San Francisco was characterized by its rival gangs and the summary justice meted out by the inhabitants, and to describe the prodigious feats of moving houses about on rollers, another example of the almost crazy boldness of the Americans. Then, little by little, things changed, and while wooden houses and dirty streets were still in evidence, new marvels made their appearance, such as the Palace Hotel, the commercial bustle of Market Street, the prodigious cable cars that made use of the city's hilly terrain, and the pervasive presence of electric lighting which, upon return, made European cities seem quite dark.

In short, San Francisco had become comparable to other American cities, with the bonus of the special magic of its site. In those years between 1890 and 1906, the French travelers followed a rather systematic sightseeing circuit, which gave them as much adventure as was still possible in circumstances of convenience and comfort. In this manner they discovered the panoramic view from Cliff House and pure exoticism in Chinatown. Going to contemplate the ocean, the seals, and an unlimited vista from this fantastic lookout corresponded, mutatis mutandis, to visiting Central Park in New York or the Capitol in Washington, D.C. It was a "must" that did not disappoint anyone:

> The birds, the sea lions, and man in close proximity to each other, and yet man does not trouble the animals; one is tempted to believe that one has returned to the early days of creation.[35]

At sunset the sight became even more splendid. As the years went by, these places became a bit more lively. One went there to eat oysters, and could even take the tramway; yet touristic exploitation could not diminish the splendor of the site.

French visitors were well aware that the presence of a large Chinese

---

35. E. M. Malézieux, *Souvenirs d'une mission aux Etats-Inis* (Paris: Dunod, 1874), p. 124.

population in San Francisco was directly related to the history of the city, and they soon learned to take their laundry to a laundryman with almond-shaped eyes. For most of them, this was their first encounter with a person of Asian descent, for few among them had gone to the much smaller New York Chinatown. So it was only natural to pay a visit to San Francisco's Chinatown in order to feel immersed in an Asian environment – an idea that was greeted with derision by the globetrotters who had just returned from China itself. Given the Californians' well-known distrust of the "Yellows" and the customs of this population, the French traveler was duly warned not to go to that part of town unaccompanied by a detective, who was easily found through the nearest police station or even through the personnel of the hotel. This practice tended to make the visitor quite tense and earned the detective a few dollars, but not every traveler was taken in.

Most of the time, this visit took place toward the end of the day, when the light of Chinese lanterns over the shop windows added to the disturbing atmosphere. The tour consisted of stopping by at a restaurant, often just to take a look; entering a temple where a statue of the Buddha shone softly in the half-darkness; taking a quick look at an opium den; sometimes watching, very briefly, a Chinese play, acted only by impassive men proffering guttural cries; and, as the height of daring, visiting a low-down brothel, in which case the traveler made it clear that he had not done anything there. At the end of such a tour, everyone expressed the same judgment. The Chinese were the "corrupt descendants of the sons of Heaven," done in by drugs and alcoholism; their habitat was disgusting and they did nothing to improve it; and so on. The visit thus exactly confirmed the opinion of San Francisco's whites and the manner in which it was conducted contributed to this convergence. Moreover, most of the observers were convinced that they had discovered an intact piece of the Celestial Empire that refused to be assimilated in any way into American society.

The presence of a fairly sizable French colony, consisting of approximately 6,000 individuals in the city of San Francisco alone, also attracted attention. At the end of the journey it provided the opportunity of meeting cordial compatriots, to eat French food, but also to comment on the splintering of these French people into multiple associations, a situation that prevented them from wielding political influence commensurate with their numerical strength. Despite these handicaps, the small French community had in the last years of the nineteenth century been able to endow itself with a French hospital without any help from France, from the state of California, or from the city; it was working beautifully and provided French travelers with American health care delivered in

French.[36] This achievement was food for thought, for it proved that the French were able to profit from American methods without losing their own personality.

San Francisco also provided a chance to visit the universities at Berkeley and Stanford. Here Jules Huret made ironic remarks about the puerility of the students' uniforms and on the "huge pedestal topped by the whole Stanford family, Monsieur, Madame, and Baby in bronze, a monument of the purest naivete, thoughtlessness, and bad taste imaginable."[37] This form of patronage was surprising to the French, who remained skeptical about these pretentious institutions, whereas they found those of the East more easily comparable to what existed in Europe.

All these activities, pursued in an ideal climate, delighted the French travelers. They found that people in the streets were much less in a hurry and friendlier than in the East, that smiling faces were not rare, and that there were even people out for a stroll. Urbain Gohier found that they resembled the Parisians, and as he walked in the parks, he wondered "whether it was worth it to come all this way from the Bois de Vincennes or Joinville le Pont." This atmosphere, on which everyone commented, made the charm of San Francisco and California; more than compensating for the disturbing aspect of certain streets, it was not found anywhere else.

Then, on 18 April 1906, an earthquake, followed by a terrible fire, destroyed most of this attractive city. The steamer carrying the Roulleaux-Dugage brothers arrived in the bay the next day; far offshore, red clouds billowing in a sky filled with terrified seagulls already announced a catastrophe. There was no question of landing; the brothers heard explosions and saw the gothic steeple of a church collapse under their very eyes. "The sea is liquid fire," and refugees who reached the ship spoke of looting. "This is a debacle, the titanic agony of a twentieth-century city!"[38] They finally disembarked at Oakland, where reconstruction planning was already under way. In Chicago, newspapers offered fortunes for photographs and news of the martyrized city.

What travelers like Abbé Klein and André Siegfried found over the next few years was above all one huge construction site, where building shacks stood side by side with brand-new skyscrapers and where

---

36. Thérèse, *Impressions d'une Parisienne sur les bords du Pacifique* (Paris: Juven, 1902), p. 196. She was the only one to use this facility, which was also admired by U. Gohier and F. Klein.
37. Huret, *En Amérique*, p. 69.
38. G. Roulleaux-Dugage, *Paysages et silhouettes exotiques* (Paris: Plon, 1908), pp. 246–47.

churches were built of wood. By 1914, a new and completely American-ized city was in place, but the adventure and the picturesqueness of the past were gone. Nevertheless, the Mediterranean atmosphere that made the charm of the city was still there, so that the 1906 disaster did not disrupt the French visitors' fascination with Frisco.

The other Californian place that delighted the French travelers was Los Angeles. Not many of them stopped there, for there was not much to see, but it was "a pretty little town amidst orange groves and euca-lyptus trees." Without large buildings, despite increasing activity after 1900, it had elegant, flower-lined avenues, and was blessed with an extra-ordinary climate year-round. An oasis of peace and beauty in a country that the French usually found lacking in both, Los Angeles received nothing but compliments. Picturesque excursions could be made from its residential neighborhoods; in 1903, Hollywood consisted of "one hotel, a few cottages, and a bank." Everything was so beautiful that one no longer felt like working, or even moving about:

> Sometimes automobilists come speeding by; why do these madmen come here? It seems to me that only peaceful people should be welcomed here, people who like to contemplate and to live in peace.[39]

This was a far cry from Chicago, its hectic pace and its smoke; refer-ences to the Côte d'Azur or Andalusia make it clear why the French travelers were happy here. They felt almost as if they were at home, and the exotic part of it was that they had this impression 9,000 kilometers away from Europe.

Returning to the East from California or on their way to it, French travelers often liked to take a detour to Salt Lake City. Of course, this was prompted above all by the wish to encounter some Mormons and to check out on the spot the effects of their much-decried polygamy; yet the city, compared with other American cities, was generally appreciated. As early as the 1870s, at a time when pioneers still traveled through the barely traced streets bordered by rudimentary wooden sidewalks, the French visitors were impressed by the abundance of trees and by the con-stant running of water in the streams along the main roads. In the years thereafter, the city modernized and adopted electric tramways, but it never lost its harmony and its cool air, which was all the more astonish-ing because the surrounding area was almost desert-like. The successful development carried out by the Mormons was considered all to their credit.

---

39. Huret, *En Amérique*, p. 17. How hard it is to make predictions!

By contrast, the famous Tabernacle, which took so long to build that it was completed only in 1893, was unanimously disliked. Tortoise back, dish cover – these and other qualifiers were used to cast aspersions on this strange specimen of church architecture. Beyond this decor, the visitors tried to scrutinize the faces of passers-by or of their hosts. They usually found that the women looked sad and that the men were stone-faced, if not outright threatening – which was in keeping with their own prejudices.

All in all Salt Like City, a green oasis in the mountains that was sometimes compared to Damascus, was not like other cities. It was pleasant and had neither elevated trains nor skyscrapers.

The West, aside from its cities, afforded the French visitors marvelous glimpses of nature, which was the other attraction of America.

## AMERICAN LANDSCAPES

On American soil, the air seemed fresher, the light sharper than in Europe, and this made people long to be out in nature, especially since "there is no horizon and not enough air in the city of New York, where during the summer one can hardly breathe." Yet as soon as they got off the boat, the immense size of the Upper Bay of that same New York or of San Francisco Bay and the power of the Hudson were very striking to Europeans accustomed to limited horizons and to the patchwork patterns of their own countryside: "In America, brooks are as large as rivers, rivers as large as lakes, and lakes as large as seas."[40] Moreover, the world-wide renown of the Niagara Falls, and later of other marvels such as Yellowstone National Park or the Grand Canyon, was bound to attract the visitor. But landscape also meant the countryside: endless stretches of fields, monstrous machinery, and lonely riders.

All of these eminently visual experiences were fundamental ingredients of the impact of the United States.

### Is There an American Countryside?

The French travelers were not in a very good position to answer this question. After all, their train rides from city to city rarely provided the opportunity to go into rural areas; for the most part they simply observed the landscape through the windows of their railroad cars.

Nonetheless, the French visitors soon realized that in the United States

---

40. J. Leclercq, *Un été en Amérique* (Paris: Plon, 1877), p. 178.

there was no countryside in the European sense of the word. This had to do, first of all, with the absence of real villages along the rail lines. To be sure, in some areas of Pennsylvania or Connecticut one could find a few small towns that might play this role, but elsewhere there were only farms without the network of villages that gives real structure to a countryside. At best, there might be some kind of railroad station, without any businesses or dwellings around it:

> Dusty or muddy roads go off from there in a straight line, bordered by trolley tracks, telegraph lines, and warning signals at the points where they cross the railroad tracks. These trails are traveled by those light vehicles perched on high wheels that one sees from one end of America to the other as the instrument best adapted to the most imperfect public road system.[41]

The appearance of this countryside, so well observed here by Vidal de la Blache, was common in the East and even more so in the West. The adventurers who traveled in the latter regions, Mandat-Grancey or de Woelmont, noticed these isolated farms without intermediary agglomerations before they came to towns filled with planks and canvas, the true sign of their temporary status.

On the other hand, rural areas seemed almost urbanized; thus in the region around Chicago, town and country were so interwoven that it was hard to say where one ended and the other began. Moreover, in the East, farms often contrasted sharply with their environment; frightful foundries and children in frayed shirts and pants could be seen close to impressive machines operated by farmers "dressed like lawyers," who changed their clothes after work. The most attentive observers realized that these farmers bought everything in the neighboring town, which had a general store; none of the merchandise there was of very good taste but one could find everything, and the organization equaled that of the biggest department stores – something that would be inconceivable in France.

Given this way of life, the rural landscape was profoundly different from that of any French region. There were no fences, but, by the same token, hardly any kitchen gardens either, and the "hideous" agricultural machinery seemed totally out of place. The houses seemed set up almost as they were in town and featured some elements of comfort, such as mechanical washing and ironing machines to help the housewife. Some even reported that American farmers read a great deal and that their daughters sometimes played the piano.

41. Vidal de la Blache, *A travers l'Amérique du Nord*, p. 518.

Such phenomena were amazing to contemplate, even if they were not common and by no means characteristic of American farmers as a group.

As one went West, the countryside became more and more different, and comparisons with France no longer made sense at all. The farms became larger and larger and far removed from everything, which further justified the use of enormous machines such as the mechanical cultivators observed at a ranch in the Dakotas as early as the 1880s. Herds also were enormous, and while traces of clearing were still visible, grand and untamed nature was always in evidence. These were no longer farmers, but *rancheros*, whose life – as popularized by Theodore Roosevelt[42] – seemed a passionate adventure, far from any peasant tradition and any roots in a particular piece of land. In California, things were different again, as they were in certain parts of Texas or Louisiana; here the traveler was impressed by gigantic orchards. This landscape was magnificent, filled with an air of opulence under the sun; at the time there was nothing like it in Europe. The term *peasants*, with its archaic connotations, was no longer applicable to this soaring development of an industrial organization of production.

The rural American landscape was thus completely exotic to the few French travelers who thought about this matter. To be sure, everything was not as well organized as they saw it on the major travel axes, but their impressions were strong and lasting. A certain admiration often gave way to worry about a rural way of life that did not seem to care about the virtues of tradition and stability. A visit to Puebla, a place strongly marked by Spanish influences, brought these deeply felt words to the pen of Frédéric Moreau:

> With what pleasure we greeted them, these modest thatched huts, for one feels that an ancient people lives here, loving its ancient customs and creating works that take their color and their originality from tradition. One must have traveled in the United States to really understand this feeling.[43]

All in all, the French travelers were well aware of the powerful impact of natural phenomena on this landscape; they had experienced intense summer heat, some of them also extremely cold winter temperatures, and they had noticed the poor quality of certain soils and the hard work of clearing. The very scope of the natural landscapes was bound to make a deep impression.

---

42. *Ranch Life* was translated into French in 1903 (Paris: Dujanic); *American Big-Game Hunting* the following year.
43. F. Moreau, *Aux Etats-Unis* (Paris: Plon, 1888), p. 65.

### Hudson and Niagara

The spectacle of nature, though perceived from the moment of arrival, took on its full dimension only in the country's interior.

First came the Hudson Valley, whether one traveled upstream or downstream, by steamer or by train. The site, of course, was impressive – the width of the river, the terraced banks covered with green vegetation – but it inevitably made the French traveler think of the Rhine Valley, here without medieval ruins but with a much higher volume of river traffic. The comparison was made by three-fourths of the French travelers; to some, this relative similarity was disappointing, for it failed to produce the surprise effect everyone expected from the American landscape.

The trip through the Hudson Valley often led to the Niagara Falls, a visit to which was one of the high points of every journey. The travelers arrived there duly prepared, both for the splendor of the site and the insensitive methods of those who exploited it. These abuses did not disappear when, owing to the pressure brought to bear by Frederick Law Olmsted, the falls became a state park in 1885. The unauthorized exploitation of the immediate surroundings of the falls was forbidden, but the visit itself was so thoroughly organized – the obligatory circuit, the raincoat-covered ride under the curtain of water, the coach ride, sometimes the approach by a little steamboat whose name, *Spirit of the Mist*, suggested strong emotions – that there was no hope of discovering the site on one's own. Yet the visitors' opinion was just about unanimous; the splendor of the view overruled all other considerations:

> Whatever men may have constructed around the falls in the way of bridges, staircases, or handrails, whatever they may have traced by way of paths or pasted on by way of signs has been unable to touch the intact and fierce beauty of these two enormous cascades.[44]

Some said that words failed them in the face of this phenomenon; others felt that the actual sight went far beyond anything that had been said about it. In any case, the impression was always very strong; the "caving in of a river," the muted roar heard from a distance, the spray of water and its green color, the power of the tumbling mass – all of these astounded the visitor. Often it was those who spoke of indescribable beauty who let themselves be carried away to the most effusive literary ravings at the sight of this "glaucous and white cataract." For most of the

44. P. Bourget, *Outremer* (Paris: Lemerre, 1895), vol. 2, p. 22.

visitors Niagara Falls constituted the first manifestation of the power of American nature, and what fascinated them most was indeed that "domesticated Titan" evoked by Paul Adam.

Nonetheless, a few of our travelers were disappointed or blasé. The former found it intolerable that the beauty of the site was spoiled by the omnipresence of human activities. "The vandals . . . some day they will build us a refinery right on the cataract,"[45] or do even worse. The latter, often women, had little use for this exuberance of nature; a nice waterfall, but equally nice ones could be found in Savoie or Dauphiné.

Aside from these few misgivings, the general impression was altogether favorable, particularly after the excesses of commercialism had been somewhat curtailed. This success explains why Niagara Falls became the natural site most frequently visited by the French as well as by other Europeans throughout the period 1870–1914 and much beyond.

### Plains and National Parks

The great plains the French visitors discovered when setting out from Chicago were impressive, not for their beauty but for their immense monotony. Many writers found themselves using maritime terms. Nothing but the ocean could give an idea of this "slightly undulating plain, without a tree, without a hill on the horizon. One might be in the middle of the sea!" The telegraph poles along the track even evoked the masts of ships, and the train rushing through a thunderstorm was likened to a ship caught in a storm. Yet the traveler, comfortably installed in his coach, was oppressed most of all by feelings of solitude and ennui conveyed by this landscape that seemed stuck in perpetual immobility. Pierre de Coubertin evoked the "infinite sadness of the American West," and others had little appreciation for these "three days of wheat fields."

The ride through the plains also provided a glimpse of cowboys, if only from afar, and especially the chance to see the railroad car filling up with rough men of brusque manners, with muddy boots, who spat all over the place without embarrassment or restraint. This was the height of picturesqueness, for here the visitor came face to face with that famous Westerner popularized in literary works, and besides, sociological observation was a welcome break from the monotony of the journey. Stops in railroad stations, aside from the chance to move one's legs or to satisfy one's hunger, also made it possible to see the first Indians, squatting next

---

45. P. Toutain, *Un Français en Amérique* (Paris: Plon, 1876), p. 63. Today an electric generator makes use of the power of the falls without disfiguring the site.

to tumble-down shacks draped in red blankets. This, surely, was American exoticism at its most exciting.

The Great Plains, even when partially cultivated, struck the French travelers by their aridity, especially in the Southwest, which some of them compared to the Crau region of Provence. Equally striking were the outsized dimensions and the wildness of the land, which made them understand what hard work was required of the men engaged in clearing or construction. There was a pervasive air of struggle here – against the soil and severe weather, against buffaloes and Indians.

Beyond the plains, great natural sights were revealed in the marvels of the Rocky Mountains. From the train, the traveler saw a great many mountainscapes that were impressive, but still comparable to those of the Alps or the Pyrenees. It took an extra effort to get a closer look at the old mining towns, particularly Virginia City in the early years of our period, and also the great natural sites, Yellowstone National Park and the Grand Canyon. Before the 1890s, the adventurous traveler had to climb up on some frightful charabanc or even one of the diligences which, resembling those of the days of Louis XIV, traveled on barely traced, bumpy, and dusty paths. Shelter could be had only in round billets. Thus, in 1879, the Lyonnais geographer Augustin Séguin, invited to Yellowstone by the park's "inventor" Ferdinand Hayden, had to travel 300 miles in ten days in one of these stagecoaches, escorted by a military guide,[46] but the spectacle was certainly worth it. Not many of the French travelers were ready for such experiences. Even when the completion of the transcontinental railroad lines made it easier to reach the site of Yellowstone Park, the Colorado River, or the Yosemite Valley, very few decided to make this detour, as Marie Dugard and Léo Clarétie did.

These natural wonders did not disappoint the French visitors, and their more or less inspired descriptions evoked staircases for Titans or "glass mountains" in connection with these massive rock formations and these gigantic geysers. Yellowstone Park, with its bubbling sulphur springs, was everyone's favorite.

In these majestic sites, the travelers were also struck by the continual presence of human activities. The gold diggers of the 1870s, who often looked like gallows birds and "talked about gold as our peasants would talk about turnips and cabbages," were succeeded by crushing mills and other mechanical digging equipment. Everywhere, even in the most remote places, innkeepers were ready for business; everywhere one also

---

46. A. Séguin, "Dix jours aux sources du Mississippi," *Bulletin de la Société de géographie de Lyon* IV (1881).

found traces of campfires. Canned food was omnipresent; the cans provided food for the visitor but spoiled the landscape: "blackened patches
and silvery cans" showed where a trapper, a gold digger, or a tourist had
passed:

> Cans of food are the great American expedient, they litter the ground of
> every campsite and are piled up in heaps that are less neat but just as high
> as those of the rag pickers of Paris.[47]

In a park like Yellowstone, such behavior seemed to be at odds with
the rules that obtained there. In fact, the French travelers were quite
surprised to see the prohibitions against camping, picking plants, or
approaching the animals.

> Such a decree certainly runs counter to the ways of a population given to
> using everything that can be used; but the devil will get his own anyway:
> the losses to cultivation will be made up a hundredfold by the spending of
> travelers who are attracted by this purported curiosity and who will also be
> attracted by the most bombastic advertisements.[48]

The very concept of the national park was unfamiliar, and consequently it was easy to suspect hypocrisy; moreover, it was surely less
moving to contemplate nature protected in this manner than a landscape
perceived as totally wild:

> ... here we have a wildness that is guaranteed, patented by Congress; it is
> officially protected barbarism, it is the maintenance of the uncultivated, it
> is the religion of nature. ... the beavers sleep in freedom under the watch-
> ful, paternal eye of the State.[49]

The French did not understand this kind of conservationism, and
besides, they felt that it was flawed by a contradiction. American nature,
they were given to understand, was threatened by human excesses to the
point of needing protection, and yet this very protection was likely to
attract even larger numbers of visitors. It was also true that these areas
of protected nature were in stark contrast with the activity and the
energy of the Americans that marked the land wherever one looked. The
only two persons in the group studied here who went to Alaska were
surprised to find intense activity in this quasideserted region. On the one
hand the town of Skagway, a vibrant center when Mathilde Shaw visited

47. H. Golliez, "Le parc national de la Yellowstone River aux Etats-Unis," *Nouvelle Revue*
   (May–June 1892): 532–33.
48. P. Rouget, "Une visite à Yellowstone Park," *Nouvelle Revue* (Nov.–Dec. 1894): 162.
49. Clarétie, *Feuilles de route*, p. 82.

it in 1897, had subsided seventeen years later when André Siegfried was there; on the other, Juneau, where he arrived at night, was brightly lit, bars and dives were open, "movie houses [were] playing, and the aggressive noise of player pianos fill[ed] the air...."[50]

The marvels of the landscape were thus always seen in association with the Americans' astounding capacity to make use of what it had to give. This could be the rampant commercialism at Niagara or the interior of a protected park like Yellowstone where, by way of another contradiction, one could nonetheless find a comfortable hotel.

Although the travelers' first impressions remained at the surface of things, they gave them a chance to taste the country's ambiance, to become aware of the strangeness of certain behaviors and the differences in customs. All of this led to reflections about the nature of American society with respect to its most exotic elements, blacks and Indians, for whom there was no equivalent in France.

50. André Siegfried, *Deux mois en Amérique à la veille de la guerre* (Paris: Colin, 1916), p. 108.

# 3

# *Western*

To a European, nothing is more exotic than this term, which evokes the landscapes of the American West, complete with roaming cowboys and Indians. Thanks to the cinema, this is still true at the end of the twentieth century, but the legend was created in the Gilded Age, when it arose out of real clashes, sometimes of epic proportions. The opening of the West, which had been started before the Civil War, resumed with renewed vigor thanks to the railroad, and in one generation new states were carved out of these vast spaces. Their native inhabitants, rounded up and placed into reservations, gave way to pioneers, miners, ranchers, and farmers. French witnesses to these changes were impressed by the American achievement, yet nostalgic about the passing of the old order.

Ever since the sixteenth century, the Indians had been part of the collective imagination of the Western world; by the early nineteenth century the dreams of Europeans were shaped by Leatherstocking and the other heroes of James Fenimore Cooper. In France, the considerable success of the works of Gustave Aimard perpetuated notions of the romantic and rugged American West until the 1870s. The French were therefore bound to be passionately interested in the fate of the Indians, who in those years experienced, even more than the blacks, their absolute nadir,[1] despite their fierce struggle, from Little Big Horn in 1876 to Wounded Knee fourteen years later. But were the French, as faraway observers, not likely to adopt the Americans' haughty contempt for the Redskins?

Crèvecoeur had seen the man of the West as part of a tradition of liberty and simple values, rough manners but big hearts. Now, in the second half of the ninteenth century, that image was renewed and sharp-

---

1. During this period, the American Indians were reduced to about 300,000 individuals, the lowest number ever.

ened. The figure of the cowboy became the mainstay of the legend of the frontier, an inextricable mixture of reality and imagination. The French would soon discover the various facets of this new hero; would they follow the American vogue and adopt him immediately, or would they keep their distance from a figure and an experience that were totally new to them?

The Far West thus fed, in a very immediate manner, into the tradition of American exoticism. And it did so by stressing not so much the struggle between Indians and pioneers as the conflict-laden juxtaposition of these two antagonistic worlds, a situation in which the apparently irreversible decline of one side gave impetus to the prodigious rise of the other. Were the French prepared to choose between them?

## A LACK OF PASSION

### *Little Interest in Cowboys and Indians*

No French observer devoted an entire book to either of these two groups, so that they appear only incidentally. Major works of synthesis, such as those of Claudio Jannet, Auguste Carlier, Henri Gaullieur, Elisée Reclus, and Baron Estournelle de Constant, treated the Indians in a few pages.[2] We thus have only five authors, writing over the course of the entire period, which is very few. These few works say nothing at all about the cowboy, whose reputation was not yet sufficient to entitle him to a place in prestigious scholarship.

There are also accounts of travelers who visited the West. Most of them only briefly evoked the fate of these populations in connection with the few individuals they may have seen from the train. However, a certain number of authors, about ten in all, lived among cowboys and Indians and observed them very closely. Some, roughly half of them, were almost professional explorers during the first half of the period. Among them were Louis Simonin, who precisely described life in the West.[3]

---

2. C. Jannet, *Les Etats-Unis contemporains* (Paris: Plon, 1876), pp. 439ff. Jannet makes frequent reference to the studies of A. Carlier, which were collected in his definitive work *La république américaine* (Paris: Guillaumin, 1890). This work devoted some hundred pages of its book 15, vol. 4, to the Indian question, examining it historically in a rigorously balanced and solidly documented manner. H. Gallieur, *Etudes américaines* (Paris: Plon, 1891), dedicated one fourth of his study to the "red race." E. Reclus, in his *Nouvelle géographie universelle* (Paris: Hachette, 1892), pp. 680–90, presented a well-documented assessment of the Indians' situation until Wounded Knee. See also P. E. de Constant, *Les Etats-Unis d'Amérique* (Paris: Colin, 1913), pp. 333–41.

3. In addition to his *Grand ouest* (Paris: Hachette, 1869), which contained his basic infor-

Then, in the 1880s, writers like the brothers Verbrugghe or Arnold de Woelmont went hunting in the Denver region,[4] and Edmond de Mandat-Grancey spent two months with friends in the Black Hills of Dakota.[5] A few years later, one can add Mathilde Shaw of the *Nouvelle Revue*, who published in that paper a series of articles devoted to her various stays among the Indians, whom she studied almost in the manner of an anthropologist.[6] The opinions of this small group of observers are particularly valuable.

And finally, other authors made occasional contributions to the knowledge of the groups who populated the West. Paul Bourget, who published the "Confessions of a Cowboy" in *Outremer*, certainly helped to popularize the subject,[7] and Marie Dugard and Saint André de Lignereux took a lively interest in the Indians.[8]

All in all, the small number of available sources is a first indication that there was not a great deal of interest in the American West in the France of that era.

### Mixed Messages

Not all of these contributions constitute rich sources. Some authors, such as Auguste Carlier or Elisée Reclus, were well informed about current American events and assembled precise information on the Indians and the policies concerning them, yet their reports remain distant and abstract. Among the travelers, only Mathilde Shaw had personal experiences with the tribes of the North, the Central Plains, and the South; the others only encountered scattered groups in the Rocky Mountains, Utes of Utah, or Shoshones further to the south. Others saw only a few ragged-looking Indians loitering around the railroad tracks. A visit to an Indian reservation was not usually included in the circuit, unlike in Canada, where Old Lorette near Quebec and Caughnawaga on the outskirts of Montreal brought Indians within the reach of even the laziest

---

mation, L. Simonin treated the same themes in articles in the *Revue des Deux Mondes*, *Le Tour du Monde*, and other publications of the 1870s.

4. L. and G. Verbrugghe, *Promenades et chasses* (Paris: Calman-Lévy, 1879); A. de Woelmont, *Ma vie de nomade aux Montagnes Rocheuses* (Paris: Didot, 1878).

5. E. de Mandat-Grancey, *Dans les Montagnes Rocheuses* (Paris: Plon, 1885); see also J. Leclercq, *Un été en Amérique* (Paris: Plon, 1877).

6. M. Shaw, "Chez les Indiens de l'Oklahoma," *Nouvelle Revue* (July–Aug. 1893): 785–802, and (Sept.–Oct. 1893): 102–116; "Au pays des Moquis pueblos," *Nouvelle Revue* (March–April 1894): 823–39; "Avec mes amis iroquois," *Nouvelle Revue* (Sept.–Oct. 1894): 776–98.

7. P. Bourget, *Outremer* (Paris: Lemerre, 1895), vol. 2, pp. 22–70.

8. M. Dugard, *La Société américaine* (Paris: Hachette, 1896), pp. 75–90 and 106–115; Saint André de Lignereux, *L'Amérique au XXe siècle* (Paris: Taillandier, 1909), pp. 250–90.

traveler.[9] Under these circumstances, the French had no first-hand information and relied largely on American opinion, whether expressed in personal conversation or in published local sources concerning these matters.

One proof of this state of affairs is provided by the references that came to the minds of journalists when they reported on the Buffalo Bill show in Paris or of travelers who saw Indian shows at the Chicago World's Fair. Seen as no more than "living illustrations" of the stories of Fenimore Cooper and Gustave Aimard, these performances promised to "explain Leatherstocking and Faithful Heart to you."[10] It is true of course that such events purposely cultivated this folkloric aspect, but the reactions of the French show that very little had been added to their knowledge of the Indians. It should be added that the great events of Indian history, such as Little Big Horn or Wounded Knee, found little resonance in the French press, which referred to them only in the most indirect manner.

Things were somewhat different with respect to the cowboys, despite the small number of articles devoted to them. Clashes between cattlemen and farmers and the exploits of outlaws in the mushrooming settlements of the West were the ingredients that gave impetus to the legend of the West that had begun to take shape around 1860. One must therefore try to find out how the French learned about these events. In 1897, Pierre de Coubertin indicated that for him the Myth of the West was associated with the names of Hepworth Dixon and Edmond de Mandat-Grancey.[11] Dixon, the English author of *The White Conquest*, enjoyed considerable popularity in France in the 1870s; his short plays described the most picturesque aspects of American life and many readers must have discovered the West through them. The work of Mandat-Grancey, a former navy officer from Savoy, had the same success and was serialized in *Le Correspondant* before it was published in book form. In fact, when Paul Bourget gathered the confessions of his cowboy, his protagonist was none other than the Duc d'Auzias-Turenne, the friend with whom Mandat-Grancey had stayed in 1883. Thus Bourget's book served to reinforce his predecessor's popularity, which had been confirmed when Buffalo Bill brought his act to France. Others subsequently continued this relay.[12]

9. S. Simard, *Mythe et reflet de la France* (Ottawa: University of Ottawa Press, 1987), pp. 150–51.
10. "La bande de Buffalo Bill," *Le Temps* (20 May 1889).
11. P. de Coubertin, *Souvenirs d'Amérique et de Grèce* (Paris: Hachette, 1897), pp. 20–21.
12. Mandat-Grancey was mentioned in *Le Temps* of 20 May 1889, and the role of H. Dixon was confirmed by P. Toutain, *Un Français en Amérique* (Paris: Plon 1876), p. 101. Later evidence is P. Passy, *Dans le Far-West* (Paris: Librairie populaire, 1897), and then in the translations of the works of Theodore Roosevelt and many other authors.

The cowboys and their exploits thus seem to have become known in France thanks to this small number of persons, who must be credited for the adoption of this new hero, a major figure to this day.

## COWBOYS: ADVENTURE AND FREEDOM

Cowboys were thus but variants of those Westerners who had fascinated the Old World all along.

### *Rugged Men*

> Peddlers, miners on foot or riding on donkeys, that whole crowd of intelligent and bold-looking people with their tanned skin and their strong arms, whose life is one continuous struggle against nature; men whom we have agreed to call pioneers of civilization.[13]

This little picture, painted by Baron de Hübner and echoed by other authors in a more philosophical vein, evoked a breed of "modern crusaders" who to some of the French constituted the "true America." Such a view is in the direct lineage of the tradition going back to Crèvecoeur and Jefferson.

Yet for the most part, the French were more ambiguous about this Westerner. On the one hand, the most attentive observers realized that under the rugged exterior, the rough manners, and the Californian overalls that protected him from the dust, there was a fiercely determined worker who spared himself no trouble. He might be a miner who had no insurance or retirement fund or he might be a true cowboy, one of those men who never took time off during the roundup, when they stayed in the saddle all day long for meager wages.[14] It was understandable that such men sometimes needed to relax and that by week's end they went to the saloon nearest to their ranch in order to waste their few hard-earned dollars, rather like sailors who like to go out on the town at every port of call.[15] And yet the work of the cowboys involved a certain waste of natural resources, disregard for the most elementary forms of social conventions, and an aggressive egalitarianism that offended even the

13. Baron de Hübner, *Promenade autour du monde* (Paris: Hachette, 1877), p. 82.
14. Mandat-Grancey, *Dans les Montagnes Rocheuses*, pp. 43ff. Coming from this ultra-royalist author, the remarks about the absence of retirement funds are surprising.
15. A very pertinent remark by Abbé Etienne, *Choses d'Amérique: De Cherbourg à New-York au Yellowstone*, lecture given to the pupils of the Institution Saint Etienne at Chalons sur Marne, 29 Feb. 1904.

most favorably disposed French traveler: Dirty clothes, spittoons, and adulterated whisky were particularly objectionable in railroad cars or in hotels. At the same time, these men were quite picturesque. In order to grasp the exotic flavor of Rapid City, South Dakota, in the summer of 1883, one should read Mandat-Grancey's pages on the saloons populated almost exclusively by colonels and majors, given these people's pronounced taste for prestigious titles.

On the other hand, the cowboys had had to struggle with the Indians, a danger that was not yet very remote in the 1870s, and before they were able to settle down, there had been clashes between rival bands and encounters with pilferers looking for a quick buck. This aspect of the legend of the West developed very early, and Americans liked to share it with foreign visitors. Thus, Louis de Turenne was shown in Nevada City the rifle that had been used to kill three men who had robbed the famous Wells Fargo Company three years earlier, in 1866. Paul Toutain was told about Bob Wilson, the legendary sheriff of Denver County in its heyday. Similarly, the James brothers, who had cleaned out the passengers of mail coaches and trains in the 1870s, were featured in the tales told by Americans to French visitors around 1880. The cowboys were presented as the scourge of the West and reputed to be more dangerous, armed, and given to drink than even the Indians.

These characters, who also appeared in popular American novels, therefore struck the imagination of visitors, although attentive travelers were sometimes disappointed: "... desperado gamblers are much rarer than is imagined by people who have visited the country only in books."[16] But this warning sounded by Arnold de Woelmont fell on deaf ears, and the show presented in Paris by Buffalo Bill in 1889 further embroidered the image of a brutal and truculent way of life. So much did the legend feed upon itself that Paul de Rousiers, traveling in 1890, calmly and deliberately acquired a revolver before going out West. He felt quite ridiculous when he found this object in his luggage, for the mining towns where he spent time were perfectly calm and far from the commotion that was attributed to them in old Europe.

Gradually the figure of the cowboy was to become more familiar as the symbol of a violent and picturesque adventure rather than of regular work. This legend prevailed, and the role of Edmond de Mandat-Grancey was essential to its adoption in France.

16. De Woelmont, *Ma vie de nomade*, p. 309.

Western                                                                   93

### The *"Fleur de Lys"* Ranch

When all is said and done, the life of the pioneers of the West was viewed with a certain detachment by the French, who found it too far removed from their own experience. However, a small group of Frenchmen who had left France for the American West actually lived the life of a cowboy; they served as models for Baron de Mandat-Grancey and for Paul Bourget. Readers in Paris or Romorantin thus learned about the life of the American West by reading about French cowboys.

What happened was that Edmond de Mandat-Grancey and his companion went to Dakota in 1883 at the behest of a company that sought to promote the raising of half-breed horses in the United States. They therefore went to see the Duc d'Auzias-Turenne, who had been trying to develop such a stud farm in the Black Hills of Dakota for several years. This aristocrat had settled in the West because he could not abide the French Third Republic, the detestable *Gueuse*. Calling his ranch "Fleur de Lys," he also marked his horses with that symbol. Not far from there, at Little Missouri, lived Baron de M., who had taken the same course. The writings of Mandat-Grancey and the "confessions" collected by Paul Bourget provide a fairly clear picture of the itinerary taken by this astonishing personality. Auzias-Turenne left France when all hope of a restoration of the monarchy seemed lost, that is, after 1877. He hated New York and went West to start a new life. In these years he found there an extremely rough way of life, complete with brawls in the saloons of Custer City and horse thieves. Once he had settled at his own ranch, he often had to contend with bandits and organize his own defense, setting up his own swift and no-nonsense justice. He even won fame when he and his cowboys arrested a particularly dangerous outlaw and was written up in the local newspaper, which was not accustomed to seeing this role played by a pure-blooded aristocrat.

The duke thus lived an exciting, hard, but healthy life and was able to prosper without being hampered by governmental constraints. He assembled a team of cowboys who were all equals in their work, even one black man who lived just like everyone else. Sometimes he would show an amazed visitor his large Dakota saddle. About fifteen years after Mandat-Grancey's visit, some young Frenchmen eager to embrace the grand life of the horse breeder came to the Fleur de Lys Ranch, but the Duc d'Auzias-Turenne had already moved on to new horizons.[17]

---

17. Comte G. des Etangs, *L'Amérique laborieuse, l'Amérique croyante*, lecture, church of Gros-Caillou, 22 Dec. 1889, pp. 9–11.

Anecdotes aside, however picturesque they may be, the popularity enjoyed by the works of Mandat-Grancey and Bourget shows that their readers liked these adventures of a Frenchman, which kindled the imagination of even the most stay-at-home among them. It should be added that the author of *Outremer* considered this individual destiny proof that the "French race" could be a conquering power on an equal footing with the Anglo-Saxons, that it could beat them at their own game. More precisely, he felt that this life at the ranch might suit a certain aristocratic ideal that Auzias-Turenne claimed as his own. Here was a seigneur who controlled the fate of his companions, who had to lay his own life on the line and make his mark before he was accepted, but who did not have to contend with either the weight of the state or the perversion of organized democracy. Defended by all who lived and worked there, the ranch was thus akin to a castle of the early Middle Ages.

At the very time when the life of the frontier was considered, following the theses of Frederick J. Turner, as the incubator of American democracy, certain Frenchmen seem to have been led by these few examples, vastly inflated by their literary popularity, to see it as the favored terrain of a new aristocracy, a place of total freedom where there were no constraints. In such a view, the American Republic had very little in common with the French Republic.

The cowboy, then, in whatever guise he was presented – as "hypochondriac of the West," glum and unwashed loner, highway robber, taciturn rider with a big heart, democrat or aristocrat – unquestionably had the typically American qualities of simplicity, energy, and self-confidence. The Indian, even when he was feared, was seen as his exact opposite.

## INDIANS: CONTEMPT AND NOSTALGIA

By 1870, a cultivated Frenchman who had read Chateaubriand and Catlin might ask himself a few questions upon arrival in Omaha, the threshold of the West:

> What has become of the Redskins? Are there still wigwams and tomahawks? Do they still scalp their prisoners? Or has all of this fallen into the realm of Ancient History, along with the exploits of the Egyptians and the Medes?[18]

The answer was not long in coming, and it was unanimous. Travelers who encountered Indians and armchair writers alike were convinced that the

18. E.-M. Malézieux, *Souvenirs d'une mission aux Etats-Unis* (Paris: Dunod, 1874), p. 93.

first inhabitants of North America were a vanishing species. The figures were there, and they seemed to indicate an irreversible decline. The prospects were not good.

### A Contemptible People?

The French observers who were interested in the Indians drew their information from three sources, each of which purveyed a very distinct image. The first was the "Cooper-Aimard tradition," the second was direct contact in the field, and the last was censuses and reports produced by the United States government.

The traditional folkloric image did not stand up to scrutiny for long. Travelers did not encounter any fringed leather pants and moccasins, and even those who watched Buffalo Bill's show, delighted though they were to see the embodiment of their youthful dreams, could not help but wonder:

> I do imagine that it will be better to see them over there, in their natural surroundings. Here they look somehow foreign. I was wrong to talk of Chateaubriand's Indians; at best, they are Gustave Aimard's.[19]

But once the traveler was on the spot, the Indians were not even as good as the already discounted images purveyed by the popular novelist:

> How much better the Redskin looks in a grand spectacle at the Châtelet theater! . . . The type is animal-like and coarse, men and women seem misshapen . . . This is not a race, but a degradation of the human species.[20]

No doubt, this statement was elicited by one pitiful group seen in a Western railroad station, but the assessment is far from isolated. Throughout our period, the French travelers, whatever their views of the social problems raised by the Indians, were extremely disappointed by those they had occasion to meet.

The first thing that struck them was the Indians' ugliness, particularly that of the women, followed by their physiognomies and their attire. Usually wearing European clothing, sometimes including a battered black felt hat, they were often wrapped in red blankets of doubtful cleanliness. These poor ragged people would beg, and they rarely elicited friendly reactions; many visitors compared them to monkeys. It is true

19. *Le Temps* (2 June 1889); the journalist deplored that the Indians were always the losers in the show.
20. G. Sauvin, *Autour de Chicago* (Paris: Plon, 1893), p. 203.

that younger Indians looked more lively; some of those who worked for the railroad companies had the litheness of accomplished hunters, but their mismatched and incongruous attire and the expression of bewildered resignation that so often struck the travelers quickly spoiled such fleeting impressions. The image the visitor took away from these ephemeral encounters marked his mind forever: "the hideous Indian with his square jaw and his dead gaze . . . squatting on his heels," and he would never forget those who spoke to him, trying to sell him wool blankets with bizarre designs, "looking sad and in speaking awkward English."

Repulsive looks and wretched poverty were noted by all the travelers, in 1876 as in 1903, regardless of their ideological positions. These testimonies came from people who had seen only small groups of Indians, marginal individuals who tried to get a few dollars or a little tobacco out of passengers on trains by begging or by selling a few mediocre handcrafted items. They were by no means representative of the various tribes that constituted the Indian people at that time. But even if he knew this, the French traveler was perturbed, for the reality was at odds with his youthful reading, and the nobility of carriage and the fierce pride that had been the very hallmark of the legendary Indian seemed to have vanished. This first shock was upsetting, even for those who expected it, and often shaped subsequent reflections.

The opinions of a few witnesses who, not satisfied with these episodic and superficial encounters, learned about the actual way of life of the Indians did little to modify the prevailing views. Thus, in the 1870s, Sioux or Cheyenne camps were depicted as miserable, populated by filthy women and children, with idle men loitering about. The decor consisted of smoke-filled wigwams and dead bodies hanging in trees; and here too one read about those red blankets, those battered hats, and a general air of poor health.[21] Given this picture, how could anyone not believe the officer who spoke of savagery, pillage, and inveterate laziness, particularly since it was he who had brought the very recent news of Custer's death at Little Big Horn, caused, possibily, by his own recklessness but more likely by the violence of people who seemed to have been crushed once and for all? The best one could do here was to appreciate the skill of the occasional Indian guide who still killed buffaloes with bow and arrow.

But as the noise of the Indian wars quieted down, a few observers came to nuance these lugubrious impressions. Thus, around 1890, Mathilde Shaw made a clear distinction between the state of the inhab-

21. A. Seguin, *Dix jours aux sources du Mississippi*, offprint of the *Bulletin de la Société de géographie de Lyon* (1881), p. 28.

itants of the Indian territory, "degenerate and brutalized by drink and excesses," and the gentle and balanced life of the pueblo villages, the special culture and qualities of the Iroquois, who told her the story of Hi-a-watha. And in 1902, Father Baudot encountered in his parish near Spokane a number of half-civilized Nez Perces of noble bearing. But very few travelers paid attention to such isolated remarks, which inevitably did not circulate widely.

Thus the general impression, fleeting and incomplete as it was, remained very negative. The contrast was just too great between a ranch and an Indian camp, a train and these ragged wretches. This had nothing to do with any legend, whether it came from Chateaubriand, from Cooper, or from Aimard.

The information furnished by American documents did little to modify these direct observations. The census showed declining numbers of Indians, and the comments of white Americans emphasized their laziness, whereas in the first years of our period, there was more talk of their barbaric violence. This being the case, one was naturally led to wonder about this people's intrinsic unfitness for life in the United States at the end of the nineteenth century.

The best-informed French travelers were well aware that before the Indians had extensive contact with the whites, they had shown a remarkable ability to adapt to a difficult environment, and that they had shown great courage in the fighting of 1875–76. These events had even aroused the admiration of certain military men who had been involved in them; the Sioux in particular had undeniable warlike qualities that were part of their nobility. Another episode also proved the courage and the dignity of these disparaged populations; this was the famous 1881 march of the Nez Perces who fled northward in the worst conditions imaginable. A few years later, Henri Gaullieur did not hesitate to walk the same way.[22]

Yet the Americans felt that these very aptitudes explained the savagery of which they accused the Indians. Around 1875, the travelers were sometimes shown a man who had survived a scalping – it always seemed to be the same man – and stories of particularly horrible tortures were told. These examples, which were simply mentioned in travel diaries, were embellished and developed in the more popular published travel accounts. Directly based on American sources, these French accounts

---

22. Gaullieur, *Etudes américaines*, pp. 32–33. The heroism of these Utes on their 2,800-kilometer trek was also evoked by A. de Chenclos, "Peaux-rouges et visages pâles: Les réserves indiennes de l'Oklahoma," *Revue des Deux Mondes* (15 June 1889): 833–59; and it was depicted in many Westerns.

dwelled at length on the savagery of Indian life in its most horrible and hence most picturesque aspects.

The fact is, however, that little by little the Indians had succeeded in adapting as best they could to the conditions of life on the reservations; good examples are the Cherokees and even the Sioux of the 1880s. Various French observers, such as Auguste Carlier, Elisée Reclus, or Henry de Varigny, were fully aware of these partial successes, and Mathilde Shaw explained very clearly that the Indian "savagery" was by no means gratuitous, but part and parcel of their traditional system of thought, in which physical strength was paramount.[23] Nor were these tribes devoid of a sense of religion, as could be seen in their ghost dances and their totems: "Do not laugh at these noses in the shape of a pelican bill, nor at these round apple-shaped eyes, nor at these crimson red cheeks. Be respectful: these are gods."[24]

But of course these qualities did not constitute the best assets with which to succeed in American society; moreover, most observers paid no attention to them. Indeed they felt that the main flaw of the Indians was, as the white Americans said, their unwillingness to work, and they were struck by the contrast between the permanent activity of the whites and the "incorrigible sloth" of the Redskins. To give them land to cultivate seemed pointless, since all they thought about was hunting; attempts to educate them were of little use, since they were unable to go beyond a certain level. These typical American arguments were repeated by the French, for they were in keeping with the most prevalent racial prejudices of the time. This is why in the end even people favorably disposed toward the Indians accepted the view that they were fundamentally inferior. This seemed to be the source of an apparently ineluctable decline:

> Ignorant of the laws of economics, the Indian accuses the Whites of a social phenomenon for which nature alone is responsible. Here we have 300,000 people who need an area as large as central Europe to live on. In such an area 10 million people could live, provided they fertilized it by their sweat. ... These 100 million people will in the end overcome these 300,000 savages; this is prescribed by the ineluctable power of things or, better, by the law of progress and of civilization, which is the only law of History.[25]

This explicitly Darwinian opinion of Louis Simonin is rather overstated and by no means shared by all other French travelers; nonetheless, it is

23. Mathilde Shaw, while sympathetic to the Indians, nonetheless reflects a certain paternalism, which was typical for her time.
24. G. Stiegler, *Le tour du monde en 63 jours* (Paris: Société d'Imprimerie et de Librairie, 1901), p. 306; the same attitude was expressed by F. Klein a few years later.
25. L. Simonin, *A travers les Etats-Unis* (Paris: Charpentier, 1875), pp. 370–71.

the underlying assumption in many commentaries. The Indians, it was often felt, were too weak to survive in a difficult world, but a large part of the responsibility for this situation must also be attributed to the American authorities.

### An Oppressed People

The fact is that the French visitors, whatever their attitudes toward the Indians, were almost unanimous in condemning their treatment by the government of the United States.

All these observers noted that alcoholism was ravaging the communities, that the agents of the Bureau of Indian Affairs were often corrupt, that the various treaties between the President and the tribes had not been respected, that the territory of the reservations had shrunk like the proverbial shagreen leather, and that the opening of Oklahoma to white settlers had been extremely hurtful to the Indians. In this context, there was nothing fundamentally surprising about the 1890 revolt of the Sioux. Carlier and Reclus launched veritable indictments, presented in precise and well-documented form; Claudio Jannet did not hesitate to speak of an "indelible blemish" in denouncing this "systematic destruction of the Indians"; and travelers and magazine writers used even stronger language.

The Verbrugghe brothers, visiting a Cheyenne encampment, denounced the Indian as "sly, . . . ferocious, and vindictive," but at the same time were indignant that he was denied his most unquestionable rights, beaten down as soon as he raised his head: "this is not a matter of grafting; here we have a tree that uproots another and takes over its hole."[26] Baron de Mandat-Grancey, having earlier compared the Indian to prehistoric people who were lacking "the final touch," exclaimed: "The Americans' policy concerning the Indians in general is abominable. Its aim is their extermination. The politicians make little effort to hide this."[27]

Those French travelers who had a certain sympathy for these populations found the attitude of the American government even more hateful; if the Indians disappeared altogether, that would be the cause. Thus Auguste Carlier, and around 1905 Laborer, writing in the *Nouvelle Revue*, described in detail the measures taken by the authorities to dispossess the Indians of the subsoil of the reservations, along with the maneuvers of the swindlers who robbed them. The laziness of which the Redskins were accused, they said, was due at least as much to these actions as to their

---

26. Verbrugghe and Verbrugghe, *Promenades et chasses*, p. 169.
27. Mandat-Grancey, *Dans les Montagnes Rocheuses*, p. 22.

natural temperament. The authorities wanted to keep them in idleness and purposely risked outbreaks of ferocity provoked by the intolerable constraints to which they were subjected.

This condemnation of the American methods found its way into the mainstream Parisian press when the famous editorialist Jean Frollo wrote of these Indians in the *Petit Parisien* that they were "the most unfortunate and the most disinherited of people."[28]

Such unanimity calls for some interpretation. For one thing, it allowed the French to compare, to their advantage, the treatment meted out to the Indians in the territories dominated by the Anglo-Saxons with conditions in Latin-controlled areas. Thus, the conservatives were pleased to celebrate the humanity of French policies in the old Canadian territories. On the other hand, condemning the Americans made it unnecessary to draw more timely comparisons with the situation of certain native populations in the French colonies. Louis Simonin was the only one to admire the settling of the West founded on the basis of total liberty for the settler, but Paul Estournelles de Constant had a more subtle view of things:

> The same problem exists in all the European colonies to this day. Think about it: if we had listened to all our bad instincts in Tunisia only thirty years ago, we would have agreed to reducing the natives to the same state as the Redskins. It is easier to exterminate or abase a people than to instruct it; but when one tries to replace it, one realizes that one can run into worse, and one is sorry.[29]

Despite all these problems, the action of the American government had had a few positive secondary effects. One did find Indian schools, even if they were not very good; certain tribes, like those of the Tuscarora Reservation near the Niagara, almost lived like Europeans; others had been Christianized, and on certain reservations one could find Indian college graduates who had little in common with those of Fenimore Cooper. By the beginning of the twentieth century, was it still possible to speak, as Henry de Varigny had done in 1893, of a "race on the way out"?

### A Future, Nevertheless?

By and large, the French, like most Americans, were convinced that the Indians would eventually disappear. However, within this consensus, one must distinguish between the realists and the nostalgic souls.

---

28. "Les strips," editorial of 11 Sept. 1901, evoking the settling of Oklahoma.
29. Constant, *Les Etats-Unis d'Amérique*, pp. 336–37. His opinion is particularly interesting because he also wrote about Tunisia. But since he was a radical pacifist, his positions had little influence.

The former, even if they did not go as far as Louis Simonin, who postulated a Darwinian mechanism, expressed little regret. Thus the prefect Félix de Biancourt wrote in 1886:

> Aside from the pity one always feels for the former masters of the land when they have been dispossessed by violence and conquest, these poor, ragged, debased, and mindlessly indolent beings who whine for alms cannot possibly inspire any sympathies.[30]

This categorical judgment found a strange echo in the words of the anarchist journalist Urbain Gohier in 1901: "They are ugly in a gentle and servile way. They accept slavery on the soil where their forefathers lived free: they are undeserving of any interest."[31] The Indians' failure to move in the direction of progress explains why many French observers preferred to stay with their memories of Fenimore Cooper or Gustave Aimard.

The nostalgic souls, who were actually in the majority, deplored the vanishing of a people that had been the inspiration for literary exoticism. Indians were the last remnants of a primitive humanity which the denizens of the early twentieth century must not forget. It should be noted that some, while considering the Indians lamentable specimens, felt that this did not justify their disappearance. That would be a grave injustice, for even an "inferior" people had a right to live. Their loss would be a real loss for humanity, and indeed deprive the white race of potential enrichment. Thus pity and nostalgia sometimes crept into these pages, and these poignant sentiments were best expressed by women. Thérèse recalled the past dignity of the Indians of the Northwest; noble and brave before the conquest, they knew nothing about theft, and it was tragic to see them now aping the whites. At a different level, Mme. Grandin compared the Indians with the blacks and found them much superior, for they had preserved their pride as free people, even though they were "tracked down like savage beasts."[32] Marie Dugard for her part felt "compassion mingled with respect" in the face of their "ineffable air of fierce pride and tired resignation"; she was certain that a whole piece of the history of the United States was disappearing with them, "the poetry of the past marching across the plain." Mathilde Shaw, with her better knowledge of the Indians, went beyond such sympathies:

30. F. de Biancour, *4,000 lieues aux Etats-Unis* (Paris: Ollendorf, 1888), p. 222.
31. U. Gohier, *Le peuple du XXe siècle* (Paris: Charpentier, 1903), p. 299.
32. Thérèse, *Impressions d'une Française sur la côte du Pacifique* (Paris: Juven, 1902), p. 60; Mme. L. Grandin, *Impressions d'une Française à Chicago* (Paris: Flammarion, 1894), p. 80.

A race that believes in the immortality of the soul and in filial love should not perish! But if it is indeed destined to vanish, all enlightened minds and all kind hearts must wish that the courage and the indomitable valor of the red men will meld with the qualities of moral uprightness of the white race.[33]

The Americans, however, did not have this tolerance for the Redskins and were likely to forget that Indian blood flowed in the veins of many of them. Moreover, this kind of assimilation, however improbable it might be, would amount only to a different form of disappearance. That is why certain French observers felt that the tribes must survive as the last valuable vestiges of vanished human races and that this was the only way to create a rich and varied humanity.

The nostalgic souls, then, were not all of one mind; some simply noted the bitter facts, while others looked for some hope of survival. Saint André de Lignereux, an isolated voice, even felt that the inhabitants of the old continent might play a special role:

It is impossible for a European of any sagacity and cultivation to see, approach, or frequent the Indians without feeling for them the most sympathetic interest and the most intense curiosity.[34]

All of these sympathies remained ambiguous, for some of the observers remained faithful to the Indian of legend, while others pretended to believe that he could be assimilated into American society.

The French felt completely powerless to stop this probable extinction, although, in the end, the Indians did not altogether disappear.

By the eve of the First World War, most of the French travelers still believed that the Native Americans were doomed, although a few good observers began to doubt this. In fact, the publication of the census figures for 1910 and certain American studies indicated that the number of Indians had begun to rebound; they now numbered about 400,000. It was also becoming increasingly clear that a distinction had to be made between those who wanted to preserve their traditional way of life by serving as tourist attractions and a minority of others who, without becoming fully Americanized, accepted education and certain forms of social organization. Moreover, it was clear that since Indian uprisings were no longer a threat, the certainty of their systematic extermination had also been eliminated. Estournelle de Constant even noted that a "reaction in their favor" was setting in, and that the Indians were finding

33. Shaw, "Chez les Indiens de l'Oklahoma," p. 116.
34. Saint André de Lignereux, *L'Amérique au XXe siècle*, p. 290.

a certain balance on their reservation. "Soon people will be sorry that there are so few of them."[35]

These few remarks are not indicative of any real optimism; it was just that a seemingly inexorable decline had been slowed down somewhat, although the Americans' fierce desire to dispossess the Indians had not disappeared. The French, largely unaware of the major efforts made in the United States to protect the Indians, had no way of reassuring themselves that the American dynamism that so impressed them would one day find a just and satisfactory solution to the Indian problem.

By the beginning of the twentieth century, the exoticism of the West was no longer what it had been fifty or a hundred years earlier. The French had discovered a new hero, the cowboy, whose name sounded better than *bouvier*; but on the other hand the first inhabitants of these regions were not nearly as romantic as those of earlier days.

Although the French found the Indians they encountered repulsive, they could not approve of the way the Americans treated them. But of course there was no way of knowing how French people in France would have reacted in the face of an analogous problem. Condemning the American methods made it possible to avoid such questions, and this was particularly necessary because the shock of the first contacts with this legendary people had shattered dreams engendered by childhood reading. By castigating the conduct of the Americans one could at least free oneself of this most disturbing impression.

The French travelers' opinion about the Indians is thus necessarily contradictory, for some criticized the Americans without appreciating the Indians, while others respected the Native Americans without really understanding them. These mixed feelings, made up of anger and pity, account for the periodic resurgence of the Indian question in some segments of the French public, both then and now.

In looking at these problems of the West, the French went beyond exoticism and discovered new facets of American activity. The scope of these problems often outweighed mere picturesqueness:

> . . . a long time from now, when history pronounces its general verdict of an era. . . . What will it say of this twofold madness that prompted us to empty America of its natural population and to replace it with Negroes torn from another world? What will it say when it has to see what has become of these Negroes in the United States?[36]

35. Constant, *Les Etats-Unis d'Amérique*, p. 341.    36. Ibid.

# 4

# *Les Nègres*

The term *nègre*, which has become derogatory today, was the one most frequently employed by French travelers in the second half of the nineteenth century. Revealing the racial conceptions of the period, it corresponds best to the American word *negro* and even *nigger*. This point needs to be made, for the existence of a large population of black race was indeed a specifically American phenomenon that forcefully struck French and other European visitors before the First World War brought more frequent contacts with black troops from Africa and America.

The sons of Ham certainly did not, or only marginally, walk the streets of Paris, and it was a rare Frenchman who had had the opportunity to travel to the French colonies in Africa or to the Antilles to meet such people. And yet French travelers, immediately upon landing in New York – amazed, not to say stunned, to begin with by the decor of the Empire City and by the vehemence of daily life – would come in contact with black people by just turning a corner, by boarding a public conveyance, and especially in the halls of their hotel and later in the Pullman cars of their trains. In most cases, this was the very first of such encounters, and it generated astonishment and many questions. If the traveler went on to Washington, not even to mention the Deep South, where such encounters became more and more frequent, there would be less astonishment but more sustained reflection.

## DOUBLY BIASED OPINIONS

### *The Weight of the Past and the Difficulties of the Present*

The French travelers' interest in the black American population had its roots in French tradition. By the beginning of our period, the generation that had passionately followed the debates leading up to the Civil War and the vicissitudes of that conflict was still alive.

Victor Hugo's 1859 appeal in support of John Brown[1] was no doubt still present in many people's memory, and the tremendous and undiminished success of *Uncle Tom's Cabin* had had a profound impact. First published in France in 1852, the book was an immediate triumph, with twelve different translations appearing in a single year. The Republicans exhibited great sympathy for the poor slaves,[2] and young Clemenceau, at the age of eleven, wept when he saw a play based on the novel at Nantes.[3]

Yet by 1870, the Civil War was over, and the end of slavery had also ended the emotions aroused by slavery. French interest in the United States and the struggle that had taken place there had had a great deal to do with domestic French politics, but these concerns had disappeared with the collapse of the Second Empire and the advent of the Third Republic. Nonetheless the echoes of that period had not yet died down completely, and so the fate of the American blacks could be evoked on certain occasions, as it was at the time of Harriet Beecher Stowe's death.[4]

However, renewed interest could also arise when the American situation was compared with that of the French colonies, even if analogies were not easy to establish. In order to produce a valid analysis, one would need to know both the United States and the French colonies very well, and this combination was necessarily very hard to come by among the French.

Thus, a traditional interest, rekindled by contact with the American reality, was bound to lead to reflections that could be particularly rich because they were not deformed by strictly French preoccupations. At a different level, in speaking of the "Negroes," French travelers in the United States had to test their general principles against what they learned from their sporadic contacts with this group of people who by and large remained unknown to them.

Yet during the years between Reconstruction and the First World War, the evolution of the position of blacks in the United States was not highly visible, and a foreigner could easily miss it altogether. More than 90

1. A poem similar to his "Message to Grant" cited in the Introduction to the present book.
2. S. Jeune, *De F.T. Graindorge à A.O. Barnabooth* (Paris: Didier, 1963), p. 16.
3. T.A. Sancton, "America in the Eyes of the French Left, 1848–1871," D.Phil. Diss., Oxford University, 1978, p. 29.
4. Her death on 1 July 1896 was the occasion for a number of articles in the press and the major reviews. Noteworthy is that of D. Halévy, *Revue de Paris* of 1 March 1898, along with a few others; but in general these analyses did not go beyond the author's personality and have little to say about the black problem.

percent of the blacks still lived in the South, where very few of these travelers went, and were employed in agriculture, which commanded only limited attention. Segregation was a daily reality that a hurried tourist might not even perceive. This period, which is often considered the nadir for the black population,[5] was punctuated by few great events, and with the exception of Booker T. Washington, few great men emerged. The movements that existed within the black population were for the most part subterranean, marginal, and rarely perceptible to a European.

### Limited Interest

It is significant that not one book was exclusively devoted to this subject. At best one finds substantial chapters in general works, grand overviews,[6] or the best travel accounts,[7] but for the most part the subject was broached only episodically. Consisting of picturesque reflections, descriptions of an encounter, or even the outline of a more or less superficial analysis, these notations often sound most credible when they deal with daily life and the first encounters between American blacks and the French. The major news magazines, finally, also treated this subject from time to time.

In short, we have regular data throughout our period, appearing at a rate that matches that of our documentation as a whole. However, this regularity must not be allowed to mask the relative meagerness of this set of data. The blacks were no longer of much interest to the French, who, without actually ignoring them, no longer spoke of them with passion. And even though these travelers had the advantage of direct contact, only a third of them wrote about blacks, a fact that can only mean that the French were not bursting with curiosity about them.

5. R.W. Logan, *The Negro in American Life and Thought: The Nadir, 1877–1901* (New York: Dial Press, 1954).
6. C. Jannet, *Les Etats-Unis contemporains* (Paris: Plon, 1876), devoted his chapter 22 to the "Questions of race and the antagonism between different parts of the Union," thirty pages out of almost 500, but he also spoke of the South in a more general manner. L. Weiller, *Les grandes idées d'un grand peuple* (Paris: Juven, 1903), evokes the black problem only incidentally. A. Carlier, *La République américaine* (Paris: Guillaumin, 1890), devotes forty-five pages of his 620-page volume 2 to "the human races in the United States" and some ten of these to the blacks. H. Gaullieur, *Etudes américaines* (Paris: Plon et Nourrit, 1891), devoted ninety pages to a comparison of the black race in the Antilles and in the United States.
7. G. de Molinari, *Lettres sur les Etats-Unis et le Canada* (Paris: Hachette, 1876); almost 100 pages deal with the South. J. Huret, *En Amérique*, vol. 1: *De New York à la Nouvelle Orléans* (Paris: Fasquelle, 1904), devotes four chapters and fifty pages to the black problem and to the South.

Moreover, when it came to this subject, the French essentially depended on American sources. These could be the regular publications of the Census Bureau or other American works, such as those by F. L. Hoffman and Kate Brousseau or Booker T. Washington's book *Up from Slavery*, which was translated into French in 1903 and very favorably received.[8] As the years went by, these primary sources were complemented by the major French syntheses, which successive readers used again and again. On the basis of such more or less accessible source materials – some of it was in English and some of it was difficult to obtain – anyone who made the effort was able to find out about the contemporary situation of blacks in the United States.

Added to these abstract data, finally, were travel accounts, but a reader who relied only on the information he took from such works was not necessarily aware how biased they often were. After all, travelers usually only met blacks in service occupations in transportation and hotels, and almost never in their more natural environment. Very few of the French visitors traveled to the South, and among these, even fewer had anything substantial to say about the black population. Thus the reality of the life of this population in the rural areas of the South did not come to the attention of the French visitors, who encountered large groups of blacks essentially in such places as Washington and Baltimore.[9]

Moreover, except for a few words exchanged with the porter or the conductor on a train, French travelers did not speak much with blacks, but they did talk about the blacks with whites. Certain travelers even reproduced their conversations with planters, while others made up

8. F.L. Hoffman, *Race, Traits and Tendencies of the American Negro*, a publication of the American Economic Association (August 1896). The author was an actuary of the Prudential Company, and his work was the basis of G. de Molinari's article, "Le Negro problem aux Etats-Unis," *Journal des Economistes* (April 1897): 3–21. K. Brousseau, *L'éducation des nègres aux Etats-Unis* (Paris: Alcan, 1904), is a thesis of the University of Paris directed by Dr. H. Nadeau, and the author was an American woman. Booker T. Washington's book was translated by O. Guerlac under the title *L'autobiographie d'un noir* (Paris: Plon, 1903). Among the various reviews of this book, one can cite that of T. Bentzon, who reviewed the original version in the *Revue des Deux Mondes* of 15 October 1901.

9. The population of the federal capital was already 40 percent black:

| | White population | Black population | Total population |
|---|---|---|---|
| 1870 | 88,000 | 43,000 | 132,000 |
| 1890 | 155,000 | 76,000 | 230,000 |
| 1900 | 192,000 | 87,000 | 331,000 |
| 1910 | 236,000 | 94,000 | 331,000 |

Source: *Historical Statistics of the U.S., Colonial Times to 1970*, U.S. Department of Commerce, Bureau of the Census (1975), part I, p. 26.

dialogues between a Southern segregationist and a theoretical defender of the Rights of Man à la française; this was done by Marie Dugard, Gustave de Molinari, and Jules Huret.[10] But none of them had the experience of living in contact with a different race. In every case, the French observers more or less consciously reproduced the concept of the black held by white Americans at that time – not exactly the way to arrive at a balanced judgment. It is true that by the beginning of the twentieth century, some French travelers had the occasion to meet Booker T. Washington, who provided them with a different view of things, but it is not certain that reading such authors as Thérèse Bentzon, Jules Huret, Urbain Gohier, or Saint André de Lignereux was sufficient to counterbalance so many consistent testimonies issued from identical sources.

The scant information we have makes it clear that one must be careful in assessing French opinion about the blacks, for it was divided and rarely neutral. One must also keep in mind that the major outlines of this opinion were formed under the influence of current American events.

### Illusions That Did Not Last

In the first years of our period, one still encounters the enthusiasm that many French people had felt when the end of the Civil War brought the emancipation of the slaves. When Albert-Edouard Portalis returned from the United States in 1869, he felt that the racial prejudice he had observed was unjustified, and that the inferior position in which the blacks found themselves was relative and temporary; it was bound to become attenuated and finally disappear, just as slavery itself had disappeared.[11] For his part, Edouard de Laboulaye, writing the preface to the book of one of his students, had lost none of his fervent admiration for the achievements of the Americans and his certainty that the great liberation undertaken by Lincoln and his allies would be a success:

> Regenerating four and a half million Negroes kept in ignorance and brutality ... that is certainly an evangelizing task that reduces all missions to faraway places to insignificance. ... Already the harvest has yielded more than just hope; as soon as yesterday's freed Negro has received any education he begins to work on the emancipation of his brethren.[12]

10. M. Dugard, *La société américaine* (Paris: Hachette, 1896), judges the situation in a very balanced and nuanced manner; the analysis of Molinari, *Lettres sur les Etats-Unis*, is particularly thorough, and the positions of J. Huret are sometimes hesitant or ambiguous, and the arguments he advances for both sides seem more theoretical than sincere.
11. A.-E. Portalis, *Les Etats-Unis, le self-government et le césarisme* (Paris: A. Chevalier, 1869), p. 185.
12. E. Laboulaye, *L'Amérique actuelle*, preface by E. Jonveaux (Paris: Charpentier, 1870).

While there is no doubt some truth to such a picture, this vision also conveys an impression of euphoria that the facts were to dispel only too soon. Nonetheless, in the next few years, the *Grand Dictionnaire* of Pierre Larousse continued to perpetuate this particularly optimistic vision. It praised the American people who, by freeing the slaves, "at the same time honored humanity and liberty," and called the development of the South "admirable," since black schools there were accepted by everyone, since everyone was willing to recognize "the perfect aptitude of the black race for the sciences and civilization."[13] Clearly, these French observers, however sympathetic, were not "plugged in" to the American reality. Launched in this particular direction, they continued to create their own image of America.

These few testimonies harked back to an earlier time and were given by men who had identified the outcome of the American Civil War with their own struggle for liberty. Many of their compatriots had not thrilled, as they had done, to the sound of slaves breaking their chains. As they closely followed the episodes of Reconstruction, some of them did not hesitate to adopt the illusions that pervaded the South. These were antithetical to earlier illusions, but equally ephemeral.

The end of the Civil War and the abolition of slavery had initially caused whites to fear surging crowds of vengeful blacks descending on their plantations. Subsequently they came to hope that the freedmen would somehow, gradually and naturally, disappear. Accustomed to constraint, they thought, the blacks would not be able to get used to liberty, families would break up, the birth rate would fall, and diseases would spread without the paternal protection of the planters, and as a result the black race would become extinct.

Such a vision, or rather phantasmagoria, could not be upheld for long. The end of federal involvement, the relative "normalization" of the South, the fact that the blacks, impelled by sheer necessity, had gone back to work had brought it home to the white population that it would have to live with the blacks for many years to come. Yet until the 1880s some French testimonies still echoed this curious way of envisaging the future. A rational mind like Louis Simonin, despite his thorough knowledge of the country, exactly reproduced the Southern arguments and confirmed the black's inability to work, predicting that an evolution analogous to that of the Antilles would lead to anarchy until such time as the dynamism of American society would bring about the extinction of the black race on United States soil.[14] Occasionally some hurried or

13. P. Larousse, *Grand dictionnaire universel du XIXe siècle* (Paris: Larousse, 1870), vol. 7, p. 1019.
14. L. Simonin, *A travers les Etats-Unis* (Paris: Charpentier, 1875), p. 34.

ill-informed traveler of the 1870s would adopt far-fetched opinions and assert that the Negroes would not survive, since they would become part of "that amalgam of peoples, leaving no more traces than a dirty river that flows into the sea and from a distance barely makes it look brown."[15]

Before long, however, the facts reclaimed their right, and there was no more talk of what for a time may have been "the obscure object of desire" for the Southern whites.

### The Nefarious Effects of Reconstruction

When the French, whether traveling in the United States or staying at home, wanted to know what had been happening in the South since the Civil War, they almost invariably adopted the explanation given by the Americans themselves, long before William A. Dunning systematized this explanation and for some decades established it as the historical truth.[16]

When Gustave de Molinari, touring the South in 1876, witnessed the troubles that were still agitating South Carolina, he often managed to remain neutral, but even so, his diagnosis was very clear:

> The Negroes may have become their masters' masters, but for all that they are conscious of their inferiority, and the day the *carpetbaggers* [in English in the original] stop exploiting their ignorance for political and especially financial reasons, everything will return to its proper order: the white conservatives will reconquer the power that they alone are capable of exercising, and the Negro politicians will go back, as the case may be, to their razors, their feather dusters and fly swatters, or their frying pans.[17]

In language that remained moderate, this said it all. The adventurers from the North and their accomplices, *carpetbaggers* and *scalawags*, were solely responsible for keeping the blacks in power, where they committed errors and exactions to harm the natural elite, the whites. If the correspondent of the *Journal des Savants* remained very moderate in his language, this was not the attitude of those who spoke directly with the planters. Lucien Biart, who had spent time in the United States before the war, returned convinced that this war had been a good thing, but it took no more than meeting a former slave owner who unveiled to him

15. G. and L. Verbrugghe, *Promenades et chasses dans l'Amérique du Nord* (Paris: Calman-Lévy, 1879), p. 216.
16. W.A. Dunning, *Reconstruction, Political and Economic, 1865–1877* (New York: Harper Brothers, 1907).
17. Molinari, *Lettres sur les Etats-Unis*, p. 196.

all the horrors to which he and his likes had been subjected to open his eyes and reconcile him with slavery.[18] The same metamorphosis transformed Jules Leclerq when he listened on a train to a Louisiana planter who told him about the ravages caused by black politicians and the interventions of the federal government.

These testimonies, confirmed by information directly received from the United States, prompted French analysts to conclude that Reconstruction had failed because of the attitude of the North. Claudio Jannet was one of these analysts, but he also brought his own certainties to bear, and they were very close to those of the Southerners.

> The Americans have done both too much and not enough for the Negroes: too much when they gave them complete liberty and the right to vote; not enough by failing to attach them to the soil by permanent ties. The true solution would have been a system analogous to serfs bound to the land.[19]

Over the next few years, Paul Leroy-Beaulieu, Emile Boutmy, and Auguste Carlier all concluded, despite differences of opinion on many points, that the Republicans had made a mistake when they declared the blacks to be citizens and imposed this policy by force. "Congress offended the instinctive sociability of the white populations of the South, and even those of the North, who are just as vigorously opposed to this mendacious equality."[20] The quasi-unanimous assertion that the North had erred in seeking to impose equality between blacks and whites inevitably involved the certainty of the blacks' inferiority. This position too was almost unanimous, whether it was based on arguments of the scientific type, on the assertions of American whites, or on direct contact between French visitors and American Negroes.

## INFERIORITY AND SEGREGATION

The French partook directly of the climate of racial distinctions that pervaded the Western world in the second half of the nineteenth century. This was understood, and none of the French observers of the United States made any reference to one of the race theoreticians, from Gobineau to Spencer.

18. L. Biart, *A travers l'Amérique, nouvelles et récits* (Paris: Biblio. du Magazin des Demoiselles, 1870). The author was a notary from Normandy who had known the antebellum United States.
19. Jannet, *Les Etats-Unis contemporains*, pp. 14–21.
20. P. Leroy-Beaulieu, "Blancs et noirs dans l'Amérique du Nord," *Le Correspondant* (25 Oct. 1886); E. Boutmy, *Etudes de droit constitutionnel* (Paris: Plon-Nourrit, 1885);

## Statements of Principle

These often came from the opinions of the Southerners themselves; thus Claudio Jannet, who greatly admired them, did not hesitate to evoke "an inferior race of dubious morality," but in 1886 a man like Pierre Leroy-Beaulieu spoke from what he considered a more solid basis. A comparison among the respective weights of the brains of whites, mixed-bloods, and blacks led him to a categorical conclusion concerning the last group: "a race placed at the lowest rung of the anthropological scale and moreover morally degraded by four hundred years of slavery."[21]

After all, were not the Negroes satisfied with the lowest wages, were they not accustomed to obeying, bowing, and scraping, and adapted to the countryside, which they must not leave because "in short, the Negro is made for the planter and the planter is made for the Negro"? It was therefore perfectly understandable that the whites refused to let them play a political role, certain that their intellectual inferiority was a given:

> In this body, which seems to combine the features of a gnome and a satyr, there moves a rudimentary, fretful and excessively imaginative intelligence which, totally absorbed by momentary sensations, is incapable of modifying them by looking even slightly ahead.[22]

For the Swiss jurist Henri Gaullieur, the matter was equally clear-cut: The blacks were destined to hold inferior jobs, they did not know how to fight, since they had not freed themselves, and, *ultima ratio*, they had not produced a single genius.

In 1876, Gustave de Molinari returned to the "Negro problem" on the basis of American statistical documents. He noted a physical and moral degradation of the population of color since the end of slavery, contrary to the hopes of those who might have believed that there would be an indissoluble link between emancipation and social and moral progress. This development was manifest in a death rate higher than that of the whites, in greater susceptibility to disease, in a general "apathy" which did not, however, prevent a criminality three times as high as that of the rest of the population. The blacks had thus become a burden to the whites, and although the author refused to approve the extreme positions of the Americans, he did think that this was indeed a "minor race":

> The Negroes, then, are still, for the most part, children; such moral strength, control over their appetites and exercise of foresight as they possess is still

Carlier, *La République américaine*, p. 321, is much more favorable to equality than the other authors.
21. Leroy-Beaulieu, "Blancs et noirs," p. 234.   22. Ibid., p. 243.

in an embryonic state, and yet this is the quality most needed by a free man responsible for his own destiny. That is why the tutelage of slavery, however oppressive and onerous, was more advantageous for them than a regime of self-government for which they were not ready.[23]

The same arguments appeared regularly, in 1905 as in 1910, in the most diverse writings, and no one felt the need to present new proofs.

To be sure, a few authors did discuss specific aspects of this alleged inferiority, but no one questioned the intellectual and theoretical aspects of the entire concept. Yet it is difficult to distinguish the role of the "French passions" from that of the direct influence of the United States, the source of the data and frequently the analysis as well.

To these so-called scientific arguments presented by a small number of intellectuals and journalists, one must add the opinions of French "colonials," who had known the black race in Africa and were inevitably compelled to make comparisons that did nothing to attenuate the peremptory opinions of the first group.

As far as Baron de Mandat-Grancey was concerned, blacks were supposed to go naked with rings through their noses, and to him it was an apocalyptic thought that they had been able to hold whites for ransom after the Civil War. Father Croonenbergh found a striking resemblance with the tribes he knew in the Congo and deduced from this that the blacks of the United States were no more ready for freedom than their African cousins. The journalist Octave Uzanne for his part was surprised by the number of blacks in Washington: "Never had I seen so many of them even in the Orient and even in our African possessions."[24]

### Proof Found in the Street

For the travelers who stayed in the cities of the Northeast before going to Washington, and for those who were received in American homes, blacks were only waiters, domestic servants, bootblacks, or railroad employees; they always appeared in subaltern roles.

Most travelers were amused and pleased to be served by blacks, who seemed to be part of the decor. One person was struck by the tall black man who was the first of a whole "squadron of Negroes" to serve him; for many others the most vivid memory was the always good-humored conductor of the railroad car, whom a tip rendered even more helpful.

23. Molinari, *Lettres sur les Etats-Unis*, p. 20.
24. E. de Mandat-Grancey, *Chez l'Oncle Sam* (Paris: Plon, 1886), p. 20; C. Croonenbergh, *Trois ans dans l'Amérique septentrionale: Les Etats-Unis* (Paris-Lyon: Dehoumme et Briquet, 1892–93), vol. 1, p. 208; L.O. Uzanne, *Vingt jours dans le Nouveau Monde* (Paris: May et Motteroz, 1893), pp. 101–2.

After all, he made up the couchette and dusted you off with a little horsehair broom as you got off the train after he had helped you with your coat. The travelers truly enjoyed being thus served at all times by Negroes, "who go around either in their uniform or wearing a huge white apron; they are like luxurious animals, a fancy touch of the railroad company that for me completes the exoticism of the decor." Paul Bourget expressed this notion so well that a few years later Ferdinand Brunetière was "enormously pleased . . . to see a Negro in the Pullman, and terribly disappointed to be staying in a hotel . . . without a Negro!"[25]

It is true that Paul de Rousiers claimed that the blacks of the Pullman cars had been "drilled" until they were perfect, but most travelers thought that these were "the best servants one could possibly find," conscientious, eager, and obliging. But then, were they not condemned to be nothing but servants, given their characteristic "absence of spirit and energy"?

For most French visitors, these servants were simply "easy-going and funny, all looking alike with their goggle-eyes," although some were repulsed by seeing a "monkey hand" wielding the little horsehair broom on the station platform or had to "overcome a certain repugnance at being served by them"; and besides, were not many of them "hideous"?

Once the French had gotten over the amusement of such first contacts, the feeling that came to dominate was in fact discomfort, especially if the traveler ventured closer to the South. To be sure, there was still a bit of exoticism in fancy dresses shimmering "in all the colors of the rainbow," or in the street scenes of New Orleans:

> . . . old man with shaky head, tall women with supple waists walking with balanced grace, wooly-headed pickaninnies jabbering away or absorbed in the pleasure of a stream . . . half naked, but always clean because they are so black and shiny.[26]

But, at first sight, the sheer size of the black population was as disquieting as it was amusing. After all, one had to come close to "one of these Negro scoundrels who thanks to Lincoln are multiplying in the minor jobs of American administrations like worms in a Roquefort cheese."[27]

Abbé Vigneron was simply taken aback when he visited Baltimore:

25. F. Brunetière, "Dans l'Est Américain: New York, Baltimore, Bryn Mawr," *Revue des Deux Mondes* (1 Nov. 1897): 95.
26. H. de Varigny, *En Amérique* (Paris: Masson, 1895), p. 173.
27. D. Bonnaud, *D'océan à océan, impressions d'Amérique* (Paris: Ollendorf, 1887), p. 157.

Masses of Negroes! Masses of Negroes! Men and women, boys and girls, Negroes of every shade, from yellowish white to pure ebony! Negroes richly dressed, Negroes in rags; I feel as if I were in Africa or in the American South.[28]

But Paul Bourget betrayed a certain diffuse fear in Florida: "Negroes and more Negroes. It is as if the city belonged to them, the sidewalks are covered with them." And if by chance a traveler came a little closer, he was usually not too pleased. The same terms – "hideous," "ugly," "uncouth" – are used again and again and one had to admit that "they have their own smell," which Gustave de Molinari found unbearable, comparable to that of "a fish market after a violent thunderstorm."

These instinctive reactions show that the French had as yet had very little contact with a different race. But they can also be accounted for by the nature of the places where these travelers, eager for picturesque sights, encountered black people. They did not seek to meet members of the black petite bourgeoisie, which existed in Washington and in certain other cities, they only saw blacks loitering in railroad stations, in markets, by the docks. Such a sample of the black population was hardly representative of the group as a whole, but definitive conclusions were made just the same. These blacks, who were among the poorest, most disadvantaged, and most marginal inhabitants of these cities, quite naturally confirmed our travelers' prejudices.

When Gustave de Molinari traveled throughout South Carolina and Louisiana, the agitation of Reconstruction had not yet ended, the towns still bore the stigmata of the war, and the number of refugees was considerable. But the horrors Molinari described had nothing to do with physical misery:

This poor *colored people* [in English in the original], a shapeless model that looks as if it had been turned out by a clumsy helper on a day when the sublime artist of the creation left his workshop to play hooky!

But then his description of the poor of Charleston went beyond the picturesque:

The female workers of New York are ladies compared to this Negress who hawks shrimp and crabs, with a worn-out man's hat crushed on her head, or that other one, who looks like an enormous truffle wrapped in a dirty napkin. Nobody mends any holes or cleans off any stains, and they all keep their clothes until the clothes refuse to keep them.[29]

28. L. Vigneron, *De Montréal à Washington* (Paris: Plon-Nourrit, 1887), p. 179.
29. Molinari, *Lettres sur les Etats-Unis*, pp. 197, 205, 189.

When traveling, voluntarily, in a "colored" coach, he had the same reactions. The only person who to some extent found favor in his eyes was "a young Negress of brownish black complexion, a Congo Negress, whose turned-up nose, big, sensuous lips, and shining, moist eyes were not lacking a certain attractiveness."

More than ten years later, when abbé Vigneron was riding around Baltimore in a carriage with one of his Sulpician hosts, he exhibited the same kind of disdain, albeit with more paternalism and less libido:

> What can they do, these good people, all day long? They don't eat much, dress in practically nothing, and have few needs. So they certainly spend their entire life doing nothing at all. Through the black and smelly holes that serve as doors to their dwellings, one can see that the inside is in lamentable disorder: pots and pans lying around, orange and banana peels on the floor, rags hanging on pegs, miaowing cats. Pouah! It looks like the Congo![30]

Twenty years later, when Paul Adam described the blacks he had met in Saint Louis or along the Mississippi, he was less peremptory and better informed about nuances, but he also dwelt on the marginal groups of "sad devils . . . the prey of gnawing sadness and hatred," who "had, in a word, lost everything along with the condition of their enslaved ancestors." He gave a heavy-handed description of sordid dwellings teeming with pickaninnies clinging to the skirts of chattering and ridiculous matrons, "agile, cheeky, and noisy boys" and "skinny girls, throwing out their chests in their short petticoats and their black stockings . . . their brown and laughing faces peeking out from every hole, leaning out of every attic window. And one begins to understand the American terror of this proliferation." Leaving Saint Louis for New Orleans, he saw from his train nothing but miserable shacks, with a few scrawny chickens scratching for food, a "fat dusky woman" appearing surrounded by a "bunch of half-naked brats," or a poor old fellow who "casually scratched the soil with a kind of iron stick pulled by an emaciated mule," and he philosophized,

> What do they have in common, these litters of primitive beings and the American farmer who walks behind his turn-wrest plough with its helix-shaped blades that cut deeply into the humus, turning it over at the fast clip of intelligent, nervous, and smart horses[?][31]

Beyond a writer's stylistic excesses, this author's attitudes and reflections were analogous to those of his less talented and more hurried

30. Vigneron, *De Montréal*, p. 221.
31. P. Adam, *Vues d'Amérique* (Paris: Ollendorf, 1906), pp. 150–55.

predecessors. They all liked to emphasize the bestiality and the animality of the blacks who enjoyed dressing up as whites, "as the true descendants of monkeys which, unable to invent anything, are perfect imitators."[32]

Although not many observers had the courage of an Othenin d'Haussonville, who, having arrived in the United States favoring the principle of equality between whites and blacks, subsequently felt obliged to admit that he had found many Negroes physically repulsive and always obsequious,[33] many others must have reacted very similarly in their secret consciousness.

A very small number of travelers bucked the trend of these judgments ranging from paternalism to hate-filled fear, but they did so quite timidly. Both Marie Dugard and Thérèse responded to the "supple walk" of the blacks, their "polite tone," and their "tranquil manner," even though they did seem to worry that they were, as was constantly said, but big children liable to get out of hand. Jules Huret, having completed a more thorough study that had brought him into contact with more people, expressed a more nuanced view of the alleged physical inferiority of blacks:

> There were indeed some heads that looked more savage than others, prognathous and thick-lipped heads with bulging eyes and with ebony-black skin, yet without anything servile about them. But side by side with these too pure offspring of Sudanese Negroes, you would have seen a parade of the most accomplished specimens of the human race.[34]

He looked with delight on women "with swelling breasts, slender and supple waists, small and distinguished hands" and felt that in Paris such women would be surrounded by men. The experience of Huret, special correspondent of *Le Figaro*, had been the opposite of d'Haussonville's; he had arrived filled with prejudices, but contact with a certain reality had caused him to evolve. However, his newfound appreciation was limited to the students of Tuskegee, who had been improved by education. The only other observers who expressed positive opinions, incidentally, were those who had come in contact with black children. These struck them as bright and lively and, unlike the adults, did not inspire any kind of repulsion. Only Pierre de Coubertin went beyond that when he noted the educational progress of black children, which might not, to be sure, presage the further course of their studies. He asserted that black inferiority, so often evoked by the Americans themselves, was "nothing

32. J. Desfontaines, *A travers l'Amérique* (Bordeaux: Imprimerie Mellinet, n.d.), p. 15.
33. G.-P.O. Cléron, comte d'Haussonville, *A travers les Etats-Unis: Notes et impressions* (Paris: Calman-Lévy, 1883), pp. 152–53.
34. Huret, *En Amérique*, vol. 1, pp. 392–97.

less than proven," and his opinion was not only theoretical: "They are nice, nicer than the unwashed and drunken characters that sometimes sat down next to me on American trains, when I would have preferred to be sitting among well dressed Negroes."[35]

Thus the great majority of French travelers were convinced of the inferiority of blacks. Their scientific ideas were part of the dominant trends of their time, and, except in a very few cases, this certainty was confirmed and accentuated by their direct and physical contacts with blacks.

### A Segregation of Astonishing Proportions

When they discovered the blacks, the French, whether they traveled in America or not, also discovered the black problem. They therefore had to adapt to what was called segregation – a term they did not use – as it was practiced more and more openly in the South and in a slightly more underhanded way in the rest of the country.

Everyone noted that racial prejudice was widespread in the United States, that it was impossible to breach, and that although it ran precisely counter to the American liberties, it constituted the "political and social catechism of the people of the United States," even in the federal capital. What would be the reaction of people who were, at least officially, committed to equality as citizens of the French Republic? Political segregation could be judged as a matter of principle, whereas social segregation spoke more directly to emotional attitudes.

For the most part, the French saw nothing wrong with the blacks' exclusion from voting; similarly, they condemned the legislation by which Congress wanted to impose equality, and also the granting of citizenship to the blacks, which at the very least they considered premature. Citizens were equals by definition, which is why the inferiority of the freedmen practically ruled out their becoming citizens: ". . . if they stepped down one step on the political ladder, they would rise by that much on the social ladder." This view exactly matched that of the Southern whites, but it also showed that a French person would consider citizenship for the blacks unnatural.

In the years after Reconstruction, the blacks were generally presented as a divisive force against whom the whites had to unite, if only to deprive them, as was only natural, of their suffrage. This was the thought of Comte Louis de Turenne, who even evoked a confrontation between "blacks and whites" after he had spent some time at the home of a

---

35. P. de Coubertin, *Universités transatlantiques* (Paris: Hachette, 1890), p. 259.

wealthy Southern landowner.[36] The same solution was advocated by Baron de Mandat-Grancey, who, fearful of the growth of the black population, could see only one of two alternatives: either the end of universal manhood suffrage or the establishment of a permanent Ku Klux Klan.

That two antidemocratic aristocrats should adopt such a point of view is not surprising, but when they were joined by the founder of the Ecole libre des sciences politiques, Emile Boutmy, one might expect a greater impact. Boutmy in fact presented the blacks as *"outlaws"* [in English in the original] and spoke about the danger that a black majority would mean to certain states in the South. Perceiving a "struggle between two races that do not want to have the same country," even though only one was available, he ended by expressing his satisfaction that the Republicans and the Supreme Court had averted the danger by enacting measures creating political segregation.[37]

During these years, Auguste Carlier was the only Frenchman to believe that the blacks were capable of exercising their citizen's right. He blamed the federal government for allowing itself to be dominated by "racial instincts" and the Republican party for giving up its opposition to violations of equality.

Yet, by and large, very few French observers dwelt at length on this situation. Black voting rights were, in principle, an established fact, and the violations of universal suffrage perpetrated by certain states were not always comprehensible to the French, who were unfamiliar with the arcana of federalism. Only diplomats posted in the United Sates, a few newspaper articles, or Georges N. Tricoche writing in the *Journal des Économistes* were reasonably precise in mentioning the process of exclusion, such as South Carolina's adoption in 1900 of a clause designed to eliminate illiterate voters. It should be added that when the worker-delegates to the 1904 World's Fair at Saint Louis were astounded to note that one man was not as good as another because of his race, they were struck above all by the social aspect of this racial prejudice.

The French in fact paid more attention to the development of segregation in daily and professional life than to its political aspects, no doubt because its manifestations were more spectacular and intelligible in that area.

Even those who accepted the inferiority of the blacks were struck by the scope of racial separation practiced in the United States. Jacques

---

36. L.G. de Turenne d'Aynac, *Quatorze mois dans l'Amérique du Nord, 1875–76* (Paris: Quantin, 1879), p. 33.
37. Boutmy, *Etudes de droit*, p. 73.

Offenbach merely spoke ironically about the sincerity of the Americans, those paragons of liberty, who did not allow blacks into their restaurants,[38] but Gustave de Molinari sought to understand. Although by no means willing to accept the equality of the races, he was appalled by the violence of the whites' positions.

Playing the devil's advocate in speaking to them, he asked whether they would be willing "to receive in their home an impeccably clean and highly educated colored man," arguing from the fact that he had "many times, in Europe . . . met men of color who would not have been out of place at any white gathering . . . ," but every time the response was as hard as if he had asked these people to "invite a monkey or a pig to dinner."[39]

Marie Dugard, filled with optimism after visiting a black school, where she had found pupils by no means inferior to others, even began to dream that "since prejudices have to yield to the equality of intelligence . . . they would soon become Americanized," but then she saw a "girl with silky blond hair, a European profile, and a pure white complexion, who was thrown in with the Blacks . . . because she had a few drops of Negro blood in her veins. . . ."[40] The French workers who looked into the question also noted the wide scope of the phenomenon, which reached even the unions, with the short-lived exception of the Knights of Labor, "an almost unique example in the United States, where many workers consider the Negroes as a race of inferior quality with which they do not care to associate."[41]

The only nuances in this finding were added by those who discussed the regional spread of segregation. Both Pierre de Coubertin and Abbé Félix Klein described a phenomenon limited to the old Confederacy:

> In the North, whites and blacks are on the same footing; there are even quite a few mixed schools, and racial prejudice is declining more and more rapidly. But here it continues full strength. The Negroes have their own cafés, their separate railroad cars, separate places at the theater. They must step aside for the whites everywhere, even in church![42]

By contrast, Gustave de Molinari, or *Le Temps* a few years later, in 1897, felt that the North was at least as harsh as the South, which according to them had a certain tolerance, at least in daily life:

38. J. Offenbach, *Offenbach en Amérique* (Paris: Calman-Lévy, 1877).
39. Molinari, *Lettres*, pp. 198–99.      40. Dugard, *La société américaine*, p. 160.
41. S. Jousselin, "Les chevaliers du travail," *Revue Socialiste* (Jan. 1893): 44.
42. Coubertin, *Universités*, p. 257; see also F. Klein, *Au pays de la vie intense* (Paris: Plon, 1904), p. 290.

... it is in the emancipating states of the North that today it [race preju-
dice] is strongest and harshest, and that it inflicts on people of color, even
if they have but an infinitesimal dose of black blood in their veins, the most
unjustifiable social exclusions and the most humiliating affronts.[43]

There are two ways to explain these differences of opinion. The testimonies that place the core of the problem in the South are those of
people who were able to verify the intensity of racial prejudices on the
spot, in Washington and in the Southern regions. In the North, the situation was more diffuse because of the small number of blacks and the
absence of institutionalized segregation; information came for the most
part from the inhabitants of the South, who considered it a way to prove
that they were not the only ones to abhor the contact with former
slaves and their descendants. And the fact is that in October 1901, when
President Roosevelt invited Booker T. Washington to share a meal with
him at the White House, the Southern reactions that ensued were fairly
close to those evoked by Gustave de Molinari twenty-five years earlier.
The observers who took note of this uproar attributed it to the "excitable
Southern press," and Jules Huret asked his Southern hosts the same
questions his predecessor of the *Débats* had asked, and was given the
same answers.

In 1906 the French consul in New Orleans could note, correctly, that
"the question of race remains as unsolved and as critical as ever, even
though more than forty years have passed since the Civil War."[44]

### *Excesses of the Blacks or Excesses of Segregation*

The very scope of segregation gave the observer pause, but its frenzied
manifestations, violent assaults and lynchings, provoked even more vivid
and more explicit reactions.

When Paul Bourget was in Georgia, where a colonel, an old friend of
Lincoln, showed him the degraded state of the blacks, for whom he felt
responsible, he participated – albeit passively – in a manhunt. A black
man, accused of a crime, was found and executed on the spot. The writer
could not help admiring the simplicity of this incident and depicted the
energetic figures of these men, who showed neither disdain nor pity for
their victim. He subsequently felt free to evoke from his lofty height the
"tamed race" which, in a savage state when it arrived, benefited from all
the good things invented by the whites.[45]

43. "Bulletin de l'étranger," *Le Temps* (3 Dec. 1902), and Molinari, "Le negro problem,"
    p. 14.
44. Archives des Affaires Etrangères, NS E.-U., III, 1904–1906, fol. 1096.
45. P. Bourget, *Outremer* (Paris: Lemerre, 1895), vol. 2.

As Pierre de Coubertin was leaving Florida, he witnessed a less serious incident. In the train where he had taken his seat, a slightly black young woman was forced by white passengers to leave the carriage where she was and sent to the one reserved for people of her race:

> Watching this ignoble scene, some Americans who were present merely gave a coarse sneer. If the Southern states are stupid enough to uphold this ingenious legislation much longer, it is likely that they will pay dearly for it; unless the federal government decides to intervene and whip them as one whips naughty children.[46]

Such vivid indignation was unusual. Other travelers, who had to judge the practice of lynching from afar, were clearly torn between the a priori condemnation of an excessively summary justice and their contempt for the simian Negroes who inspired very little sympathy. But none of these witnesses had been able to judge for him- or herself the behavior of the blacks in criminal situations. As a result, their judgments were inevitably shaped by what they had heard or read in the United States.

Thus the blacks were often depicted as lazy and lacking a sense of morality, even when it was granted that they had a certain intelligence. But Abbé Vigneron was the only one to admit that he had heard this from an American priest whose guest he had been. When Stephane Jousselin spoke of the "nervous tic" of the Negroes, who constantly committed rapes; when Urbain Gohier asserted, "They are obsessed by the idea of white women and this obsession frequently leads them to the most despicable crimes. Their ambition is to be considered great seducers of white women";[47] and when Saint André de Lignereux cited medical reasons for the growing number of rapes of white women, claiming that blacks were unable to behave or control themselves, they did not invent anything. They simply passed on the dominant opinions of the white Americans of the time, taking the assertions of the newspapers and of many of their interlocutors as gospel truth.

That this was the case is shown by the testimony of Georges N. Tricoche, many of whose letters dealt with the matter of lynching, since these events became more numerous in the first years of the twentieth century. In principle he unequivocally condemned these summary judgments, which nullified the moral pretensions of the United States and were totally unjustifiable, but on the other hand he did not particularly trust the "Afro-Americans." He also explained how in the South, where justice was slow and where the accused could easily get away and meld

46. Coubertin, *Universités*, p. 267.
47. U. Gohier, *Le peuple du XXe siècle* (Paris: Fasquelle, 1903), p. 251.

into the black population, these practices might be understandable: "Anyone who has lived amidst black people and has studied them even superficially will recognize that the procedures of regular courts and ordinary punishments do not have any long-term preventive effects."[48] Yet he remained relatively optimistic, counting heavily on education as a means of reducing the number of "rapists" [in English in the original] in a rapidly growing black population – he predicted that there would be 33 million blacks by the year 2000! This would be the only way to eliminate "a horrible danger for white women."

Thus the French, often skeptical about blacks to begin with, had their convictions reinforced by the American environment, which was bound to have a major impact, especially when it came to issues as emotionally charged as sexuality. Few observers expressed their opinions as sincerely and profoundly as Urbain Gohier:

> This is one of the points about which a European, a son of the French Revolution, feels most troubled when his doctrinal convictions meet up with reality. . . . But this Negro, way down on the social ladder, has a very nasty way of looking at women and little girls at the top . . . we resolutely proclaim that we consider lynching excessive . . . as long as the attack does not involve our own wife or our daughter.[49]

From abject approval of the excesses of segregation by some to discussion and reflection by others, one encounters the entire gamut of opinions. These throw a special light on the variety of attitudes the French would adopt when they themselves had to deal with this kind of situation.

Although the rather somber view the French had of the situation of the American blacks did not change dramatically, it did undergo a certain evolution. Over the period as a whole, more than a third of the French opinions expressed were in favor of segregation, and only a minority registered its firm opposition to it. However, in the early years of the twentieth century, criticism of racial separation became more frequent, until it equaled its approval.

## IF THE FUTURE COULD SING

The predominance of a critical attitude toward the blacks and the repulsion that contact with them provoked in many of the French observers

---

48. *Journal des Economistes* (Aug. 1903): 249; (Oct. 1899): 94; (May 1907): 244.
49. Gohier, *Le peuple*, pp. 244 and 254.

did not prevent them from ascribing to the blacks certain aptitudes that might brighten their future prospects somewhat.

## A PEOPLE OF MUSICIANS

While visiting the United States, travelers had the opportunity to attend typically black events, whether they happened to pass a black church and stopped to listen to the singing that burst forth from it or were taken to a concert by their hosts. The happy few who experienced this were unanimous in their delight and their recognition of the musicality of the American blacks.

While dismissing the *minstrels*, that is, whites in blackface who parodied black music, as ridiculous, crude, and mediocre, French visitors were completely won over by black singing and black rhythms, to the point that one of them, upon witnessing a funeral complete with singing, keening, and praying was obliged to confess: "we had better leave, for this madness might get to us. . . ." The opinion of Comte de Turenne is particularly significant; here was a man who showed the greatest contempt for the blacks, espoused the extremist positions of the South, and yet was carried away:

> The group was composed of four women and five men. One of the men played the harmonium and accompanied the singers. What they did first had a very strange character and a peculiar poignancy. These are special kinds of religious chants, interspersed with the most effective recitatives. God and the Devil, Jesus and Satan appear one by one, followed by choruses of angels and disciples. Here, as in the Medieval mystery plays, the principal events of the Old and New Testament are reenacted and, as in the old mysteries, the naive and the sublime exist side by side . . . witness one of the songs entitled "Ride on, King Jesus!" These Negroes belong to the Methodist sect. Their sense of music seems to be highly developed, and their voices have admirable sonority, timbre, and pitch.[50]

The fact that this concert, which took place in Tennessee in 1876, was organized by the blacks to raise money for the construction of a school was not mentioned, but the French aristocrat's ear did react.

In the early twentieth century other travelers, such as Abbé Félix Klein

---

50. Turenne, *Quatorze mois*, p. 181; these were probably the Jubilee Singers, a highly successful group whose tour was commented upon by several travelers, among them F. Buisson. René Rémond points out that the French discovered black music around 1845: *Les Etats-Unis devant l'opinion française* (Paris: Colin, 1962), vol. 2, p. 457.

and Pastor Charles Wagner, were also seduced by black music. Both were interested in the religion of black people. Klein experienced a baptist service filled with singing and shouting, a moving and unfamiliar but by no means ridiculous world. Wagner was invited by a black pastor to give a lecture in a black church in Chicago; he was struck by the spirituality that pervaded the congregation, and the profundity of the singing, a sign of "rare musical development" that evoked a veritable "human organ," was deeply moving to him.

A race that had such qualities could not be totally inferior, and perhaps music was one of the opportunities for blacks to assert themselves. Paul Adam, who liked to harp on the bestiality and the erotomania of the blacks, thought that their musical talent should be put to use by the whites, in Sunday services, for instance, for assimilating and thereby civilizing them:

> Almost all the Negroes have a good ear. Nothing is more astonishing than to hear a fat matron sitting on the steps of a humble abode sing as she trims her vegetables. Out of this shapeless and pitch-colored mass comes a crystalline voice and enchants us.[51]

More directly, Jules Huret asserted: "... as I said, the Negroes are admirably gifted in music, and I am sure that if one day America produces musicians, they will be black."[52] Jazz was not yet known in France, but such reactions foreshadow the reception that this music would be given in France a generation later.

These reactions do not of course really resolve the inherent contradiction between making the black an uncouth brute on the one hand and a potential artist on the other. But certain questions were beginning to be asked.

Gustave de Molinari already considered the black "a musician, a storyteller . . . a bohemian," all of which was rather favorable, but also depicted him as "lazy, gluttonous," and "without a sense of tomorrow," which was not so favorable; but at least he did not make him into a monster of lubricity whose conduct would justify all the excesses of segregation. Others also had second thoughts:

> ... with their mobile features and their expansive physiognomy, they seem incapable of sustaining the high energy of the Americans, the "fight for place" [in English in the original] their pastors urge them to undertake; when dealing with him they look like big children. However, one likes to look at them: their supple movements, their shiny faces, and their big smiles make for a happy contrast with the steely gestures and the grave demeanor

51. Adam, *Vues d'Amérique*, p. 169.   52. Huret, *En Amérique*, vol. 1, pp. 396–97.

of the American and add an exotic note to this already too European society.[53]

Although Marie Dugard, a teacher of English at the lycée Molière, did not say so, she seems to have sensed that the qualities of the blacks were often seen as flaws by the Americans. Jules Huret was more explicit: ". . . next to the Americans in the narrow sense, that ambitious and positive race . . . the Negro is a dreamer and an idler! But is not Europe full of such people?" Such opinions were too isolated to warrant any general conclusions, but they do show the complexity of French reactions. The influence of white Americans was certainly strong, but it does not provide answers for everything. Furthermore, the gentleness and sensitivity that certain visitors were pleased to ascribe to the blacks were also evident in their school experience.

### *Generally Positive Views of Schooling*

The French observers' opinions about education for the blacks was important, for all of them considered the school as the key to advancement. It would surely play that role for the freedmen and their children, who, during slavery, had been deprived of all access to education. At first sight, the French readily acknowledged the Americans' efforts to educate the blacks right after the Civil War. But then the most thorough investigations emphasized the remaining insufficiencies, especially in the South. Whereas Célestin Hippeau had nothing but praise in 1869, Ferdinand Buisson, seven years later, felt great sadness as he saw the state of the schools in the former Confederacy. To be sure, the blacks themselves performed marvels raising funds that neither the federal government nor the states were providing, but the road they had to travel was long and difficult.[54]

A few years later, there was no longer any doubt; the full extent of school segregation had become obvious. Since it concerned children, it provoked lively responses, even if they were indicative of a great ignorance of the American realities. Thus, Paul Edouard Passy noted the backwardness of the black schools, which he attributed to their separation from the white schools – even though he had doubts about the blacks' real aptitude for learning – and hoped that the federal government would intervene to remedy this situation.[55] At the very end of the

53. Dugard, *La société*, p. 164.
54. F. Buisson, *Rapport sur l'instruction primaire à l'Exposition universelle de Philadelphie en 1876* (Paris: Imprimerie nationale, 1878), p. 147. The author was careful not to make any hasty judgments, knowing that everything could change quickly.
55. *L'instruction primaire aux Etats-Unis* (Paris: Delagrave, 1885), pp. 208–9.

nineteenth century the same questions were asked again, which proves that little had changed in the United States, but also indicates that in waxing indignant about the "incredible indifference" of the federal government, the French betrayed their lack of understanding of federalism. Accustomed to centralization, the French were greatly upset by the American school system, which lacked the power and the coherence to reduce these abuses. Nonetheless, the question of the Negroes' ability to benefit from education continued to be debated.

Although it was hard for black schools to develop and prosper, the French visitors were initially rather favorably impressed by the obvious qualities of the black students. To be sure, they visited mostly the best institutions, such as Hampton or Tuskegee, or a good school in Washington, D.C., and rarely saw a rural school – but how high-spirited, how lively these students were! Marie Lozillon, Marie Dugard, and Félix Klein were unanimous:

> ... they seemed willing to accept discipline, and eager to learn; their answers were lively and correct, their physiognomies intelligent. I picked up some of their writings at random, and they showed an intellectual level that was no lower than that of other students.[56]

But visiting a classroom does not allow the observer to find out whether the education received there is good enough to permit the student to go on to more advanced studies after grade school. It was therefore only natural for the visitors to consult the Americans around them, the white teachers. And at that point all of them became skeptical about the results of this education. One said that the blacks had little perseverance and no mathematical ability, others claimed that the qualities of vivacity and cleverness disappeared very soon after adolescence, making further education impossible. These arguments were exactly those of the whites who supported segregation and wanted to show the inferiority of the blacks. Here again, the opinion of Georges N. Tricoche is most revealing:

> It is of course extremely useful to polish, even "clean up" the Negroes, but once again the push of the philanthropists has overshot its goal. . . .
> The black will improve above all through the influence of his milieu; his intelligence is indisputably slow, and he is more adept at imitating than at assimilating knowledge.[57]

It is understandable that in the face of such arguments the French modified or nuanced their rather favorable first impressions

---

56. Dugard, *La société*, p. 160.
57. G.N. Tricoche, "Lettre . . . ," *Journal des Economistes* (May 1900): 242.

and wondered whether the education the blacks received was a genuine benefit.

> Seeing these Negroes with their supple feline bodies lined up in front of school desks, imprisoned in our overcoats and in the tight clothing of civilization, with their frizzy hair shorn or tightly braided, with their swift eyes riveted on the grammar of the English language or the history of America's civil government, one has the feeeling of an anomaly; they are made for a very different kind of life, these creatures of freedom, a more simple existence, closer to nature, for long spells of *farniente* in the sun of Africa.[58]

Despite these reservations, no observer questioned the usefulness, even the effectiveness, of primary education for the blacks, but these reservations explain their misgivings when it came to higher education.

Some felt that higher education for blacks was not desirable because it would be not only useless but actually harmful to them. It would only give them illusions about their possibilities of social advancement, and it was hardly in keeping with their character, which attracted them to "fancy clothes, red fabric . . . big drums and brass instruments." Others thought that black universities were premature, given the incomplete network of primary and secondary schools. The success of Fiske and Howard Universities, of which many French observers were not aware, were only the exceptions that confirmed the rule – admirable but impossible to generalize.

The only path that seemed to lead to success was the one opened by Booker T. Washington with his Tuskegee Institute, whose reputation owed as much to its achievements as to the fame of its founder.

Booker T. Washington was indeed an example of remarkable social success, and it is understandable that he was the only black figure to attract the attention of the French visitors; after all, he was the most popular black person among his own people. He was the living example of what can be achieved by a Negro, living proof of the inanity of the theory postulating the inherent inferiority of the black race.

But the French were interested in the author of the Atlanta Speech from the white more than from the black point of view. All those who studied what he had done at Tuskegee felt that it avoided creating misfits by valuing manual labor and humility, which they considered particularly suited to the blacks. This reasoning was a superficial version of what Booker T. Washington himself had said, and it satisfied the French, who were conscious both of the blacks' need for education and of the limits beyond which they were unable to go.

58. Dugard, *La société*, p. 160.

It is in this direction, then, that the admirable Booker T. Washington steers the eleven hundred students of his Tuskegee Institute, where young women are taught housekeeping as much as bookkeeping, where the science of housekeeping is studied more carefully than the science of history, and where the young men themselves have constructed the buildings of the school and built the furniture for their rooms.[59]

Félix Klein's opinion concurred with that of Urbain Gohier and Saint André de Lignereux, or even Jules Huret, who described the Alabama institution at length. Here again, the remarks of Georges N. Tricoche form a kind of counterpoint, when he explained why Booker T. Washington was right not to demand integral voting rights for blacks and to work for keeping them in the South, despite the wishes of "white negrophiles more ardent than himself." The French, who knew nothing of the tactics of these agitators, wholeheartedly agreed with judgment of the correspondent of the *Nouvelle Revue*.

The actual person of Booker T. Washington was very attractive to the French. The impression was generally favorable, even if some were astonished by the contrast between the man's typically black appearance – "wooly hair, flat nose" – and his lofty views. Thérèse Bentzon, who reviewed his book even before it was translated into French, stressed his evangelism, but Jules Huret went beyond the strictly educational aspects and tried to assign the head of Tuskegee his proper place as the symbol of the blacks' progress.

He addressed the "great Negro . . . apostle and . . . mover of crowds" whose limits were apparent in his "narrow general culture" and "fairly obscure artistic tastes," but whom he nonetheless compared to Emerson:

> . . . your compatriot [Emerson], a great man whose name and works will live longer than those of the billionaires, was unable to make money, but he leaves behind ideas and sentiments that may well serve the glory of America better than the billions of Rockefeller or Carnegie. And you yourself, I insisted, if instead of concerning yourself with the future of the Negro race, you had dreamed of getting rich, you would not have become the head of the Tuskegee Institute, you would not be Booker T. Washington.[60]

This example balances a rather more somber vision expressed elsewhere.

### Highly Uncertain Perspectives

In reviewing the diverse testimonies about the future of the blacks throughout the period, one notices that the French were not optimistic.

59. Klein, *Au pays*, p. 294.   60. Huret, *En Amérique*, p. 394.

Furthermore, those who were most strongly in favor of segregation were also the most pessimistic; as if segregation, though considered necessary, were not a real solution to a problem that looked very much like an impasse.

In the first years of the twentieth century, the situation of the black population of the United States was appreciably different from what it had been in the immediate aftermath of the Civil War. The great majority still lived in the South and worked in cotton, but social advancement had occurred and produced teachers and some members of the liberal professions living in the cities. This development led to stricter social and professional segregation and also gave rise to discussions about assimilation or the forced departure of all blacks. In the face of an increasingly complex situation, it is not surprising that the French, depending on their own inclinations, focused their attention on this or that specific aspect.

Some thought that the future was completely blocked because the chasm separating the two races was just too deep. Abbé Klein, for instance, felt that the Europeans must become fully aware of "the antagonism between whites and blacks or, rather, of how difficult it is to make two peoples who are as different as can be imagined live together." Paul Adam also insisted on the profound difference between the "citizens of the Union and the 'African race'" – forgetting, it seems, that the blacks too were citizens – and did not see a way out: "Nothing will do away with this prejudice. It will keep on growing. In certain states, the reciprocal hatred has assumed tragic proportions." Taking the example of the racial incidents that had occurred in Texas, he concluded that "the problem can only get worse."[61]

The threat of racial conflict had been hovering over the country since the Civil War, and some of the travelers focused on the renewed specter of an onslaught of unfettered and vengeful Negroes. This "Negro race . . . the plague of America," aside from being unpleasant in itself, also undermined the well-known Yankee energy and perseverance, since its influence propagated "the poison of black blood" that originated with the "African microbe." Such language, which Paul Adam borrowed directly from the most extremist Southerners, was not used by everyone, but it does reveal how far the pessimism about the racial problem in the United States could go. No solution seemed possible; the blacks would remain "pariahs," something that was unknown in Europe:

> Will these primitive outcasts of African origin, now that they have suddenly come under the rule of half-Roman and half-Anglo-Saxon laws, remain

---

61. Adam, *Vues*, p. 371.

unreasoning, unruly, and vicious children, a nefarious element, proof of the errors of the conqueror and his guilty attempt to violate nature? . . . Or will they find a way to assimilate the benefits of their uprooting and rise to a moral level that will eventually lead others to forget the stigma of their race?[62]

This question asked by Saint André de Lignereux has a tragic ring to it, and most other observers spoke in more measured terms.

The fact that forty years after the Civil War the problem of the relations between blacks and whites involved so much violence forced the French to look into the reasons for this state of affairs. The inferiority of the Negroes, though generally assumed, could not be the only answer.

The very great harshness with which the whites treated the freedmen was perhaps not the best way, for it prevented the achievement of a lasting and satisfactory balance. Such an assessment appeared as early as 1876: "They are good people, the people of the South, except that they are a bit too Darwinian when it comes to their younger brother the Negro, and rather too quick to draw their revolvers."[63] Therefore, some regrets were heard over the years that followed: Would not the blacks have benefited from a "paternal, firm, and gentle tutelage," from being organized in associations, labor unions, even the military? This protection would have allowed for the advancement of the best and offered a solution that was "more humane and actually more economical than the laws of lynching and mass expulsion." But the Southerners were not the only ones responsible; the Yankees, convinced that they had done everything for the blacks when they abolished slavery, had since lost all interest in the problem. Jules Huret said this very clearly:

> As long as it was decided to free the Negroes, was it not logical to allow them to develop? The work of emancipation would be no more than a paltry hypocrisy if they were eternally kept in a state of inferiority and subjection.[64]

The French who thus felt that responsibilities should be shared were astounded by the solutions envisaged by certain Americans, considering them totally unrealistic. Henry de Varigny succinctly stated the problem that would not go away: "The Americans have slaughtered one another for the Negro; at this point they would pay a big reward to anyone who would rid them of him: this, in two words, is the situation."[65]

62. Saint André de Lignereux, *L'Amérique au XXe siècle* (Paris: Taillandier, 1909), p. 272.
63. Molinari, *Lettres*, p. 276.      64. Huret, *En Amérique*, p. 371.
65. H. de Varigny, *En Amérique*, p. 222. The author vividly objected to segregation but at the same time agreed that the blacks were inferior.

The most determined Southerners' plans to send the blacks to Liberia
or any other faraway territory – and these were simply new versions of
the hope they had had in 1865 to see them disappear "naturally" – were
seen by all the French observers as totally unreasonable, however much
they mulled over this question. Never would the blacks agree to go to
Africa, for their destiny had definitively rooted them in America, and
there was no need to find out, as Pierre Leroy-Beaulieu tried to do,
whether they would be good or mediocre settlers. In point of fact, only
white politicians, "street corner orators," evoked this "voluntary" expa-
triation, which was not in the nature of things. The most traditionalist
French observers like Claudio Jannet felt that the blacks should stay
attached to the land they worked, for that was where their future lay,
that is what they were meant for, and those who went to the cities would
not be happier there. Other, more realistic observers, such as Elisée
Reclus, knew that mass departure was impossible because the blacks had
become too Americanized:

> ... despite their former masters, they have become completely American
> in language, education, manner of thinking, and even patriotism with all its
> prejudices. . . . When visiting with North American Negroes and talking to
> them, one is astonished to see how very little originality they have within
> the nation which, having formed, molded, and imbued them with its spirit,
> is nonetheless intent on rejecting and getting rid of them.[66]

The perspective of a conflict between the ever-growing number of
blacks and the degenerate Southern whites, which would lead the
United States far away from the "political Arcadia" of which George
Washington had dreamed, was not the only eventuality envisaged by the
French observers; some of them were able to distance themselves from
the excessive rhetoric of the Americans.

Given that the blacks had accomplished real progress in certain fields,
some observers rather hastily concluded that optimistic and even frankly
idealistic views of the future were justified.

Auguste Carlier, writing around 1890, was aware of the difficulties, but
still close to the views of the generation of Frenchmen who had known
the Civil War: ". . . the race question is bound to become less urgent in
time. Education, more polished manners, and a better understanding of
social conventions will allow the Negroes to make their way in white
society, as they have done in Brazil. . . ."[67] Anatole France rapidly evoked
the progress accomplished by the blacks in the "capitalist civilization"

66. E. Reclus, *L'homme et la terre* (Paris: Librairie universelle, 1908), "Le Nouveau
    Monde," p. 108.
67. Carlier, *La République américaine*, p. 328.

and in other areas: "They were illiterate. Today fifty out of a hundred can read and write. There are black novelists, black poets, black economists, black philanthropists."[68] Thus, the future was open to them, both in terms of their own development and in their relation with the whites. Elisée Reclus, usually a more lucid observer, did not hesitate to foresee a vast reconciliation between the races:

> ... the population of the United States, red, white, and black, is preparing for that dreaded evolution called "miscegenation." The union of the races will take place mostly at the lower levels. They will be few and far between, to be sure, but there will be among the sons of the abolitionists a few warm-hearted men who, able to rise above the prejudice of caste and color, will not be afraid to found a family whose children may add a brown hue to the glow of their cheeks. But in the big cities, where the crowds are becoming thicker every day, foreign-born girls ... will not always allow themselves to be bound by unreasoning repugnances, and more than one among them will be glad to become the mate of the black man whom she admires for his healthy good looks, his strength, and his kindness.[69]

This opinion stands alone and probably owes more to the generous attitudes of a former participant in the Paris Commune than to a precise observation of the American situation. In this sense Reclus was indeed the precursor of his twentieth-century counterparts who also were to believe that the race problem is only a secondary component of the overriding social question.

Eschewing this somewhat unreasoning optimism, some admirers of the United States, though fully aware of the difficulties it faced, trusted the country's intrinsic qualities. Pastor Wagner wanted to believe that racial prejudice was not as violent as people liked to claim and that this problem could be worked out. On the eve of the War, Baron d'Estournelles de Constant adopted more or less the same attitude. He knew all the elements of racial prejudice and even criticized the Americans for their overly rigid positions, for he foresaw the role that the blacks might one day play in the electoral politics of certain states. For a long time he considered the situation hopeless, but eventually "admirable men" convinced him that today's blacks were much superior to their fathers of the preceding generation: "Yet the Americans do not give up hope; they never do. They tell me: we have gotten over the worst."[70]

68. A. France, *Sur la pierre blanche* (Paris: Calman-Lévy, 1905), pp. 222–23. France even envisaged the following: "Perhaps he is already born, the mulatto of genius who will make the children of the whites pay dearly for the blood of the Negroes lynched by their fathers!"
69. Reclus, *L'homme et la terre*, p. 109.
70. P.-E. de Constant, *Les Etats-Unis d'Amérique* (Paris: Colin, 1913), p. 347.

Halfway between the pessimists who, following the lead of the Americans, could see nothing but impending doom, and the excessive optimists, who saw all the obstacles fade away as if by miracle, one also finds more measured observers.

### Common Sense and Comparison

Without denying the scope of the black problem, a few realists thought that some day the Americans might arrive at a certain balance. Félix Klein summarized this point of view well: "They will not be allowed to lead, but they cannot be excluded," a view that was further detailed by Elisée Reclus: "what protects the Blacks is the fact that their work makes them indispensable to the very people who are planning to exile them." This common-sense opinion was not expressed very often, for most of the observers were blinded by the tensions and the passions of the moment, but it does point to one of the few possibilities for the future.

Once a certain coexistence was established, white Americans might gradually be led to stop seeing blacks only as inferior. But few French observers were capable of envisaging such a development, which ran counter both to the reality they were observing and to their own prejudices. Hence, they came up with some striking and unexpected comparisons with the French situation.

Was the black problem uniquely American? The vast majority of the French observers thought so, but some tentative comparisons with the French colonies were also made, not only superficially, as we saw, but in a more evolutionary perspective. Elisée Reclus was the only one to refer to a specific case:

> This phenomenon is analogous to what can be observed in Algeria, where so many settlers rail against the Arabs and constantly talk about driving them out into the desert, but nonetheless trust them to do all the work in their homes and on their farms.[71]

Without attaching too much importance to this simple remark, it should be pointed out that this is what an unconventional understanding of the situation of blacks in the United States could have been. In a more superficial manner, M.-A. Leblond of *L'Opinion* compared the evolution of the American blacks since slavery with that of the indigenous peoples in the French colonies. He felt that the Americans were too impatient, and that forty years were not enough to bring the two races closer together, especially in a country of violent passions and a hetero-

71. E. Reclus, *L'Homme et la terre*, p. 695.

geneous population. He also thought that the problem might be solved "more easily in the French Antilles."[72] Musings of this kind, while not indicating a thorough knowledge of the American milieu, are interesting as signs of a way of thinking that prefigures how the French might react if they ever had to deal with a race problem in their own country, and not only in the colonies.

The private statements of persons as dissimilar as Vicomte d'Haussonville and Urbain Gohier make it clear that egalitarian principles and lofty sentiments did not always stand up to a brush with reality. Tolerance was much easier as long as one looked at things from a distance. Lazare Weiller was one of the few to make a conscious effort to put himself in a different place. He wrote after stopping in Washington, which he found too crowded with blacks, and where he saw

> ... the profound antipathy for the Negro, an antipathy we Europeans do not understand, first of all because we have taken seriously the theory of the equality of all races, and perhaps also because the image of the Negro, whom we only see in the theater, in the *café-concert* and in the circus, is forever tied to happy memories in our brains. It is, in fact, very probable that if Negroes came into our domestic lives and caused the same problems there as they do in the United States, they would arouse in us the same repugnance and be martyrized in our popular press and our vaudeville shows.[73]

Without having visited the Deep South, the French industrialist had understood the nature of the problem, but it would be hazardous to conclude from this that the French were well prepared to face situations that no longer had anything exotic about them in the twentieth century.

Despite some perceptive remarks, the experience of the American blacks remained largely foreign to the French observers. They were no longer passionately interested in the fate of the freedmen, and none of them took the trouble of going into the black community, satisfied, it would seem, with what white opinion said about it.

These observers behaved as typical nineteenth-century Europeans, calmly conscious of their esthetic and mental superiority. This attitude, which often had paternalistic aspects, was not limited to a specific social or political group but was shared by most of the French concerned here. It is remarkable to see convergent opinions expressed by Claudio Jannet and Elisée Reclus, by Othenin d'Haussonville and Urbain Gohier, men

---

72. Leblond, "La question des Noirs en Amérique," *L'Opinion* (9 July 1910): 51.
73. Weiller, *Les grandes idées*, p. 351.

who otherwise had nothing in common. Beyond prejudices, the element of discovery was essential; nothing else can explain the firm stance against race prejudice taken by a Pierre de Coubertin, or the profound insight sometimes shown by Jules Huret. The French, in fact, reacted as much by emotional reflexes as by principles.

This ambivalence explains why the French, though quite open to the views of this matter held by the Americans, whose general mindset they shared, could also express considerable misgivings about the excesses of segregation. Of course the blacks were inferior, even dangerous, but there was no need to treat them as pariahs.

To be sure, such thoughts remained quite rare, but they may well presage the attitude the French were to adopt toward American blacks thirty years later. The black *Sammies* would find a welcoming country, whose inhabitants did not show them the slightest hostility, but by that time they were American soldiers first and blacks second, and their stay on French soil was brief. By contrast, the attitude toward immigrants, both between the wars and afterward, is a direct continuation of the majority opinion toward the American blacks before 1914.

However, not many French people were aware that such a development was possible. To this day, the "Negroes" are one ingredient of the exoticism of America.

# 5

# A "Manipulated and Mechanized Life"

After their first few weeks in the United States had brought them in contact with the country's day-to-day realities, the travelers began to go beyond the most superficial impressions. Through personal experiences at the hotel or in the street, on the occasion of a train trip or a Sunday in the park, a certain less fragmented and even relatively coherent image of the organization of American life began to emerge.

The exotic character of American life gradually became intelligible, as did the awareness of how it differed from French life.

> Where are our hackney coaches, our cleaning ladies, our workmen in smocks, our street sweepers, our water-cart men, our hawkers, our nursery maids, our soldiers? There is almost none of that in America. This street in Denver speaks to us of a very simple and very new, active, and hurried world, of a brand-new and imported civilization where the barbaric exists side by side with the refined.[1]

These few lines by André Chevrillon bespeak the widespread feelings of French people who had the opportunity to experience the way of life of the United States first-hand.

Remarks of this kind can be grouped together under a few major headings that summarize the dominant impressions. The first is unquestionably the industrialization of everyday life that repelled most observers; the second had to do with the strange leisure activities of the population, and with the fact that the organization of leisure was by no means incompatible with the constant pursuit of efficiency. On the basis of these observations, the French could ask their questions about the quality of the American Way of Life [in English in the original].

---

1. A. Chevrillon, *Etudes anglaises* (Paris: Hachette, 1901), p. 31. The author reviews the works of P. de Rousiers, C. de Varigny, and M. Leclercq before traveling to the United States himself.

## AN EXCESSIVE PURSUIT OF EFFICIENCY

### *"The Comforts" and Their Machines*

The American hotel amazed the French traveler by the various technical innovations it could feature, and one might think that these were limited to luxury establishments for a select clientele. This, however, was not the case, and the search for "the comforts," as people said at the time, took all kinds of other forms.

The omnipresence of electricity as early as the 1880s not only made all the European cities look dark to the returning traveler, it also permitted the use of all kinds of equipment travelers had not seen before. Elevators surprised by their frightening speed, but they were nothing more than an improvement on their hydraulic or steam-propelled predecessors, which were well known in Europe.[2] By contrast, the telephone, though known in France at the prototype stage, stupefied the visitor by its widespread use in households and offices in the cities. The ease with which the Americans were able to call firemen, and even delivery men, from their own homes was definitely appealing, but since this convenience was accessible only to a very small number of people, at least at the beginning of our period, it still had a somewhat folkloric aspect. By the beginning of the twentieth century, the general use of this means of communication brought new questions. Were there not, in 1899, more than 2,000 telephones in the city of Washington alone, whereas only ten times as many could be found in all of France? It seemed unreal. Besides, at the same time, "household matters, business, meetings, everything is arranged by telephone" in Seattle as well. In view of these advantages, the annoyance of a ringing phone or the inopportune character of certain calls did not weigh very heavily. Telephoning had ceased to be a luxury and had become a daily necessity.

Another instance of these comforts that made life so much easier, especially in the hot summer, was the "big fans hanging from the ceiling to keep the working girls cool" in a factory,[3] in other words, ventilators, which were also compared to "thin . . . overturned windmill wings." Such innovations benefited everyone; these were luxuries to which one could easily become accustomed, as were bathrooms with hot water in univer-

---

2. Those of the Eiffel Tower, for instance, were installed in 1889. They were replaced by electric elevators only in 1985, but the reaction of the French had to do with the height of the American buildings.
3. Marquise San Carlos de Pedroso, *Les Américains chez eux* (Paris: Librairie de la Nouvelle Revue, 1890), p. 107. H. de Varigny used almost the identical words.

sities and hotels. The contrast with one's usual habits was so stark that Pierre de Coubertin felt called upon to express some reserves:

> The shower bath is not used much in the United States; many persons take a hot bath every morning. In such a stimulating climate, this may be a good custom; but it does not suit ours, where nothing can take the place of the cold morning shower.[4]

Nothing tells us that French schoolboys, if indeed they took cold showers, agreed with this eminent pedagogue.

Less useful for all and sundry, typewriters, whose proliferation could be seen in offices, hotel lobbies, and even on a few trains, were eyed with a certain bewilderment; the same reaction took place in front of the Remington booth at the Paris World's Fair of 1889. In Washington it was quite a sight to watch squadrons of young women banging on these strange keyboards in the offices of federal departments; proof, once again, that this was no longer a marginal accessory for the use of a few trifling dreamers.

There were many more examples of the intrusion of machines into everyday life; some washed clothes, others dried them; and at the stock exchange, the fluctuations of the stock prices were posted automatically on a special tape. The observers were well aware, of course, that not many Americans used all of these contrivances; but the fact that they were common enough to be found on a simple walk or in any ordinary public place did show that they were an essential part of American life, whether in the factory or in the home. At the Philadelphia World's Fair, many visitors already had the opportunity to discover all these marvels of technology:

> ... machines to twist the thread, weave wool or cotton, break or forge iron; machines to clear the land, harvest grain, transform the harvest; machines to hurt or heal, to kill or restore life, to do away with suffering, labor, and even effort. There is no longer one corner of human activity where the need to convert inertia into intelligent and diligent energy is not openly asserted.[5]

In the face of such feats of prowess and their intrusion into private life, opinions were divided and ambiguous; was this helpful or confusing? On the one hand, one finds that the visitors admired the deployment of so much imagination and such great resources, for the most part

---

4. P. de Coubertin, *Universités transatlantiques* (Paris: Hachette, 1890), p. 36.
5. Eggermont, *Voyage autour du globe* (Paris: Delagrave, 1892), p. 45. On this point the author's observation was still relevant, even though he published the book almost fifteen years after he had written it.

in the service of the general well-being. In this spirit, a certain number of travelers felt called upon to make the trip to Menlo Park, where they were received by Thomas Edison, the very symbol of American inventiveness and of the omnipresence of electricity. Edison was so adept at self-promotion that some of the visitors were embarrassed.[6] But Chicago, Philadelphia, and even Saint Louis were also veritable Meccas of technology, which justified a visit to these places and left the visitor stunned.

However, there was a considerable difference between marvelous inventiveness and the regular use of machines. That is why many travelers' abstract admiration had an admixture of terror, not unlike what they had experienced when visiting the Chicago slaughterhouses. Marquis de Chasseloup-Laubat, an engineer by profession, could not quite hide this feeling when he evoked "all the most recent applications of all the sciences, leading to a material civilization that is very advanced, much more advanced than anywhere else."[7] It is not surprising that a European of the late nineteenth century, faced with the speed of the tramways, with the density of the network of communications, and with the omnipresence of technology, should have exclaimed from the bottom of his heart: "Bravo, that's enough!"

And indeed, these mechanical excesses and these technical refinements did more than generate comfort, they also made for a waste of resources for maintaining it and a dependence on the superfluous that made the French uncomfortable. Paul Bourget for one complained about American excesses in every area – everything had to be taller, bigger, faster, more expensive than everywhere else – and his intimate enemy, Urbain Gohier, agreed with him but widened the scope of his criticism: "What the people of America call superfluous, what they ruin, and what they throw away as unworthy of their delicate ways would probably be welcomed and even turned into wealth by ours."[8] The French visitors, almost in spite of themselves, shared a common discomfort with the development of an increasingly industrialized way of life, whose comfort and convenience had to be paid for, in their opinion, in one way or another.

Consequently, remarks praising the agreeable comforts of daily life – Félix Klein even admitted to a certain tolerance for the soft life of the

---

6. O. Uzanne, *Vingt jours dans le Nouveau Monde* (Paris: May-Matteroz, 1893), p. 59. Those who visited the great inventor were for the most part members of delegations and journalists; ordinary tourists rarely made the extra effort.

7. Marquis de Chasseloup-Laubat, *Voyage en Amérique et principalement à Chicago* (Paris: Cité Rougemont, 1893), p. 77. Such admiration inevitably bred a certain terror.

8. J. Huret, *Le peuple du XXe siècle* (Paris: Fasquelle, 1903), p. 15. The author here echoes P. Bourget's *Outremer* (Paris: Lemerre, 1895), p. 66.

seminarians of Rochester – were always interspersed with expressions of concern about excessive reliance on the machine where it seemed out of place. Jules Huret, neither archaic nor anti-American in outlook, came to wonder: "What will it be fifty years from now, this race of people, saturated with electricity and trained for speed, whose ideal state seems to be the paroxysm?"[9]

Such bewildered fascination with the invasion of machines into daily life in the late nineteenth century foreshadows the real alarm that would be spawned a few generations later by the advent of the robot. But American extravagance also flourished in other areas.

### Aggressive Commercialism and Advertising

Inevitably our travelers had occasion to do business with storekeepers and to look for certain kinds of goods. Wherever they went, they dealt with people who deployed an astonishing energy in these normal activities, acting as if their very future were at stake.

Their reactions to "advertising" perfectly illustrate this situation, and in fact quite a few authors devoted entire chapters to this particular manifestation of the American genius. It was not too surprising that Broadway should be the paradise of advertisement; this was New York, where one had to be prepared for everything, but advertising was invading the entire landscape. Along the railroad tracks one saw painted rocks and aggressive billboards. In the towns sandwich men strolled up and down the sidewalks – and sometimes there were other devices, like the dead horse in a New York street, which according to many witnesses was covered with competing advertisements. In hotels and restaurants, free matchbooks bearing the name of the establishment were the epitome of this pursuit of publicity, but also a fine example of wastefulness. Among the many examples provided by our travelers as frequently in 1870 as in 1914, one can pick two that summarize all of them. In the first instance, Gustave de Molinari witnessed in 1876 the struggle between a brand of toothpaste and a particular throat syrup that was fought out throughout the countryside:

> At one point I had believed, I must admit, that Gargling had won: all the
> horizontal billboards that form a wall along the Pennsylvania Railroad cel-
> ebrate the glory of Gargling Oil, but when I saw the name Sozodont
> imprinted on the most inaccessible rocks and even on the dark underside
> of a bridge, I understood the superiority of Sozodont. But what difference

9. J. Huret, *En Amérique* (Paris: Charpentier, 1813), p. 322.

does it make, it really gets you down, Sozodont, Sozodont! Why should I care?[10]

Thirty years later, Paul Vidal de la Blache felt harried by gigantic and imperious electric advertisements, and in particular by a "monstrous eye" that pierced the night recommending the services of an oculist in Chicago:

> One reads this as one rushes by, almost without turning one's head. But it has captured one's attention for a moment; it has hit home. The American looks more than he speaks and in a fleeting moment takes in more than he understands.[11]

Here were two rational men who accepted modernism, and yet both were struck in the same way by American advertising, even though they encountered different techniques. They had the impression that the advertisement was addressed to them personally; it forced itself on them and made them uncomfortable. The problem, they felt, came from the commercial aggressiveness of the Americans, which in these two cases was successful, as it often was. This was bound to worry these staid Frenchmen, who relied above all on their reasoning faculties. Underlying the sometimes picturesque aspects of other references to prodigious advertisement efforts, one finds the same feeling of being taken over by insidious and sometimes brutal means.

To be sure, a certain form of advertisement was not unknown in France, but it was contained in circumscribed spaces, under the famous law of July 1881, which forbade the posting of notices; no such regulations existed in the United States. This was compounded by a commercial energy that encouraged any act of sale, wherever and whenever it might be. As many French observers noted, advertising was not always directly involved. On the trains, the constant passing of the pushcart might be irritating, but for the vendor this was a way of showing his persistence until his quarry gave up and bought something. The same attitude prevailed among the shoe-shine boys and the petty newspaper vendors in the cities, who followed a potential customer around, threading their way among the tramways and looking more eager and determined than their Parisian counterparts. This too was a manifestation of commercial drive, whether it was ordered by a boss or freely chosen.

---

10. G. de Molinari, *Lettres sur l'Amérique* ... (Paris: Hachette, 1876). This fierce struggle between two products is described in almost identical terms in many other travel accounts.
11. P. Vidal de la Blache, "A travers l'Amérique du Nord," *Revue de Paris* (March–April 1905): 523–24.

In the eyes of the French, this impetuous commercial activity was the main characteristic of the New World; they knew this before they went there, but contact with the daily reality showed them that this behavior was not confined to businessmen but was also at work in the humblest activities conducted in the street. There was general astonishment at the intensity shown by all these people; Léo Clarétie, for instance, found it hard to take that the shopkeeper accosted the customer even in the street, whereas traditionally the customer was king when dealing with a passive and helpful, even servile tradesman.[12]

The wide gap that separated the two countries in this area says a great deal about their different economic methods and characterizes these two societies very well. In fact, the few French shopkeepers who traveled to America had the same reactions as the journalists and the gentlemen of leisure, even when they admired the effectiveness of the various commercial practices: "Beware of the American, for when it comes to business he has a very special mentality," exclaimed Georges Fromage, the owner of a small factory, in 1910, deploring in the same breath the lack of initiative of the French.[13]

In every area of life, the Americans seemed intent on saving time and on doing away with every superfluous gesture:

> This is a salient feature of the American character: cutting down on all agents and middlemen. All their inventions, large or small, tend to do away with a task or save a second. . . .[14]

This general attitude even affected sectors of American life where one would not expect to find it.

### The Press

The French travelers' first contact with the American press was the reporter who came to interview them as they arrived. For prominent travelers this scene would take place on the New York pier at the foot of the gangplank leading from the steamer; for the others it came as they got off the train or, at worst, in their hotel room in a town whose impor-

---

12. L. Clarétie, *Feuilles de route aux Etats-Unis* (Paris: Dentu, 1895), devoted an entire chapter to "Advertising" (pp. 275–90), in which this remark occurs. It is very revealing of his attitude; and indeed, to this day, Americans visiting France are sometimes surprised by the passivity of sales women, their lack of commerical drive in dealing with customers.
13. G. Fromage, *Notes sur un rapide et court voyage aux Etats-Unis et au Canada* (Rouen: Imprimerie du Journal de Rouen, 1910), p. 20.
14. L. and G. Verbrugghe, *Promenades et chasses dans l'Amérique du Nord* (Paris: Calman-Lévy, 1879), p. 11.

tance diminished with their own celebrity – ranging from Saint Louis to Laramie.

Very soon they were asked *the* question: "What do you think of America?" The travelers did not know how to answer, since they often had not yet seen anything, but the reporter was unrelenting, trying to find out everything about a person who had come from so far, especially some picturesque details that would make a hit in his paper. At first the visitor was flattered by this proof of his reputation, although the better informed knew that in the West, lists of passengers likely to be of interest to the newspapers of the next town were passed on by telegraph. But they were soon disillusioned. The journalist's questions actually seemed absurd, and he showed no respect for a traveler who was increasingly uneasy when thinking about what he would read about himself in next day's local paper: "You can consider yourself very lucky if the reporter does not have a codak [*sic*] in his pocket and if the next morning the picture of your wife or your daughter does not appear in the newspaper."[15] What shocked the French most was not the content of the article – not many would read it anyway – but the manner of the reporter, his brusque and offensive questions.

The logic of this unusual behavior became clear to the nonplussed visitor only after he had taken the trouble of reading these strange newspapers. Advertisements took up more space than politics, minor incidents of the day – the expression *fait divers* (crime column) had just come into use in France – were frequently given front-page honors, and the headlines were always eye-catching and vague, so that an interview could be a godsend. If the ingenious reporter had neither a great criminal nor a famous artist to write about, he could fall back on a French traveler, especially if he bore a noble title or a name "with some extra syllables"; this would add spice. The result was a big pile of paper filled with "motley ramblings to satisfy the appetite of a people with the souls of little children," as Paul Adam put it. One would not forget the obnoxious reporter, but sometimes his article was acceptable; the advertisements were irritating but picturesque and supplied storytellers with an inexhaustible mine of American extravagances in every area. And it did appear that the American public was particularly fond of this type of "rapid, sensational, and universal" journalism. But none of these observers wished that this kind of press would become established in France, and some were seriously worried about it. Urbain Gohier realized that a certain development had already taken place:

15. S. Jousselin, *Yankees fin de siècle* (Paris: Ollendorf, 1892), p. 78.

The American papers are very American, excessively so; they have their ways of doing things and we have ours. Theirs are probably good, for they captivate the American public, and their methods, when exported to Europe, now captivate the English public and the French public.[16]

With this one exception, the French observers had strong reservations about the American press, particularly since in France they read just one paper with a specific editorial policy that gave them "its clever, moralizing, and intriguing columns, and its reviews of art and literature," so that they knew nothing about the cheap French dailies that were more comparable to the American yellow press [in English in the original]. What they knew of the press was *Le Temps*, *Le Figaro*, or *Le Journal des Débats*, for they had not yet become aware of the advances and the technical means of *Le Matin* or the *Petit Parisien*, which also sent reporters all around the world and featured stories of crime and passion. Not that American journalism did not have its own special characteristics, but the difference was not what most of the observers thought. Despite what those who visited the printing presses of the *New York Herald* or the *World* may have said about them, their equipment was in fact hardly more powerful than that of their Parisian counterparts. For once, machinery did not put the American ahead.

The difference was that the American press was part of the business world, a fact that also accounted for the ruthlessness of the journalists, the slightness of the articles, the spicy titles, and the inevitable abundance of commercial advertising. Boni de Castellane, who visited Pulitzer's *World*, was one of the few to understand this phenomenon fully; a newspaper, he said, must attract attention and be talked about, it is "a news business as there are grocery and guano businesses."[17] No wonder, therefore, that the journalists were more interested in information than in commentary, and that their main objective was to provide news, from which the reader could chose what he wanted; the masses of advertising met these criteria perfectly. Under these circumstances a newspaper was bought like any common merchandise, which meant that it needed a very large number of customers, whereas the French papers, often ideologically committed, were satisfied with a narrow and selected readership.

16. Gohier, *Le peuple*, p. 196. Gohier was the only author to remark on the role of journalists in the uncovering of scandals, although he did not give any precise examples.
17. Marquis de Castellane, "Quinze jours aux Etats-Unis," *Revue de Paris* (15 April 1895): 894; his comparison was intentionally contemptuous, but he found this journalism effective, just as these other businesses could be effective.

## THE AMERICAN WAY OF LEISURE AND SPORTS

Could people as rushed as the Americans, in their constant pursuit of efficiency, really relax and enjoy leisure?

### *Do Americans Know How to Enjoy Themselves?*

As they participated in certain official ceremonies, visited the amusement parks of the world's fairs, and followed the crowds at Coney Island and similar places, the French travelers found the answer to this surprising question.

The organization of official ceremonies regularly struck them by its apparent disorder and the mediocrity of the various arrangements. The Americans were not particularly concerned about any official rank order and placed their guests almost haphazardly; the stands were shaky, the decorations either absent or tacky. Everything looked unfinished and makeshift. Such instances of poor taste and disdain of the forms were also found at the celebration of the centenary of the Battle of Yorktown, at the inauguration of the Statue of Liberty, or at the opening of the world's fairs. These were official occasions, for which the Americans had little use and very little experience, but the same impression was also conveyed by the public amusement parks.

The best example of this was the Midway Pleasance, which featured the attractions and distractions of the Chicago World's Fair. Here visitors found a concentration of refreshment booths, shooting ranges, a ferris wheel, and all the shows of which the Americans were so fond. But the French were not enchanted by what they saw; it seemed to them that the crowd was morose and stone-faced, showing none of the signs of pleasure that such places should naturally bring forth. There was no genuine gaiety, and indeed a certain austerity seemed to prevail: How different this was from the memory of the Paris World's Fair of 1889! What could be the reason for such an attitude? No doubt it was the didactic design of the fair; the Americans did not visit it to enjoy themselves; their pleasure remained serious and they smiled peacefully instead of laughing out loud. Moreover, the atmosphere was not that of a fun fair, and there was not even a vaudeville show, much to the chagrin of impenitent French men-about-town. Some felt that one should blame the "cold national character" for this lack of zest, which may also have been related to the huge expanse of the fair.

So now it was important to find out whether the same tendencies characterized the usual leisure activities of the Americans. Coney Island, which attracted so many New Yorkers on summer weekends, made a strong impression. Here the populace could be seen frolicking on a beach of dirty sand amidst sandwich wrappers and hot-dog vendors. An enormous elephant dominated the beach, making a strange hotel for the lovers who came there in droves. Modesty seemed forgotten, and the American puritanism suddenly became extremely tolerant; Baron de Mandat-Grancey even found the bathing costumes quite lacking in modesty![18] Looking at this land of milk and honey, the destination of packed ferry boats, the French had the same reactions that would be elicited in France, even among the French middle class, by the first paid vacations in the summer of 1936. The sight of people enjoying themselves was watched with a certain paternalism; besides, the French took note of the difference between the relative license that prevailed in these places and the equally excessive prudishness that dominated the more high-class beaches of Asbury Park or Ocean Grove, where the women bathed in full-length garments to avoid stirring up temptations, and where bathing was forbidden on Sundays – to the indignation of passing French tourists.[19]

Moreover, the Sunday pleasures of the New Yorkers seemed to be a high-energy undertaking. Upper-class families went to the country to entertain and to engage in sports:

> I think there are very few who go to the countryside simply to walk around and quietly enjoy the pleasure of being outside in the fresh air, amidst the greenery of a beautiful landscape. Americans let loose in nature still need the same fever of activity and combativeness that spurs them on the other six days.[20]

Between the implied criticism of the hypocrisy about the beaches and the description of leisure time that was too frenetic to be restful, the French clearly felt out of step with the Americans. The theater plays they saw were also too highly charged, relying more on good organization – well-constructed scenery, fire safety – than on the quality of a text. As for the art of swinging a leg, "it took the place of dancing."

Such examples make it clear that in the eyes of the French, the Americans did not know how to enjoy themselves or to relax. It seemed as if their perpetual need for activity could be appeased only by sport, in which they engaged to excess, unless they went in for camping, a new

18. E. de Mandat-Grancey, *Chez l'Oncle Sam* (Paris: Plon, 1885), p. 105.
19. M. Shaw, "Quelques plages suburbaines de New York," *Nouvelle Revue* (Jan.–Feb. 1892): 554–64. These French travelers swore that they would never again set foot in these places.
20. C. Huard, *New York comme je l'ai vue* (Paris: Rey, 1906), p. 192.

activity that developed, as Félix Klein noted in 1908, as a kind of return to Indian ways. Both activities seemed extreme, but all in all, sport was the most astonishing phenomenon.

### The Excesses of Sport

Organized sports came to France rather late, often by way of Great Britain, as in the case of soccer or rugby,[21] and *Le Temps* inaugurated a regular sports column only in 1886. For many of the French who went to the United States, this was their first encounter with the practice of organized sports.

Travelers who were interested in sport thus "discovered" boxing in 1888, then, in the 1890s, football and baseball, and finally a football match in the water, which must have been water polo.[22] Their first reaction was astonishment about these activities for which there were no French words; as for regattas and horse races, they were known to them but practiced rather differently than they were in Europe.

Another source of astonishment was the passionate interest that these "amazing contests" of walkers, boxers, and riders aroused. Everyone was intensely interested, and the telegraph made it possible to transmit the result of a given match to the newspapers, which turned it into a front-page headline:

> The vicissitudes of a ball game are noted with as much exactitude and discussed with as much gravity as the vicissitudes of the Battle of Gettysburg. If a student had outshone Pico de la Mirandola in his examinations, no one in the neighboring town would care; but all of America is informed of how he has hit a baseball with his bat or kicked a football with his foot.[23]

The popularity of sports was demonstrated by the number of spectators at important games, and also the rhythmic chanting of the fans that accompanied the moves of football teams. More than 2,500 persons were

21. Soccer, which was first played in Great Britain in 1863, was slowly being introduced in France. The soccer club of Le Havre came into being in 1872, that of Paris in 1879, but the first championships were held only in 1903–4. Rugby, which began to be played in 1871, was introduced in France by a group of Englishmen in 1880, and the French team played its first international match in 1906. French interest in sports was marginal, particularly among intellectuals such as those who wrote about the United States.

22. First French reference to boxing in F. Moreau, *Aux Etats-Unis* (Paris: Plon, 1887), p. 217; of football in A. Lambert de Sainte Croix, *De Paris à San Francisco* (Paris: Calman-Lévy, 1884), p. 67; baseball for the same year in P. Trasenster, *Aux Etats-Unis* (Paris: Ghio, 1885), p. 50. J. d'Albrey was the only author to mention water polo, played in California, in *De Tonkin au Havre* (Paris: Plon, 1898), p. 205.

23. Gohier, *Le peuple*, p. 222.

present at the boxing match that Paul de Rousiers attended, and the passion of the public and the reporters at a college football game left the staid Paul Bourget stupefied.

This vogue explained the astonishing fact of the existence in New York of professional baseball, a "kind of cricket" that Estournelles de Constant described with great precision and dreamed of introducing in France. All the testimonies stressed the importance of this sport in the United States, where by the end of the nineteenth century it had become *the* national sport. Another demonstration of the importance of sport was the attention it was given by colleges and universities; in fact all the games the French attended were intercollegiate matches, for instance, between Harvard and Yale. These events, which were inevitably compared to the famous contests between Oxford and Cambridge, remained incomprehensible to the French. Why mix sports with studying; does it not distract those who engage in it from their regular work, and what is the use of "strong muscles and big fists"? The French did not understand this way of thinking, nor did they approve of the Americans' spending so much on the organization of boxing matches, which gave rise in the country to a frenzy they considered all the more unwholesome as popular fervor in turn influenced the behavior of the players and boxers. Having to meet the spectators' expectations, the contestants were led to deplorable excesses.

Once they had gotten over their initial astonishment, the French observers did not, in fact, enjoy the sports events they attended. Baseball was not too bad, they did not understand what was going on, but the game remained dignified. By contrast, the violence of boxing matches and football games struck them as absolutely revolting.

At the end of the nineteenth century, boxing was undeniably violent and often gory. The French had the opportunity to see the great matches of Jim Corbett versus Mitchell or Sullivan. They did not have the vocabulary to describe these fights, calling the ring a platform and the boxer shorts swimming trunks. There was a sort of ceremonial that meant nothing to them: Taking off the bathrobe at the start, trainers sponging off the contestants, these were new scenes that called for descriptions as precise as those of an entomologist.[24] But when they had overcome the shock of the smoky hall and the screaming public and understood the meaning of the different operations, the dominant reaction was horror:

24. That of P. de Rousiers, *La vie américaine* (Paris: Didot, 1892), pp. 123–24, is the most precise and striking, for it painstakingly describes a spectacle that is now perfectly familiar to us. See also Clarétie, *Feuilles de route*, p. 258, about the Corbett–Sullivan match, which was transmitted throughout the United States by telegraph.

... the spectacle of two men hurled against one another like two fighting cocks for the greater amusement of the public has left me with nothing but a feeling of revulsion against those who enjoy it.[25]

Another observer said that "these savage fights are a shame on civilization," and Paul de Rousiers perfectly expressed the general opinion of these few witnesses: "I feel terribly cold amidst this tumult; the skill of these gladiators seems great, but the spectacle is too brutal for a Frenchman of the nineteenth century."

To be sure, not many of the French attended a boxing match, but in 1888 and 1893, both a diplomat like Louis Vossion Serre and a literary figure like Léo Clarétie reacted with total rejection. On these occasions the Americans took pleasure in spectacles that seemed to them barbaric and without any moral or esthetic justification. This was an enigma that the French were not yet ready to decipher, one more shadow on the kind of leisure activity enjoyed by the citizens of the Great Republic.

Finally, one might understand, though not appreciate, that an individual fight between two boxers could turn violent, but it seemed totally unacceptable that a collective sport, football, when played by young men, should usually end with broken noses and legs, as French spectators unanimously noted. Yet such clashes occurred in California as well as in New England, between major and minor teams, and our authors talked about them much more than about the rules of the game which, as they freely admitted, they did not understand at all. Paul Bourget, revolted by the brutality of the clashes that seemed to be spurred on by the passion of the spectators, was nonetheless fascinated by the spectacle:

... young mastiffs trained to bite, to rush for their share of the quarry; game of a race made for savage attack, violent defense, implacable conquest, and struggle to the death.[26]

If students showed such desperate eagerness in what was after all only a game, it was because they had been trained for it, taught to win at any price, and the noisy support of their fellow students, the will to raise their college's colors above all others, were signs of this attitude. Under these conditions, was this still sport as the French understood it? Most of the observers did not think so, but they still watched these spectacles as dilettantes, often without being really interested in sports, which had not yet

25. Moreau, *Aux Etats-Unis*, p. 217. Boxing, which was truly regulated only in 1891, was admitted to the Olympics in 1904. Before these dates it was extremely violent and practiced withoout much restraint. Hence the shock of the French observers.

26. Bourget, *Outremer*, p. 146; these fights did not have the aristocratic gentility Bourget considered so French.

become popular in France. Under these conditions everything seemed to them even more excessive and objectionable.

The opinion of one expert is particularly interesting in this context. When Pierre de Coubertin came to the United States for the first time, he had just been commissioned to study the development of physical education. His opinion was nuanced and balanced; he admired the sports facilities of the colleges he visited, wished that France would adopt the system of showers and athletic clothing, and also noted that there were considerable differences in the manner of conducting sports activities from college to college. He felt, for example, that athletics were not well conceived at Cornell, where not enough emphasis was placed on effort, and too much on hygiene, whereas at most other institutions the exact opposite was true. In his report to the minister of education he criticized the exaggerated emphasis on discipline and the scientific nature of American physical education. In fact, he was stupefied both at Harvard and at Yale to discover methods of muscle building and training that seemed more suitable for horses than for humans: "All this is not education, it is animal husbandry!"[27]

This would mean that sport would become nothing more than a savage competition that would have little in common with the growth of the individual envisaged by the founder of the modern Olympics. It explained the frenzy of athletic events and the pursuit of success at any price that generated such popular enthusiasm and nonplussed the French. Thérèse – who otherwise appreciated the freedom American women seemed to enjoy – was even indignant about the development of women's sports; the contortions of sweating bodies literally made her feel sick.

Thus there was an immense time lag between the concept of leisure and sport in France and in the United States. In activities where the French looked for quiet and personal enjoyment, the Americans seemed bent on creating sound and fury. This confirmed the impression of an overcharged society, whose comforts seemed to be partially canceled out by the use the Americans made of them.

## TO LIVE IN THE UNITED STATES?

After these various, sometimes superficial and sometimes more profound assessments of American life, one can now ask the travelers whether they

---

27. P. de Coubertin, *Universités transatlantiques* (Paris: Hachette, 1890), p. 90. Coubertin was at Harvard at the time, and at Yale he spoke of a gym that "looked like a stud-farm."

have found daily life in America attractive and whether it has made them feel like settling in that country. They have not yet, to be sure, given their opinion about education or politics, but they have gained a feel for the general climate, to which they have reacted with immediate enthusiasm as well as with considerable misgivings. Out of such a bundle of impressions they would forge a first general idea.

However, this question remains purely rhetorical, for none of the travelers manifested the desire to settle in the United States, although there were many who before returning to France toyed with dreams to this effect, dreams that shifted from rosy to gray in various proportions, depending on the year and on the individual.

### A Seeming Lack of Conviviality

In a sense, this was the counterpart of the commercial aggressiveness and the permanent intensity of life that made many human contacts look very harsh. Already extremely alarmed by the Americans' eating and drinking habits, which any good Frenchman considered the basis of friendly human relations, and further worried by the astonishing forms of athletic endeavors, the travelers associated these observations with other surprising behaviors.

All these partial and superficial observations were used by the French to construct a first idea of the way of life of the Americans. They did not even have to evoke the extravagances and eccentricities that fed the "unheard-of-ness" with which the Americans were fairly dripping to feel amazed.

The manners, especially of American men, gave rise to never-ending and horrified frowns. The use of chewing tobacco seemed quasi-universal and brought with it the presence of those abominable spittoons almost everywhere:

> ... enormous brown tureens, shiny copper vases, earthenware or crystal bowls – one encounters them at every step, in hotel lobbies, in railroad cars, in offices, in bedrooms; the Negro who shines your shoes makes sure to place one within your reach: the spittoon seems to be humanity's first necessity.[28]

Incidentally, the bulging cheek was not exclusively male, for women had quickly found a substitute for the tobacco plug in a special gum, which when chewed created distortions to which even the most beautiful face could not stand up. Chewing gum, a notable contribution to

28. Rousiers, *La vie aux Etats-Unis*, vol. 2, p. 132.

national unity, according to Urbain Gohier, was one more proof of the strangeness of American tastes and manners.

Tobacco plugs, spittoons – which, incidentally, were mentioned less and less as the years passed, as if their use were becoming rarer – and chewing gum were only details, but they confirmed other facts of a similar nature. The Americans did not care what was said about them. The travelers mentioned again and again how much they were bothered by seeing feet on the backs of easy chairs and on table tops – although as time went on this fad seems to have become entrenched in the True West, where rough manners were almost normal – and by loud clothing; they also remarked upon the absence of formal courtesies in everyday encounters. This lack of formality did not preclude the expression of very warm cordiality, which was pleasing if the French visitor made the effort to give up his own conventions, and obnoxious if he insisted on them: ". . . American cheerfulness, Yankee gaiety, brutality and childishness, false confidences; what it amounts to is the joviality of vulgar pimps."[29]

Once these first snags were overcome, the observation of the life of city dwellers also elicited reactions. For one thing, it soon became clear that men working in the city did not go home at noon, for they could be seen in those ubiquitous bars, perched on high stools in front of a counter. At the end of their working day, they often went to their strictly male clubs and did not join their homes and families until late in the evening. This had to do with the fact that residential neighborhoods were very far from the center of the city, so that in New York as in Cincinnati or Milwaukee one had to travel several miles to reach it. Since husbands, brothers, and sons were absent all day long, wives, sisters, and daughters thought nothing of going downtown by themselves. They could be seen in department stores, in drugstores, and in public conveyances. To be sure, they were treated with the greatest respect, but the French found this sight surprising.

Such a way of organizing one's life, some felt, implied a disorganized family life, where men and women did not see much of each other and where both led almost independent lives. This fit in with what all the newspapers were saying, along with lightweight popular books: lots of divorces, unmannerly children. Eventually, after thinking about it, the traveler realized that sometimes entire families with women and children lived regularly and for long periods of time in the very hotel where he was staying. He was told that domestic servants were even harder to find for families than for hotels, so that it was more convenient – again that obsessive search for convenience – to live in one of those perfectly

29. D. Bonnaud, *D'océan à océan* (Paris: Ollendorf, 1897), p. 370.

equipped establishments. And if those who lived in houses could not count on valets and servants, they only had to push a few buttons to turn on the heat, call for a delivery, or summon the police.

This description essentially matches what most of the travelers said. Describing only the world of the middle class, where the man was occupied with his own affairs and worked in an office, they generalized from a few cases. Yet the vision of American life they culled from them is not without interest.

The fact is that French people, most of them city dwellers and even Parisians, found in the United States a way of life that had very little in common with their own. How could the Americans live that way, sufficient unto themselves, without the support of a solidly organized family cell? Did this account for their pursuit of hectic leisure activities, was it the price they paid for the admirable American energy at work in the building of skyscrapers and the tremendous growth of the cities? Did it justify taking pleasure in the various technical achievements the Americans had mastered?

The exotic character of comfort and material progress, and the fact that one could easily become accustomed to them, gave rise to fundamental questions that called for a less superficial analysis. André Siegfried expressed this quite clearly:

> Let us not be deceived by the superficial argument of elevators, bathrooms, and sixty-story houses! Some tourists are disappointed because they no longer encounter big Mexican hats . . . or revolvers . . . in the United States. They find that the street is lacking in romanticism. They only have to pierce a thin bark to find all the romanticism they want, for morally there is a great deal of Mexican mentality here, and financially a great many revolvers are still pointed![30]

This opinion, given in 1914, benefited from the advantage of distance that travelers of earlier decades did not necessarily have; less experienced than Siegfried, they did not separate the extraordinary character of the material life of the Americans from the features of their actual social organization. Most of them used such hasty syntheses to form their judgments about the attractiveness of American life.

In this manner, remarks about bad manners and the apparent hypocrisy of prudishness or alcohol consumption formed a stark contrast with others about the comfort of the trains, the pleasure of hot baths, and the marvels of electricity: It was a curious American cocktail, whose taste was a bit strong for many travelers, although it did intoxicate others.

30. A. Siegfried, *Deux mois en Amérique du Nord* . . . (Paris: Colin, 1916), p. 102.

### Better Off at Home

Visitors at the beginning of our period had decidedly more misgivings about American life than their successors in the early twentieth century. Not that they did not appreciate certain specific aspects, but they were more sensitive to the roughness of American ways and customs. They were glad to visit – "why is the America that so avidly visits us not more often the aim and object of our visits?"[31] – but hardly anyone thought of settling there. Some did not hesitate to express a categorical judgment:

> We want to be democratic but well-mannered too, and the spectacle of American society is as hard to take for Conservatives as it is for Republicans. The former are frightened to see what they consider the inevitable consequences of democracy in power, and the latter understand that they will never be able to persuade populations as sophisticated as those of Europe to adopt a system that would have these results.[32]

There were several versions of this argument. Some based it on the excessive youth of the country, although they could not say whether maturity would bring any real change; they followed the example of Baron de Hübner, who had visited America in order to uncover this evolution, not satisfied with reading about it in books. The point of view of this Austrian aristocrat was very close to that of his French counterparts who did not identify too rigidly with archaic positions. Others complained even more openly about the lack of "society" in the United States, for they did not meet people like themselves, and the luxury of the restaurants and the nouveaux riches was no help. Life was expensive and rough, and they resented its constant aggressions. Such attitudes were present among more humble travelers as well, sometimes in equally haughty form.

Over the following years, the unpleasant character of many aspects of American life did not disappear from the accounts, but it was compensated for by other things. Thus, no one could be more snobbish than Marquis de Castellane; when he went to the United States, he complained about the "aurea mediocritas" he found there and about the general brutality. "This entire America is just one big factory," he wrote, and yet he came to see the vigor that emanated from this New World, and it did not

---

31. C. Allard, *Promenade au Canada et aux Etats-Unis* (Paris: Didier, 1878), p. 9.
32. J. de Rochechouart, *Excursion autour du monde* (Paris: Plon, 1879), p. 275. The author complained particularly about the lack of domestic servants, feeling that even the machines cannot work without a human hand. Personally, this diplomat seems to have been a republican, or at least rather tolerant of the republican regime.

reflect favorably on his most cherished values: "Seen from New York, France looks like the world's Faubourg Saint Germain,* that is something, but it is not enough."[33] In other ways, he was very conscious of what this young society represented and foresaw that, for all its flaws, it was indeed one facet of the future. Perhaps Boni de Castellane was looking for a kind of rejuvenation treatment, in addition to the dollars of the Gould family. Paul Bourget expressed the same thing in almost identical terms:

> Many things in America are brutalizing and unpleasant. One often longs for the slow and gentle Europe. At times one feels real nostalgia for a historic land where the dead stand behind the living. And yet, upon leaving this astonishing Republic, one experiences an emotion made of gratitude and pity. One has learned there to shed the great fear of that mysterious tomorrow toward which the entire civilized universe is advancing.[34]

On the basis of this assessment, which matches that of Pierre de Coubertin as well as those of Paul Adam, Vidal de la Blache, and many others who put it less well, one can speak of a certain French consensus. On the eve of their return to Europe, these travelers concluded with a "Yes . . . but!" and when they arrived in France, everything there seemed small and far removed from ruthlessness and turmoil. "Here we are back to Latin tranquillity, the slow trot of coaches, a lot of talk . . . the taste for what is certain and nice. Now Paris looks to us like an archeological site, the old-fashioned work of meticulous craftsmen, of slow and fussy workmen."[35] Everyone, writers and civil servants, workers and men of leisure, was struck by the strong contrasts, between the patina of French walls and the gleaming surfaces of American skyscrapers, between orderly French streets and the noisy anarchy of transatlantic cities, and they once again noticed soldiers and dogs on the sidewalks and the dim light of the street lamps. Their reactions were similar in 1870 and 1914, as if there had been no evolution.

It was only after they had felt the natural joy at returning to their habits and their familiar horizons that their conclusions began to diverge somewhat. Were they really better off at home or did they miss the comforts of American life after all?

Roughly speaking, two groups emerged. The first rejected this America, even if it was the future; the second, more or less reluctantly, was ready to accept it along with the risks and the hopes that this choice implied. But all conceded that ". . . just as the weather service pre-

---

* The aristocratic quarter of Paris (trans.).
33. Castellane, "Quinze jours aux Etats-Unis," 876.
34. Bourget, *Outremer*, p. iii.
35. P. Adam, *Vues d'Amérique* (Paris: Ollendorf, 1906), pp. 2–3.

dicts squalls coming from the West across the Ocean, so many symptoms make it clear that it [this future] will come to our old European countries."[36]

The first group was certainly larger and more representative. The argumentation of its adherents was simple: American life was not suited to French people, and the future it was supposed to represent was not yet threatening. The journey had been agreeable and enriching, but living in the United States for any length of time was out of the question; at most one could temporarily do business there. The American form of social organization seemed overwhelming, the treatment of Indians and blacks was worrisome and might spread, and besides the ragged beggars of Italy knew a "happiness and . . . poetry" that was out of reach for the well-fed American worker who read a sixteen-page newspaper. Without going this far in his criticism, Camille Saint-Saëns expressed very well the general feelings of those who refused to make snap judgments:

> Yes, I liked America and will be glad to visit again; but would I want to live there? . . . That is another matter. Born in the first half of the nineteenth century, I belong to the past; and to all the comforts of the young nation I will always prefer our old cities and the holy relics of our old continent.[37]

Even those who were won over by the American vigor asked themselves such questions, without in fact arriving at clear answers. And it was not without some diffuse fear that the travelers, forgetting the unpleasantness of certain American customs, admired the power they had felt everywhere:

> One feels as if one had come upon something out of proportion with our normal scale of earthly probabilities or possibilities. One forgets many blots, many flaws, and even some of one's misgivings in order to keep intact this vision of grandeur and prosperity in the peaceful organization of a great continent.[38]

To some observers it also appeared that the gap between France and the United States, however wide, could be bridged, and that it would not take much to make life in the two countries quite similar; all that was needed was some polish. In fact, it was the absence or, conversely, the heaviness of this polish that provoked the most conspicuous differences of opinion among the observers. The group that was willing to put up

---

36. Coubertin, *Universités transatlantiques*, p. 236.
37. C. Saint-Saëns, *Au courant de la vie* (Paris: Dorbon aîné, 1914), p. 113.
38. E. d'Eichtal, "Quelques notes d'un voyage aux Etats-Unis," *Annales de Sciences Politiques* 21 (1906): 228.

with a certain roughness of American life in order to benefit from its various advantages was fairly diverse.

Some of these people also had their misgivings, but they appreciated the salutary shock produced by the experience of American energy. Not for nothing did Paul Adam give his book the subtitle "*La nouvelle jouvence*" (Land of Rejuvenation), and when the economist Georges Aubert wrote, "I have seen a strong people, and I felt weak," he expressed a feeling close to the elation of Vidal de la Blache:

> If that country will never give to the archeologist and the artist the past and the glorious patina that time puts on old things, the historian and the sociologist will encounter a much rarer pleasure, that of watching the future being prepared. A vitality that breaks out of the old frames, that imparts unexpected and unparalleled proportions to social and economic facts, and the tumultuous germination of seeds: all of this is unforgettable. There is something contagious in the joy that the experience of growth and life imparts to an individual. What books had told us, our eyes tell us even better: something new is being created there, and that is a phenomenon we do not often have the chance to observe in this world.[39]

But since this enthusiasm was limited to observation, it did not imply a desire to adopt the American way of life. At most, and even then only partially, it indicated a willingness to prepare for it.

Only a few travelers expressed a willingness to stay, among them almost all the women. Not that Madame Grandin, Marie Dugard, and Thérèse did not denounce specific examples of brutality or bad taste, but on balance their experience was very positive. They discovered a day-to-day freedom, an ease of living, a place and a role for women that seemed decidedly preferable to what they knew in France. All these reasons came into play simultaneously and resulted in categorical judgments: "... life seems impossible anywhere else than in the United States for anyone who has tried it," exclaimed Thérèse. As for Madame Grandin, she felt a positive wrenching when she left the United States to return to France.

These two women had lived in the United States for a long time, a fact that may in part account for their attachment to that country, along with certain personal reasons of which we know nothing. But in a more covert and implicit manner, Marie Dugard and even Thérèse Bentson or Mathilde Shaw expressed rather similar feelings. Even before we come to an examination of French attitudes toward the American woman, we should consider such a convergence fairly significant, particularly since

39. Vidal de la Blache, "A travers," 531.

very few men, even after a prolonged stay, spoke as freely. Perhaps someone like Urbain Gohier came close to it when he confessed that he had very quickly felt Americanized, completely at ease in a "wide open" life where nothing was hidden and where the most shocking details – the food served at a meal or the self-assurance of girls riding their horses astride like ordinary cowboys – became as natural as they were comfortable.

Accepting the future – and all the travelers agreed that it might well be American – was not an easy thing to do, and it was only from the 1890s or even 1900 on that a certain number of French observers declared themselves ready to face it. And even then, many did so with a certain resignation. It is therefore safe to say that the largest segment of French opinion continued to have misgivings and did not consider the American way of life enviable; only a small group was ready to fall into step without hesitation.

It should be pointed out that differences of opinion cannot be linked to any political or social groupings. At most one can say that the "Moderns" were more favorable to the American way of life than the "Ancients." But beyond this fairly banal division, the groupings were quite heterogeneous and obeyed a different logic than would be applied in other areas. What did Urbain Gohier have in common with André Siegfried, certain working-class travelers with Marie Dugard? And yet all of them were united in a certain admiring fascination with the American way of life. By contrast, the negative reaction of some of the workers joined that of the aristocrats or a man like Paul Bourget. One could multiply the examples, all of which show that choosing to live in the United States or to adopt the American way of life was not easy; essentially it was an individual decision.

However that may be, the French readers of these various works probably retained more of the criticism of the Americans' manners and the description of their extravagant ways than of the essentially favorable judgments of some observers. For the image that was too often repeated from book to book, even with all kinds of nuances, was that of a noisy, brutal, and disorderly country where "the classic Frenchman" who loved "the qualities of harmony, of measure, of the finished and accomplished" was ill at ease.

These rapid and at times superficial judgments show that there was no model of American life with which everyone could agree without discussion. This does not mean that this existence did not have its enviable or attractive facets, and many travelers were certainly aware of the complexity and diversity that constituted the United States. This enabled them, as well as the other observers, to take circumstances into account and to distinguish between those that might be adapted to French use and those that were quintessentially American. Perhaps this was the way to avoid the "manipulated and mechanized life"[40] that would threaten their children.

The shudders these travelers experienced might make us smile and often seem worthy of Flaubert's Bouvard and Pécuchet, and yet it stands to reason that they quite simply discovered in that American life the substance of the life that would be lived by the denizens of France in the late twentieth century. They saw the future, but they did not quite recognize it, and the France to which they referred looked more archaic and backward to them than it really was. Thus the two ways of life, the French and the American, seemed to follow parallel paths, as if they were never to meet. Hence the constantly repeated observations, unchanged over forty years: The United States was once and for all the land of speed and of comfort. Yet at the same time the French also discovered exotic aspects of American life in places where it had not been found in the previous period, in the industrial world rather than in the savage customs of the West.

Imperceptibly, the United States came to show to an industrializing and modernizing France some interesting examples and, perhaps, new models.

40. G. Lordereau, *Du Havre à Chicago* (Lyon: A. Rey, 1894), p. 18: "impression of a manipulated and mechanized life," made up of motors and noises; "if this were to be our future civilization, I would feel sorry for our grandchildren." His opinion is to be taken all the more seriously since he was himself a civil engineer, and thus unlikely to favor a systematic archaism.

# Part 2

# MODELS FROM
# THE UNITED STATES

The world is moving toward a kind of Americanism which offends our refined ideas, but which, once the crises of the present hour have passed, may well not be worse than the old regime when it comes to the one thing that counts, namely the freeing and the advancement of the human spirit.

Ernest Renan, "Souvenirs d'enfance et de jeunesse" (1883), in *Oeuvres complètes de Ernest Renan* (Paris: Calman-Lévy, n.d.), p. 717

# 6

# *A Truly American Democracy*

At least since Tocqueville's book, the French associated the United States with democracy, without always asking themselves too many precise questions about this subject. Yet the institutional tribulations that forced them in 1830 as in 1848, and again in 1870, to consider the problem of the timeliness of a Republican regime quite naturally led them to study the only great democratic republic of the era, and even to develop strong feelings about the established form of government of the United States.

Thus the Second Republic made use of the American example, at least for the election of the President by universal manhood suffrage, and it is not without interest that in the Constituent Assembly Tocqueville was among the supporters of this measure. However, the Coup d'Etat of 2 December [1851, Louis-Napoleon Bonaparte] and the ensuing repression contributed to a clear decline of admiration for the United States, especially among the Republicans, and it was only after 1860 that Republicans once again became propagandists for American-style democracy. By way of strengthening their attack on the Second Empire, even after it had become liberal, they decked out the Great Republic with all the virtues; this continued until 1870, when the new imperial constitution actually came closer to the American model than the drafts proposed by these same zealous Republicans.[1] How would French opinion feel about the democracy across the sea once the Republic had been restored in France itself? In the few years preceding the consolidation of the Third Republic it was not at all clear whether deputies and jurists would turn to the American example, as their earlier stance would indicate. Would the Republicans see it as a model, and the royalists as the hell of democracy?

---

1. T.A. Sancton, "America in the Eyes of the French Left, 1848–1871," D.Phil. thesis, Oxford University, 1978, p. 168.

Yet in the end the articles of the constitution of 1875 seemed to show few traces of borrowings from the American institutions. Would French opinion in subsequent years once again seize on the American example or, on the contrary, consider it in a more detached manner?

## THE LAST GASP OF THE MODEL

A good way to appreciate the strength of the American political model is to gauge the interest it could command in French opinion.

### *Limited Interest*

Books devoted to American political life were neither very numerous nor very original, especially after the publication of James Bryce's *American Commonwealth*, which served as the more or less acknowledged basis for most of them. Nonetheless, those who made the requisite effort could acquire a solid knowledge of the functioning of American institutions, thanks to the volumes of the Duc de Noailles or Emile Boutmy, to cite only the most important.[2]

To these titles one must add the remarks concerning the American political system to be found in the many travel accounts. The travelers, even the most earnest among them, were not particularly passionate about this subject, but they always made some comment, usually in anecdotal form, for example, when they had gone to a campaign rally or shaken the President's hand at the White House, or else in very judicious-sounding commentaries. This never amounted to more than a few pages, at best a short chapter that never constituted the most important part of the book. One of the rare exceptions is André Tardieu's book *Notes sur les Etats-Unis*,[3] half of which is devoted to a rather complete description of the country's government, no doubt inspired by a kind of professional solidarity.

And finally, articles in revues and daily newspapers more or less closely followed the current events of American politics, which often gave them the opportunity to recall, briefly, the major rules governing

2. E. Boutmy, *Etudes de droit constitutionnel (France, Angleterre, Etats-Unis)* (Paris: Plon-Nourrit, 1885), and *Eléments d'une psychologie politique du peuple américain* (Paris: Colin, 1902); P. duc de Noailles, *Cent ans de république aux Etats-Unis*, 2 vols. (Paris: Calman-Lévy, 1886, 1889). These were the major works, but there were others, many more than are cited by M.-J. Toinet, "Juristes et publicistes français face aux institutions américaines sous la troisième République," in *L'Amérique dans les têtes* (Paris: Hachette, 1986), pp. 231–50.
3. (Paris: Calman-Lévy, 1908).

that regime. Essentially, though, these articles covered only presidential elections and major events, such as the assassinations of Garfield and, later, McKinley. This was often done in simple columns that were not free of errors or summary judgments concerning the separation of powers or the personal qualities of individuals. Nonetheless, anyone who was informed to begin with could, *grosso modo*, stay in touch with the help of the dispatches of the wire services, although he would have trouble obtaining election results for individual states, not to mention for midterm elections, which were totally ignored, as were most politicians unless they were declared or presumed candidates in a presidential race.

This rapid overview of the various resources available to French opinion concerning American democracy necessarily leads to some significant observations.

One great difference existed, as it did in other areas as well, between a small group of persons who were very well informed about American institutions and current events and most others, who took a more distant interest.

The former, of course, were members of the group of "Americanists": Jannet, Noailles, Carlier, Laugel, Boutmy, and a few others. It was only natural that these authors should be interested in the institutions and the political life of their favorite country, but this does not mean that their attention was much more focused than that of their predecessors or their successors,[4] which would indicate that the United States hardly constituted a political model. This is not to detract from the richness of the principal titles, which were certainly superior to those of the first half of the nineteenth century.[5]

Other works by journalists and travelers were much more superficial, and many of the authors could have endorsed the formulation of Max O'Rell: ". . . when a people lives happily and in complete security, its politics is probably not very interesting." And indeed, a system of such stability, which functioned like clockwork, and whose debates were incomprehensible to most outsiders, did not necessarily arouse passionate interest, even if there was agreement about the excellent qualities of the constitution governing it. No wonder that the authors of the first group derided, as Boutmy did, the few pearls one might find in the writings of one of the second group and the highly fragmented nature of many of their commentaries.

However that may be, these few examples make it clear that

---

4. Cf. Toinet, "Juristes et publicistes."
5. R. Rémond, *Les Etats-Unis devant l'opinion française (1815–1852)*, 2 vols. (Paris: Colin, 1962), complains about many errors.

American democracy was viewed in a rather detached way, as if from a distance, another proof of the limited interest it commanded in this forty-five-year period.

Another characteristic of the expressed opinions about the American Republic had to do with their common political origin. It appears that most of the books, brochures, and articles about institutional and political issues came out of conservative circles and almost never from the Left.

Thus the royalist and ultra-Catholic Right was well represented by Claudio Jannet and, in a somewhat more nuanced manner, by the Duc de Noailles, while the moderate Republicans had Emile Boutmy and one pamphleteer who early in our period admitted to his admiration for Thiers. In a similar vein, the most regular columns appeared in the *Revue des Deux Mondes*, *Le Correspondant*, and the *Nouvelle Revue*, but current American events were most thoroughly treated in *Le Temps*. By contrast, neither the authors known for their leftist ideas, Elisée Reclus and Paschal Grousset – two former adherents to the Commune – nor the *Revue Socialiste* nor even the Socialist dailies gave much space to these issues and often ignored them altogether. Moreover, the worker-delegates to the various world's fairs adopted a similar attitude and almost totally ignored these issues.

Before examining what influence an American model, if any, might have had at the time of the founding of the Third Republic in France, the division among observers deserves to be more precisely delineated. Institutional questions no doubt often fascinated people attached to Law and Order, whereas the Left was preoccupied with social and economic issues. Thus the free worker-delegates at the Philadelphia Fair asserted very clearly that although the American institutions did have some virtues, they were nonetheless "bourgeois" in nature and therefore favored "capitalist oppression," a fact that canceled out their possible theoretical advantages.[6] This attitude is perfectly understandable, but the silence of frankly Republican authors is more surprising, considering that the French Left liked to stress its presumed veneration for American democracy.[7]

The next task is to find out whether, on the fleeting occasions when it was invoked, the American example was used by the Right, as the sources indicate, or by the Left, despite its apparent silence. This

6. Cf. *Délégation ouvrière à Philadelphie*, "Tailleurs d'habits," p. 116, or "Mécaniciens": "Capital and government have gradually become the *ultima ratio* and have in practice done away with all the benefits spelled out in the Constitution of the United States" (Paris: Association ouvrière, 1879), p. 202.
7. F. H. Saeger, *The Boulanger Affair* (Ithaca: Cornell University Press, 1969), p. 186.

question can be asked for two occasions that gave rise to a sudden but short-lived revival of interest in the American form of government.

## An Ephemeral Resurgence of the Model

The first of these occasions arose between 1875 and 1877. On the American side, these two years saw the celebration of the country's centennial – with the Philadelphia World's Fair as its high point – followed by the contested election of Rutherford B. Hayes. Visitors flocked to the United States and there was a great deal of comment about the American form of government that had weathered such jolts. The French were particularly interested because they were in the midst of an institutional debate that eventually led to the crisis of 16 May 1877 and the resignation of President MacMahon as a result of the adoption "at the last whistle" of a set of constitutional laws that became the true foundation of the new regime. So there was a momentary Franco-American analogy.

A similar, though less obvious, phenomenon occurred between 1887 and 1889, in response to a more exclusively French problem. The United States was of course celebrating the hundredth anniversary of its Constitution, but in France this would have gone by almost unnoticed if the subject of a reform of the French institutions had not been brought up under the pressure of Boulangism. Once again, newspapers and reviews briefly looked into the American example.[8]

No later event, whether French or American, brought the matter of the transatlantic political model into such sharp focus. Throughout our period, as well as before and after it, hasty observers showed a superficial and childlike envy for the American constitutional text:

> Nine changes of government, eleven constitutions for a fourteen-centuries-old and therefore more mature people; whereas the United States of North America, a young people in whom one would easily forgive instability and inconstancy, still has its first constitution of 1787.[9]

Others wondered, not without ulterior motives, how such institutions could survive the Civil War without suffering real damage. They could

8. Important are L. Vossion, "Le centenaire de la constitution américaine," *Nouvelle Revue* 19 (1887): 69, and above all the series of articles by the Duc de Noailles in the *Revue des Deux Mondes*, "Le centenaire d'une constitution" (15 Feb. and 15 April 1889): 852–85 and 795–829. See also E. Masseras, "Nos essais parlementaires et la constitution américaine," *Nouvelle Revue* 19 (April 1887): 641–63, or C. Jannet, "Ou en est la démocratie américaine?," *Le Correspondant* (25 April 1888): 205–36, as well as several articles scattered in *Le Temps*.
9. Abbé Gagnol, *Histoire contemporaine, de 1789 à nos jours* (Paris: Librairie Poulssiègue, 1889), p. xii.

not help admiring their value and their vigor, albeit usually in the form of strictly rhetorical references and absolutely not as a model.

The painful process of preparing the constitutional laws of the Third Republic could furnish the occasion for thinking more deeply about the American example, as was done by the Duc de Noailles:

> In the present state of France, should we not first of all focus our careful attention on America? Where could we study the conditions and the consequences of our new institutions more profitably than in the living body of a vigorous and prosperous republic, a republic, in short, that has never been equaled by any other. Without question, it is a model of its kind and sets a lasting standard, a superior and unique prototype to which we would do well to refer.[10]

The deputies felt obliged to follow the advice of the eminent political scientist more or less closely, and so they also cited American and English examples. And how could the apparent simplicity of the Founding Fathers' writings and the Cartesian rigor of the political calendar fail to appeal to Frenchmen wearied by constant change? Yet in the end, after some fanciful proposals, they chose a system much closer to British parliamentary democracy.

It is not without interest that the Laboulaye amendment of 29 January 1875, stipulating that "the government of the Republic shall be composed of two chambers and a president," however innocuous and formal it may have sounded, was rejected as too close to the American example with which everyone was bound to associate the name Laboulaye. Yet what this fervent admirer and extremely knowledgeable expert on the institutions of the United States had in mind was not a slavish copy of these institutions. Wanting, at most, to preserve their spirit, he eventually rallied to the idea of a regime based on ministerial responsibility.

In fact, the Republicans altogether turned their backs on all American references and did not use them in the masses of tracts and pamphlets they circulated at the time, leaving a few mavericks to make use of them.

In the course of the debates that accompanied the definition of the powers in the brand-new Republic, Léon Gambetta made himself perfectly clear:

> Some have made a great deal of to-do about the American senate. They even went so far as to commission from an American (laughter on the left), whom I suspect of being from Seine-et-Oise (general hilarity), a consulta-

10. Noailles, "Les publicistes américains et la constitution des Etats-Unis," *Le Correspondant* (25 May 1876): 569.

tion on the analogies that might exist between the French senate and the American senate. . . . There is no way to compare America with France, and on this occasion it would have been better to go simply from Paris to Versailles than from Paris to America (approval and laughter on the left).[11]

This brief incident is very revealing of everyone's position. In 1870, Laboulaye had supported the liberal Empire, appreciating the tenuous resemblance of the texts that governed it to his beloved American Constitution, and was therefore still trying to save as much of its spirit as could be saved in the constitution of 1876. Gambetta, by contrast, who in 1868 had unhesitatingly praised the Great Republic beyond the Atlantic to the skies, now defended a totally different regime, in which the executive would be weak and the Upper House would represent the people as a whole, rather than only the states, as in the United States. The success of his ironic remarks about Laboulaye's projects clearly shows that the Left repudiated any kinship, except its ceremonial side, with the regime of Washington or Lincoln.[12]

The crisis of 16 May 1877 confirmed this evolution, for the only lawmakers to find some advantages in the American system, specifically in the strength of its executive, were the conservatives and the monarchists who had lined up behind MacMahon. According to his supporters, the latter would, by carrying out his own policy independently of that of the National Assembly, and by endeavoring to form his own cabinet, act like a President of the United States, for the Republic would not necessarily have to be a parliamentary regime. At this point *Le Temps* fully assumed its role as the semiofficial paper by coming to the defense of the regime established in 1875 and denying any similarity with the Great Republic beyond the Atlantic. The American President – and at that very moment Hayes presented an example – used "power not to perpetuate conflict but to appease it," contrary to what was happening in France; there was no comparison between the two countries, "whose constitutions are different in every point, without exception." Moreover, had not the National Assembly "meant to found a parliamentary republic precisely in contrast with the very republic of the United States whose example is being invoked today"? Those who wanted to deny this were making an enor-

---

11. Session of the Chambre des Députés, 28 December 1876, *Journal Officiel* (29 Dec. 1876): 9829. The allusion to Laboulaye is transparent; the "Lettre d'un Américain" in the *Journal des Débats* of 27 December 1876 had vaunted the harmonious relationship between the two houses of the American Congress; the response, a "Lettre d'un Anglais," published in *Le Temps* of 29 December 1876, came quickly and refuted any analogy between France and the United States.

12. It was also in 1879 that the municipal council of Paris named two arteries of the capital after Washington and Lincoln.

mous mistake, which could be understood only as a vulgar "partisan invention revealing . . . the secret preoccupations of the enemy."[13]

Far from being a model for the Republicans, the United States was used as a counterexample by their adversaries, who seized on the aspect that most frightened Republicans, that is, personal power, which inevitably revived the memory of Louis Napoleon's coup d'état of 2 December 1851. Neither of the two camps really analyzed the functioning of American democracy, and its example was trotted out like a bogeyman in connection with strictly French issues. The parliamentary tradition going back to the July Monarchy and familiarity with the less remote British example did the rest. The Republicans made a strenuous effort to eliminate any similarity with the form of government on which they had heaped praise a few years earlier; the election of the President by the Parliament, ministerial responsibility, the right of dissolution, not to forget the right of pardon, all show that nothing was borrowed from America. Only bicameralism might be considered a borrowing, were not the analogy ruined by the refusal to accept any kind of federalism. The Republicans were convinced they had made "the right choice," particularly when in 1877 their adversaries had made use, albeit very fleetingly, of the reference to America.

The choice made in 1875 was justified by the stability of the regime. When certain associates of "good old General Boulanger" in their turn seemed to invoke the American example, this seemed to be a repetition of the debates of 1877, but in a more tense climate that confirmed the pernicious character of this foreign import.

By the end of the 1880s the great republican élan had run out of steam in France, and in view of scandals and mediocrity in government certain questions were revived:

> Having run out of expedients and nostrums, some people are once again looking to remedy our political troubles by a closer assimilation of our institutions with those of the United States. There they are hoping to find, through an increase in the power of the executive, guarantees for a more steadfast direction and greater stability. The theme is not new, but it seems to have been set aside.[14]

The splintering of the parties and the excesses of the parliamentary regime created a need for a stronger power. As a result, Alfred Naquet, senator from Vaucluse, had issued in 1883 a formal statement in favor of a constitutional revision leading to the total separation of the executive

---

13. *Le Temps*, 5 and 23 Oct. 1877. This article analyzed the basic features of the regime.
14. Masseras, "Nos essais," p. 644.

from the legislative and a strong President. The positions of this man of the Left would not have risen above the level of the anecdote if Naquet had not become General Boulanger's advisor for constitutional issues;[15] although he did not push the American example, it seemed to become increasingly important. Thus, in the partial elections of spring and summer 1888 in the departments of Nord, Dordogne, Somme, and Charente-Inférieure, considerable sums were spent – 200,000 francs in Nord instead of the usual 8,000 – on the distribution of leaflets and the manufacture of objects (pipes, plates) bearing the picture of the day's hero: It was a full-fledged American campaign, or at least people thought so. The fact that on this occasion Boulanger celebrated the great American freedom, which he was in a position to appreciate when he represented the French government at the centennial of the victory of Yorktown, was enough to provoke talk about the Americanization of French political life.

The defenders of the Republic, led once again by *Le Temps* as well as by people such as Louis Vossion, immediately and strongly insisted on "the many disadvantages of the constitution for which many adversaries of parliamentary government in Europe and particularly in France profess to envy them [the Americans]." This was said only a year after the centennial of the famous document had provided the occasion to praise its solidity and its many good points, such as the balance of powers and an independent judiciary. Now, every example showing the dangers of the American system was brought in; the fact, for instance, that the Senate in Washington modified a duly negotiated and signed treaty with China in order to please the voters of the West Coast:

> This shows what becomes of the interests of the country, the continuity of its policies, and the adherence to its treaties in a regime that every four years hands over to the entire people the election of its head and gears all of the parties' policies to this objective. It shows whether it is true that the absence of ministerial responsibility will free the debates of the houses of Congress of the excesses of a partisan spirit.[16]

Actually, Boulanger had never called for the adoption of an American-style regime, and the constitutional options advanced by Naquet were extremely hazy, but there had been talk of a *spoils system*

15. A. Naquet, *Questions constitutionnelles* (Paris: E. Dentu, 1883), p. 90.; Saeger, *Boulanger Affair*, p. 75, exaggerates the importance of a few very secondary articles in an effort to prove the attraction of the American Republic.
16. "Bulletin du jour," *Le Temps* (19 Sept. 1888); also *La République française* (11 Feb. 1889).

because Boulanger had brought a large part of his staff with him from the Ministry of War, and his election campaigns were masterminded by Comte Dillon, a great connoisseur and great admirer of American business methods. This was enough to raise the specter of an impending constitutional reorganization, inspired more or less directly by the American example; the Republicans geared up for action. Even if this aspect of *Boulangism* was never more than marginal and noted by only a few experts, it was best once again to dismiss the American example by placing heavy emphasis on its flaws and the problems it caused.

In the years following these turbulent episodes, the American institutions ceased to be relevant. The nature of the regime was no longer an issue in France, and the major crises, such as the Dreyfus affair, were too specific to respond to a foreign model. The French no longer needed the model of the American Constitution; the Left repudiated it and the Right used it in a superficial manner. It is remarkable indeed that neither Jaurès nor Clemenceau ever referred to the founding text of the United States and that the only politician to take a closer look at it was André Tardieu.

This shift to the right in the French view of the American Constitution was, strictly speaking, not new. In 1848 already, and then at the beginning of the Second Empire, the Republicans had distanced themselves from it, and it had taken their desperate struggle against Badinguet (Napoleon III) to make them evoke it briefly and almost hypocritically.

## PECULIAR INSTITUTIONS

For at least one generation, the reasoning underlying Toqueville's *Democracy in America*, which considered the advent of a democratic regime in France as well as in the United States inevitable, was prevalent, and even though the American Constitution had no influence whatsoever on the writing of the French constitution of 1875, the simple parallelism of the two regimes sometimes brought forth this theme:

> To be sure, the distance is great and the differences are numerous between the United States and France; but since we have become like them, a democratic nation, we share with them perils we must fear and avoid.[17]

17. A. Langlois, "L'élection présidentielle aux Etats-Unis," *Le Correspondant* (10 March 1877): 784.

### A Conservative Constitution

In the 1870s the American form of government, while not actually in jeopardy, experienced a particularly somber period, marked by the convulsions of Reconstruction, multiple scandals in the Grant administration, and the disgraceful election of Rutherford B. Hayes, to mention only the most glaring facts. The French observers wondered about the direction American democracy was taking.

Whereas Ferdinand Le Play and Claudio Jannet resolutely grappled with the democratic principle itself, which did not prevent them from praising the virtues of a George Washington or a John Adams and of the Constitution as it functioned in their time, the Duc de Noailles was more subtle. Still, as early as 1876, he distinguished between two periods in the application of the text adopted in Philadelphia:

> ... even this young America is already seeing the end of its old regime, of that tempered, liberal, religious, and conservative democracy such as it was instituted by its true great men, the Franklins, the Washingtons, and many of their contemporaries.[18]

Institutions allowed society to flourish as long as the "natural" elites played their role, but they were unable to prevent the excesses of universal manhood suffrage and radicalism in the aftermath of the Civil War. Yet the nature of the regime was not modified, and the fears of "caesarism" that were sometimes voiced at the time of Grant's reelection did not materialize. Thus the United States was able to preserve a certain balance and to avoid the anarchy that seemed to threaten it in circumstances which in France would surely have provoked riots or even real revolutionary "days." Indeed, the French wondered how a truly egregious electoral fraud of the kind committed in 1876 could be accepted so calmly, and how the conduct of the radicals in the occupied South, though always violently denounced, did not reawaken the conflict between North and South, for which there was still a great deal of support.

To be sure, French predictions were particularly alarmist at that moment. The institutions of democracy seemed to be definitively perverted or even moribund, a situation that gave malicious pleasure to the fierce scorners of the Republic and caused the defenders of the regime to back off a little more from the American example. But it soon became evident that the United States had succeeded in overcoming these diffi-

---

18. Noailles, "Les publicistes," p. 572.

culties, and in 1881 Cucheval-Clarigny gave a good summary of a fairly widespread feeling:

> Such a situation justified the worst fears; yet on the occasion of this crisis the United States showed that fearful ordeals can be passed unscathed by a democracy in which religious principles and conservative sentiments have kept their power and which preserve within the population respect for the legal system and obedience to the laws.[19]

This explanation was repeated and sometimes developed further by the best commentators, such as Noailles, Boutmy, or Chambrun. They were struck by the various brakes on absolute democracy provided by the Founding Fathers, those veritable "democrats in reverse." After all, the Senate and the Supreme Court were not chosen by direct election, even though the powers assigned to them were considerable; it almost looked as if the extent of their power were inversely proportionate to the democratic character of their election. Thus the House of Representatives did not have much prestige, even though it was elected by quasi-universal manhood suffrage at relatively short intervals; by contrast, the presidential veto or the famous impeachment, to mention only these examples, were powerful political tools over which the people had no control. In the same vein, the inexorable regularity of the electoral campaigns seemed designed to prevent any spontaneous manifestation of the popular will.

This restrictive concept of democracy seemed to hold one of the keys to the country's stability and to its ability to cut off crises before they turned into tragedies. This type of reasoning was developed in France as early as the 1870s, but came into its own by the end of the following decade. The American Constitution, it was said, offered a certain protection from popular excesses, even if it did not prevent them altogether. Claudio Jannet had to admit that in the United States this text, respected as it was by everyone, played the role that monarchy played elsewhere, that of providing assurance, permanence, and stability. Noailles, who until then had placed greater emphasis on people and their behavior, came to modify his judgment: "When the needs of the moment require it, the American people will approve any expedient, any subterfuge, rather than allow a modification or revision of the Constitution, the Ark of the Covenant before which they like to dance."[20]

Not that these authors were unaware of the amendments that had

---

19. M. Cucheval-Clarigny, "Les années de l'histoire des Etats-Unis. I, L'administration de M. Hayes," *Revue des Deux Mondes* (15 Feb. 1881): 818.
20. Noailles, "Le centenaire," p. 810.

been passed after the Civil War, but they insisted on the complicated nature of the revision process, which made hasty or demagogical steps impossible. Thus, a great rigidity of the texts went hand in hand with a great suppleness of the practices and a very realistic understanding of the functioning of democracy, all of which was very different from the absoluteness of the French constitutions. Royalist commentators were not the only ones to underline this difference; it was also noted by such authors as Boutmy and Chambrun, who were closer to a liberal and moderate Republic.

These virtues of the American Constitution were not those of democracy in general, but of one particular text of essentially British provenance. Such features as suppleness in applying texts, general respect of the law and of other clauses, such as the *habeas corpus*, and the vitality of local institutions were clearly part of the Anglo-Saxon heritage. Adolphe de Chambrun therefore went to some length to show how much the American institutions owed to the Magna Carta and to English common law:

> ... I believe that there is infinitely more analogy between the republican form of government of the United States and the English monarchy ... than between that same republican form of government and the Republic such as it exists at this moment in France ...[21]

The English origin of the American institutions was generally agreed upon, even if certain authors, such as Boutmy, also found in it aspects close to the "heroic and idealistic impulse of our revolution of 1789." This provided an explanation for the general stability of the system, its adaptability to many different circumstances, and its pervasive liberal spirit, which seemed more important to many observers than the performance of democracy itself at the level of individual states. Indeed, the discovery of Woodrow Wilson's theses in *Congressional Government* allowed them to buttress this explanation, since Wilson emphasized the functioning of a parliamentarianism whose ideal was at Westminster.[22] At the time when this set of ideas developed in France, James Bryce's masterpiece, *American Commonwealth*, was well known there, and it was he who first found in America "an improved England."

Most of the subsequent analyses of the American institutions did little more than repeat the explanations of the future ambassador of His Majesty to Washington, thereby accentuating the fundamental differ-

---

21. A. de Chambrun, *Droits et libertés aux Etats-Unis* (Paris: A. Thorin, 1891), p. 358.
22. E. de Leveleye, "La forme nouvelle du gouvernement aux Etats-Unis et en Suisse," *Revue des Deux Mondes* (1 Oct. 1886): 626–50. This is a lengthy review of two books, one of them by Woodrow Wilson.

ences that separated the two republics. This general explanation also contributed to diminishing the admiration that Tocqueville's work had enjoyed in the preceding generation. References to this book did not, of course, disappear but became a matter of mere ritual, except when it was criticized, either for some points of detail, as in the case of Boutmy, who continued to admire the work as a whole, or for the entire underlying conception of *Democracy in America*, as in the case of Jannet or Carlier, who refused to accept the universality of the victory of democracy. Tocqueville was no longer up-to-date, and it was thought that he had been superseded by Boutmy or Noailles, reinforced by Bryce, all of whom developed an entirely different analysis that did not ascribe the essential function to democracy.

Aside from the satisfaction at showing that Tocqueville was wrong – Bryce's shortcomings were excusable, since he was English and not French – Boutmy also enjoyed criticizing him and pointing out that he, Boutmy, would have proceeded differently.[23] Still, one lesson had to be drawn, and that was the special character of the institutions of the United States. But these did not necessarily show the way to universal democracy. Auguste Laugel clearly expressed this thought in 1890, in a review of the work of the Duc de Noailles:

> The government of the United States is truly a government *sui generis*, and it would be a glaring mistake to believe that all democracies will copy this model. They have already found, and they will find, other forms of democratic government, ranging from the most revolutionary and leveling demagoguery to the delegation of sovereignty to a single individual.[24]

Formulated around 1890, this analysis became the standard one until the end of our period. It accommodated everyone; conservatives could admire the text of 1787 but disdain its daily practice, and moderate Republicans came close to the same attitude, though perhaps with a better understanding of subsequent developments. Yet the transformations wrought in the United States in the early twentieth century by imperialism and the advent of Presidents with strong personalities inevitably led observers to wonder about the fate of the institutions. It became increasingly clear that despite the undeniable intrinsic value of the constitutional text, it evolved through the use the Americans made of it: "... circumstances and the common sense of human beings have

---

23. Boutmy, *Eléments*, 3rd ed. (Paris: A. Colin, 1911), p. iv.
24. Laugel, "Un ouvrage récent sur les Etats-Unis, " *Revue des Deux Mondes* (15 March 1890): 433. The author was a liberal Orléanist who knew the United States well.

completed this text." This was what caused admiration for the constitution if not to wane, then at least to be put in perspective.

### The Balance of Federal Powers

Once they had judged the Constitution as a whole, the French analysts took a look at its functioning. It is striking to note that except for the authors of scholarly studies, very few were interested in Congress or the Supreme Court and other judicial institutions, and that all the attention went to the presidency. But this must not prevent us from examining how these few French scholars judged the interaction of these powers, beyond some simplistic remarks about their mechanical separation.

Noailles considered the American Constitution, far from simple, as "a complex instrument equipped with multiple keyboards and pipes" and showed the extent to which the three branches were interwoven at every level. Thus the famous impeachment, which attracted a great deal of attention at the beginning of our period – the attempt to apply it to President Johnson was still fresh in everyone's memory – was no longer used at the highest level because it exposed the entire system to the danger of demagoguery. On another point, the Senate's control over presidential nominations was also proof of the complex interaction among the powers which, depending on the circumstances, could turn to the advantage of one or the other. However, the separation of powers was a fact, for the President could not interfere in the legislative process, was not surrounded by a cabinet, and had a frequently used veto power. Again, the complexity of this balance was obvious.

Boutmy, who described this situation, pushed his findings to the point of paradox; in his opinion the Constitution was deliberately designed to set up conflicts between the powers, even to exacerbate them, instead of doing its best, as one might expect, to avoid them. He then pointed out that a Secretary did not have to worry about one hostile chamber, but that the two-thirds majority by which the Senate was required to ratify treaties gave exorbitant powers to a minority. To a Frenchman, these were genuine design flaws, and illustrated by current events; strangely enough, however, they did not produce dire consequences. The different partners acted with moderation and did not seem intent on gaining a decisive advantage for themselves.

In this manner the different crises that punctuated this period – the unsatisfactory election of Hayes, the hostility of Congress toward Cleveland in his second term, or the impetuous acts of Theodore Roosevelt, which were initially presented as major dramas – could in the end be quite easily resolved. One could of course explain this by the conservative argument, but it was undeniable that constitutional dispositions of this kind

> . . . are to be recommended, not for the good they do but for the dangers they avert. They are, to say it all in one phrase, *the least of evils* in a federative organization; but they would be the worst of evils in a centralized organization.[25]

This was indeed the crux of the matter. The analyses of Noailles, Boutmy, and a few others, though correct on many points, solidly argued, and neither frankly hostile nor blindly favorable, reveal just how foreign the American institutions still were to French traditions. This being the case, some authors might well endeavor to praise the special virtues of the Supreme Court or of the Senate, full of admiration for their restraint and their moderation, and even wishing for the adoption in France of a Supreme Court that would regulate the functioning of parliamentarianism. But, as Noailles understood perfectly, the French would not possibly allow a law passed by the representatives of the people to be overturned by five out of nine judges! This would call for such modifications that the original institution would become unrecognizable. As for the Senate, it attracted the French more than the House, for it was closer to the French assemblies, both in manner – its members conducted themselves rather like their counterparts on the banks of the Seine – and in its role; yet its nature was not clearly understood. The U.S. Senate did not represent the notables or a nonexistent aristocracy, yet acted as if it did. Moreover, and this too was surprising, it had more prestige than the directly elected House; the fact that it represented the states was not sufficient to explain this enigma. In France, power and means were given to the representatives of the nation [in the Chambre des Députés], whereas the House of Representatives seemed to be hemmed in by suspicion and hampered by constraints. No doubt these various observations were biased by preconceptions on the part of the authors, who could also read in Wilson's book that Congress was not so different from other parliaments, despite its sometimes perplexing rules.

The American presidency truly fascinated the different observers. This was related to a French tradition of interest in great men and in personal power, and although the latter always seemed to lead to unfortunate experiences in France itself, it did leave behind a kind of nostalgia. In addition, the Right was always given to emphasize this position of power, which echoed the monarchy, or at least the kind of authority with which the country could identify. The United States provided one of the rare

---

25. Boutmy, *Etudes*, p. 158.

examples in which these characteristics were combined with an electoral principle that came into play with clockwork regularity.

In addition to this very French attitude, one must also mention the variations undergone by the institution between Ulysses Grant and Woodrow Wilson. The texts did not change, but it was clear that the presidency of Chester Arthur had little in common with what it would become at the time of Theodore Roosevelt. This was a matter of personalities, no doubt about it, but also of the different functioning of the branches of government.

Actually, a division among the French analysts of the American presidency soon became apparent. To some, the President seemed invested with very considerable power, and the memory of Lincoln showed that he could make use of it, as, incidentally, did the initiatives of Theodore Roosevelt. To others it looked as if everything were set up to make him into nothing but a "subaltern," whose every nomination had to be approved and who was reduced to the role of chief administrator rather than of governing authority. This was the view of the observers of the 1880s. The others were carried away by the potential or real vigor of the presidency. They were struck by the wide range of powers available to an American President, powers that seemed more comparable to those of a true sovereign than to those of a constitutional monarch or a President of the French Republic. The Duc de Noailles was pleased to underline the monarchical origin of the institution due to the influence of Alexander Hamilton, of whom he often spoke with approval. To be sure, American Presidents did not always use the tools at their disposal, but such power could not be left unused for long. The weight of the parties could lead to mediocre choices, and even limit the scope of presidential action; yet the President was by definition a great man: "In the United States the nation does not distrust the President. It has brought him to power by its own will and sees him as its representative, its living image."[26]

In addition to the preponderance he had obtained through his election, the President had prerogatives that were not only less restrictive than those of the houses of Congress but also spelled out in the Constitution; it was as if the Americans feared the demagoguery of their assembled representatives more than the tyranny of one individual. Such privileges would be inconceivable in France where, on the contrary, everything was designed to limit the powers of the President, the object of the most watchful distrust.

26. A. Desjardins, "Le président de la république aux Etats-Unis," *Le Correspondant* (25 Feb. 1897): 622.

The accession to power of strong personalities in this different context made this situation much clearer to the French observers. When the anomaly of weak Presidents who failed to use their tools disappeared, the Americans returned to normalcy: A President with such powers was made to rule, and so the French observers liked to depict Cleveland or McKinley in the full splendor of the great man. When Roosevelt arrived on the scene, things became even clearer; one could apply to him what the French historian of Andrew Jackson had said about that President: "He understood his duties as the head of a great nation and fulfilled them without violence or weakness";[27] besides, it was reassuring that the American people were not different from others, and that ". . . however enamored they might be of their liberty, they nonetheless like to feel a governing hand."[28]

The extension of federal powers brought about by the country's expansion, imperialism, and the problems raised by the trusts tended to strengthen the role of the presidency even further and to accentuate a still very moderate centralization. Yet for some French observers it also reawakened the fears of excessive presidential power that had been expressed during Grant's last term. Furthermore, the institutional dispositions were conducive to instability:

> . . . it seems doubtful to me that a system which, in America, keeps the whole country in a state of agitation for a whole year every four years, will be judged preferable to the proceeding which, in our country, can reduce the crisis to a single day every seven years.[29]

Around these themes, divergent views appeared in French opinion. Left-wing Republican circles were most reluctant to approve of such an extension of personal power, although this did not prevent many of them from frequently expressing admiration for Roosevelt; the conservatives, by contrast, saw it as a means of restoring a little vigor to the French Republic. Very telling indeed was Tardieu's opinion in this matter: Not content to celebrate Teddy's personal qualities, as so many others did, or to describe the mechanism of the American presidency, he reflected on what could be done in France. He contrasted the American President's veto power to the inevitable passivity of his counterpart at the Elysée

27. A. Gigot, "La présidence d'André [*sic*] Jackson, *Revue des Deux Mondes* (1 March 1984): 188.
28. J.P. des Noyers, "Le pouvoir exécutif aux Etats-Unis, les fonctions présidentielles," *Revue des Deux Mondes* (1 Oct. 1901): 643. Des Noyers was the pseudonym of J. Patenôtre, who made the same point in his book *Souvenirs d'un diplomate* (Paris: Aubert, 1914), vol. 2, p. 328.
29. H. Wallon, "Coup d'oeil sur la constitution actuelle des Etats-Unis," *Revue des Deux Mondes* (1 Aug. 1900): 720.

Palace in the face of legislation that displeased him and also evaluated the influence of the State of the Union message to Congress, which in Paris would provoke rioting, as well as the President's free choice of collaborators, which ensured the existence of a true presidential policy, and came to the following conclusion:

> We have humiliated the executive power before the legislative power. This cannot continue with impunity. Politics in France has become a body without a head, but the headless living never have a long career.[30]

While the future prime minister certainly did not wish to copy the American Constitution, he did find in it examples of what could be done within the framework of a Republican regime. He was one of the very few who felt that the American presidency could be a source of inspiration, and one can be sure that he did not forget this when the economic crisis of the 1930s once again brought these kinds of issues to the forefront.

Meanwhile, the organization of the branches of government in the United States, while well understood and fairly accurately analyzed, remained puzzling and very foreign to French customs; it is obvious that the institutional model met with no more than polite approval and did not inspire envy, except of the most superficial kind.

Nonetheless, the federal institutions were easy to understand, indeed comparable to those of the central French government. However, things became more complicated when the French observers looked into the intrinsic functioning of American democracy with respect to suffrage and local government, for here nothing looked like France – everything was truly American.

### Federalism and Democracy

The weight of France's centralizing mentality, in conjunction with the absence of information about local life in the United States, explains why the French too often neglected this facet of the country's political life. The reverse, of course, was also true, for the travelers complained about the Americans' ignorance regarding French life. The fact is that the municipal elections of Romorantin or Mont-de-Marsan were not discussed in the United States any more than those of Kansas City or Atlanta were discussed in France. The real difference was that

---

30. A. Tardieu, *Notes sur les Etats-Unis, société, politique, diplomatie* (Paris: Calman-Lévy, 1908), p. 207. The author carefully accounted for his positions by citing his various contacts with American senators and aides of the President.

local politics was much more important in the United States than in France.

Moreover, any discussion of the Senate or the American electoral system involved the ups and downs of political life at the state level. Even the best-informed French chroniclers had trouble understanding that the contested election of Rutherford B. Hayes was decided by a single voting place in Louisiana, that women could vote on local issues in Wyoming, and that the modalities of suffrage could differ so much from state to state, even though all were called upon to elect the President or the national representatives. Suffrage in the United States was universal for white males, yes, but it lacked the strictly regulated and absolute aspects it had in France. This astonished the French Republicans, and more conservative observers deplored the fact that men of "ability and knowledge" who were naturally entitled to the vote had seen fit to share it with the ignorant masses. Yet they also found the wide range of elective offices at the level of judges and sheriffs in the smallest localities very satisfactory, since it allowed populations to be represented directly and without intermediaries.

In this manner the most astute observers gradually came to understand the great importance of the political life of individual states and the power of self-government [in English in the original], a characteristic feature of the United States. Discovering the motley world of the states and the vigor of their political life was not a new thing, for Tocqueville had already depicted its full scope, yet this work had to be done again and again because centralism was so deeply embedded in the French mind. The Duc de Noailles, for all the sophistication of his analysis, which did not overlook the role of local government, was always fascinated above all by national politics. Without question it was Boutmy who resolutely stressed the vital importance of this reality. Eventually Bryce, as well as to a lesser extent Chambrun, helped create a better understanding of the deep "attachment to self-government and local liberties" that constituted one of the principal assets of the United States.

In point of fact, if the federal Constitution seemed to have become frozen in time, a kind of "fetish," the state constitutions were diverse and changeable and therefore reflected more accurately the adaptability of American institutions to social and economic change; as for the citizens, they might well spend their life without coming in contact with federal laws. It was therefore important not to study one constitution without the others: "One must go even further and say, not that the state constitutions are the complement of the federal Constitution, but that the federal Constitution is the complement to the state constitutions."[31] This was how Boutmy explained the precedence of the colonial charters over the text conceived at Philadelphia, as well as their relative autonomy vis-à-vis that text. Other commentators noted the development in certain states of "local option" initiatives concerning railroad and labor legislation, and also found that the first steps to combat corruption and political demagoguery were taken by the states in the early nineteenth century.[32]

The few French observers who became aware of these movements were somewhat flabbergasted by the dynamism of local politics, and the most knowledgeable took a malicious pleasure in mocking the ignorance of their compatriots – as when the municipal council of Paris saw fit to send its request for pardon of the condemned of Chicago to the governor of Illinois instead of the state supreme court, as if the governor had the right to pardon. The French could see that the Americans did not constantly turn to the "welfare state" as people did in the old centralized countries: "To the omnipotence of the state the Americans oppose *self-government*, which implies that everyone will respect the liberties of everyone else."[33] This kind of situation appealed to the royalists because of their attachment to regional liberties, which, they felt, the Revolution had attempted to strangle in their own country; yet others saw it as one of the foundations of democracy. It was at this level, where it was free of the weight of the central state, that democracy seemed most alive to Paul Bourget. His feeling was shared by the Republican magistrate Louis Jacolliot, who discovered it in California at the very beginning of the period, when he listened to a Frenchman who had settled there: "Over the last sixteen years I was three times elected mayor by my fellow citizens, and I have just been sent to the state legislature by almost unanimous vote."[34] Jacolliot was inspired to a vibrant hymn celebrating the community as the basis of this democracy.

There was a certain contradiction here, for those who scorned democracy, no less than certain Republicans who venerated it, admired the

31. Boutmy, *Etudes*, p. 109.
32. E. de Laveleye, "La transformation du gouvernement local aux Etats-Unis," *Revue des Deux Mondes* (1 Aug. 1889): 638–59. The author largely follows Bryce, but he is one of the few authors, along with Boutmy in the *Eléments*, to mention these changes.
33. Noailles, "Le pouvoir judiciaire aux Etats-Unis," *Revue des Deux Mondes* (1 Aug. 1888): 573. Noailles used the expression "welfare state" (*Etat-providence*), which was to come into its own later but passed unnoticed at the time. It is a sign of the perceptivity so often shown by the duke.
34. A. Jacolliot, *Voyage au pays de la liberté, la vie communale aux Etats-Unis* (Paris: G. Decaux, 1876), p. 19. The contrast between France and the United States was particularly great because this author had gone to live in California at the time of the Second Empire.

same America of counties and townships. To be sure, the monarchists denounced the abuses of universal manhood suffrage, which were even more glaring at the local than at the national level, whereas the Republicans looked only at principles, but the reality was the same. The only plausible explanation for this was the existence of local liberties, and thus of basic democracy, before there was a federal state. The few observers who were interested in these questions realized that this was very different from the French situation, and that there was rich promise in the spread of democracy born of more traditional liberties:

> The first ships that arrived on the shores of the refuge brought the seeds of democracy from Europe. Planted in virgin soil, it germinated vigorously. The plant grew and freely let down its roots. When the day of the American Revolution came and it was exposed to the great tempest, it was found to have grown into a mighty tree that clung to the very entrails of the soil and could give shelter to a state.[35]

This vigorous local activity constituted a large part of the political gulf that separated American from French democracy and ruled out any influence of the former on the latter. Moreover, it remained surprising to the French that such a system, founded on "the disintegration [and] . . . dislocation" of the use of the law, as Boutmy put it, could function properly. This could happen only under a most unusual set of conditions that would not be found elsewhere. The whole setup did seem a bit disorderly to Cartesian Republicans, while awakening a certain nostalgia in more conservative observers.

Actually, this local democracy was no longer out of reach of the weight of the federal state, which had gradually increased, although it still seemed quite bearable. In 1881, Auguste Carlier was pleased to show that Tocqueville had been wrong when he predicted the gradual weakening of the federal state. Over the following years centralization grew apace. If certain states reacted vigorously to this development, they were not always able to muster enough defenses to escape the powerful hold of big companies and trusts, which was felt even more strongly at the local than at the national level. Thus, Estournelles de Constant, a fervent admirer of American democracy, was extremely concerned about the role played by these companies in a state like California, which was still free and democratic.[36] Such concerns were not expressed often, but they

---

35. C. Borgeaud, "Les premières constitutions de la démocratie américaine," *Annales de l'Ecole Libre des Sciences Politiques* 6 (1891): 212.
36. P.E. de Constant, *Les Etats-Unis d'Amérique* (Paris: Colin, 1913), p. 487. The author also calls the federal state an "abstract and hazy confederation" (p. 300). A long stay in the States made him aware of a vigorous local life, whereas the Parisian observers were more attuned to the centralizing tendencies of the federal government.

indicate that the French still found it difficult to fully understand the nature of local democracy.

It is clear, then, that in the great family of democracy, the American institutions belonged to a different subspecies than their French counterparts. Therefore it was said, "We have nothing to take from it, but we have much to learn from it." The difference did not have to do only with the nature of the two constitutional texts, nor with their origins, but with the radically different experiences of these two countries. It was unfair to blame the Republican regime in France for its imperfections and its unfinished character by comparing it with the harmonious and well-regulated functioning of the United States, which had experienced only one major test in the course of its history, the Civil War, and even that had not threatened its institutions as a whole. Thus the French could only "... reject an overly invidious comparison between a regime that has risen to this fortunate condition and the parliamentary regime with which we have to contend...."[37]

Not only was the issue of a model moot by the end of the nineteenth century, it was also understood that the history of the two countries made it impossible to push the comparisons between the two democracies any further. The Third Republic, now that it was firmly established and founded on true universal manhood suffrage, had no need for lessons. This development, which marked a great change from the preceding period, was almost definitive; except in very unusual circumstances, the French would never again look to the American institutions. Besides, the manner of interpreting them would henceforth be conventional and devoid of real originality. Tocqueville was not and would not be superseded.

Furthermore, American democracy was not necessarily always virtuous; the French did not find the men who ran it, the famous politicians, and the parties to which they belonged very attractive. In stark contrast with the "admirable edifice of the Constitution," they sometimes made American political life seem unbalanced, founded on great principles that were poorly applied.

37. "Bulletin du jour," *Le Temps* (30 Jan. 1894).

# 7

# *A Political Life without Grandeur*

The French were naturally interested in the practice of American politics. In many ways, they found it strange, especially the nature of the parties and their functioning, to which must be added the behavior of politicians. Images of unbridled corruption, shameless demagoguery, and feet on tables almost inevitably came to mind; it was a far cry from the majesty of the Founding Fathers.

## FROM THE DONKEY TO THE ELEPHANT

In view of the manifold elections in the United States, from the county level to the presidency, the French considered the existence of parties fully justified; it was just that these parties bore no resemblance to what was understood by this term in Europe. Their small number was intriguing: Democrats and Republicans had held center stage for years without being troubled by serious competition, and the role they played was also surprising, for they were both omnipresent and lackluster. To be sure, the prestige of the party of Lincoln was great, but how much was left of it for French observers who tended to be unaware of American political references? Had the Democrats recovered from their wrenching quarrels in the wake of the Civil War? These were the questions asked at the beginning of our period, before the 1890s overturned old patterns with the advent of new themes and new political balances.

### *1870–1896, the Democrats, Perhaps*

In the 1870s and '80s, the American political parties were not conspicuous for the loftiness of their confrontations, as the French were quick to notice. The high fervor of the Republicans had soon waned, and their program tended to founder in dreariness, becoming less and less distinct from that of their adversaries, who seemed to be quite weakened themselves. However, the spoils system had not diminished – quite the contrary was true – and at first sight this was an essential activity of the parties. Indeed it seemed to be their only *raison d'être*, rather than the development of new initiatives for improving the country's government, which the French considered the normal function of a party.

One example of this surprising conduct was provided by the French Republican Duvergier de Hauranne in 1872. This observer had trouble understanding how the Democrats could have chosen as their presidential candidate the former fierce abolitionist Horace Greeley, and that he had accepted the nomination. This was such a reversal of position that it could be justified only by reasons of crass electoral politics; by contrast the Republicans projected the image of being united behind Grant.[1] Yet in the years that followed, the Republicans also seemed to lose all moderation and behaved with a brutality and a contempt for all propriety that left the observers aghast.

They were unanimous in their condemnation of the scandals that totally dishonored the party in power and its leader at the time of the celebration of the country's centennial:

> By an unfortunate coincidence, the many foreigners bidden to attend the centennial celebrations were in fact invited to witness a strange display of political, financial, and social scandals of such egregious immorality that one no longer dares speak of the corruption of courts and courtiers.[2]

While the Duc de Noailles was not displeased to demonstrate the nefarious effects of universal suffrage, such Republican travelers as Gustave de Molinari, who were favorably disposed toward American democracy, returned home absolutely terrified by what they had seen. These reactions are understandable, since the scandals of Grant's second term stand out in a political history that had a full share of them. But they had the effect of destroying the last vestiges of sympathy that still existed in France for the party of Lincoln. Added to this were the particular problems raised by Reconstruction in the South, a matter that tarnished the image of the Republicans even further. In fact, no French observer disputed the Radicals' responsibility for the desolation that reigned in the erstwhile Confederate states, described in graphic detail in most of the French press of the time. The French were horrified by the behavior attributed to the carpet-baggers [in English in the original], who

---

1. E. Duvergier de Hauranne, "L'élection présidentielle aux Etats-Unis, le Général Grant et M.H. Greeley," *Revue des Deux Mondes* (1 Dec. 1872): 513–59.
2. Duc de Noailles, "Les publicistes américains et la constitution," *Le Correspondant* (10 Feb. 1877): 377.

in their minds represented the party as a whole. While the conservatives were quick to denounce the dire results of radicalism which ". . . here as everywhere . . . having first destroyed morality, the laws, and the institutions, has produced nothing but anarchy and is not likely to spawn anything but despotism in the future,"[3] French Republicans found it hard to mount a spirited defense of Grant and his supporters. The best they could do was to put things into some perspective by pointing out that the situation was not always as somber as conservatives liked to say.

The circumstances of the election of Hayes served to confirm the poor opinion that the French, along with many Americans, had of the political behavior of the Republicans. The most passionate of the French supporters of democracy loudly expostulated against the prospect of a third candidacy of the victor of Appomattox and were heartbroken to see the wheeling and dealing and the denials of justice surrounding his successor's election; here again the French simply did not understand a system that allowed a candidate who had not obtained the most votes to win.

The fact that the Democrats accepted their defeat without any real protest – at the time the reasons for this attitude were not known[4] – confirmed to the French that the American parties had no dignity and no ideological principles, a failing that made them absolutely contemptible. Moreover, the observers were nonplussed to see that in the hard-fought campaign of 1876 the platforms of the two major parties were very similar.

The moderation of Hayes and the restoration of calm throughout the country did not help. The French were totally turned off by the American parties, which they could not take seriously, and in 1879 Cucheval-Clarigny made fun, without understanding it, of the strange vocabulary they used: "whig, hard-shells, soft-shells, know-nothing, loco focos, kuklux, grangers" – all of this was the stuff of folklore.[5] Not much was left of the old distinctions between supporters of a strong central

---

3. J. Gervais, "L'expérience du radicalisme aux Etats-Unis," *Le Correspondant* (10 Nov. 1876): 545. Gervais was one of the managing editors of this Catholic review, writing about the recently translated book of the American conservative Ezra Seaman, *The System of American Government*. This book was one of the essential sources for C. Jannet.

4. Cf. K.M. Stampp, *The Era of Reconstruction, 1867–77* (New York: A. Knopf, 1964). The articles in the *Revue des Deux Mondes* or *Le Correspondant*, which regularly followed the course of American politics, show that the French were dimly aware of the compromise of 1877 between the two parties.

5. M. Cucheval-Clarigny, "Une campagne électorale aux Etats-Unis," *Revue des Deux Mondes* (1 Nov. 1879): 178. This article lacked depth and even showed a certain confusion; the KKK, for instance, had never been a political party, any more than the Grangers and other groups that corresponded to specific moments in American political history.

state and the defenders of states' rights, and the vicissitudes of the elections of 1880, 1884, and particularly 1888 did nothing to change this situation.

Finally, in watching these rather dismal episodes, the French tended to side mostly with the Democrats. Not that their program was all that wonderful, but it seemed only fair that they should finally accede to executive power after having so narrowly missed the presidential boat in 1876 and 1880. The Democratic Party, perhaps because it had been out of power for so long, seemed from the outside to be a little less afflicted with the gangrene of corruption. But this view was not related to any political division in France itself, it was simply adopted by most French observers, who had no reason to get excited, and even less to become divided, over something that finally left the Americans quite calm, except in the throes of the campaign itself. In 1884 Auguste Moireau gave a good description of this absence of a great debate between the two parties:

> Democrats and Republicans have voted everywhere with their customary discipline, conforming to the injunctions of the party leaders with docility but without enthusiasm, and convinced that the destinies of the Union do not depend in any way on the success of one or the other candidate.[6]

The most interesting interpretation of the American parties was given by the Duc de Noailles. Noting the absence of durable third parties and the absence of a real Left, since in the end the episode of radicalism had only been ephemeral, he also pointed out, quite correctly, that the major parties were structured vertically, not differentiated by classes, but incorporating all of them. This, he contended, was the reason for the natural dominance in each party of "capital, intelligence, and property," which was conducive to stability but also to a certain listlessness:

> The most curious trait of American democracy during the hundred years of its existence is the organization of two right wings, one in power and one in the opposition, and taking turns. Differing in nuances, they are in agreement on fundamental doctrines and essential principles, even when they are fiercely fighting over the issues of the day.[7]

If one replaces the notion of the right wing with that of the center, the reflection of the royalist analyst is quite appealing and original for its

---

6. A. Moireau, "L'élection présidentielle aux Etats-Unis," *Revue des Deux Mondes* (15 Nov. 1884): 448.
7. Noailles, "Le centenaire d'une constitution," *Revue des Deux Mondes* (15 April 1889): 799; another excellent formulation: "the country still has two conservative strings in its democratic bow" (p. 800).

time. It makes it more understandable that the French, who were much more ideologically committed than the Americans, did not pay much attention to these indistinct parties that clashed only over secondary questions and seemed to avoid the great debates over ideas in which the French delighted.

This state of affairs did not disappear in the 1890s, but there was a certain renewal of American political life that allowed the French to discover other aspects of the activities of the parties.

### After 1896, the Republicans, Nevertheless

Their return to favor was by no means immediate and, in fact, quite unexpected. The most attentive French observers of American political life, though continuing their partiality for the "wise, progressive, and liberal" party headed by Cleveland, discerned the changes caused by the birth of the People's Party and even, a little later, the first political manifestations of Socialism. Did this constitute a threat to partisan stability? Would third parties actually have a chance? For the most part, the French observers, except the Socialists, who were looking hopefully for the birth of the American Socialist Party, were worried about the risk of disequilibrium posed by such a development, which would invalidate their analyses of the United States.

But for all that, the French were caught completely off guard by the passions unleashed by the election of 1896, which shook the United States. All of a sudden the peaceful Democratic Party, which could at most be criticized for a certain conservatism, took on a quasi-revolutionary bearing under the prompting of William Jennings Bryan. This came as a sudden shock because, except in a few premonitory articles, the full scope of the confrontation had not been revealed until electiontime. Not that the Republicans were dressed up in all the virtues by the touch of a magic wand, but the evolution of Jefferson's party was extremely worrisome. At the Chicago convention, a minority of anarchists, even Communists, seemed to have taken over the party under the leadership of the governor of Illinois, John P. Altgeld, depicted in the French press as a dangerous plotter, and the demagogue Ben Tillman. The Democratic platform, imbued with "free silver heresy," was composed of "resounding and hollow formulas, of all the fighting words of demi-Socialist populism," and the "incendiary and blasphemous"[8] peroration of Bryan's acceptance speech was given a frenzied reception by

---

8. "Bulletin de l'étranger," *Le Temps* (21 July 1896), which presented the most precise account.

"prophets with long beards." To some observers the situation seemed analogous to what they had seen on the eve of the Civil War, when the rabid proslavery forces had also hijacked the old party.

To deal with such a situation, no Lincoln was in sight, and no one had the bad taste to compare McKinley to him. The task at hand was to avoid the barbarous ways of the West and financial turmoil for the United States. To the French the choice was clear, and the abrupt judgment of the Republicans appearing in the *Petit Parisien*, while not accepted by everyone, did represent a widely shared opinion:

> Against the radical platform propped up by Socialist propositions constructed by M. Bryan and his friends, they [the Republicans] have constituted themselves as the champions of social conservation. And it is above all this opposition of two systems, which is shared by the New World and the Old, that gives such capital importance and such palpitating interest to the contest of 3 November.[9]

Not that France had much to expect from the excessive protectionism espoused by the Republican candidate, but it would have to fear at least as much from a victory of the inflationist theses preached by Bryan, for these were bound to lead to even more detrimental adventures. A McKinley victory thus appeared to the French to be a victory of common sense, of "civilization," for the Democrats represented a true danger.

In this almost unanimous chorus, one finds little more than shades of opinion; *Le Matin*, for instance, was more reserved than *Le Figaro*, and *Le Temps* made an effort to discern the specifically American aspects of the phenomenon. As for the *Petite République*, it did not rally as easily to the Republican cause, which it denounced as "prohibitionist," "protectionist," and "interventionist" – with respect to Cuba and Venezuela – but it could not go along with the Democratic theses either. So the best L. Dubreuil could do was to take into account what the Americans themselves wanted:

> Do we now have to say that we regret this outcome? We do. Without turning this matter into a tragedy, and without making M. Bryan into a Socialist, it is clear that a large part of the American proletariat wished for the victory of this candidate.[10]

The question is whether this change of French opinion in favor of the party of the elephant would last or whether it was related to the very special circumstances of the election of 1896. The fact is that the French

---

9. *Le Petit Parisien* (5 Nov. 1896), reporting McKinley's victory.
10. "Aux Etats-Unis," *La Petite République* (6 Nov. 1896); here Bryan is considered as a pioneer who might, perhaps, clear the way for Socialism.

realized fairly quickly that Bryan was not as violent and extremist as had been said, and that the two major parties, once they had digested the populist episode, once again ran in their habitual grooves. The great confrontation left an aftertaste of simple demagoguery. Yet the scope of the Republican victory, the endorsement by the American people of the choice of financial security, even when accompanied by the excesses of the capitalists, gave the French pause. When all was said and done, was not McKinley's party closer in its options to a conservative party in Europe than those Democrats who had let themselves be swept off their feet by a crazy idea?

Launching the war against Spain and the assertion of the United States' power that followed did not shock the French on the strictly political level. The Republican administration had acted in a manner that did not strike anyone as extravagant, and Jules Cambon expressed very well a sentiment to which only the most leftist opinion could object, just as it had objected to choosing between two parties that in the end were closer to each other than had been believed for a moment:

> In Europe we tend to be more favorable to the Republicans than to the Democrats, for the Republicans are more often men of government in the European sense: their ranks include most of the influential, wealthy, and educated men whom foreigners are glad to meet here.[11]

This did not mean that the French approved or endorsed all the positions of the Republicans, but in a certain way the victory of 1896 and the war of 1898 had raised that party above the profound mediocrity of the preceding years. Conversely, the Democrats had a hard time recovering from their adventuresome direction. Yet the gulf between the two parties was still not fully understood in France, and French judgments expressed about one or the other were still distant, and often only concerned moral issues.

Thus the growing imperialist appetite exhibited by the McKinley administration, the actions taken in the Philippines, and also the excesses of the trusts caused the French to judge the Democratic propositions more indulgently and sympathetically. To be sure, Cambon could make fun of the reversal undergone by Bryan and his party, but there was a feeling that in their opposition to the government's policy they represented the country's true tradition, from which they had strayed only for

---

11. Archives du Ministère des Affaires Etrangères, Nouvelle série, Etats-Unis, I: Cambon to Hanotaux, 10 June 1898, fol. 55. The ambassador was later commended for his analysis of the American parties, in which he had once again stressed the theme of centralization.

a short moment. Before the election of 1900, the French chroniclers could therefore allow themselves a few puffs of idealism, while never doubting that McKinley and the Republicans would win, given his better organization and amazing financial resources:

> ... the entire part of the nation that cares about the past, about the Constitution, and which dreads the fatal slope toward an imperial presidency (*"le césarisme"*) in a democracy, which hates the corruption of morals and fears the revenge of the anonymous crowd against the excesses of the trusts and of speculation, has opened its eyes. All secondary quarrels disappear before the great struggle between imperialism with all its dangers, its sacrifices, its mirages and the republican tradition that remains faithful to the spirit of Washington, Jefferson, and the fathers of the Republic. If M. McKinley embodies the first trend, no one is better qualified to defend the second than M. Bryan.[12]

Yet realism soon regained the upper hand, and French opinion, while not in sympathy with the Republicans, was nonetheless fairly impressed with their success and took its distance from the other party, which could not get back on its feet.

The assassination of William McKinley on 7 September 1901 and Roosevelt's accession to the presidency totally eclipsed the Democrats, so that the French had eyes only for the Republicans and their chief. The trend that had already carried them willy-nilly toward that party was reinforced and widened, but this time it was the powerful personality of the colonel of the Rough Riders that masked the reality of the party. To be sure, it still had fierce opponents in France, who refused to pay any attention whatsoever to a representative of these bourgeois parties whose policies were guided exclusively by the great capitalists, and who now could no longer even see a future for Bryan, but on the whole, French opinion sided with the Republicans because so many people were so taken with Roosevelt.

However, once the great man had gone off hunting in Africa, the craze slowly began to subside. The programs of the two major parties were still as close to each other as they had been twenty years earlier. Moreover, the Taft presidency had brought out into the open the worst defects of the trans-Atlantic parties, scandals and the excessive power of the party machines and their bosses, all of which had been masked by "Teddy's" exuberance. In this context, the splitting off of the progressives was hardly noticed; from afar, this seemed a rather futile ploy, for the phe-

---

12. "B.E." *Le Temps* (7 July 1900). This was a review of the history of the parties; but by November of that year the same paper had forgotten all its praise of Bryan and painstakingly dissected all of his weaknesses.

nomenon of third parties was never properly understood in France. And besides, if the choice of the name *Bull Moose* amused the French for a moment, it seemed to prove the superficial character of this new political formation.

At the time of the 1912 election, Taft's Old Guard had little support among the French, and the opposition between the Progressives and the Democrats seemed rather artificial, since both had done their best to loot the other's program or at least to dip into the same well: combatting the trusts, combatting corruption, and so forth. Here again, the party machines were the center of attention for the French. Most of their commentaries resumed a distant and moral tone, saying that a victory for the Democrats would be only fair, given that they were facing a party that had been ruined by the full impact of power and scandals.

Hence the return to power of the Democrats, while eliciting a certain interest in the unknown person of Woodrow Wilson, did not give rise to any new positions. There was a certain satisfaction about promises to lower the tariffs and rein in imperialism, but nothing more. Without indulging in the heavy-handed irony of Jean Longuet writing in *Humanité* – "His [Wilson's] election has not troubled the sleep of J. Pierpont Morgan, nor the notoriously difficult digestion of John D. Rockefeller"[13] – most French commentaries once again turned away from the American parties. Only the rise of Debs's Socialists produced some interest; a sign of weariness with the excesses of the trusts and the tariff and of disgust with the two major parties for some, it was seen by a few others as a victory in the struggle against capitalism that would bring a better future.

The French, then, were not enthusiastic about the American political parties, understanding neither their confrontations nor their functioning. What astounded them was the formidable effectiveness of these parties, their ability to produce massive voter turnout and in the absence of any true debate to create an excitement and an enthusiasm that seemed totally artificial and relied on details and anecdotal material to keep up the momentum. In 1900, for example, the campaign started amidst general apathy, and then the tension mounted:

> ... people all excited, intoxicated by the endless speeches of both parties' orators, by the thousands of ingenious and grotesque means used to seduce, hypnotize, and sweep them off their feet in support of McKinley or Brian.[14]

13. J. Longuet, "Les élections présidentielles aux Etats-Unis," *L'Humanité* (7 Nov. 1912). The caption of a cartoon read: Capitalism says: "Democrat or Republican, you too will take orders from me."
14. A. Viallate, "W. Mac Kinley," *Revue de Paris* (15 Nov. 1900): 318.

But this agitation subsided as soon as the results were known, proving the seemingly superficial nature of the debates. In the absence of ideological debates, all attention was fixed on the personalities of the candidates, whose choice was governed by a set of clever manipulations: "It is a curious phenomenon that in American politics the personal element plays such a preponderant role."

## INFERNAL MACHINES

Understandably, the French observers' opinions about the conflicts within the American parties were relatively neutral, but the ways in which the parties were run could not leave them indifferent. Thus, the conduct of political rallies and the role played on such occasions by party members presented the problem of a veritable perversion of democracy that distressed its defenders and more or less secretly delighted its adversaries.

### *An Ongoing Folkloric Spectacle*

Ever since the de facto establishment of universal manhood suffrage in the United States, voting had been attended by picturesque practices. The need to obtain the votes of a huge and very heterogeneous electorate and the practical importance of an election victory for gaining access to innumerable national and local offices had early on excited the imagination of the party leaders. These men compensated for the absence of a class of notables who in Europe, and particularly in France, acted as a filter between "the people" and power.

Many of the French observers who looked into what seemed strange patterns of behavior had a dignified and austere conception of democracy, a system obtained after painful struggles, which had little room for fantasy and exuberance. They therefore expressed the same amazement mixed with indignation at every election throughout the period – and far beyond it. Their various commentaries focused on the presidential elections, for these involved the largest number of participants and were without doubt the most spectacular.

The active participation of the voters throughout the campaign was one of the first things to strike them. What they saw was a steady succession of parades in support of this or that candidate, with posters and portraits held aloft, preceded by fanfares, all of this with fanciful uniforms or at least jerkins of uniform color to identify the party. These noisy crowds were happy to mount a torchlight parade and exhibited an apparently boundless enthusiasm. This was a far cry from the gravity of the elections of 1848 in France, when voters had walked to the urns behind their landlord or their mayor to symbolize the composure they owed democracy. American campaigns bathed in an atmosphere of vulgar celebration that particularly shocked the French because the slogans used on these occasions were so simplistic, and because "the whole procedure was put together, it would seem, to get the votes of poor stupid Negroes rather than to capture the minds of intelligent citizens [*sic*]."[15] This general impression is found again and again in the writing of most observers, whether at the beginning or at the end of our period. They were shocked by the circus-like atmosphere, and those who were most hostile to democracy saw this as the specter of a revolting "dumbing down," while those who favored it pointed out that the country was astonishingly calm despite these occasional outbursts. But both refused to recognize the usefulness or the benefits of such practices, realizing that there was nothing spontaneous about them and that they were obviously manipulated by the party leaders.

Their role was even more apparent in the other aspects of the campaigns. Everywhere in the country, professional orators came to spread the good word and to vaunt the "virtues" of their candidate, while the candidate himself did not show himself too much, the first exception being William Jennings Bryan in 1896. The deployment of such means throughout the country presupposed a prodigious organization and considerable financial resources. The phenomenon was already well under way by 1872:

> ... from the great halls of the cities of the populous North to the forests of the West and the South, the entire territory resounds with the names of Grant and Greeley, which are constantly linked and repeated in the most varied tones, from the grossest insult to the most extravagant panegyric.[16]

But over the next years the system was perfected, millions of brochures were sent to every state, advertisements appeared in the press or on the panels of sandwich-men, and "they advertise a candidate just as an industrialist advertises a new product, and an election is launched just as a new stock is launched on the stock market." To the French of that time, such an attitude toward politics was totally unacceptable, and they now began to understand why in the confrontations between the major parties, and indeed the minor ones, real debates of ideas were lacking. Money became

15. A. Moireau, "La lutte pour la présidence aux Etats-Unis," *Revue des Deux Mondes* (1 Feb. 1889): 649.
16. Hauranne, "L'élection présidentielle," p. 539.

the essential lifeblood of an election, and it was almost scandalous to learn that the election of 1900 had cost $25 million; such sums were bound to weigh heavily on the free expression of the will of the people. Subsequent elections went even further along this road, with the candidate's train crisscrossing the country for six to eight months, greeted at every stop by local activists. Everywhere he owed it to himself to shake hands, interminably, with crowds of people, an activity that did not seem exactly sanitary or even necessary to the functioning of democracy.

The large expenditures were caused, in part, by the conventions, frequently described by the French observers, who also regularly detailed the process by which candidates were nominated by delegates chosen in a way nobody quite understood. These people exhibited an altogether extraordinary enthusiasm for the hero of their choice, wearing his insignia until one of the candidates obtained the majority and everyone rallied to him. The convention was also the opportunity to explain once again such strange terms as *dark horse, favorite son,* and others, which constituted the specific vocabulary of these gigantic events attended by several thousand persons. The speeches delivered by the party leaders gave rise to ovations, even though, physically, only those in the very first rows could hear a few of the words that were said. This was presented as proof that these addresses were totally devoid of content, for not many French observers were aware that because of the telegraph these speeches were not lost to everyone and that they were carried in all the country's newspapers on the same day.[17]

Such spectacles left the observers perplexed and uneasy. The complexity of the procedures used at the local level to choose candidates and convention delegates was bewildering to minds accustomed to centralization – and then there was the never-ending problem of money that invaded all stages of the election. Was this related to the practice of democracy in general, or only to its American version? The second hypothesis was more reassuring, and more in keeping with the idea the French had of "... this people that is so different from us in the brutal exercise of individual citizen's rights," but nonetheless these practices were totally unacceptable:

This immoral bidding, this colossal trafficking around principles, this universal venality are possible only because of the exorbitant powers that the constitutional mores give to the president of the Republic.[18]

17. J.-P. des Noyers, "Une campagne présidentielle," *Revue des Deux Mondes* (1 Oct. 1900): 559–87; not many observers noted such details. See also J. Bardoux, "Les conventions nationales américaines," *L'Opinion* (29 June 1912): 807–09.
18. J. Huret in *Le Figaro* (7 Nov. 1904).

Jules Huret pretended not to know that the phenomenon was not
limited to the presidential election, even if this was indeed its apogee,
and that the money of companies, along with that of private individuals,
irrigated the entire body politic of America. To be sure, French democracy was also acquainted with the – most often hidden – influence of
money, but there was nothing even comparable to this riot of funds, this
display of wealth mobilized in a rational, almost industrial method to
show the sovereign people what choice to make.

Added to this, the length and the scope of the American campaigns
brought to the fore all forms of scandal, all kinds of accusations against
the opposing candidate as a means to catch the attention of the citizen
and give an edge to people's enthusiasm. Torrents of mud were poured
out by professional slanderers, scandalous invasions of private lives were
made in hopes of unearthing things that would ruin a career. Politicians
used whatever it took to win the prize of victory and the chance to
reward themselves for their troubles.

These practices produced groups of men who used their expertise in
this field to sell newspapers or make book on the winner, and also an
apparatus that paid them and assigned tasks. This was indeed, as André
Tardieu remarked, "the most highly organized democracy in the world
when it comes to election campaigns." A democracy so embroiled in
underhanded schemes could not remain pure, he said, and despite
appearances the people did not express themselves in a truly free
fashion. The responsibility for this state of affairs fell on the parties that
had set up these monstrous organizations.

### *The Party Organizations*

Most French observers simply described these political phenomena
without really understanding their origin. It was much easier to wax
indignant about the pervasive corruption in New York than to understand the complex role played by the party organizations. The only true
exception was the political scientist Moïse Ostrogorski, who in a series
of articles in the *Annales de l'Ecole Libre des Sciences Politiques* of
1888–89[19] presented a very subtle analysis of the party system in the
United States which, though based on bosses and on spoils, provided
social services for some of the poorest segments of the population.

The public impact of the articles and the book of Ostrogorski, one of

---

19. M. Ostrogorski, "De l'organisation des partis politiques aux Etats-Unis," *Annales de
    l'Ecole Libre des Sciences Politiques* (15 April 1888); (15 Oct. 1888): 520–38; (15 Jan.
    1889): 12–30.

the founders of modern political science and the scholar who had fully understood the originality of the American situation, was extremely slight, not to say nonexistent. As a result, most of the other commentators were not aware of anything but certain pieces of the puzzle constituted by the life of these extraordinary political organizations. It is in fact remarkable that the principal political studies, those of Noailles, Boutmy, and Chambrun, treated this subject cursorily – the parties did not warrant lengthy disquisitions – or in very general terms. Prior to the twentieth century France did not have party organizations; the Republicans played an important role in the governmental apparatus of the 1880s, but they never had a full-fledged organization at the level of the voters, nor a system for selecting candidates. In seeing developments in this direction, the French inevitably thought of the unavowable deals and underhanded maneuvers that characterized organized politics and failed to understand the complex functions of the parties.

Because of this attitude, French observers viewed the organization of the American parties in an extremely superficial manner. No one, for instance, mentioned the remarkable figures of voter participation the parties of that era were able to obtain; yet voter participation is one of the essential elements in the functioning of a democracy.

The French absolutely did not recognize themselves in these aspects of American political life, certain that they were not threatened by these ills, which they did their best to describe with rather facile irony.

Corruption, of course, riveted their attention. It was indeed one of the outstanding features of American political life at the end of the nineteenth century, and related to the spoils system as well as to the negligence of City Hall. American testimony on these subjects was plentiful, even at the time, and served to confirm the judgments of the French observers.

Thus, the example of Tammany Hall was brought up regularly, from the beginning to the end of the period, and it took a long time for the shadow of Boss Tweed to disappear from the horizon of the Empire City. In the early 1870s, the memory of the formidable master of Tammany Hall was still very much alive, and it was trotted out to shed light on the full turpitude of the Grant presidency, although the French writers failed to provide a convincing explanation of his past fortune or to distinguish between the Democratic machine and the Republican administration. Claudio Jannet saw corruption as proof of the iniquity of democracy, whereas other less sectarian observers were nonplussed that an organization of this kind could wield so much power over a such a prestigious city. In the course of the years the Tweed case became a veritable standard against which to measure other New York bosses, such as Kelly and

Croker, although it was never quite understood how such a system could be perpetuated:

> What are the devious paths, the mysterious means that allow a man whose name is unknown . . . , who has in his favor neither an official position, nor social prestige, nor a mandate conferred by the vote of the people, to acquire this enormous weight in the balance of the political parties and to take uncontrolled charge of the richest and most populous state in the Union . . . ?[20]

This "strange despotism" exerted by the bosses was used as an indicator for the absolute power of the party "machines," which integrated the membership into a perfect network reaching from the poorest tenement house to the district office. And this was as true in 1880 as it was in 1910:

> No army in the world is better disciplined and better staffed. At the time of an election campaign, perfectly prepared agents, each knowing his district or subdistrict like the palm of his hand, leads his people to the polls with the irresistible authority of an old sergeant in bygone days.[21]

And the strangest part of all was that such a system, based as it was on corruption and on coercion by a few, could function, apparently without too many glitches, and that although its very principles, being devoid of any ideology, were to be condemned, it was actually efficient. It was also clear that good citizens who opposed these practices were rarely successful in the long run.

The example of New York was the most frequently used and seemed applicable to almost all the large cities, and in fact the articles of a Lincoln Steffens, who was known by only very few observers, such as the correspondents of the *Journal des Economistes*, seemed to confirm this somewhat hasty conclusion.

The cities thus fully revealed the sway of the party organizations. The French observers were horrified to learn about the dues public officials were made to pay and about the role of local committees and the national committee, which was run for many years by McKinley's mentor, Mark Hanna. Decidedly, the healthy rural democracy dear to Washington and Jefferson seemed to have survived only in a few remote areas of the West. The corruption of the cities had taken over the entire machine, and neither party had reason to envy the other. If the Democrats of New York stood out for being "lucky" enough to have a Tweed

---

20. C. de Varigny, "Tammany Hall et la vie politique à New York," *Revue des Deux Mondes* (15 Aug. 1894): 878.
21. G.N. Tricoche, "Lettre," *Journal des Economistes* (May 1910): 428.

who had become a kind of brand name for Tammany Hall, the Republicans were not slow to pay off voters, to steal votes, and to make deals with big business.

Such commentaries failed to take into account local conditions and to approach matters systematically: ". . . one wonders where slavery ends and the sovereignty of the voter begins. . . ."[22] Here was a fundamental flaw of American democracy, and while the scandals of Grant or Tweed remained exceptional, rampant corruption and vote-buying still existed in the early twentieth century. To be sure, the French observers took note of the first civil service reforms, but their effects were slow in coming; the "machines" kept their power, and even Theodore Roosevelt's greatest admirers had to admit that in this area his efforts, praiseworthy though they were, had had little effect. In 1903, for instance, this President, who had been able to make the mine owners yield at the time of the recent coal miners' strike, could not prevent the nomination of a district attorney in Delaware once it had been decided by a local party boss: "If American democracy is not cured of this ill, it will die of it. . . ."

To be sure, Progressive efforts to break the machines and to clean out the Augean stables of certain cities were not altogether ignored by the French observers, but they looked marginal and pusillanimous. Would not the referenda that certain states hoped to introduce fall into the hands of the parties? And would the management of cities, either along business lines or according to the principles of a paternalist Socialism as at Toledo, be able to satisfy the better class of citizens and at the same time respond to the crying needs of the population without ruining these cities more surely than the worst graft?[23] The observers were skeptical about this, as also about the multiplicity of primary elections before the election of 1912; indeed one can say that the French showed "ironical curiosity" for this democratic craving. Born of a pleasing idealism, it was insufficient for resolving such serious, deep, and tenacious problems.

The parties, then, were a major blemish on America, and their methods and machinations acted like a cancer within institutions that they perverted in depth. The diagnosis of French observers of all stripes was particularly bleak. When C. Malato of *L'Aurore* joked about the election of 1900 – "MM. Mac Kinley and Bryan cannot fail to be flattered by the gusto with which the voters kill each other in their honor" – he went further than most of his colleagues but what he said did not really shock anyone.

22. "B.E.," *Le Temps* (21 April 1900), but also C. Anet, "La corruption municipale aux Etats-Unis," *Nouvelle Revue* (1 Jan. 1906): 27–36.
23. Living in the United States, Tricoche and Laborer were most fully aware of the situation, but highly skeptical about these efforts.

The revulsion the French felt for the American parties is rather easy to understand, for it sprang from their very different concept of democracy and political life. This concept was fully apparent when it came to the men who ran these parties, the sinister "politicians," who must never be confused with "political leaders."

## Politicians

The formidable efficiency of the parties rested on the shoulders of a rather large number of men. They were the ones who made the speeches, who knew all the people in their neighborhood and made them vote the right way, and who, when victory was at hand, hurried to get their reward, the famous spoils: "clusters of them descend upon Washington, with no more luggage than an overnight bag, hence their name of 'carpet baggers' ... after the quarry has been brought in."[24] Without their energy and their skill with people, the parties could not achieve anything. These politicians, for that is what they should be called, did not all operate with scrupulous honesty nor at a very high intellectual level, and in the aftermath of the scandals of the 1870s and the assassination of Garfield, horrified onlookers pointed their fingers at them, even in the United States. Moreover, the Pendleton Act of 1883 and the various reform movements of the Progressive Era were intended to break the "machines" and to substitute the true will of the citizenry for that of these ward heelers and stump orators.

Under these circumstances the reaction of the French, who had major misgivings about the politics and the methods of the parties to begin with, was not likely to be favorable when it came to these individuals. These people actually made most of the observers feel nauseated, in 1870 as in 1910, for they constituted a veritable political class which, in its profound mediocrity, was quite unlike the dignified "political leaders" in France.

Thus it was said in 1872, when a group of Republicans talked abut the possibility of a third term for Grant:

> The truth is that for the first time and momentarily, there was within the American Republic a cause and a new class, along with powerful interests willing to identify their security with one man's power.[25]

In fact the phenomenon went back to the Jacksonian era, but had subsequently been reinforced by the takeover of the South by the Radicals,

---

24. C. de Varigny, *Les Etats-Unis* (Paris: E. Kolb, 1892), p. 234. He even spoke of "the democratic leprosy."
25. "La crise présidentielle aux Etats-Unis," *Revue des Deux Mondes* (1 Sept. 1876): 6.

which had popularized and exaggerated the image of the rapacious carpetbaggers. These men, it was said, colonized not only the parties but the very state apparatus by becoming public employees, and their recruitment was necessarily questionable:

> ... class of unenlightened men without morality, who consider politics a job and running an election a means of personal advancement ... deplorable lowering of the intellectual and moral level of the administrative personnel, a corruption impossible to combat, and the public employees' lack of responsibility toward the government they serve and, as a logical consequence, their absolute dependence on local politicians who can make and unmake them.[26]

This was a harsh assessment, which pointed to the close connection between politicians and public office. The gradual adoption of competitive examinations for the recruitment of public officials did little to modify this diagnosis given in 1884. The French observers felt that the existence of political appointees was the reason why "honest men ... almost always keep away from activist politics," since all positions were taken and tightly controlled by people who, though perhaps open to criticism, were after all professionals.

This was the crux of the problem, for the politicians were indeed professionals, and this was something that deeply shocked the French: "Most chose to become politicians as they might have chosen to become farmers, railroad engineers, lawyers, or bankers. What they want is to make money."[27] In the French conception of politics, there was something profoundly incompatible about this. A politician who was doing a job inevitably had to accommodate everyone, had lost all deep convictions and all true sincerity, and was no longer capable of any true hatred or enthusiasm. This kind of situation filled a militant like Urbain Gohier with indignation, but other more moderate observers felt the same way. These professionals of politics could not, by definition, be considered respectable.

This reaction to the professionalization of politics would not have led to a complete rejection of politicians if these men had not done their job in the worst possible way, and without even being worthy of doing it. Thus Gustave de Molinari wondered why the Americans, so ingenious in other ways, could fail so completely in the domain of politics and tol-

---

26. A. Gigot, "La présidence d'A. Jackson," *Revue des Deux Mondes* (1 March 1884): 163. The article describes the origin and the continuity of the phenomenon.
27. C.-M. de Limousin, "Une excursion aux Etats-Unis à l'occasion de l'Exposition de Philadelphie," *Journal des Economistes* (Feb. 1877):263. The identical terms are found in de Varigny and de Rousiers some twenty years later.

erate being "at the mercy of the politicians, that society of foxes organized to live at the expense of the democracy of crows."[28] Twenty years later, Paul de Rousiers waxed indignant about the "repulsive work" of the lobbyists and the ignominy of Tammany Hall, explaining both by the mediocrity of those who chose this line of work:

> ... the American politician is a loser in private life; he has not made it in cultural, industrial, or commercial activities, being unfit or disinclined to live by working, and therefore unable or unwilling to create his own business; his business will be politics.[29]

On the basis of this finding, it was not surprising to see that the United States had "the most fleeced and poorly administered population." Some of our observers did not hesitate to say that in France political leaders were chosen among the best, whereas the politicians of the United States came from the humblest layer of society, from among the losers.

What was meant here was not so much democracy itself, as the royalists believed, but the role of men of politics in a republic. The French criticized the American politicians for coming from the people, for not being different from the voters, so that in an Irish neighborhood they were Irish, and Yankees in a Yankee neighborhood. They were no better educated than their constituents, whose simple and sometimes brutal pleasures they shared. Thus – for shame! – the local organizer was often the pub keeper. In France, political leaders owed it to themselves to be above the people; highly visible and identifiable, they were supposed to guide their constituents, rather than represent them. Details such as the simple and unadorned dress of the representatives and senators, even the Speaker himself, who might come down from his presiding seat, his vest unbuttoned and busy with lighting a cigar, never failed to strike the French, for this would be totally inconceivable on the banks of the Seine, where the black frock coat and a dignified bearing remained de rigueur.

This elitist conception was held not only by the conservatives – who, believing that politics should be handled by the notables, expressed indignation at the social level of the American politicians under the cover of attacking corruption – but also by the Republicans, even the most progressive among them. As far as these last were concerned, politics belonged to activists motivated by their convictions and their ideals

---

28. G. de Molinari, *Lettres sur les Etats-Unis* (Paris: Hachette, 1876), p. 159. [This image refers to La Fontaine's fable of the fox who tricks the stupid crow out of a fine cheese – Trans.]

29. P. de Rousiers, *La vie américaine* (Paris: F. Didot, 1899), vol. 2, p. 183.

rather than by the pursuit of employment or advantages of any kind, except that of improving the lot of the people, which they alone were capable of guiding. Neither the notables nor the activists saw themselves as professionals; they were either amateurs devoted to the public good or selfless idealists, and both were completely devoid of personal ambition.

This was the picture that emerged from most of the French observers' reactions to American politicians. It did not by any means correspond to the actual situation that obtained in France, but only to the image that people saw from afar. But it does make it easier to understand the rejection of the campaign methods of a Boulanger, which were immediately branded as American, that is to say, synonymous with corruption and soulless professionalism. By way of comparison it was pointed out that in Great Britain the methods of a Joseph Chamberlain, who had introduced the system of caucuses, were also criticized for bringing the hell of American politics into the pure British system.

Without attempting to make too little of the frequently distressing nature of certain American political mores, on which all historians agree, it must be said that the reaction of the French, and indeed of the Europeans, is striking in its profound hypocrisy. After all, everyone knew that the European parties were composed of full-time professionals whose ambition could be savage; yet all of these people were certain that they formed an elite that understood the people without mingling with it. There were scandals as well, but they had a different origin, involving as they did the highest strata of society. And so the French talked of two different forms of democracy, each shaped by its own traditions that were not governed by the same principles.

If such were the views to which most French observers subscribed in all good conscience, a small group was able to come to more nuanced and in the end more tolerant conclusions. The correspondents of the *Journal des Economistes*, the first to point to the abuses of American democracy, also remarked that the spoils system existed, albeit in an unsystematic form, in France as well, and that corruption was not totally unknown there; but then they reacted almost like Americans irritated by the regular criticism voiced by the French. More interesting are the opinions of Pierre de Coubertin and Lazare Weiller, who, without whitewashing the politicians across the sea, felt that these men were rather conscientious about carrying out their task and less despicable than was often said. As a meticulous analyst, Adolphe de Chambrun showed that the scandals involved only a minority: "The ensuing investigations brought out in most of the cases that this was a perfectly honorable *corps*."[30] Louis Vossion, for his part, was afraid that the projected reforms making public employees into civil servants would bring worse ills, those of an excessive bureaucracy, that "phylloxera of administrations" of which free societies were dying. But in what had to be a unique editorial, *Le Temps* went further than anyone in 1902, when it showed how the "populace" was protected from the worst exploiters by the politicians who, needing to be elected, distributed certain bounties. The organization of Bill Devery in New York, for instance:

> [was it not] . . . close kin to the dregs of the people, but also full of solicitude for it, identifying with its tastes and its destiny? Did it not have the courage, the combativeness, and the power of sarcasm that are the virtue and the weapons of this American "camorra"?[31]

But how much weight did these reflections of more knowledgeable observers have, what chance did these efforts to understand a rich and active political life have when they met an onslaught of criticism founded on national political pride? At most, these reflections showed that in dealing with these problems, French opinion did not divide along political lines but, rather, according to different moral conceptions of democracy. And despite the fears and the sinister prophecies of French observers, the American Republic survived these abuses ". . . inelegant and uneducated, but full of the sap and strength of youth."

In fact, the mediocrity of the political personnel did not preclude the emergence of great politicians; great not in terms of money but of their ideas – just as in France, where both categories were also represented. The great figure of Lincoln was compelling, as that of Roosevelt was soon to be as well. This was one of the contradictions that few of the French observers sought to resolve, easily fascinated as they were by strong personalities.

## LOOKING FOR GREAT MEN

Among the major political figures who attracted the attention of the French – who promoted some of them to the rather meaningless status of statesmen – were only the most outstanding protagonists, along with, as we have seen, a handful of political bosses. This lack of diversity is not surprising, considering that the Gilded Age did not produce a flourishing of admirable men. There was little to say about Presidents without

---

30. A. de Chambrun, *Droits et libertés aux Etats-Unis* (Paris: E. Thorin, 1891), p. 22.
31. "Bill Devery," *Le Temps* (22 Sept. 1902).

stature, whose administrations have for the most part fallen into deep and often deserved oblivion, about gray and ephemeral congressmen and colorless mayors. It was only at the end of the nineteenth century that the French could observe the emergence of Bryan, especially Roosevelt, and Wilson, whose eminence was enhanced by the contrast with their predecessors.

### The Time of Mediocrities

During the period between the end of the Civil War and the election of 1896 Lord Bryce was wondering why the great men of America did not become President, and many of the French asked that same question, without coming up with Bryce's pertinent answer. The fact is that from Grant to Hayes, from Arthur to Harrison, the level did not improve much, so that when Grover Cleveland appeared, he looked like a shining light. Among the officials in secondary positions, only James G. Blaine attracted some attention. This small group was not viewed favorably in France.

As much as Grant had been celebrated at the time of the Civil War and when he succeeded Andrew Johnson, his popularity in France was completely wiped out by his unfortunate telegram to the Emperor of Germany in 1870. Nor did the scandals that racked his presidency enhance his prestige, even if no one impugned his personal honesty. The French were almost relieved by the election of Garfield in 1880, which ended the specter of a continued Grant presidency. His brief private visit to France in 1879 did not attract attention, except for some brief reminders of his anti-French attitude. Only Grant's death after an eighteen-month struggle redeemed him in the eyes of Cucheval-Clarigny,[32] who certainly spoke for the few Frenchmen who took an interest in this personage. Most people, however, felt that he would have done better to retire in 1865.

His two successors were pure products of the political in-group, candidates of the "election managers" who controlled the conventions – the French liked to speak derisively about the nomination of Garfield on the 33rd ballot – and elected for reasons that had little to do with their personal qualities. Yet the assassination of Garfield, several months after his inauguration, almost made him into a hero. His agony in the hands of

32. Cucheval-Clarigny, "Le Général Grant," *Revue des Deux Mondes* (15 Oct. 1885): 824–58. A few years earlier E. Masseras in "L'élection du deux novembre aux Etats-Unis," *Nouvelle Revue* (Dec. 1880): 682, had not hesitated to reproduce a passage of Hugo's *L'Année terrible* (cited in the Introduction to this book).

incompetent and competing physicians – "you don't get to use your scalpel on a President every day" – elicited a certain sympathy, and he was suddenly invested with all kinds of virtues. This was a kind of promotion by assassination, repeated twenty years later in the case of McKinley, which had a much greater resonance due to the development of the French press and the increased coverage given to the United States.

Under normal circumstances, American Presidents, along with their unsuccessful competitors, came and went almost unnoticed. The two elections of Cleveland, separated by the surprise victory of Harrison, which took place in a climate of increased personalization of politics, were much more interesting to the French.

The case of Harrison was given short shrift: He was called "pale and insignificant," as well as ice-cold in his approach, and said to represent the worst aspects of the Republican Party: "a rigid Presbyterian, a small mind well versed in the chicaneries of party politics."[33] The French were not about to come to the defense of a man whom the Americans themselves did not exactly praise to the skies, and to this they added their contempt for all those "pettifogging politicians" without prestige or grandeur:

> ... high spirits won't be making their entry at the White House, and we are not about to see, at least not through efforts from on high, the lifting of the heavy veil of boredom that covers the United States from the East to the West like a leaden garment and makes a stay there so difficult for people of Latin stock.[34]

Grover Cleveland was a perfect illustration of the proverb, "Among the blind the one-eyed man is king!" There was something refreshing about a Democratic victory, and the fact that his opponents had dug up an old love affair and that, for once, he had a charming wife were precious assets that made the first Democratic President since Buchanan attractive to the French public. Cleveland, incidentally, was the first President of the period whom the French liked to visit when they traveled to the Chicago World's Fair, and many of them were charmed by the reception they received and also by the absence of formality.

Added to this was their interest in the initiatives of a man who seemed to be less tied down by the party apparatus than his predecessors. Was he not taking measures to accelerate the reorganization of public

33. H. Kern, "La Convention républicaine de Minneapolis," *Nouvelle Revue* 47 (July–Aug. 1891): 180.
34. L. Vossion-Serre, "Cleveland et Harrison: La dernière Campagne présidentielle aux Etats-Unis," *Nouvelle Revue* 57 (March–April 1889): 41–99.

employment, did he not seem willing to resist the pressure of office-seekers, and did he not, in his second term, put brakes on annexationist adventures? All of these actions warmed the hearts of the French, who mistook sheer obstinacy for personality, and being out of touch for political acumen. This is why in 1893 *Le Temps* could praise the qualities of this President, saying that he had left a deeper mark on the office than anyone since Lincoln, why de Rousiers could evoke his "great example," and why D. Guibert of *Le Figaro* could write, à propos of the refusal to recognize the Cuban insurgents: ". . . this proves that in addition to internationalist muddle-heads, America has a pool of wise men who strictly abide by the rules of conscience and reason."[35] Such rather excessive comments reveal that the French felt a great need to admire strong personalities and could not care less about their actions.

Aside from Presidents, a few other names also appeared in French writings. None attained the stature of a Charles Sumner whose memory Auguste Laugel evoked most emphatically in 1874. This man of "emancipation and the Union" belonged to the generation of the great figures of American history, to whom it was difficult to compare the contemporaries.[36] Such people as Conkling, Seth Low, or even Henry George did not attract any real attention and affection. At most Henry George and his altogether desperate attempt to run for mayor of New York against Tammany Hall elicited some favorable reactions, but in the final analysis these were due more to his status as a writer than to his standing as a politician.[37]

The only other statesman to compete with the Presidents, although he had run against Cleveland in 1884, was of course James G. Blaine. His multifaceted personality, his gift for maneuvering, and his ambition could not go unnoticed. He was a talented speaker – an essential asset in French eyes – but he seemed superficial and fickle and seemed altogether too American, too "magnetic," and too tied to the party machine: ". . . the true assets of a statesman, an unfettered spirit, an alert intelligence, but he has no idea of what a scruple is. . . ." As it happened, the French observers knew what they were talking about. They could not forget that in 1881, when he was Secretary of State, Blaine had, purely as a matter of election politics, included the Germans in the celebration of the cen-

---

35. D. Guibert, "Le message américain," *Le Figaro* (9 Dec. 1896).
36. A. Laugel, "Le Sénateur C. Sumner, un homme d'état américain," *Revue des Deux Mondes* (15 June 1874): 721–49. The author had met Sumner in Paris in 1884, and then in Boston ten years later. A fervent abolitionist himself, he asserted with considerable emotion: "He has freed a whole race."
37. L.V., "Un grand américain, Henry George," *Nouvelle Revue* 110 (Jan.–Feb. 1898): 629–36.

tenary of Yorktown. The French held his pro-German sentiments against him until he died; this was enough to disqualify him, and it did not seem to be at odds with the concomitant reproach of fickleness. The fact that he never reached the heights for which he seemed destined seemed to confirm the French prejudice.

French observers used these few examples for the sole purpose of illustrating the harmfulness of the party systems, which methodically and obstinately seemed to eliminate the best and the brightest.

### Bryan, No! McKinley, with Reservations

The election of 1896 generated relatively clear-cut reactions within French opinion, given the ideological choice it seemed to embody. But the main protagonists were hardly equal to the fight in which they were involved. On the Republican side, a well-known but not well-respected man, Governor McKinley, had gained notoriety by his sudden and excessive support of absolute protectionism; he symbolized a party machine firmly in the hands of his manager, Mark Hanna, a figure of doubtful integrity. On the other side was a totally obscure young lawyer, pushed into the limelight by his oratorical gifts and his frenetic, perhaps demagogic, support of the free-silver doctrine. Neither of these two personages corresponded to the ideal image of the statesman that so fascinated the French. McKinley, they felt, might have the proper stature and moderate views, but his propensity for seeking to be compared to Napoleon seemed rather childish, and his breadth of vision was not impressive. Bryan was able to excite a crowd and deployed a staggering energy, but he was really too young and too much of a mad dog to be taken seriously, and besides, his ideas struck most observers as dangerous. Decidedly, this combat, however important, seemed pretty mediocre because of the "valor of the opposing champions."

William Jennings Bryan unquestionably interested the French, who admired his energy and his dynamism and compared his oratorical skill to that of Camille Demoulins, or even Jaurès. The French tried to understand the reasons for his initial success while firmly rejecting his ideas:

> Young, handsome, and athletic, he was liked by everyone, even if his ideas often ran into what he called prejudices. Never in the history of the United States had a presidential candidate given more of himself and made more manly efforts to bring about his party's victory.[38]

---

38. Marquis de Chambrun, "La campagne présidentielle aux Etats-Unis – Les programmes et les hommes – Bryan et Mc Kinley," *Le Correspondant* (10 Jan. 1897): 67.

Some, however, wondered whether he was not simply endowed with an extraordinary "magnetism" and devoid of deep convictions. This question was frequently raised, for this man, whose total abstinence from alcohol the French stressed again and again, absolutely did not fit the usual schema of the politician; and while such traits might make him attractive, his inflammatory speeches and his permanent agitation eventually became worrisome. The best *La Petite République* could do was to assign him a momentary role as a trailblazer for the Socialist cause, but the French certainly could not recognize themselves in such a phenomenon. His speeches were too revolutionary for the conservatives, who liked to categorize him as an anarchist or a Socialist, and not serious enough for left-wing circles, who saw him as nothing more than an ordinary liberal trotting out certain popular themes.

In 1900, and also in 1908, his repeated failures and his changing positions did little to enhance his image, even if the French did concede the sincerity of his anti-imperialist stance, and Jules Cambon rather crudely expressed a fairly widespread attitude: ". . . M. Bryan's personality is controversial and his program looks more like that of a street-corner orator than that of a statesman."[39] Very soon, moreover, the speaking tours he undertook to refurbish his finances gave rise to ironical comments of French observers who reminded him of his free-silver doctrine and his earlier denunciations of Eastern gold.

Under these circumstances it is not surprising that his appointment as Wilson's Secretary of State was greeted with sarcasm, particularly since he remained in the lecture circuit on his own behalf: "If I were an American, I would be one of those who feel that the government benefits rather than loses by the time M. Bryan devotes to his lectures."[40]

To the French, William Jennings Bryan thus represented the height of extravagance in American politics, and this prevented them from perceiving the forces of renewal that were very slowly making their way within the Democratic Party. Quite understandably, only the excitement of 1896 had attracted attention. The lack of measure and the frenzy of the campaigns conducted by the "boyish orator" [in English in the original] flabbergasted the observers; at most they were willing to recognize that he had given his party some hope, but he was just too childish and too simplistic.

Little wonder, then, that most of French opinion rallied to Governor McKinley, not with much pleasure but because he represented a known

---

39. Archives du Ministère des Affaires Etrangères, NS, Etats-Unis I, Cambon to Delcassé, 20 Feb. 1900, fol. 158.
40. Ibid., E. de Peretti, chargé d'affaires, to S. Pichon, 23 Aug. 1913, p. 198.

and reassuring policy. *La Petite République*, of course, denounced him as an incontestable representative of the most unfettered capitalism and had nothing to say about his personality, but the rest of the press noted his personal honesty, even though he had gone bankrupt when he was in business. When all was said and done, he represented the serious America of that moment, and that would have to be enough, even if he was known to have been produced by his party. The French preference for the Republican candidate really came about by default, and analysts sometimes had to make a little extra effort to find some good qualities in him.

And indeed, the man was not particularly attractive, and there was nothing exciting about his biography, although it did reveal certain merits. He would certainly have joined his Republican predecessors in purgatory if a special concatenation of circumstances had not, paradoxically, enhanced his popularity.

Whatever the French might have thought of the war of 1898, it did propel McKinley into the ranks of the victorious heads of state and suddenly increased his stature far beyond his personal qualities. Thus, despite the presence within the Republican Party of the Anti-Imperialist League, which could take votes away from him, he was the natural candidate for 1900. The French might reproach him for his "pretentious banality" and his close ties to the trusts, but he was the undisputed favorite who, as *Le Figaro* said, stood for security, experience, and public wealth. C. Malato of *L'Aurore* could rant all he wanted against imperialism, *Le Temps* could affect disdain, the fact is that the outgoing President reaped the full benefit of his first term and of his country's power. The French resigned themselves to McKinley without much enthusiasm, but they considered him worthy of his office, as if the office had shaped the man.

There is no question that it was the assassination of the twenty-fifth President of the United States that afforded him, in a classic amplifying effect, the sincere and ephemeral recognition of the majority of French opinion.

In November 1900 the editorialist of *L'Aurore*, looking at the mediocrity of the American presidential election, had exclaimed: "Kings, alas, come and go, but presidents stay!"[41] He certainly did not think that he was to be proven wrong so soon. The attack in Buffalo on 6 September 1901 became known in France almost immediately, for *Le Matin* had for some time been proud of its ability to publish news from across the Atlantic less than four hours after it happened. This was very different

41. C. Malato, "L'élection américaine, un avertissement," *L'Aurore* (8 Nov. 1900).

from the assassinations of Lincoln and Garfield, whose details had not been known for some time. Nonetheless, comparisons with these two previous Presidents were made immediately, and it should be added that no one insisted on calling this a typically American violence.

Throughout McKinley's agony and until his death on 14 September, the French papers were filled with information about the circumstances of the attack, the personality of the attacker, the presidential physicians, who were criticized for hesitating to act, and with overly optimistic bulletins. Assessments of the dying President and his successor were also featured.

On the one hand, *Le Figaro* and *Le Matin* immediately aggrandized McKinley's person, stressing his simplicity, the trust that caused him to plunge into crowds by himself, and returning again and again to his integrity and his dignity:

> M. McKinley occupies his high office with the simple majesty that becomes the first magistrate of a democracy of which the universe henceforth expects an essentially peaceful and civilizing conduct.[42]

These papers were incensed at the hateful attack against the "most democratic head of the freest people," but they said little about his ties to the trusts or the negative aspects of the imperialism that had come into its own during his watch. A head of state, especially if he was assassinated, simply had to be a great man.

A more centrist paper, *Le Temps*, carefully balanced its arguments between the reference to the leader who "inaugurated the new America" and veiled criticism of the man who, in the end, was rather too beholden to his friends and to public opinion. To this it added various thoughts about political assassination, the danger that anarchists represented both in America and in Europe, and the need to restrict access to the American President who could now be threatened like any ordinary monarch.

On the other side, *La Petite République* and *L'Aurore* were indignant about the excessive condolences addressed to this "happy bourgeois, the champion . . . of the plutocracy, of protectionism and imperialism" and saw McKinley as no more than the man on whose orders the Cubans were put to the sword and the Filipinos massacred, and who had systematically defended the employers against the workers. No, the assassinated President was not a tyrant, but Czolgosz, the assassin, was neither a Socialist nor an anarchist, but simply a lost soul:

---

42. G. Deschamps, "Une audience de Mc Kinley," *Le Figaro* (14 Sept. 1900).

There happened to be a man who naively thought that he could finish off the entire regime by doing away with the one who is its soul. This man is mad, for the regime is held together by an infinite number of causes and circumstances that have nothing to do with the President. But what has produced this madman, other than the very causes that have brought forth this regime and have made M. McKinley the most visible representative of an abhorrent policy?[43]

With the exception of such systematic denunciations, which had little to do with McKinley as a person, his sudden death thus gave him a certain historical stature and saved him from total oblivion or serious obloquy, even if one perfidious pen suggested that he would be more advantageously compared to the obscure conservative prime minister of France, Jules Méline, than to Napoleon.

The French thus counted McKinley, for a time, among the great men since Lincoln, but the fact is that he did not really stand out amidst the general mediocrity. The insignificance of his Democratic opponent, which was a lucky break for him, propelled him into the limelight, but this did not enhance his charisma. This situation changed abruptly with the advent of his successor, whose conduct was of great interest to the correspondents who covered the death of the "high priest of the Golden Calf."

Here, finally, was the rich and powerful personality for whom the French had long been waiting, the kind that was to belie Bryce's thesis, a man of different stature than those pale imitations of great men, Cleveland and McKinley, who had been all there was.

## AND THEN, ROOSEVELT, AT LAST

Although Theodore Roosevelt had held several important offices, he was little known by the French before he was placed on the Republican ticket in 1900. To be sure, the very best connoisseurs of American politics had heard of him in his role as head of the Civil Service Commission, then about his firm measures against the "machines" during his term as governor of New York, and finally about his flamboyant activity at the head of the Rough Riders, but for most French observers he was still a name that did not mean very much.

It was not long before the French recognized his name and his face on

43. M. Charnay, "Les raisons du fou," *La Petite République* (10 Sept. 1901). The paper protested against the dispatches that depicted the assassin as a Socialist and against the search for accomplices that suggested the possibility of a conspiracy.

a large number of books and brochures and before he was frequently seen on the front pages of the French dailies. Teddy was to stay at the top of the French list of important Americans until he was supplanted, much later, by Woodrow Wilson.

## The Irresistible Rise of Roosevelt

When the former undersecretary of the Navy accepted the nomination as Vice-President, most of the French commentaries simply ignored him, and none of the dailies mentioned his existence. All eyes were fixed on McKinley, and everyone knew that Vice-Presidents rarely played an important role. The French foreign minister Delcassé therefore had to ask Ambassador Cambon for some information about this individual:

> M. Roosevelt is very ambitious, very intelligent, and totally committed to the imperialist and military policy he has supported in his writing and in his actions. He is an excellent representative of that young Anglo-Saxon race celebrated in the poetry of M. Rudyard Kipling and inspired by the history of M. Seeley.[44]

The diplomat Cambon did not hide the fact that despite many good qualities, among them "energy and uncompromising integrity," the man was often "excessive and adventurous." This judgment did not become widely known, but it reveals that Cambon was impressed by this personage, although he never expected him to be President by 1904.

It was in September 1901, when his rise to the presidency became very probable, that the French became fully aware of the rich and multiple talents of the Vice-President. They suddenly seemed to recall that he had played a very active role in the campaign of 1900, sometimes outshining McKinley, and they closely studied his biography, which revealed the facets of a rather unusual personality. In the weeks after his move into the White House, the French correspondents carefully watched his first initiatives and closely examined his first State of the Union address, delivered in December.

This phase of observation yielded an extremely favorable image of the new occupant of the seat of power in Washington. In the very beginning,

---

44. Archives du Ministère des Affaires Etrangères, NS, Etats-Unis, 1, Cambon to Delcassé, 8 May 1900, fol. 173. The ambassador had once before, in July 1889, drawn attention to the eccentric personality of Roosevelt, who sought popularity at any price but was "by no means a vulgar personality." On 5 March 1901 (ibid., NS, Etats-Unis 2, fol. 6), he repeated his warnings: "It is to be hoped that M. Roosevelt will never come to power, for there is no way of knowing where his desire for popularity and his passion for the extraordinary will lead him."

most of the commentaries were inclined to see continuity, as Roosevelt himself had announced, but very soon the new President showed his mettle. During the transition he exhibited qualities on which *Le Temps* enjoyed expanding: ". . . in everything he did he showed a rarely found energy, composure, fearlessness, refusal to care what people will say, and confidence in his own abilities."[45] *Le Matin*, for its part, envied the Americans for having replaced a "prudent, upright, and knowledgeable head of state" with, quite simply "a man"! The tone was beginning to be set; the French could not see Roosevelt as another McKinley, except for Jean Longuet of *La Petite République*, who depicted him as "one of the most unscrupulous men among the American politicians," who would follow the same imperialist policy dictated by the "capitalists of the great trusts."[46] This was one of the very rare dissenting opinions to be heard at that point.

The prudence with which Roosevelt proceeded in this period reveals how well he had been prepared for his office, and how different he was from the much reviled politicians whom he had not hesitated to fight; this was a decisive asset that gained him the respect and sympathies of the French. But then Roosevelt's literary talent, which they soon discovered, was another and most important asset. The quality of the American Presidents' writing had not often attracted the attention of the French public, which had always set great store by the complementary relation between politics and literature. Now the successor to McKinley had a considerable body of work to his name, and although none of these books had yet been translated into French, Edouard Rod immediately set out to read them. Skeptical at first, the Swiss writer was soon seduced by "strong thinking," a "well-furnished and solid intelligence," and by this "canticle of triumphant strength." In October 1901 it was not yet clear, of course, whether the new President would be able to apply his sometimes contradictory ideas as a "proponent of state intervention," a "practical-minded doctrinaire," and a man of "great and noble aspirations,"[47] but such a man was certainly fascinating.

In the course of his first term, Theodore Roosevelt asserted himself in many areas, whether he directed strong words against the abuses of the trusts, tried to mediate in the long coal miners' strikes of the fall of 1902, or loudly demanded a place for the United States in the world, and

45. "Les débuts d'une présidence," *Le Temps* (15 Sept. 1901).
46. *La Petite République* (8 Sept. 1901); then J. Longuet, "Le Président Roosevelt," *ibid.* (16 Sept. 1901)
47. E. Rod, "Le Président Roosevelt d'après son oeuvre littéraire," *Le Correspondant* (25 Oct. 1901): 242–75. This was the first serious article on this subject before the translations of the President's books came out.

particularly in Central America. On all these occasions, the French reacted in keeping with their political divisions and their own concept of French national interest. Yet the enthusiasm most observers had for the person of Roosevelt continued to be strong and consistent.

Thus, *Le Temps* was particularly full of praise for the policy Roosevelt had followed with respect to monopolized industries. This paper did not hesitate to devote its "Bulletin from Abroad" column to him under such titles as "A Man" or "The Lincoln of the Trusts" and to depict him as a true hero:

> M. Roosevelt will have against him all the giants of finance and their allies, the politicians. All he will have for him is his conscience, public interest, and the lukewarm sympathies of indifferent citizens.[48]

Similarly, the press and the news magazines for the most part admired the moral pressure and the mediation the President exercised during the great strike of 1902, waxing ecstatic over the skill with which he opposed the big employers without yielding to the unions and over the novelty of his approaches. Only the publications of the extreme Left, being mainly interested in the development of the American Socialist movement, wanted to show that despite all his bluster, Roosevelt had been humiliated by J. P. Morgan. Thus it was clear to the French that Roosevelt was an uncontested, young, and popular head of state who had done many good things for his country, and that it was to him that the Republicans, a worn-out party, owed their victory in the election of November 1902.

This great favor is somewhat surprising. For in his first year Roosevelt had mostly just talked about the evil of the trusts and about the tariff and had done no more than evoke a foreign policy based on the Monroe Doctrine. His only undeniable success had been the negotiations to end the strike. Nonetheless the French, especially the French press, were almost excessively enthusiastic about him, even though until then their attitude toward the United States had been rather cool. The correspondents particularly liked the President's appeals to national unity and the lofty views that appeared again and again in his speeches and messages. This way of exercising executive power was attractive, and the ideas of the occupant of the White House, typically American though he was, definitely appealed to the French.

This state of grace between the French and Theodore Roosevelt was well established by the end of 1902 and the situation changed little until the presidential election of 1904. The ups and downs connected with the

---

48. "Un homme," *Le Temps* (18 Sept. 1901).

building of the Panama Canal in the autumn of 1903 were not held against the President but considered the legitimate outcome of his action. The French were glad that their favorite was almost certain to win a second term: "a unique, honest, and energetic candidate . . . whose policy has given his country a luster that flatters the pride of the Americans."[49] *L'Aurore*, no longer as virulent as in the early years, still considered Roosevelt the "champion of the plutocracy and of imperialism" but had to acknowledge the widespread popularity he owed to his largely illusory struggle against the trusts.[50] The few reserves that were de rigueur in the Socialist press were found, curiously enough, in *Le Figaro's* columns by Jules Huret, who, with little appreciation for the personality of the "bear hunter," brought a more nuanced tone to a paper that otherwise remained very favorable to the former Rough Rider.

### A Flood of Adulation and One Sour Note

During his first term, Roosevelt not only became a prominent actor on the national and international political stage, he also formed lasting personal ties with a wide variety of French personalities who came to constitute a group of truly fervent devotees.

Starting in 1903, translations of all his works were published in France, along with several books about him, which made him a veritable mentor in matters of philosophy and morality.

Emile Duthoit admired his "marvelously full life" and reproduced long passages of *The Strenuous Life* on such topics as the education of girls or the role of the state and deplored only a certain lack of mysticism in his hero.[51] Albert Savine, Roosevelt's translator, was totally carried away by his author:

> To Holland, Theodore Roosevelt owes his sedate habits and his solid attitude; to Scotland, his subtlety; to Ireland, his combative and generous aspects; to France, his vivacity, his imagination, and his boldness. Such a mixture of blood is bound to produce a virile, original, sincere, and balanced being.[52]

49. Archives du Ministère des Affaires Etrangères, NS, Etats-Unis, 3, Jusserand to Delcassé, 3 May 1904. Here again the ambassador's warm feelings for the President are obvious, but his attitude was widely shared in France. Parker, the Democratic candidate, was almost totally ignored.
50. "L'élection de M. Roosevelt," *L'Aurore* (10 Nov. 1904). The criticism remained sharp, of course, but *L'Aurore* had to accept the fact that the American people, and not just some horrid plutocrats, favored Roosevelt.
51. E. Duthoit, *Les idées du président Roosevelt* (Lille: A. Amorel, 1903).
52. A. Savine, *Roosevelt intime* (Paris: Juven, 1904), p. 2.

The anecdotes taken from the President's public and private life yielded the portrait of a man full of energy and vigor who knew how to breathe a new spirit into everything he touched. He brought civic spirit to New York, patriotism to Cuba, and efficiency and innovation to the administration he directed. Léon Bazalgette was not to be outdone when he devoted a hagiographical brochure to this remarkable man who created around himself "an atmosphere of freedom and heroism":

> All told, he presents a fine example of modern man, who loves the present, whose eyes are not turned inward, backward, or heavenward, and in whom the spirit of free rather than fictitious democracy acts powerfully. A born leader, he has remained simple despite his fierce demeanor; he is in touch with himself and with humanity, and his natural boldness is counterbalanced and controlled by a fundamental wisdom and a vigorous common sense.[53]

That a few overenthusiastic hack writers were taken with admiration for an American President who made every effort to project a favorable image is fairly easy to understand, but the admiration Roosevelt aroused was much more widespread than that.

Before long, Roosevelt became a veritable cult figure for travelers of very diverse backgrounds, people who had no professional reasons to seek contact with him. Minor authors spoke of him with reverence, and such writers as Abbé Félix Klein, Pastor Charles Wagner, and the very Catholic Thérèse Vianzone considered themselves so close to their shared hero that they did not hesitate to dedicate their books to him, complete with extravagant dedications.[54] What did they have in common, a priori, the priest who admired all things American, a Protestant pastor who deeply appreciated their value, and an intimate woman friend of the prominent right-wing nationalist and anti-Semite Paul Déroulède? Yet all three were much taken by this man who received them most graciously, using a few words of French, and who struck them as the very incarnation of American energy, and moreover endowed with nobility of vision as well as practical wisdom.

---

53. L. Balzagette, *Théodore Roosevelt* (Paris: Sansot, n.d.), p. 10.
54. F. Klein, *Au pays de la vie intense* (Paris: Plon, 1904), pp. 237–42. Klein asked the President for permission to dedicate his book to him; its title was taken directly from one of Roosevelt's books and the dedication reads: ". . . from an admirer of his ideas and his courage." C. Wagner, *Vers le coeur de l'Amérique* (Paris: Fischbacher, 1906), is also dedicated to Roosevelt, "a magnanimous and peaceful man," as is T. Vianzone's *Impressions d'une Française en Amérique* (Paris: Plon, 1906). In addition to the dedication, this book features a frontispiece showing a photograph of the author's hero with a reproduction of his signature.

Félix Klein said that this was the most interesting person he had ever met – along with Cardinal Lavigerie – someone who constantly sought to elevate and ennoble his fellow citizens and to inspire them to generous actions; he felt that the President endeavored to do the right thing in every domain. In Charles Wagner's opinion, the man was "decisive," "careful," and brimming over with "concentrated strength"; the worthy pastor positively purred at the contact with this cordial man of power, particularly when he was invited to spend the night in the White House, where his host congratulated him for his book *La vie simple* (The Simple Life), which had even been translated into English. Thérèse Vianzone, who was more interested in the familial virtues of the President, expressed similar feelings and was delighted to be welcomed in this manner.

These few persons were not representative, of course, and many other testimonies were rather more discreet; yet it is a fact that between 1903 and 1904 there was a group of loyal French "Rooseveltians" who spread the good word everywhere. It was as if, unable to find a man of such stature in France, they set out to amplify what most of the dailies were saying. Even men as different from the host of the White House as the worker-delegates to the Saint Louis World's Fair could appreciate the example shown to them there: ". . . he makes me feel a little better about the presidency of a truly democratic Republic,"[55] one of them exclaimed!

It appears, then, that a majority of French opinion, regardless of political divisions, was very favorable to Roosevelt from the very beginning of his presidency, but this does not mean that so spectacular a figure did not also elicit a few rather sour judgments, even outside the extreme Left, whose ideological condemnations were as terse as they were definitive.[56]

Roosevelt's forceful personality was bound to irritate a few people who were turned off by this well-orchestrated exhibition of manly force, national pride, and civic preaching. Some ironic comments about the great man "who pronounced himself to be one" or Anatole France's accusation that so outraged Jusserand, to the effect that Roosevelt wanted to create "an America that was mistress of the world"[57] – all of

---

55. J. Malbranque, *Exposition de Saint Louis, délégation ouvrière* (Paris: Cornély, 1907), p. 255. His fellow workers were more discreet, but never very critical of the American presidency.
56. These were systematic and long-lasting positions which, first adopted at the time of McKinley's assassination, continued to be held until 1912, with *L'Humanité* simply taking them over from *La Petite République*. For *Le Matin* any American President was automatically a great man; for the leftist papers, he had to be a baneful bourgeois.
57. A. France, *Sur la pierre blanche* (Paris, 1905), p. 236.

this remained marginal. By contrast, the statements of Urbain Gohier, Jules Huret, and Paul Adam went much further; all three, with their very different backgrounds, criticized the President of the United States for his excessive activity:

> In his speaking tours, M. Roosevelt gives as many as eight speeches a day to tell the American people that he is the greatest, most glorious, most intelligent, most energetic, most generous man in the world. To this he adds the most hackneyed commonplaces of everyday morality and bourgeois aesthetics. The crowds love him.[58]

Paul Adam, for his part, felt that despite all the wreaths the French were weaving for him, Roosevelt did not have the culture, nor the subtlety, nor the breadth of vision of his Parisian counterparts from Doumer to Poincaré, from Clemenceau to Jaurès, and that he would not be as successful if he were at the head of a European country that was less privileged than the United States. As for Jules Huret, he characterized the President as a "muddle-headed braggart" who was too pleased with himself, too proud of his country, and possibly dangerous because of his fascination with force. None of these critics cast doubt on Roosevelt's democratic disposition – even if Urbain Gohier claimed that he was unintentionally fostering his country's transformation into an "imperial demagogy" – nor even on his sincerity, but they found him too flamboyant, too much of a swashbuckler, too American, and lacking the refinement and the sophistication of a European.

Thus the criticism of Roosevelt was never unqualified and did not amount to outright condemnation, but it did express a shying away from an individual who did not conform at all to the French ideal of the statesman. That is why the influence of the French supporters and admirers of the President of the United States remained preponderant, for they found in him qualities and examples that would be just as valuable in France, where divisiveness and derision were excessively cultivated to the detriment of efficiency and simplicity.

### *Triumph and Competition: Paris and Wilson*

Roosevelt's second term was marked by great achievements: the Peace of Portsmouth, which brought the President a Nobel Peace Prize in 1906; initiatives to promote the international meetings at The Hague that envisaged outlawing war; the discreet support for France at the Algésiras Conference; and sending the American fleet around the world. All of this

---

58. U. Gohier, *Le peuple du XXe siècle* (Paris: Fasquelle, 1903), p. 185.

was attentively watched by the French and further enhanced his standing. By contrast, the uncertainties of America's domestic situation, marked by the recession of 1907 and by the problem of the trusts, while followed with a certain interest, did not fundamentally hurt Roosevelt's popularity in France. No, he had not succeeded in every area, but he had continued to show a fierce determination and had never given up, and so his qualities as a man won out over strictly political judgments.

This general attitude became fully explicit when Roosevelt's term came to an end and he seemed ready to retire from active political life; it was time to take stock.

Some observers asked questions about the scope of "Teddy's" achievements; and while everyone agreed that his had been a "historic presidency," it was also clear that the exercise of power had taken a certain toll. The President had seemed to deploy little activity during the economic upheavals of 1907 and had let things take their course, and the fact that he still unleashed his tirades against monopolized industries in his last State of the Union address was also cause for concern. Did this mean that his action over the last seven years had been ineffective, that he had confined himself to demagogic speech-making? The machine seemed to be falling apart, and certain initiatives of the President, such as sending the Navy around the world, looked rather like a flight forward.[59]

Yet such skepticism did not last long, and the final evaluation was very positive. How could one fail to admire a man who voluntarily decided not to seek another term? This was an indication of democratic rectitude that greatly impressed the French, even if in America some malicious tongues claimed that this was nothing but a maneuver in preparation of a later candidacy. André Tardieu eventually also became a fervent admirer of the host of the White House, which he visited in 1908; he was particularly impressed with this decision, which is rarely seen in politics. Besides, had not Roosevelt seen what needed to be done before anyone else and pursued his goal with determination despite a great deal of criticism when he loudly and clearly asserted his country's place in the world? Had he not fully played his role by "stretching to the point of exhaustion the energies of the American nation"? His successor, Taft, for all his administrative talents and affable demeanor, looked rather dull and gray next to him, a Sancho Panza after Don Quixote. In fact, the personality of the outgoing President dominated the election, and he managed until the very last days of his term to appear everywhere with astonishing energy.

59. R. Michaud, "Lettre d'Amérique," *L'Opinion* (9 Jan. 1909): 54–55.

The French did not understand why Roosevelt had to deal with so much opposition in his country – the Senate, business, the unions – concluding that "the Americans have not been easy on Roosevelt, who is as it were one of the glories of Europe." André Tardieu did not hesitate to declare:

> Europe, which holds President Roosevelt in high esteem, has judged him better than some of his compatriots. It has discerned from afar the strongly drawn outlines of the goals and the results of his action. It has understood that the eight years of his presidency will mark a most important period in American history.[60]

Very soon, little attention was paid to Taft, and many of the French began to miss his predecessor's face. What a wonderful surprise it was therefore to see him alight on the Parisian pavement in person during the first visit of an American ex-President, whose presence attracted almost as much attention as if he were still in office.

In addition to the extremely warm welcome he was given by the population and by the authorities, Roosevelt's stay in Paris in April 1910 afforded all the newspapers the opportunity to express their opinions about him without having to worry about possible repercussions on the domestic or foreign policy of the United States. The usual misgivings were still present, so that the press of the extreme Left almost totally ignored the visitor, while some of the conservative papers spoke with a certain disdain of this "semi-barbarian," but the general tone of the press was highly favorable.

Many journalists only now discovered Roosevelt's personality; all of them were struck, just like the people who had visited him, by his frankness, his simple and direct manners, and by his apparently sincere expressions of positive feelings for France. The papers frequently recalled the positions he had taken during the crisis with Germany four years earlier, but they always coupled such considerations with the certainty that they were dealing with one of the strongest personalities of their time: "Truly, few men have attracted more widespread attention, and few, we hasten to add, have deserved it more." Sentiments similar to this one expressed by *L'Aurore*, which had now become less strident, were also found in *Le Temps* and *Le Figaro*. The man was actually much more famous than any office he might have occupied, even if French traditionalists were by definition uncomfortable with the visit of a great man without title or protocol.

For those who celebrated his presence, Roosevelt represented a rare

---

60. A. Tardieu, *Notes sur les Etats-Unis* (Paris: Calman-Levy, 1908), pp. 101–2.

triumph in the democracies of the time, that of the concept of authority firmly associated with the meticulous safeguarding of liberty, as well as the demonstration that a strong man can wield power without becoming a tyrant. The President of a republic could really preside without creating a dictatorship. For this reason the example of the American ex-President was of universal value and could be followed in France itself. Roosevelt's speech on "the Duties of the Citizen" at the Sorbonne was so well received precisely because it met the public's expectations. Beyond that, Roosevelt turned out to be an excellent speaker, which was rare in an American politician and constituted an extra asset in the opinion of the French, who attached great importance to rhetorical flourishes.

France might overcome its divisions and abandon its habitual distrust of the true American elites whom Roosevelt had shown in such splendid light: ". . . he is a man who never comes unstrung. May his visit and his 'case' inspire us with some salutary thoughts."[61]

By the end of his visit, the former colonel of the Rough Riders thus reached the apogee of his popularity in France. He was seen as a well-rounded human being, the image of the "honnête homme" of the early twentieth century, "impetuous, as brave as a buccaneer, as cultivated as a scholar, as hardy as a cowboy, and intractable in matters of honor."[62] A more versatile, complex, and subtle figure than many had thought, he was an extremely telling exemplar.

The harmonies of this concert of praise almost drowned out all criticism of the hero. All that could be heard was Georges N. Tricoche, acting like an American, who felt it useful to recall that for all the grand phrases that were so well received in Europe, the "demagogue-dictator" had accepted campaign money from the reviled trusts and had demolished more than he had built during his presidency. *Le Correspondant* echoed Tricoche by insisting on the imperialist and "jingoist" character of the personage, who had gotten along perfectly well with the party machine he had vowed to eliminate. These isolated and sporadic criticisms were not devoid of truth, but how much could they mean to an opinion dazzled by the vivacity and the reputation of this unusual statesman, for whom many French envied the United States?

Yet the circumstances of the infighting within American politics during the last two years of Taft's term inevitably tarnished Roosevelt's pres-

---

61. *Le Figaro* (28 April 1910), just before he left for Brussels.
62. R. Millet, "T. Roosevelt et la constitution américaine," *L'Opinion* (23 April 1910): 514. The ambassador compared the day's hero to Washington and Lincoln and spoke of the first "president of the world."

tige. He was blamed for having made a very bad choice when he designated as his successor a man who represented the worst aspects of the Republican Party. Moreover, the resurgence of old problems served to demonstrate the truth of what certain malicious tongues had asserted years earlier, namely that the actions of the former President had little effect. Then too, Roosevelt's attempt to split from the party, while showing that he had lost none of his energy or ambition, also demonstrated that the Republican Party no longer had anything in common with him. And finally, the relative radicalization of "Teddy's" way of speaking was cause for concern; the conservatives who had appreciated his moderation saw him take a turn toward extremism; as for the Socialists, they sneered as they watched him align himself with certain positions of their American comrades and their evocation of his "neo-boulangism" carried more weight than it had done earlier. To be sure, many of the French still liked this daredevil fellow who had so often surprised them; he was the only real national leader, and almost above the parties.

Until the Democratic convention in Baltimore, Roosevelt's chances of gaining another term did not seem too poor, but that body's laborious choice of Woodrow Wilson placed him into a well-nigh inextricable situation.[63] The two men appealed to a very similar constituency, and his rival impressed him as a truly remarkable opponent.

In early 1912, Woodrow Wilson was still unknown to almost all French observers, as well as to many Americans, but they all soon discovered a most capable man, whose positions on combating the trusts or reducing the tariff were more forceful and outspoken than those of the former President. At this point the French journalists asked their American colleagues for information, and on inauguration day one of them was able to enlighten the readers of the *Revue des Deux Mondes* about the new President. What gradually emerged was the image of a genuine, "thoughtful and sagacious" intellectual – more solid than his predecessor – deeply influenced by progressivism, even radicalism, but not devoid of practical sense, as shown by the positions of university president and state governor he had held earlier. The man had convictions and the means to implement them.

Under these circumstances it would take some extraordinary events to make Roosevelt win the race. *Le Matin* still pretended to believe it possible, but after the attempt on his life in which the ebullient colonel was slightly wounded, *Le Correspondant* said ironically: "Well now, if

63. "La convention de Baltimore," *Le Temps* (4 July 1912). This was a particularly lucid and pertinent analysis; the paper, despite its fondness for Teddy, spoke of a "terrible blow" to him.

M. Roosevelt with his taste for noise and theatrical effects were pushed into the presidency by a pistol shot, that would really be American!"

Wilson's victory was welcomed in France, for he represented a different and more pro-French policy, but although he was respected, he remained virtually unknown and no one seemed to care. Yet his accession to power was seen as symptomatic of an important development in American political mores that had been initiated by Roosevelt:

> In a country where over the last twenty years politics had become the private property of a small number of unscrupulous individuals of the most mediocre intellectual and moral caliber, and where the epithet "politician" had become pejorative, the mere fact that a university professor consented to run for elective office was bound to cause a sensation.[64]

Until the war Wilson's personality remained very remote, and it was not until 1917 that the French became truly interested in him, but then it was only a few months before he overshadowed the familiar figure of "Teddy."

Despite this final eclipse, the figure of Theodore Roosevelt was the one that for a good ten years made by far the deepest mark on French opinion. Indeed, one can confidently assert that he was one of the Presidents of the United States who aroused exceptionally warm feelings in France, where he had his court and his biographers. The role played by his successor in 1918 would give rise to enthusiasm and admiration, but this had to do with the momentary situation and was not marked by strong personal sympathies. The same can be said about Roosevelt's nephew Franklin, and it was probably not until John F. Kennedy that such intense feelings of friendship were seen again. This shows the altogether exceptional place "Teddy" occupies in American political life as seen by the French.

Roosevelt was without doubt the tree that for a time hid the forest from view, for the French showed no real interest in any of the diverse aspects of American political life. Parties that became harder and harder to distinguish, with their complex, confusing, and shameful ways of doing things, politicians who disgraced the American democracy, "machines" that manipulated and corrupted the voters, all of this deeply disappointed even the most admiring observers of the institutions of the United States.

---

64. L. Aubert, "W. Wilson élu président des Etats-Unis," *Le Figaro* (7 Nov. 1912). This was a thoughtful commentary, which in similar form also appeared in the *Journal des Economistes* and in *Le Correspondant*.

In the end, the French concluded that their own system, in which the parties were no more than general staffs without troops, and in which the political leader was quite simply recognized by his talents as a speaker and legislator, was the better one, even if the President was a bit lacking in personality.[65]

65. Hence the reflection of Jusserand, who knew the United States very well, on the occasion of the death from a heart attack of Vice-President Sherman on 2 November 1912: "The kind of life led by American politicians, and one might almost say by all Americans, who must constantly be on their toes, makes this kind of illness extremely prevalent" (Archives du Ministère des Affaires Etrangères, NS, Etats-Unis, 5, Jusserand to Poincaré, 2 Nov. 1912, fol. 40.).

# 8

# *The New World of Education*

If many of the French saw the American political model as a shining example in the early nineteenth century and a little beyond, it may have been because the United States had the decisive advantage of being a democracy functioning at its best at a time when France seemed happily determined to evade any form of institutional stability. What seemed surprising was that a new country, whose remnants of savagery were often underlined by French observers, should be able to set the example of a successful school system. And surprise is precisely what French observers, many of whom were very thorough, regularly experienced as they examined various aspects of American education.

Their comments followed the development of the educational system of the United States, from preschool to the university, as it came into being, but they also studied it in relation to the educational upheaval France was undergoing at this time. The American elementary school, which had existed for a long time, actually changed with the introduction of public education in the South and with the need to include large numbers of immigrants; at almost the same time the Third Republic implemented the Ferry Laws which gave it the system of elementary education that was to serve it so well. Similarly, the American universities and colleges entered their phase of greatest growth and influence at the end of the nineteenth century, at the time when France achieved a powerful renewal of its higher education.

The dominant impression of the French observers was highly favorable, and they sought to find out what made it so and whether this example could be applied to the French experience.

## A FINE AND ENGAGING EXAMPLE
## OF PUBLIC EDUCATION

The fact that the United States had an illiteracy rate of only 20 percent, despite the diversity of its population and considerable regional differences, motivated the French to look into the American elementary schools.

### *Secular, Free, but Not Necessarily Compulsory*

What the French discovered was a school system based on these few principles years before their own was governed by them.

There was no trace of a Ministry of Public Education, all there was was an office to keep track of educational statistics. There was no national uniformity, and yet a great deal more money was spent on public education than in France. This was the first surprise:

> When it comes to expenditures for public education, America shows the exact opposite of what is practiced by the European governments. In the New World, public education takes from the war budget as much as the war budget takes from public education in the Old World.[1]

The comparison was not very convincing, but it shows how difficult it was for a Frenchman to understand how such a school system functioned. Actually, the painstaking studies of Célestin Hippeau and Ferdinand Buisson[2] had acquainted the specialists in the educational field with the great efforts the United States had made from the very beginning to set up a school system that would meet the needs of the country. What was created took into consideration both the desires of the Puritan populations of New England, for whom reading the Bible was paramount, and those of the advocates of universal suffrage, who felt that schooling would overcome the heterogeneous character of American society. The public school was thus from the outset something everyone wanted and everyone helped organize: "If this country has become what it is, it is literally thanks to the public school."

1. J. Delprat, *Compte rendu sur l'Amérique du Nord et l'exposition internationale de Philadelphie* (Toulouse: Imprimerie Viatelle, 1877), p. 7. The author headed the delegation of workers from Toulouse. Other delegations did not report on educational matters. Delprat's argument was confirmed by Hippeau or by Chotteau's *L'instruction en Amérique* (Paris: Bibliothèque des Travailleurs, 1873). All these authors were Republicans, and proud of it. Such comparisons were no longer made after these years.
2. C. Hippeau, *L'instruction publique aux Etats-Unis*, 3rd ed. (Paris: Didier, 1878); F. Buisson, *Rapport sur l'instruction primaire à l'Exposition universelle de Philadelphie en 1876* (Paris: Imprimerie nationale, 1878).

The federal government did not have to play a decisive role, except that of financing educational establishments by property taxes. Everywhere, schools were born out of the will of the citizens and the municipalities, which agreed to make them accessible to all by keeping them free of charge and religiously neutral, so that none of these schools were beholden to anyone. Such a description is rather too idyllic, even if Hippeau and Buisson hastened to point out that they had seen and studied only the schools of the Northeast, and that at the time of their writing, education in the South was a complete disaster because public schools, the famous "*common schools*," were still quite rare.

To many observers, there was something fascinating about the functioning of such a system, even if they perceived only its major outlines. In the 1870s the French Republicans saw it as a kind of model: a school for all, financed by the parents themselves, truly democratic, protected from religious pressure, where the son of the worker was the classmate of the son of the employer. But more conservative, especially Catholic, circles also saw the virtues of a decentralized school system, in which families played an essential role and in which religion, while not taught, was by no means combatted. The subsequent appearance of offices of education in various states and the few efforts to centralize school systems here and there were worrisome to these fierce supporters of autonomy, as well as to the American Catholics themselves, but in the mid-1870s French conservatives were quite favorably impressed by the system of elementary schools that had been established in the United States.

Would this broad consensus concerning the American school be helpful for dealing with the question of school reform in France? It was not well rooted or general enough to justify this hope. But the fact is that once they had come to power, the Republicans, and in particular the new Director of Elementary Education, Ferdinand Buisson, would establish a system of free, secular, and compulsory elementary schools. Catholic critics hastened to denounce the inappropriate use of the American example:

> Since we are going to be subjected, by the will of M. Jules Ferry and M. Paul Bert, to a system of public schools analogous to the American system, it is surely in order to find out what this system has produced in America.[3]

This critique went on to remark that the French ministry had taken everything that was bad in America and left aside everything that was

---

3. Abbé Martin, "Les écoles américaines jugées par un Américain," *Le Correspondant* (10 March 1881): 877–902. The author was professor at the Ecole supérieure de théologie of Paris.

good, and also that there was no hint of decentralization or of the possibility that members of the clergy could teach in public schools as they did in the United States. To this were added criticisms that certain Americans also leveled against their public schools – failure to impart elementary knowledge and poor reading materials – in order to show that "neutral and secular" schools were bound to fail always and everywhere.

This virulent Catholic critique, which tended to show that the French elementary school, the glory of the Third Republic, had some American roots, had no hesitations about exaggerating the harmful aspects of this model. But an American origin is also attested to by other sources less suspect of trying their best to bring out its nefarious influence. Indeed, if Buisson's highly laudatory report on the American system had a certain success, and if it played a possibly decisive role in his career,[4] it was because it said what people wanted to hear. The general tenor of the principles governing the organization of American schools was particularly well suited to a democratic republic like France, and Ferdinand Buisson was directly inspired by them when he was appointed head of the Ministry of Education. It should be added that the influence of the great American educator Horace Mann was repeatedly pointed out in 1880 and also by Gabriel Compayré writing in 1907:

> The recent history of the founding of the French secular public school is in more than one respect similar to that of the establishment of the American *common school* as conceived and realized by Mann a half-century ago. . . . It is not to detract from the honor due to the founders of French elementary education . . . to say that they were largely inspired by the examples and the ideas furnished by the great American educator.[5]

The French retained only what suited them in the American school and adopted neither decentralization nor the election of the administrators, any more than coeducation, even though these were fundamental aspects of the American system. Yet there is no question that the widely acknowledged success of an essentially democratic and secular school system contributed to the establishment of such a system in France.

In the years following the implementation of the Ferry Laws the relevance of the American example began to fade, somewhat as the

4. Guerlin de Guer, *L'instruction primaire aux Etats-Unis* (Paris: Berger-Levrault, 1880). Both Hippeau and Buisson made it very clear that that they did not think the French should imitate the American system but only let themselves be inspired by it.
5. G. Compayré, *Les grands éducateurs: Horace Mann* (Paris: Delagrave, 1907), pp. 6 and 7.

adoption of a republic in France had weakened the interest in the American Republic. Still, a general consensus of admiration, which did not preclude a certain amount of criticism, continued to prevail. In this connection, nothing is more revealing than the positions of such Catholics as Claudio Jannet or, better yet, the Vicomte de Meaux. Such critics had to acknowledge that the American elementary school worked rather well and that the danger of centralization that had loomed under Grant seemed to have disappeared under Harrison.[6] On the other hand, they gently reminded American Catholics who protested against paying general taxes that could not be used to finance Catholic schools that the Canadian system, in which school taxes were distributed among the various confessional schools in proportion to their student population, could not be applied in the United States, where separation of church and state was the rule. The best they could do was to advise the American Catholics to establish their own schools, making them strong and attractive without jeopardizing the school system as a whole, which was needed to "prepare and cement national unity," a task it did not have in an old country like France, where unity was a matter of course.[7]

Among the proponents of the French type of public school, the value of its American counterpart was a given that was not questioned, as long as one did not look too closely. In 1906 Charles V. Langlois, for instance, spoke derisively of the virtues that certain French commentators, such as Bourget or Brunetière, attributed to the decentralization of the American school system; he himself did not find it superior to the French centralization that avoided the abuses of local authorities and made for better control over the teachers.[8]

The American common school temporarily served as a model for the French, but thereafter the way was cleared for a more serene analysis of the specifics of the school system across the sea.

### *"The School Is the Stomach of America"*

In the United States the elementary school had a social and political function that greatly appealed to the French Republicans. As early as

6. C. Jannet, "L'instruction publique et la liberté de l'enseignant aux Etats-Unis," *Le Correspondant* (10 and 25 Aug. 1891): 422–44 and 643–70. These articles were very moderate by comparison with the author's book of 1876, even if he thought that the United States would have to reconsider the separation of church and state.
7. Vicomte de Meaux, "Les écoles aux Etats-Unis," *Le Correspondant* (25 Feb. 1891): 604 and 617. This very rich article reappeared, in a slightly expanded form, in *L'Eglise catholique et la liberté aux Etats-Unis* (Paris: Lecoffre, 1893).
8. C.V. Langlois, "L'éducation aux Etats-Unis," *Questions d'histoire et d'enseignement* (Paris: Hachette, 1906), pp. 156–58.

1863, Laboulaye had already gone into rapture: "No official lies here, this is the reign of truth. . . . The school equalizes and liberates,"[9] and many others also associated the American school with democracy. However, there was a considerable difference between the American and the French experience, even if the schools became similar. Jules Ferry's secular school was designed to implant the still fragile Republic, and it did accomplish this goal. Yet in doing so it was unable to enlist the support of all French people for this project, which involved overcoming the opposition of the Church and the reluctance of the royalists. This meant that the French school was necessarily militant.

Beyond some incontestable similarities between the two countries' public school systems, the French observers realized that that of the United States had even larger goals than their own. It was no longer a matter of protecting a regime, but of perpetually building a nation, and so it was wise not to refuse the support of religion but to enlist it in this effort: "The greatness of the United States rests on two solid foundations, a deeply religious attitude and widespread education. With this kind of support, a nation can withstand many a storm." Ferdinand Buisson clearly showed this formative role of the American school:

> Without the fusion of races, without a uniform language, without equality among social classes, without the mutual tolerance of all the different sects, and above all without the ardent love for the new fatherland and its institutions, would the United States still be the United States?[10]

His report also indicated the importance of civics and history in the curricula of American public schools. This importance was noted by all French observers throughout the period. It is therefore not surprising to see that the school was considered, even more than in France, as the "rampart of public liberty." This aspect became more and more prominent as floods of immigrants poured into the schools in order to become Americans in their turn; Jules Huret, who was not an expert in education, was struck by this phenomenon: "Here I felt a passionate endeavor to create in this very mixed and very new population feelings of patriotism that are bound to arise without much difficulty."[11]

This American need for a school that would create the nation, or at least continually cement it, did not have its equivalent in France. The web of the French nation seemed destined to last forever, even if it had to be mended from time to time, whereas that of the American nation had

9. E. Laboulaye, *Paris en Amérique* (Paris: Charpentier, 1863), p. 359. Numerous reeditions kept this work up-to-date.
10. Buisson, *Rapport*, p. 3.
11. J. Huret, *En Amérique* (Paris: Fasquelle, 1904), vol. 2, p. 48.

already been torn once and could be torn again if it were not held together by the thread of the school. This was the opinion of all French observers, and for the most unrelenting opponents of the Ferry Laws this was another opportunity to criticize the application to France of principles for which it had no need and which, indeed, were an insult to its past.

If the civic role of the "common school" was comparable, despite a fundamental difference, to that of the French public school, this was not the case when it came to the character formation of the students. American children must be able to ". . . collaborate in the work of building the young civilization, must be prepared for all kinds of action: the making of citizens and people prepared for practical life is therefore the principle of American education."[12]

This was not a strictly utilitarian education devoid of all ideals, but rather a character training that accustomed the child to expressing himself or herself freely, and to take responsibility. All those who visited a school noted that the pupils did not show excessive deference for the male or female teacher – and to their great surprise most were female – and that they spoke up freely and were spoken to as if they were adults in order to develop their ambition. No punishment, no restriction of spirited oral expression, an education "à la Jean-Jacques . . ." – these were the ingredients that would serve to form a genuine American, fearless and sure of himself:

> From kindergarten on, the school constantly calls on the pupils' initiative and makes them exercise their own judgment. Changes in method, curriculum, or subject matter are openly discussed, which puts them in the habit of constantly looking for improvements. The Americans are innovative like their schools. The Europeans are immobile like theirs.[13]

This was one of the essential differences between French and American education. In France, consulting very young students in this manner was out of the question, and furthermore, parents would not have accepted such a liberal school system. Their counterparts across the Atlantic, by contrast, liked this rather unauthoritarian system, which fostered freedom and frankness. Indeed, the treatment of children in school was an extension of the attitude prevailing in the home, where the French often observed what struck them as complete anarchy.

If the behavior of schoolchildren shocked the French visitor, he could not help envying their vitality. French children were no doubt better at

12. M. Dugard, *La société américaine* (Paris: Hachette, 1896), p. 209.
13. Laborer, "Les leçons de choses à l'Exposition de Saint Louis," *Journal des Economistes* (March 1905): 335.

doing written work, at constructing a rigorous argument, and at expressing themselves with delicate precision, but they were less nimble in using their capacities and their knowledge and not as quick to mobilize their energy. The question to be asked was therefore whether the school should produce scholars and dreamers or men of action brought up on the "living lessons of reality." The answer was a priori obvious, but it was easier to give while one was watching this vitality in the United States than after one had returned to the habitual ways of the school and the family in France.

The virtues of the American public schools were many, both on the social and the individual level, since they not only formed citizens but also built a country. The French observers saw only the surface of things, but they did not hide their admiration for "so complete, so spirited, so eminently democratic and liberal" a system of popular instruction.

Yet some felt that this remarkable system had its drawbacks, and that it attained its ambitious goals at the price of a certain excessiveness:

> The public schools, considered to be instruments of civilization functioning like huge industrial machines that produce fast and in quantity, strike us not so much by the perfection of their results as by the powerful means at their disposal. Like the great powers of untamed nature ... they create the present while preparing the future.[14]

### Overly Democratic Schools

The French would not be French if they expressed unqualified admiration for a foreign institution, especially in an area where they had certain pretensions. This unspoken rule applied to the American school system as well, although it did come out with honorable mention in the end.

One of the essential characteristics of education in America, its diversity, was not always clearly perceived by the observers who knew only the Northeastern regions of the United States, either because of the limited development of the West at the beginning of the period or because their investigation was part of their visit to the World's Fairs in Philadelphia or Chicago. Only a handful of persons, who either spent a long time in the States or wanted to find out more, pointed out that the Western schools, "the little schoolhouses on the prairie," were short of money and could not put into practice the fine principles of the typical New England common school; they really had nothing that French rural schools would envy. Some others looked into the meager development

---

14. Hippeau, *L'instruction publique*, p. 201.

of schooling in the South and also found sparse and rather insignificant educational opportunities for blacks and even Indians in only a few places, such as Washington, D.C., and Chicago. Ferdinand Buisson was of course well aware of these problems, which he very honestly pointed out, but they did not alter his idealized vision of the American school system, any more than that of even less rigorous observers.

Another problem was that such a network of establishments made the recruitment of teachers difficult. Normal schools were few and far between, and the qualifications for a teaching position were not very demanding. The great number of women teachers, moreover, which can be explained by their more advanced education and the low pay for teaching, caused an accelerated turnover in personnel. The reason was that young women were willing to teach for a few years before they were married by way of a "kind of conscription," as Paul-Edouard Passy put it. Such a system made for instability and did not allow for true pedagogical improvements. In addition, the free exchanges between pupils and teachers, however nice they might be, were not conducive to more thorough learning: ". . . the participants are charmed but come away with vague notions or false ideas. . . ."[15]

The French related these flaws in part to the decentralized character of the American school system: "It is by popular whim, by the tyranny of the parties, and by the shameful pressure of the politicians that school officials are appointed and, alas, certified as to their competence. . . ."[16] Many of the French visitors, especially those who were teachers themselves, more or less explicitly praised the virtues of the Ecole normale supérieure, the French Ministry of Education, and the inspectors general.

Whatever the causes of these problems, they did cast a shadow on the quality of the teaching that could be performed by more or less competent teachers essentially left to their own devices:

> One is often struck by the hasty, rapid, almost improvised character of this teaching, which trusts good intentions, good sense, and good will, always hopes to speak to the eyes, the memory, and the imagination, and also wants to save time over the old strictly didactic methods, but which in doing so runs the risk of becoming somewhat superficial and sometimes a little too quick to spare the intelligent pupil the severe but fecund labors of abstraction and reasoning.[17]

15. G. Weulerse, "L'éducation publique aux Etats-Unis; impressions et réflexions," in *Autour du monde* (Paris: Alcan, 1904), p. 402.
16. C. Barneaud, *Origines et progrès de l'éducation en Amérique* (Paris-Lille: Savaète Desclée de Brouwer, 1897), p. 16. The author also enjoyed pointing out the errors made by all those who had written about the subject before him.
17. Buisson, *Rapport*, p. 402. This observation made in 1876 is found in analogous terms twenty or thirty years later in the works of Weulerse and Compayré.

Some found that the work of the schools frequently presented an "air of negligence that made you wonder about its true effectiveness," while others stressed the hands-on character of American education, which produced people who knew how to read, write, and count without pushing them any further than a daily newspaper. Surely this was a leveling to the lowest common denominator, no doubt in keeping with the ways of democracy, but most regrettable just the same. Besides, the development of private schools, both religious and nonreligious, was proof that the wealthiest Americans were not always satisfied with such a system; this attitude somewhat reassured the French, who were often attached to a very elitist concept of education.

Such doubts only slightly darkened the general picture of these common schools, which met the needs of American life so well, but the elementary school was not everything.

The kindergarten attracted little attention, even if its usefulness seemed incontestable in a country where children were rather independent of their families at a very young age. In fact, it was not particularly original, since the Fröbel method it used came from Germany, and the freedom of expression was the same as in the elementary school.[18] However, kindergartens were set up by private initiative, and so the disparities were even greater than among public schools. Sometimes the visitors were full of admiration for a marvelous, airy, almost luxurious school for the little ones, at other times they saw a dirty hall where the most elementary rules of hygiene were barely respected.

It was a long time before the French took an interest in this phase of education and began to understand its great importance, and the American initiatives were not sufficient to impress them or really awaken them.

Secondary schools were much more intriguing to the French, for they offered more than just a point of comparison; since this cycle was the crowning glory of their own educational system, they could not develop feelings of inferiority as they did with respect to the American elementary school before 1880.

American high schools, still rare at the beginning of the period, were becoming increasingly prevalent. They raised a great many questions, for they appeared to be the extension of the elementary school without having the autonomy of the French lycées, which meant that there was no distinction between the masses and the elite. While Célestin Hippeau was glad to see this coherent organization, in which the secondary level continued the primary levels, since the selection by classical languages

18. Marie Loizillon, *L'éducation des enfants aux Etats-Unis* (Paris: Hachette, 1883), p. 22.

as practiced in France did not apply, most observers' opinions were much more nuanced. This was in part because the organization of American secondary education was confusing, for the last years of the French lycée corresponded to both the end of high school and the beginning of college. Gabriel Compayré found it hard to understand:

> Just imagine the disorder, the pedagogical jumble, if all of a sudden the lower grades were done away with in our secondary schools and replaced by middle schools (écoles primaires supérieures) which, partly transformed by the introduction of Latin and Greek, offered their heterogeneous teaching, half of it centered on French and the sciences and half of it on classical studies and Greek and Latin, pell-mell to all comers, whether they be the future privileged students of the humanities or the run-of-the-mill aspirants to no more than a somewhat enhanced primary instruction.[19]

In addition to this ironic report Compayré expressed his astonishment that the high schools did not charge tuition, and that this did not provoke protests from parents whose children did not attend these establishments, for most students were not bound for prolonged schooling. Compayré and Langlois, both sincere Republicans, had trouble understanding the citizens' general enthusiasm for a secondary education that was pursued by only a tiny minority of their children, and moreover not very good.

For this reason, American secondary education was no more democratic than its French equivalent, and of lesser quality as well. Given the constant mixing of genres, the teaching done in the American high school was necessarily shoddy and fostered "the inept pride of the half-educated, an intellectual proletariat." The French took careful note of American criticism of the mediocrity of high schools and the poor training they provided for the pursuit of higher education, especially when they were accompanied by praise of the French system.

The American college seemed ambiguous, located halfway between secondary and higher education, but the French appreciated it more since it was decidedly selective and closer to the final years of the French lycée; and besides, the colleges were always private and never tuition-free.

Thus even the most republican French observers were not ready to accept the democratization and the uniformity of the secondary system. If the great French school reform of 1902 that separated secondary education into two cycles bore some superficial resemblances to the

19. G. Compayré, *L'enseignement secondaire aux Etats-Unis* (Paris: Hachette, 1896), p. 5.

American system, it did not unify the various kinds of schooling, any more than it established coeducation. The French attachment to a classical education and to traditional forms of learning was too strong to envisage such an evolution, even among those who praised the organization and the value of a democratic elementary education. These reservations about the very core of the educational system shed light on the profound difference between the American and the French conception of education. However, the general admiration of the French resurfaced when it came to the other end of the educational system, to higher education.

## TRANSATLANTIC UNIVERSITIES

The American achievement in the field of elementary public education and the uncertain status of the secondary system did not prevent a veritable flourishing of universities that fascinated the French. The names of Harvard, Yale, or Stanford evoked visions of a kind of academic paradise that by the late nineteenth century already gave rise to a good bit of envy, especially among members of the French system of higher education, who were inevitably led to frequently depressing comparisons.

### *Diverse, Powerful, and Independent*

It was not until the 1880s that the French became truly interested in the world of American universities. Until then they had simply noted the coexistence of numerous academic establishments which, of a religious character or founded thanks to "charitable millionaires," did not attain a very high level. Hippeau was nonetheless quite optimistic about their development, whereas others felt that with the exception of Harvard or the University of Michigan at Ann Arbor, "true university teaching, such as it is understood in Germany for instance, is still unknown in America."[20] Such reactions were completely justified, for the first great strides of the American universities were made around 1870, when the first doctorates were awarded and improvements were made in the organization of the largest institutions.

Yet gradually the diversity and the multiple possibilities of the American university became fully apparent, despite continued widespread ignorance about them in France. Pierre de Coubertin, for instance, pointed out that around 1890 the French Ministry of Public Education

---

20. M.-C. Ladreyt, *L'instruction publique en France et les écoles américaines* (Paris: Hetzel, 1883), p. 363.

still took Harvard to be an annex of Oxford and had written to President Johns Hopkins of the university of that name.

Such lapses were inexcusable, for the world of the American universities was becoming increasingly well known in France. To be sure, and this was inevitable, the French only knew a small part of these institutions, since they focused on the Ivy League schools and a few other important ones in Chicago or California, all of which astonished them by their distinctive character.

The absence of a single model was one of the first traits to strike them, even after life in America had to some extent accustomed them to this form of permanent and diverse decentralization. The very term *university* was used to designate very different institutions, some of which were in fact colleges that seemed more akin to a secondary school, a situation that accounts for judgments that were as precipitous as they were negative. Moreover, all commentators had to explain to their readers the difference between private and public universities, explain the absence of a national university in Washington, and tell them how under the Morrill Law the federal government was allowed to help fund certain universities, such as Cornell. Once all the pieces of the puzzle were put into place, it was a surprise to find out that these universities were run like businesses, with trustees who managed large endowments and a president who played a major role: ". . . men of broad vision and powerful will, who bring to the training of the young the same ardor that some of their other compatriots expend on the pursuit of wealth."[21] French visitors who had the opportunity of calling on one of these men, Charles Eliot of Harvard, Nicholas Butler of Columbia, and of course Woodrow Wilson of Princeton, were utterly charmed.

This type of organization had absolutely nothing in common with the French university system, for higher education in America had developed mainly according to the German model. But these characteristics did not diminish the enthusiasm of the French observers, who were impressed by the power of these institutions.

The tremendous vitality of these universities was another dominant trait. They were created out of the will of the citizens or their local governments. It was as if a society whose credo was wealth, where there was little time for leisure and intellectual jousts, and where politicians were not interested in literature, was better able than other, more refined societies to pursue the serene and exalted cultivation of the mind far from the everyday passions. Pierre de Coubertin expressed such sentiments when he insisted that off the beaten path there was a "thoughtful

---

21. R.G. Lévy, *La vraie Amérique*, offprint of *La Réforme sociale* (Paris, 1894), p. 15.

and unselfish America that has a great love for learning and moral greatness":

> But the dollar absorbs all the attention, whereas learning is discreet; and travelers will continue for a long time to bypass the small university towns where scantily paid professors are content with their lot, where silent workers ardently pursue their secret aspirations. Instead they will flock to noisy cities filled with strife and speculation, and from there they will bring back the notion of an exorbitant, disorderly, and feverish country at a time when the true America is being built in the shadows, a country that they have not seen at all.[22]

Such a situation explained the total independence of the universities, even the state universities, from the federal government; donations from rich businessmen, even from state governments, served to guarantee this independence considered essential to the flourishing of university teaching and research on which no one wanted to infringe. This was the reason why most universities were so lavishly endowed; French observers were stunned by such wealth. Gabriel Compayré, for example, noted that Leland Stanford's bequest for founding the university of that name had been $30 million – the equivalent of the total assets of the French system of higher education – and continued: ". . . sustained by their enormous wealth, the Americans are positively wasteful, spending extravagant sums on education."

This munificence could have its ridiculous effects – overblown praise, unnecessary luxury – but it sustained a "powerful and constantly reinforced vigor." The origin of the funds did not seem to be a concern, and no one seriously worried about the hold of capital over the universities. Nor did it matter that some universities were still professional schools where only law or medicine were taught, because others, such as Harvard and Yale, had become towers of Babel of knowledge, "veritable academic bazaars" where all disciplines were present. Diplomas were perhaps handed out a bit too easily, classical languages were a bit neglected, and the practical aspects a bit excessive, but the fact remained that the "powerful vitality revealed by the American universities . . . foreshadows a surprising future."

### The Good Life for All

All the French observers marveled at the material conditions enjoyed by the American professors, who had easy access to sumptuously furnished

22. P. de Coubertin, *Souvenirs d'Amérique et de Grèce* (Paris: Hachette, 1897), p. 8.

libraries and comfortably appointed facilities. "It would certainly be nice to study or teach here!" exclaimed a totally charmed Gabriel Compayré. His opinion was echoed by many professors who, whenever they returned to France, praised the neo-gothic beauty of Harvard, the luxury of the University of Chicago, and the pleasant surroundings of women's colleges such as Bryn Mawr or Wellesley – "they could not possibly be more simple and do eccentric things in a nicer way" – and the friendly atmosphere of the social clubs, which were so sorely lacking at the Sorbonne; nor was there any of the bad taste of "certain frescoes and gilded images" of that same Sorbonne.[23] On the contrary, there were bright colors and light, varnished wood, which made it harder to return to France, where black paint was everywhere: "Will we remain forever the people *pledged to black* by way of a kind of mystical link to the lugubrious Middle Ages from which we are still struggling to emancipate ourselves?"

It is easy to understand that these austere men were bowled over by the charm of the grounds, the beauty of certain sites – ah! Stanford! – the handsome buildings, the lively colors. They were certain that good work would be done in such places.

And after all, they did meet American professors in their beautiful and comfortable offices, scholars who had access to all the documentation they needed, although the French were divided in their opinions about these men who often met them in shirt sleeves, without collar or necktie! Yet as they stayed a little longer on these marvelous campuses, the French academics discovered that their American colleagues were not always very well paid and that their teaching loads were much higher than their own. Emile Legouis found that he had worked very hard, putting in twelve hours a week instead of three, without even having to participate in department meetings or teaching at all levels.[24] These differences raised second thoughts about the attractiveness of the American universities, for the French professors could not count on enjoying the advantages given to certain eminent personalities. They found it strange, for instance, that ex-President Harrison was teaching law at Stanford. Could anyone imagine Jules Grévy doing that in Paris?

23. E. Legouis, *Impressions d'Harvard* (Paris: Champion, 1914), p. 20; Langlois, "L'éducation," p. 299; this was one of the few things he liked. Sixty years later the remarks of Legouis and Langlois were sometimes repeated in the same terms in connection with the Sorbonne and the American universities, but by that time the tone was one of utter despair.

24. Legouis, *Impressions*, p. 14. The same remarks are found in G. Lanson, *Trois mois d'enseignement aux Etats-Unis* (Paris: Hachette, 1912), p. 146, and in E. Rod, *Réflexions d'Amérique* (Paris: Flammarion, 1905), p. 61.

But there could not be universities without students, and those who populated the American establishments studied and played in most agreeable ways.

Although in the United States, as in France, universities only educated an elite, the matter of financial requirements was rarely broached by French observers. At most, Urbain Gohier commended President James of Northwestern University for lowering tuitions without lowering standards or admired Berkeley for admitting Californian students free of charge, but he was the only one to mention these subjects.

What struck the French observers most were the living conditions of the students; except at a very few urban universities, they were living together in marvelous places. Housed in dormitories, they had private rooms they could furnish as they wished and receive any guest they pleased, albeit at certain times only; and all of this was equipped with all the modern conveniences. To this must be added the famous "clubs" organized for students with similar backgrounds under the patronage of alumni, where one went to drink, talk, and train for formal debates. Paul Bourget, who, along with many others, greatly admired the Harvard clubs, was particularly interested in the fact that poor students worked at the most humble jobs in order to participate in the various activities, while Charles-Victor Langlois was rather more skeptical, comparing the lot of those who had to work to pay for their education to what would have gone on in France in the Middle Ages. He also felt that this situation could not last forever.[25]

These living conditions created a veritable esprit de corps that came into play whenever the honor of the university was at stake.

Sports, of course, constituted the ideal occasion, and the French were amazed to see the role played by university sports, the reverence students had for those of their fellows who were tennis or football stars, and the excessive antics of the "supporters." It was good and healthy, of course, to have sports at the university, but the French found it hard to approve of the primacy of sports over academics.[26]

Nothing here was comparable to the life of French students, who lived in rooms whose dark walls and lack of sanitation looked even more sordid by comparison, and who got together in brasseries that seemed particularly wretched when the observer was still under the spell of the "transatlantic universities." Actually, it would have been more accurate

---

25. P. Bourget and A. Tardieu were among the greatest admirers of Harvard; as for Langlois, *L'éducation*, p. 138, he assumed, more correctly, that the states would eventually have to subsidize the universities.

26. Cf. Chapter 5. The problem was stated well by H. Bargy, "Collèges et universités aux Etats-Unis," *Revue de Paris* (1 Aug. 1904): 806–26.

to compare the life of the American students, except for some material details, to that of the preparatory classes, followed by one of the *grandes écoles*, which also fostered an esprit de corps and were not totally unacquainted with sports. However, an essential difference had to do with the much more open and less narrowly elitist character of the American universities, and with the purer air one breathed there: "This contrast shows how much better the Americans understand democracy than we do."

However that may be, the impression made by these students, and by students living under very similar conditions elsewhere, was highly favorable: "Here one can breathe more deeply, move more freely, and live more independently than elsewhere," exclaimed Ferdinand Brunetière before he returned to France.[27]

Given these general features, which appealed to even the most jaundiced observers, each university had its special admirers, and it is quite likely that our observers' judgments about intellectual accomplishments were not totally unrelated to a delightful atmosphere.

While they did not draw up an actual honor roll of American universities, the qualities that French observers praised in assessing some of them are rather significant. Thus Harvard, the oldest and best known of these institutions, did not win immediate approval. In the 1890s Coubertin as well as Compayré criticized its chaotic organization into separate schools, "a confused and rather clumsy imitation of the English universities." Moreover, the reforms undertaken by Charles Eliot, the efforts to adapt the university to an industrial society, and the professional training delivered by certain schools seemed shocking to the French, who were committed to the pursuit of studies for their own sake. Yet as the years went by, the development of classical studies and the brilliant performance of the department of French literature, along with the prestige of the university, definitively made Harvard one of the favorites of the French.[28]

Cornell University was of interest from its foundation, for was it not a symbol of democratic America, where a public institution could be endowed by the millionaire Ezra Cornell, "the American Tolstoy," as Coubertin called him, with the aim of creating – oh utopia! – a tuition-free university open to all, regardless of gender, color, or religion.

27. F. Brunetière, "Dans l'Est américain, New York, Baltimore, Bryn Mawr," *Revue des Deux Mondes* (1 Nov. 1897): 119.
28. This was made possible, in particular, by faculty exchanges between Harvard and Paris. These are described in C. Cestre, *Une grande université américaine* (Dijon, 1899), and by Legouis and Langlois.

Among the others, Chicago stood out for the means, considered excessive by the French, that had been provided by Rockefeller, but the French did not really like it. Nor did Columbia, an urban university, please them, perhaps because it reminded French travelers who had become used to beautiful campuses too much of the Latin Quarter and French university towns.

Many more remarks of this kind could be cited. They all attest to the French fascination with places that so pleasantly linked high-quality education with an agreeable way of life.

### Very Ambitious, and Rightly So

As all observers pointed out, a university diploma never provided direct access to employment, and because of the diversity of these institutions, the value of an education was not uniform. Nonetheless, the role of the universities was essential, for they occupied a position that would be held by other institutions in France. Taking the place of salons, academies, learned societies, or officers' clubs, they held together the largest part of the country's elites. As Henry Bargy pointed out at the beginning of the twentieth century, the Americans' admiration for the self-made man did not mean that holders of diplomas did not reach the top of the social scale more easily, for a diploma was the country's "only title of nobility." Ferdinand Brunetière was of the same opinion when he noted that ". . . by means of these great universities, a whole segment of America is *turning into aristocrats.*"[29]

In this manner the universities contributed to the appearance of an intellectual elite that had been sorely lacking in the aftermath of the Civil War, and French observers who had the opportunity to attend a university were aware of this phenomenon. They found some students whose intellectual level was as high as or higher than that of the French, but also a large number at a decidedly mediocre level. This too was related to the more open character of the American institutions which, although they did produce an elite, were not set up to do only that; they also trained technicians and future industrial managers who were not interested in erudition but in solid, practical know-how. These students surprised the French, who were accustomed to a stricter selectivity; for the Americans came to the bifurcation in their educational path, so dear to the heart of Langlois, at the university, whereas in France this decision had to be made at the secondary level. Langlois was worried that the

29. Brunetière, "Dans l'Est américain," p. 114.

close proximity of advanced and elementary courses might turn the American university into a high school.

This two-fold level and the growth of American universities explain why around 1890 Vicomte de Meaux, a great admirer of the American system, could say: "No civilized society has as few scholars and as many educated people as the United States." Frequently heard ever since Tocqueville, this kind of remark was no longer appropriate twenty years later, for out of the ranks of the educated, scholars in various disciplines began to emerge; it was an evolution that confirmed the optimistic predictions made by Hippeau as early as 1869, by Gohier in 1903, and by many others as well.

The French, then, clearly perceived that beyond their marvelous facilities the American universities succeeded in the two areas that constituted their mission. On the one hand, the culture they purveyed was more "friendly to human beings":

> This has to do with a life of healthy habits and fresh air, and with the fact that of all the peoples on this planet . . . they are the least musty-smelling. Hence an air of health and alert vigor that stands up to the assault of the years for a long time, a freshness of spirit that preserves a taste for new things and new faces.[30]

Moreover, it was clear that "America can expect a fine flourishing from its young universities." What more could one ask; Langlois may have thought that American higher education had nothing to teach to Frenchmen endowed with a solid tradition, but very few of his compatriots agreed. Most of their comments dwelt on various examples the French university system should consider in order to make the most of its incontestable potential. This accounts for the development of mutually beneficial exchanges between French and American university professors: "We in France have a love of perfection in all things and a fine taste in literary and artistic matters that marvelously complement the spirit of enterprise and invention of the genius of America."[31]

This fairly widespread enthusiasm did not seem to stumble over one essential facet of American education from kindergarten to the university: the presence always and everywhere of girls and boys in the same class, and later the importance attached to the development of higher education for women.

---

30. Legouis, *Impressions*, p. 19.
31. R.G. Lévy, "Les étudiants américains en France," *Revue Internationale de l'Enseignement* (Feb. 1897): 111.

## FOR OR AGAINST COEDUCATION?

This question inevitably arose when the French observers came face to face with a phenomenon that called for deep, not to say intimate, reflection. The fact is that while American schools and universities, despite many and important differences, allowed for constant comparisons with the French situation, the schooling of girls was rather more exotic. Not that it was unknown in France, but there had never been a coeducation that seemed to go smoothly, nor a higher education for women that seemed to work out.

### *A Success That Seemed to Defy Morality*

This was the inevitable conclusion, and the French observers, whatever their prejudices, eventually had to recognize that this was a specifically American phenomenon.

> The absolute right of women as individuals to enjoy the same education as men and to develop to the full extent of their abilities does not encounter any opposition in the United States, and this principle is so well accepted that a number of establishments, whether schools, colleges, or universities, are open without distinction to students of both sexes.[32]

This realization could be embarrassing, especially when the traveler was in a position to verify the situation first-hand. It was not too bad in kindergarten or even in elementary school, but in colleges and universities where young men were surrounded by lively young girls in shimmering dresses who talked mathematics or literature, the most honest Frenchmen admitted that they felt uncomfortable, unlike the girls who surrounded them; they laughed at the embarrassment they saw on the brows and in the glances of their visitors. Such reactions, which were more often experienced than admitted, show that the French were facing a reality that was almost totally unknown to them. Not that since Victor Duruy France did not have secondary schools for girls, but they were never mixed and had their own specific curricula. Yet aside from a few summary and ideologically motivated condemnations that were totally out of touch with reality – Claudio Jannet, for instance, felt that coeducation inevitably "corrupted the youth" and contributed to America's demographic decline – most opinions were quite thoughtful. Célestin Hippeau and Ferdinand Buisson, the first to analyze this question in a

---

32. E. Reclus, *L'homme et la terre* (Paris: Librairie universelle, 1908), ch. "Le Nouveau Monde," p. 140.

serious manner, explained very well that American coeducation was not a matter of chance or economic necessity, but a deliberate choice that did not involve any theoretical discussion. The Americans, they said, came close to adopting equality between men and women in pursuit of "effective freedom," a quest for which it was hard to blame them. Girls were educated as if they would have to make their own way in life, and this seemed to correspond to a certain organization of American society with which the school system had to "chime in."

Actually, the schools seemed to function smoothly and even successfully, as even the most skeptical observers had to admit. The first explanation to emerge was reassuring: American schoolchildren were accustomed from a very early age to women teachers who made everyone feel good: "It is to the credit of American women that they live up to the confidence people over there have in their educational abilities."[33]

Such a female authority figure accustomed boys and girls to getting along smoothly and sometimes acted like a mother whose attention and affection was not determined by her children's gender.

Furthermore, there was no reason to doubt the effectiveness of the system. Marie Dugard, who had listened to American critics of coeducation, had to realize that schooling was conducted freely and without apparent tension. Given that the various subjects were neither specifically female nor male, both sexes could be equally successful. Emile Levasseur, who thought about this a great deal, eventually had to admit that coeducation worked well in the United States, the best proof being that more girls than boys graduated from high school, even though they had been in contact with each other from the very beginning of their schooling. Many of these commentators were troubled, but all of them came to the same conclusion as Ferdinand Buisson:

> The system of coeducation of the two sexes in America is neither good nor bad, it is a fact, it is a necessity. At all levels of the educational system, it is the only natural and rational one for this country, and particularly so in places where it would be most shocking to us.[34]

The fact is that the essential problem, the deepest reason for the embarrassment felt and expressed by most of the observers, had to do with moral positions that in their minds the apparent success of the system was unable to override. How was it possible for American boys and girls to rub shoulders in class, especially in secondary school, without

---

33. B. Buisson, *L'enseignement primaire* ... (Paris: Hachette, 1896), p. xvi; the younger brother understood this reality much better than his older brother Ferdinand.
34. Buisson, *Rapport*, p. 110.

experiencing the stirring of passion, which was bound to have a disastrous effect on the students' work and their equanimity?

The Americans seemed to have chosen to create multiple contacts between boys and girls as a way to prepare a peaceful solution to the storms of adolescence, rather than to pursue the same goal by organizing a systematic separation of the sexes as was done in France, so that in the American setting self-control took the place of repression. This was a complete success, for the absence of prohibitions seemed to accustom the two sexes in all serenity to live together without getting carried away or offending morality. A healthy stimulation fostered the studies of both groups, and the boys became more gentle through their contact with girls. There were, apparently, no complaints, and if a few marriages did ensue later, they were probably more solidly anchored than those that had to be concluded in a hurry to smother a scandal. In mixed universities and even in women's colleges it was by no means considered risqué for a young woman to go out unchaperoned with a young man; no one would raise an eyebrow. Such an attitude, surprising as it was, nonetheless seemed to be healthier, at least for young men, than that which made "men of twenty, budding intellectuals, into sighing swains to elderly damsels in the promiscuous atmosphere of a brasserie."[35]

This picture of American coeducation, compelling though it was to most of the French commentators, nonetheless struck them as rather too idyllic. In fact some of them, by way of reassuring themselves about this astounding kind of liberty, did not hesitate to point out that the American laws provided very severe punishments for the villainous seducer, forcing him to marry the abandoned girl, as if this judicial sword of Damocles were the reason for everyone's good behavior; it was the typical reaction of Frenchmen accustomed to the iron rod of the law. However, the most regularly advanced explanation held that there was an American morality that was different from the French norms:

> At the risk of being held up to ridicule, I am saying that in these matters American democracy owes to its Puritan tradition a desirable dignity, which is in itself a powerful tool in education that all societies should make part of the habit of freedom.[36]

Perhaps American morals were no better and no worse than those of the French, but the mask of propriety was always kept up, untouched by winking or bragging, and this reserve seemed sufficient to maintain calm

---

35. A. Tardieu, *Notes sur les Etats-Unis* (Paris: Calman-Lévy, 1908), p. 69.
36. C.V. Langlois, "L'éducation aux Etats-Unis," in *Enseignement et démocratie* (Paris: Alcan, 1908), p. 301. The author became more critical after his return from the United States.

in the schools, although some claimed that the façade was not enough and that it was indeed the "general decency of American morals" that kept the system from collapsing under its abuses.

This moral explanation also explained why coeducation did not seem easily transferable to France; the two societies were just too different. Their Latin passions would overwhelm the French students; the troubling presence of "shining eyes" would be everywhere, and the school system would be unable to cope. Yet the American success made the observers think; would it not be possible to find a compromise between excessive French rigidity and American liberty? Some of them, who had been converted in America, thought so. Lazare Weiller said: ". . . I would vote for coeducation, having observed its advantages in America. Before I went over there, I might have voted against it, imbued as I was with European prejudices."[37]

### What Should Girls Study?

If the French were ready to accept that girls and boys should sit on the same school benches, at least in the United States, they were more reluctant when it came to the subjects that girls were made to study, at least beyond the basic notions of reading, writing, and arithmetic, the truly ungendered subjects called the Three Rs by the Americans. Ferdinand Buisson squarely stated the problem, having seen that Virgil or higher mathematics were no more difficult for girls than for boys:

> It is to be feared that engaging girls in the superficial study of so many scientific subjects will not be sufficient to provide them with useful knowledge, yet perhaps sufficient to give them a thin coating of book-learning. This is one of the serious drawbacks that can ensue from prolonged coeducation beyond childhood. The danger is that women will make it a matter of self-esteem to equal men and to surpass them on their own terrain. And they might be unlucky enough to succeed.[38]

This kind of argument was used, in more or less veiled form, by most of the French observers, both men and women. Did girls really need as abstract and nonutilitarian an education as boys? They could succeed in it, but it would take them away from their true vocation, from the domain over which they were destined to rule: "They often ignore or even disdain

---

37. L. Weiller, *Les grandes idées d'un grand peuple* (Paris: Juven, 1904), p. 314.
38. Buisson, *Rapport*, p. 146. This reflection shows just how troubled the author was, for he was intellectually in favor of coeducation, yet unable to face its concrete consequences.

anything that has to do with the details of the domestic economy and the responsibility of running a household, which they find burdensome and give up gladly."[39] An examination of high school curricula showed that courses in sewing or cooking had totally disappeared and been inadequately replaced by courses in household management that were far removed from daily realities. Here again, the French were perplexed, wondering whether one could refuse girls this freedom on the grounds that it often led them to discard the indispensable domestic virtues.

Sometimes nature seemed to provide a solution that would satisfy everyone. Young American females were not physically able to sustain the effort and the tension demanded by an advanced education. The visitors noticed a "general air of fatigue," a "pallor," a "semi-sickly look" on the faces of female students and some of the schoolteachers, especially in the 1880s. Was it female pride that made them push themselves too hard to reach the level of their male fellow students, or was it a life of too many outside activities, what with nightly outings and poor eating habits? Whatever the answer, it implicitly served to show that studying was not really suitable for young women brought up as freely as the Americans, and by 1894 R. G. Lévy could peremptorily assert that there was a link between "higher education and female sterility."[40] Such arguments were thin disguises for the firmly anchored determination of many French men and women not to allow girls to go in for an advanced education that they simply did not need.

And yet what charm they had, these women's colleges, where girls seemed to grow anything but sickly, canoeing on the lake at Wellesley or enjoying the splendid campus at Smith. Their achievements clearly proved that they could do as well as their male fellow students when they were together at the same institution, as at Cornell, and it was an amusing thought that some day there might be an annex for men at Bryn Mawr or Vassar. But there were other surprises as well for the likes of Louis Madelin or Gustave Lanson, who discovered that these charming young ladies, highly trained in biology, were also reading the French authors of the nineteenth century, even those who were still forbidden in France; at least they would be able to make comparisons with the realities of life.

However, the French did not really approve of such marvels, for these brilliant young ladies would be able to teach a thing or two to their hus-

---

39. Loisillon, *Education des enfants*, p. 89. A similar remark was made by M.-C. Ladreyt, who meant to prove that women were not ready to accept an evolution in the role of women.
40. Lévy, "La vraie Amérique," p. 11. The same remark recurs in Buisson, Ladreyt, Passy, and others.

bands, who would admire them; and in the end all their learning would be used for little more than that. When these girls returned from college, where there was "too much luxury," they would be contemptuous of their families and not use their attainments to find work, for whether they were rich or poor, their destiny was to get married. But now they were too vain to have children – final proof that higher education for women was a failure. This apocalyptic vision did prevent the French from enjoying the time spent at these institutions, where girls were studying among themselves or in the company of boys. Félix Klein was more lucid when it came to problems of unequal education between husband and wife; being a priest, he did not approach this matter in terms of rivalry:

> Whether this is a good thing or not is not the question; and even if it were, I personally would not hesitate to say that if both the father and the mother cannot be educated, it is best for raising the children and for the public good that at least one of them be educated.[41]

Wherever one turns, one thus finds that for the most part the French were always ready with arguments to demonstrate the dire consequences of education for women over the shorter or longer run. The point is that this was a reality with which they simply could not cope, and against which they erected moral, scientific, physiological, or social barriers depending on their time and their circumstances. One senses the ever-present fear evoked by Ferdinand Buisson, the fear of competition. Very few French observers dared look beyond this fear, but Marie Dugard was one of them, for she was convinced, as was Lazare Weiller, by having seen the advantages coeducation and advanced studies could bring to girls. Similar reactions were voiced by Ernest Lavisse, who liked to see a good education for future mothers responsible for the education of their children. There were even French publicity campaigns for coeducation, which often used the American example. However, these voices were quite isolated, and it was not until after 1945 that France, despite some earlier progress, especially in the area of university study for women, established true coeducation of the kind that had so fascinated the French in the late nineteenth century.

Despite these misgivings, which had as much to do with a global conception of society as with education in the narrow sense, American education was seen as wholly admirable by French opinion. Indeed, aside

---

41. F. Klein, *Au pays de la vie intense* (Paris: Plon, 1904), p. 269. Completely in favor of women's education, the author congratulated the American Catholics for their successful efforts in this area.

from a few ungracious remarks about the high schools and the uneven levels of the universities, the admiration was almost unqualified. Elementary education was a remarkably democratic achievement, which may even have inspired its French counterpart, and the universities gave rise to long-lasting enthusiasm that only grew throughout the period; as for women's education, it seemed, if nothing else, to meet the needs of American society.

Does this mean that American education actually became a model? It did not, of course, but it presented marvelous examples that might inspire the French and from which young people could learn valuable lessons. Most revealing in this respect is André Laurie's novel *L'oncle de Chicago, moeurs scolaires en Amérique*, which shows all the advantages American colleges have in store for French youngsters whose family has come to the United States at the urging of that uncle, and these advantages are coeducation, material comforts, workshops for handicrafts, and sports. The parents of course find it hard to get used to this, and especially to give so much freedom to their daughter.[42]

And there, precisely, was the rub. The French could adapt to a system intent on providing education for the greatest number, possibly to the detriment of the most highly educated, for such was the way of democracy, but they could not possibly approve of a social upheaval that would make women the equals of men.

42. A. Laurie, *L'oncle de Chicago, moeurs scolaires en Amérique*, Series "La vie de collège dans tous les temps et tous les pays" (Paris: Hetzel, 1898).

# 9

# *La Belle Américaine*

The fascination American women held for the eyes and minds of the French, indeed all Europeans, was of long standing. It can already be seen among the first observers of the society of the New World, from François-Jean de Chastellux to the great Tocqueville himself. They marveled at the high spirits of young girls, at their poise in every situation, at "the extreme liberty that prevails in this country between persons of different sex before they are married,"[1] and at the resolute bearing that matrons kept up even in the lonely Western pioneer life of those days. This fascination did not fade over the years, and by the beginning of the nineteenth century one regularly finds positive comments on the freedom enjoyed by American women, the near-absence of constraint and discrimination they encountered, and on the role they played in politics.[2]

The continuity of this admiration, which did not preclude certain criticisms, is all the more astonishing because throughout these periods a very different tune was heard in the United States: Women protested against the inequality to which they were subjected, and some of them struggled vigorously to end it, albeit with only partial success. This gap between reality and the image constructed by the French can be explained, however, by the real discrepancy that existed in this domain between Europe and the New World.

Between 1870 and 1914, these views could have changed. American women were able to establish a certain equality in many areas of public life – except the right to vote in national elections – and to make it stick,

---

1. F.-J. de Chastellux, *Voyage dans l'Amérique septentrionale* (Paris: Taillandier, 1980), p. 126. A. de Tocqueville, *Democracy in America*, Stuart Gilbert, trans., vol. 2, ch. 9, "Education of Girls in the United States," and ch. 10, "How the Girl Is Found in the Traits of the Wife."
2. Th. A. Sancton, "America in the Eyes of the French Left, 1848–71," D.Phil. thesis, Balliol College, Oxford University, 1978, p. 244; R. Rémond, *Les Etats-Unis devant l'opinion française, 1815–52* (Paris: A. Colin, 1962), vol. 2, p. 476, for a very superficial overview.

but French women were not idle either, succeeding over the years in breaking some of the locks of their society's ironclad traditionalism. Yet French opinion remained curiously congealed when it came to its perception of the American woman, a figure endowed with extraordinary powers and privileges who fascinated everyone, for she was surely the harbinger of things to come. Looking into the upbringing of girls thus opened a vista, both on an almost unknown world and on an inevitable future.

## THE MISS

There is no doubt that it was she who was most closely watched, being very different from a French *jeune fille*. The first image of the American woman, she did not disappear and "lived on in the features of the married woman."

### *What Zest!*

In more or less explicit form, this expression flowed into the pens of the hundred or so travelers who paid some attention to this beautiful specimen of humanity and was repeated by armchair travelers who took their word for it.

The first surprise was to see young girls walking by themselves in the streets, traveling by themselves on trains, and riding horseback astride at an age when young French girls hardly ever went out without their parents or a chaperone – if they went out at all. Some travelers were astounded at the conversations they could have with one of these lively and charming young creatures: "What vivacious replies! What playfulness! What zest! And along with that, such graceful casualness in her poses, such innocence in her glances! What energy under such seeming frivolity."[3] Such easygoing behavior and apparent independence fascinated the French before it seduced them, for such traits cast a very special light on the functioning of American society. Then too, these young girls did not hesitate to speak first to boys of their own age, saying hello without giving a thought to how this might look.

Before they could ask themselves what such behaviors might mean, the French were simply amazed, for all of this was in total contrast with everything they knew, and the explanation that it had to do with coedu-

---

3. A. de Woelmont, "Une semaine en wagon," *Le Correspondant* (15 April 1879): 353; there are many examples of such brief encounters.

cation was not enough to reassure them. What made it worse was that all Americans accepted this freedom of girls and even made fun of the French for worrying about it. On the other hand, respect for women was evident everywhere, in the cities as in the countryside; indeed, it sometimes seemed excessive. It was only normal that men should rise and yield their seat to a woman in a tramway or a public place, but it seemed quite shocking that the beneficiaries of such gallantry did not take the trouble to say thank you. It was praiseworthy when a policeman helped an old lady cross a street filled with frenzied vehicles, but he really exaggerated when he stopped all traffic so that a smart young girl did not have to go to a pedestrian crossing. Yet the Americans approved totally of such doings and were entirely submissive, for all their apparent roughness, to the demands of their female companions.

> The respect bestowed on the young girl is agreed to by everyone. There is no trace ... of the thoughtless and coarse gallantry that will pursue a pretty woman who walks by herself in the streets of Paris. Whether in society or in the street, they are always treated with respect.[4]

There were of course various explanations for the origin of this widespread American behavior, for instance, that women had long been in the minority and therefore had to be protected by the law, but also that the moral code was very strict. This situation still existed in the West during the greater part of our period, and the respect that extremely rough men showed to all of womankind seemed even more astonishing than in the cities. "The rights of madame are regulated by local custom." Added to these uniquely American circumstances were some traits that were shared by all Anglo-Saxon populations and differed radically from those of the Latins. This is why young American women who went to France and wanted to behave as they did at home were reproved for being frivolous and flighty and regarded with suspicion – unless they were rich heiresses, in which case the French closed their eyes to carryings-on that were inexcusable for the less fortunate.

The next surprise was the beauty of these unrestrained *misses*. All the French noticed their grace and the way they dressed. As one of them wrote in 1876: "American girls are usually pretty and stylish and highly skilled in the art of dressing well." Twenty years later we hear of "beautiful American girls, full of vigor and radiant youth, slender, elegant, with large velvety eyes and an alluring air ...," while Paul Adam wrote: "Walking like a gymnast also gives them that smart, somewhat manly and bold look that misleads our seducers in Paris and incites them to

4. C. Anet, "New York, la ville et la vie," *Revue de Paris* (1 Aug. 1901): 644.

slander."[5] One could cite many more passages about tall silhouettes crowned by blond hair and the seductiveness of all young American girls. Only a few curmudgeons found that they looked too athletic, and some distinguished minds were upset about certain excesses, especially outside the major Eastern cities: "The women there showed off masses of blond hair, ivory-colored arms, exuberant bosoms, and colorful garments. They really use too much makeup and false jewelry,"[6] but these reservations did not prevent the French scholar from admiring the vigor of these handsome plants and their independent spirit.

Such unanimity raises a few questions. It is, for instance, rather unlikely that all girls in the United States were exceptional beauties, and it is not easy to define "the" American type. Yet from Molinari to Gohier, from the humble Toutain to Bourget, all authors expressed the same troubled admiration. What these young women represented was difference; unchaperoned, athletic, and dressed in light colors, they attracted more attention than French women of the same age, and their beauty had more to do with this ease and freedom of movement than with the delicacy of their features or the perfection of their figure. Félix de Biancour, a former prefect with a roving eye, clearly saw this: "charming glances and an incompararably supple way of moving," he said, were more alluring than "classic" beauty, which was no more frequent here than elsewhere.[7] Camille Saint-Saëns also understood the situation once he had arrived in the United States:

> I had been afraid that I would meet boyish women with short hair and hard eyes. What a nice surprise! Women rule in America, that is true, perhaps even a bit too much, they say; but they remain essentially feminine and rule as if they had a right to do so by dint of their charm, their grace, and their irresistible seductiveness.[8]

Thus the beauty of young American women was more a matter of manner than of esthetic canons, and the strong impression they made on

5. G. Desaché, *Souvenir de mon voyage aux Etats-Unis et au Canada* (Tours: Imprimerie P. Bousserets, 1877), p. 58; P. Deschamps, *A travers les Etats-Unis* (Paris: Leroux, 1896), p. 422; P. Adam, *Vues d'Amérique* (Paris: Ollendorf, 1906), pp. 96–97.
6. A. Zannini, *De l'Atlantique au Mississippi* (Paris: J. Renoult, 1885), pp. 161–62.
7. F. de Biancour, *Quatre mille lieues aux Etats-Unis* (Paris: Ollendorf, 1888). The author devoted an entire chapter to American women, as did many other travelers, who evoked "her Majesty the American woman" or all kinds of other admiring variations of this term. The opposite reaction can also be found on the part of observers who considered the demeanor of American women provocative. Georges Duhamel, much later, even spoke of industrially molded legs: "How do they manage, these American ladies, to get hold, every one of them, of the same delicious legs they so generously show off?" *Scènes de la vie future* (Paris, 1960), p. 89.
8. C. Saint-Saëns, *Au courant de la vie* (Paris: Dorbon aîné, 1914), p. 102.

the French is eloquent testimony to the advantages to be derived, at least initially, from a liberal upbringing and an easygoing manner. Besides, "the unmarried young woman is an American institution, just like the fire-hydrant, only more interesting. . . ."

### Flirts, Flirtation, Flirting

The variation in the words used – one also finds the even more exotic-sounding "flirth" – shows that despite the French origin of the term, the thing itself was not yet clearly understood by the French observers: "this undefinable word . . . means everything one can think of, from innocent child's play to the most hazardous distractions of adulthood."

Some thought that *flirt* began as soon as a girl spoke by herself to a boy in a fancy drawing room or on the deck of a steamer, as soon as she used a small part of the liberty that seemingly was hers. Others felt that a flirtation was an actual provocation to which Latin men, even diplomats, succumbed easily, although it was usually disappointing, for in the end a man obtained nothing but the most fleeting touches that were as chaste as they were furtive. Moreover, the law severely punished seducers who had been too sure of their powers of persuasion, to the outrage of some Frenchmen. But then, young men across the Atlantic did not seem to be very demanding, as Paul Adam said when he saw a couple passionately hugging in the streets of Saint Louis: "The *bachelor* courts a kind of legitimate mistress, who allows him a great deal, except to break the window. And that's enough for him."

On the basis of such findings, opinions were divided. Was the *miss* dangerous, or did she only exercise her freedom, reserving her right to yield when she was ready or when she was truly in love? "Once her heart has spoken, she will stop flirting!"

This distinction was not without importance and drew a dividing line among the French observers. For especially in the early part of the period, many anecdotes were circulating about the snares that these charming young ladies laid for their naive admirers, and about the rather hypocritical nature of their behavior, for they engaged in "a repulsive kind of husband-hunting" in which cold calculation took the place of sentiment. Paul Bourget found this touching, but he nonetheless belonged to this camp when he took a malicious pleasure in using his experiences in American drawing rooms to establish his categories: "the Beauty, the Sincere One, the Ambitious One, the Bluffer, the Lady Bachelor, the Collector, the Level-Headed One," all of them suggesting slight disapproval despite a front of admiration.[9] Decidedly, this camp felt, these young women were just too free when they played games with men the better to enchain them; they were in danger of becoming *demi-virgins* if they contented themselves for too long with the perverse charms of the flirt. Having so much fun might well make them lose their heads, at the risk of becoming self-satisfied old maids who had never found companions that were good enough for them. Such bitter thoughts were never completely absent and provided some comfort to Frenchmen who had ventured to make some advances without receiving any appreciable dividends.

Yet even more Frenchmen had allowed themselves to be captivated by the admittedly troubling charm of these astonishing young ladies. The discreet and nostalgic reflections of an Aimé Jay, who happily enjoyed their company on a California beach, of a Léon de Tinseau, or of a Stéphane Jousselin, to mention only them, might speak of a "beautiful flirter" on shipboard and hint that they had not been received so badly. They also claimed that these young *misses*, for all their machiavellianism, were not cold-hearted monsters:

> . . . the American miss is both tender and reserved, calculating and bold in her flirting, but she will wholeheartedly return to the generous instincts of her nature as soon as a sincere passion liberates her from the yoke of her assertive upbringing and the sickening preoccupation with catching a husband.[10]

At any rate, flirting, even when slightly risqué, was still the natural continuation of a shared upbringing; boys and girls did not discover each other when they reached adolescence but had been together all along in a very healthy manner. It was just that the misses sometimes seemed to be more advanced than their companions, but then, *honi soit qui mal y pense*! [Evil be to him who evil thinks.] This opinion was held mostly by French women; Madame Grandin, Marie Dugard, Thérèse, and even the devout Catholic Thérèse Vianzone saw nothing provocative or malicious in this behavior, only the simple blossoming of free and educated young women who were establishing balanced relationships with young men their own age. A man like Jules Huret, though somewhat uneasy about the tyranny of superficial and idle girls, nonetheless felt that France could use more of these emancipated misses who, "endowed with an egalitarian ambition that stands up to any ridicule, free and easy in their manner, yet always gentle

---

9. P. Bourget, *Outremer* (Paris: Lemerre, 1895), pp. 135–40.
10. Biancour, *Quatre mille lieues*, p. 106.

and gracious, would reassure the congenitally suspicious male once and for all that he will always be safe."[11]

Flirting and young American females, then, fascinated the French, and even the killjoys who waxed indignant about excessive liberty were, not always without considerable hypocrisy, attracted to the more or less pernicious charms of these females. Interestingly enough, the phenomenon of the flirt was mentioned only in connection with the misses, and boys were considered to be cold and reserved, completely captivated by their female companions, who called all the shots. And this was precisely what accounted for the misgivings, the accusations of perversity, and the more or less veiled reproof that are found so often in the comments of French men, even if they were generally favorable. For this was an apparent inversion of the traditional roles that was hard to take, even if it could be explained by educational practices or by the frenzied activities of men who might not have time to think of minor things.

In an effort to elucidate this astonishing situation, Georges Sauvin, and later Jules Huret, did not hesitate to discuss the matter – in all propriety, of course – in a correspondence with a young lady, an Eastern intellectual. In both cases the dialogue revealed the pride of self-assured misses who chided the French for being flighty and for criticizing American mores; they did not hesitate to contradict these eminent French authors in strong terms by stressing the indolence and the vices of Europe. The Frenchmen hardly knew how to reply: "I could prove to you by a thousand examples that it is you on the contrary who are being spoiled by absurd and undeserved praise and flattery" – a pretty feeble rejoinder for a sharp wit.

Decidedly, the widely recognized charm and vivacity of the misses were often offset by an excessive, almost frightening, self-assurance, and some of the French observers were ready to raise the fearful specter of feminism in connection with these seemingly innocent games.

### An Enigmatic Sensuality

If flirting, "which is to love what the preface is to the book and to passion what fencing is to the duel, finishes what shared education has begun,"[12] the problem it raised was analogous to that of coeducation in adolescence. How were the Americans able to resist temptation, not to give in to what are after all natural desires? No doubt, self-control, a typically Anglo-Saxon virtue, had something to do with it, but could one not

11. J. Huret, *En Amérique* (Paris: Fasquelle, 1905), p. 379.
12. C. de Varigny, *La femme aux Etats-Unis* (Paris: Colin, 1893), p. 87.

also detect a particular kind of sensuality across the Atlantic? This was the only way to explain how it was possible to maintain proper and peaceful mores in an environment a priori incompatible with such restraint.

Hence, many Frenchmen used a strange physiological explanation to analyze American sexuality. According to this view, the Americans were devoid of real sensuality. On the one hand, ". . . the man lacks the talent of the seducer. Timid, respectful, and sentimental to excess, he also does not have to combat the ardors of a Latin temperament,"[13] but women, in the end, were chaste because they lacked sensuality – after all, wine-drinking countries have the fewest alcoholics. In the final analysis, it was believed that this was a general characteristic of a "race" whose "physical needs were more limited,"[14] people who knew nothing of sensual delight because they were too busy with other things:

> The fierce and uninterrupted efforts these people had to make in order to conquer the land from the Indians and from nature, the nervous tension they still have to sustain to stand up to competition, their mediocre food, the absence of wine and the intoxicating effect of liquor, religious fervor and political ardor – there are twenty reasons that have prevented this race from developing a sensuous side.[15]

Bound by these constraints, the Americans would never be fortunate enough to experience the bliss of sensuality. This reasoning of Paul Bourget presents a good synthesis of a fairly widespread opinion that saw the inhabitants of the New World as naturally and effortlessly chaste beings. Under this assumption, American mores were inevitably more calm, being devoid of sex scandals and excessive sensual instincts. Boys and girls could be brought up together without risk and flirt without consequences, adultery was necessarily rare, and a superficial view made people believe that prostitution did not exist at all.

This idealized vision did not stand up to closer scrutiny, and a few observers realized that things were much more complex. The port of New York had its prostitution just like any European city, as did Seattle and various small towns in the West; nor were all the houses of prostitution Chinese. Entire streets were the theater of these activities, and in certain establishments of Chicago called "*pretty girl saloons*" "pleasant and half-naked girls . . . familiarly sat down next to if not on the laps of the cus-

---

13. Paul Adam, *Vues d'Amérique, ou la nouvelle jouvence* (Paris: Ollendorf, 1906), p. 100.
14. A. Lutaud, *Les Etats-Unis en 1900* (Paris: Société d'édition scientifique), p. 269; the author was actually a physician.
15. Bourget, *Outremer*, p. 109; there is something unreal about this reasoning, which could be applied to many other peoples as well.

tomers and even drank with them."[16] It was also said that a certain number of married women engaged in these practices, and that the close quarters in certain dwellings brought people together in ways that were not always innocent. Also, the amorous frolicking of young people returning from Coney Island was quite vigorous, yet the witnesses who showed exaggerated primness on other occasions were not shocked, any more than they were shocked by the unequivocal advertisements of "lonely heart advisers" and other providers of services. Conventional morality did not allow such things, but the newspapers were full of them.

It was clear, then, that the conduct of the misses had to be placed in a larger context and could not be reduced to a few pseudoscientific explanations concerning the physiology of the Americans. The liberty of young women and a general reserve could not completely mask a more human reality, even if many of the French observers would have liked not to know about it and to stay with an explanation that reassured them at the deepest level. People who did not live as they did could not be altogether normal; this kind of reaction was totally unrelated to ideological conviction or social position and remained a strictly individual matter.

## THE WIFE AND MOTHER

The essential aim of the flirt was to help the young woman find the husband of her choice. The institution of American marriage was another source of surprise for the French.

### *On Marriage*

Young Americans married strictly according to their inclinations, without paying much attention to the wishes of the family, which was the exact opposite of what was practiced in France, especially in the bourgeois milieu. This was to be expected, for it would be difficult to see how girls and boys, accustomed to living side by side from a very young age, could suddenly give up this freedom and submit to their parents' will. And although the French used this reasoning, they were not always serenely willing to accept its practical consequences.

This is revealed by their insistence on the extreme casualness of these unions, which were said to be concluded hurriedly, sometimes without

16. L. Simonin, *Le monde américain* (Paris: Hachette, 1877), p. 163.

any formality whatsoever, in the presence of the first preacher available, and at times even without informing the parents. Exceptional or picturesque cases are always the most interesting to foreign observers, but this tendency becomes accentuated when they want to hide their discomfort with an unfamiliar situation. That is why many French correspondents liked to make fun of more or less secret marriages, which sometimes came close to the abduction of a very young girl, or on the contrary of those young ladies who had voluntarily chosen an old man, not to forget the many baroque marriages concluded in a grotto, in a zoo, on a train, or even by telegraph! Celebrating a union in this manner was to deride marriage itself. Equally shocking was the attitude of some of these misses who were too proud to get married at all; they did not even use the liberty they had to find a husband, or did so only very late, preferring to continue the fascinating life of an unmarried girl at an age when this became almost indecent. Findings to the effect that most Americans did not marry in eccentric ways but on the contrary in the bosom of the family, with flowers and wedding cake, were actually fairly rare, indicating that the French continued to focus on alliances between two persons rather than two families.

The same tendency to exaggerate appeared when it came to divorce, which seemed to confirm the fragility of American marriages. And how could the French resist the malicious pleasure of showing that these love matches often ended in separation? Some of them sought the cause in the overly hasty way – "devoid of moderating and idealistic ideas" – of entering into a union, but this did not square with the more frequent criticism of too many late marriages. In order to explain a phenomenon indicating that American marriages were far from ideal, observers therefore had to invoke the multiplicity of laws governing marriage and divorce, which varied from state to state but always favored the woman. Actually, divorces were just as "manufactured" as marriages; agencies advertised their services in newspapers, offering to produce proofs, with photographs if necessary, of adultery and to obtain a separation, and in Nevada one could obtain an automatic divorce after a six-month stay.[17]

There was something enigmatic about this propensity of a free society, where women were respected, religion flourished, and girls wanted to get married, to go in for divorce at an ever-accelerating rate. The French could not accept the idea that this was simply another form of liberty and found this development extremely disturbing and dangerous to the stability of the family itself. This reaction, understandable in a Claudio

17. F. de Tessan, *Promenade au Far West* (Paris: Plon, 1912). This was one of the first references to the phenomenon in connection with Nevada.

Jannet or other fervent Catholics, was shared by most of the other observers, whatever their convictions in other areas.

At most, some of the more attentive and reasonable minds noted that these divorces, which allowed couples to put an end to unsalvageable marriages, were probably healthier than the situation in France, where such cases were usually covered up with a veil of seemliness. Moreover, those marriages that did survive were all the stronger and all the better for it, and in any case divorces were probably not as frequent as examples taken from the newspapers would lead one to believe. Paul Adam thus evoked "long, faithful, healthy, and prolific love-matches under the scepter of the wife. In short . . . havens of virtue." Despite these important nuances, however, divorce seemed too frequent to all French observers; it cast a lurid light on marriage itself, since it did nothing to prevent crimes of passion, even if vices and scandals usually remained hidden.

Yet in fact, divorced persons were not considered respectable in the United States at that time, and divorces were not always easy to obtain; moreover, their number represented only about 8 percent of marriages at the beginning of the twentieth century. But the French were essentially seeing only urban examples, frequently taken from an unstable high society. Nonetheless, the arguments advanced around 1900 were repeated throughout most of the twentieth century as the real rise in the divorce rate made them more pertinent. In this area, the time lag between France and the United States was so great that it did not disappear for a very long time, so that the reactions remained almost unchanged despite some modification in the relative incidence of the phenomenon. The legalization of divorce in 1884 in France did not drastically change the behavior of families, especially in the bourgeois milieu from which most of these observers of the United States had come.

However that may be, American-style marriage attracted a good deal of commentary, even aside from the spectacular and atypical cases of unions between the wealthy daughters of millionaires and "European blue-bloods" intent on restoring their fortunes.[18] Of greatest interest was the wife's role in marriage, for according to the French there was a striking contrast between the situation of the miss and that of the wife. The former had every freedom, the latter lost most of hers; after a whirlwind life filled with flirts and pleasures, here she was, subjected to the rules of domesticity, seemingly without having gained by the change. The French saw this very clearly: "Personally, here is how I feel: I like

---

18. M. O'Rell, *Jonathan et son continent, la société américaine* (Paris: Calman-Lévy, 1889), p. 91. Incidentally, various authors pointed out that the Americans were very hostile toward European marriages of wealthy heiresses.

the American woman better before marriage, and the Frenchwoman afterwards."[19] These men felt that the French wife blossomed in marriage, whereas her sister overseas was likely to fade. Even before studying the arguments to this effect, one can once again see how the different assumptions of the two countries shaped these reactions. The miss was much more visible than the young unmarried Frenchwoman and therefore alluring; conversely, the married woman was necessarily discreet, rather like a Frenchwoman.

### The Married Woman and the Home

The way of life of American couples as outlined by many French commentators was not particularly enviable. The wife, left alone for most of the day by a husband who worked like a man possessed, tended to go out a great deal, especially if she did not have children, consume all kinds of drinks, including alcohol, and have encounters that certain Frenchmen considered necessarily dubious. This existence was facilitated by the reciprocal freedom of both spouses, with the husband going to his club and the wife keeping some of her independent ways:

> If American marriage is mainly an association, it also seems that the American family is mainly a workers' guild, a kind of social encampment whose cohesion, if it is close, is rendered so by individual sympathies, as it would be among persons who are not related by blood.[20]

This certainly excessive statement was justified by what the French knew and observed of the life of American women. They constantly repeated, like a leitmotif, the remark that American wives completely neglected their household duties, and French women were not the last to repeat it, even though they greatly appreciated the freedom enjoyed by their American sisters: ". . . she does not know how to sew or cook, and it would upset her very much to wield a feather duster." Many of the French men commented on such particulars as women who had brought no dowry into the marriage, whose husbands did not want them to work, and who did not take care of their households, ". . . the gift of her person seems to be sufficient compensation." No wonder they were at loose ends and amused themselves with trivial pleasures, and that their husbands preferred the club to the cozy home.

19. G. Sauvin, *Autour de Chicago* (Paris: Plon, 1893), p. 111. The author very clearly expressed the opinion of practically all the French observers. A similar attitude is found among many European people, except the English, who seemed more fascinated by the married American woman.
20. Bourget, *Outremer*, p. 144.

Such descriptions matched only a few cases, exclusively located in certain luxurious settings in Eastern cities, yet the French observers were riveted by them. However, the frequently heard allegation of French observers to the effect that American women were not too happy with the routine life in marriage was not altogether without foundation. Statements of this kind were made by American women at the time, and it is certain that there was a stark contrast between the great freedom of the young girl and the relative dependence of the married woman who often struggled, albeit discreetly, with problems for which she had hardly been prepared.

To make matters worse, young American couples lived either in houses that were nice enough but far from the center of town, or in boarding houses shared by several such couples, or even simply in a hotel. Throughout the period, most of the French travelers spoke at length about this strange way of life, which practically became the identifying mark of the American couple.

Such an existence horrified them. In the first case, the separate life of the spouses was accentuated by physical distance, and the second led to the most degrading lack of privacy or else a nefarious idleness, caused in part by the disdain for housework that was the reason for moving into such an establishment in the first place. The figures advanced by some of the French authors were startling and excessive, for it was said that in New York or Brooklyn "the entire middle class is condemned to boarding," which would mean as many as three-quarters of all families.

This picture of the life led by the Americans seemed totally unbelievable; how could anyone survive without servants, for the lack of domestic help was the reason given for this exodus to the hotels and other boarding places; how could anyone do without a home; and how could women put up with such a life? Moreover, this situation had some extremely unfortunate consequences, since it was "notorious that the married women of the East are more and more inclined to . . . avoid" motherhood;[21] this phenomenon was even thought to be brought about by the "moral corruption favored by urban life and by a more social than domestic upbringing compounded by peculiar housing arrangements." No wonder, then, that a Frenchman would prefer the French to the American wife.

What are we to make of this almost unanimous presentation? It was certainly excessive, but it was also based on facts that were not so much

21. E. d'Eichtal, "Quelques notes d'un voyage aux Etats-Unis," *Annales de Sciences Politiques* 2 (1906): 206. The author only repeated a widespread opinion, which can be found in most books of the time, that speculated on the basis of a real decline of the birthrate.

wrong as incomprehensible for middle-class Frenchmen of the late nineteenth century.

The boarding house was nothing more than a kind of *pension de famille* where young couples who would not even consider moving in with their parents and who had no dowry went to live for a while after they were married and before they had children and enough money to buy a house or find a good rental. There was nothing particularly revolting about such an always temporary arrangement, where lack of privacy was no worse than in a middle-class French household where several generations and the servants lived under one roof. Besides, the owners of these establishments were usually very vigilant with respect to their boarders' morals. This life in boarding houses made many superficial observers believe that the Americans were living in hotels. Limited in fact to New York and a few other major cities, this lifestyle was by no means characteristic of American society as a whole.

Indeed, some of the more attentive observers protested against what they considered to be lies, having met women who took care of their households without foundering in sloth or excessive independence.[22]

The majority, however, readily generalized on the basis of a few examples gathered in the cities and felt that such an existence was contrary to all principles of good order within families and mutual help between parents and children. This was similar to the sometimes veiled discomfort created by the overly free demeanor of women and by the seemingly casual nature of American morals.

This incomplete view of the life of American married couples, then, was based on certain facts, but also on a great deal of distortion. One may wonder whether this was also the case with respect to the problem of domestic help; their almost complete absence in American homes, and the poor quality of domestics who did exist, was attested to by almost all the French observers. Paul de Rousiers told of how he had handed a letter of recommendation he was carrying to the lady of the house, believing that she was the maid. Others reported that American women complained about their servants, saying that they were entitled to have Sunday off, received anyone they pleased in their masters' home, and talked back when reprimanded. Urbain Gohier personally found Irish maids particularly unsatisfactory, and black manservants altogether dreadful; he felt sorry for the poor ladies who had to run a house,

---

22. C. Wagner, *Vers le coeur de l'Amérique* (Paris: Fishbacher, 1906), p. 304. This book can be compared to the more nuanced studies of C. de Varigny and P. de Rousiers. See B. Buisson, *L'enseignement primaire au congrès d'éducation à l'exposition scolaire de Chicago* (Paris: Hachette, 1896), pp. xv–xvi.

although he also felt that every American's unwillingness to serve others was proof that everyone wanted to be free. After all, servants tried to behave and dress just like their employers.

The problem seemed to be so serious that, in addition to lamentations about the absence of domestic servants or their manners, constructive suggestions were made by the French. Lazare Weiller, a practical and efficient man, having noticed that maids and servants were rarely Americans and often a bit unpolished, suggested the founding of a training school for these European immigrants.[23] Others were worried for themselves, wondering what might happen in France if servants were no longer available, for the Americans could at least – better than nothing – count on the Negroes to do this kind of work.

The lack of domestics to some extent explained the inelegance of American domestic life, the helplessness of the women in the face of all the work to be done, and the search for alternative solutions, such as hotels or other arrangements, all of which were wrought with perils.

This finding is rather astonishing, considering that we know from other sources that more than half of the female Americans were employed in domestic service, whereas the proportion of foreigners was relatively small.[24] What was true, however, was the rapid turnover of domestics, which made it necessary to pay them fairly good wages – as most observers noted – so that they were in a position to set up housekeeping on their own, thereby accelerating this development. In addition, Americans liked to explain that they sought to avoid domestic service, which would curtail their freedom, that girls who did go into service did so hoping that they would not stay long, preferring to do other, less directly supervised and less degrading work, and that it was actually embarrassing to admit that one was a maid or manservant.

The French, listening to what their hosts were saying, did notice that the service was less impeccable than what they were used to, and that there was much less deference, and so they quickly jumped to conclusions and on the basis of a few cases developed an almost apocalyptic vision of social relations in the United States, notwithstanding the advances in daily living:

> All that is very nice; but you can push all the buttons in the world, no hot water will come out if someone has not gone to the trouble of lighting the boiler; and lots of people go through life without ever needing a fireman,

23. L. Weiller, *Les grandes idées d'un grand peuple* (Paris: Juven, 1903), p. 194.
24. E. Levasseur, *L'ouvrier américain* (Paris: Maisonneuve, 1898), p. 412; also Deschamps, "A travers," p. 18.

whereas the lack of domestics is a woe one suffers every day and at every moment.[25]

To be sure, such remarks were made by people accustomed to being served, aristocrats and bourgeois, and the French workers who visited the United States did not have the same reactions; still, they found it hard to understand that their American counterparts refused to let their wives work as domestics. The fact is that the French of all backgrounds were accustomed to living with domestics, which formed a stable and specific group. They therefore had trouble with the idea that the Americans did the job of domestic service, and other jobs as well, with the intention of changing as soon as possible.

The French and the Americans thus had different views of the problem of service, and the way it was solved in the United States – not as easily as the French thought – led them to believe that there was no problem, and that the Americans could get along without domestics. Without realizing it, they once again seemed to discover on the basis of a distorted vision of the American reality what their own future might hold.

### Mothers and Children

Meeting schoolchildren who freely interrupted adults and appeared to be quite self-assured, not to say brash, had been the first hint that discipline was probably not too ferocious in the home. This tolerance was actually one of the characteristic traits of the American family, and all the visitors commented on the liveliness of the children and their responsible attitude. To be sure, the most superficial observers attributed this state of things to the carelessness of the mother and to the hotel life that ruled out a healthy upbringing: "She only takes care of herself and does not have a minute to devote to her children, who in fact don't ask for it either. . . . " But the issue was much deeper, much more rooted in American life: "In Europe we say that an unruly child or an insufferable adolescent girl was brought up in the American fashion."[26]

Every one of the French observers cited examples to confirm this state of things. The child was king; he was not scolded, he was not forbidden anything, and even the slightest corporal punishment was out of the question. He was allowed to do whatever he pleased, although he

25. J. de Rochechouart, *Excursion autour du monde* (Paris: Plon, 1879), p. 275; the author was clearly very upset.

26. A. Saint André de Lignereux, *L'Amérique au XXe siècle* (Paris: Taillandier, 1909), p. 154. He was the only one of these authors to be equally interested in American children, whom he uses as examples from the very beginning.

had to take the consequences. Thus a boy of seven was capable of order-
ing a meal by himself and of carrying his own luggage; if he went
horseback riding and fell, the mother and father did not rush over to
pick him up;[27] and this was not even to mention the freedom of girls.
Children went to school by themselves, crossed cities by tram on their
own, chose and freely saw their own friends, seemingly without having
their parents concern themselves about anything but watching out, from
afar, for their safety. Children were not surrounded by "timorous
tenderness," which explains why the mother sometimes seemed to be
more of a "big sister":

> Everyone must watch out for himself; for her that is the long and short of
> maternal solicitude, and she applies it in all tranquillity, not as a reasoned
> principle but from habit, and without imagining that this could give rise to
> even the shadow of criticism.[28]

It was therefore not surprising that boys often worked at the early age
of twelve, and that they were even free to spend their earnings as they
saw fit; it also explained why students did not hesitate to work in order
to pay their tuition and why the sons of millionaires were willing to do
very humble jobs.

Such views are not exaggerated, and, as we know, little Americans had
these privileges long before the famous Doctor Spock came along in the
1960s. French attitudes on this issue were at the very least ambiguous.
Their first reaction was to find these children perfectly impossible and to
think that they needed a good spanking. This was a source of conflict for
couples where the husband was French and the wife American. One
hapless father, for instance, who insisted on his right to forbid his
thirteen-year-old son to go by himself and without permission to play in
the countryside with some neighbors, was firmly put in his place: ". . .
their mother and her family felt that he was claiming a tyrannical authority."[29] The first reflex of the French, and one that they never quite over-
came, was to act sternly and to forbid, and so they felt deep down that
American parents made it too easy for their progeny to use them as
beasts of burden. Upon more careful observation, however, they came
to respect the results obtained by these apparently distant fathers and
these mothers who refused to hover over their children.

They realized that, for the most part, American children seemed to be

27. Weiller, *Les grandes idées*, p. 182. Weiller found American children altogether insufferable, and moreover very expensive, what with their own rooms, their special chairs
in restaurants, and their regular visits to a specialized doctor.
28. P. de Rousiers, *La vie américaine* (Paris: Didot, 1892), p. 4.
29. M. Dugard, *La société américaine* (Paris: Hachette, 1896), p. 214.

happy and thriving, for society had not put off the "blossoming of their personal lives"; they were conscious of their dignity and did not put up with absurd and humiliating rules, whether it be at home or at school. If they were not shy about answering back to adults, this was not meant as a provocation but as a legitimate assertion of their equality. Moreover, everything was done to develop in the child a "fruitful sense of responsibility, dignity, and manliness," and nothing could be more telling than the answer to a question R. G. Lévy asked one of his hosts in New York: Asked what plans he had for his son, the man said: "You mean, what plans does my son have for himself?" In the same vein the adults did not involve themselves in children's clubs in the schools, where the children, on their own, developed an admirable sense of patriotism.

The French could not help marveling at such forms of upbringing, which did not smother the children's personalities and gave them a sense of responsibility at a very early age. Indeed, the young Americans whom the French met in their travels, both in France and in the United States, struck them as self-assured but not boastful, full of curiosity, and resourceful when in a tight spot. This was certainly a reason to forget the irritation caused by the whining of the little ones and the ironic remarks elicited by the American parents' admiration for their offspring.

Marveling at how well American children turned out did not preclude certain doubts. Would this "improved child" make a better adult? This was not at all sure, and furthermore, while the independence of children was desirable, might it not contribute to the disintegration of the family that the French believed they had discovered in the behavior of married couples, as well as to the excessive freedom to which American women were accustomed? Did children not leave the maternal bosom too soon? And while doing away with tyranny in the family might be a good thing, was this individualism not excessive? The French observers who essentially favored this mode of child-rearing came to ask themselves these questions, for they were totally surprised by what they discovered and found that everything was different from what they knew, although it did seem to work reasonably well.

## WORKING WOMAN AND YET A QUEEN

The independence of the miss, the education she received, and the relative autonomy of the mother, all of this provided a place in the working world for the American woman.

## Paradoxes of the American Woman in the Workplace

If we believe the French observers, American women had access to almost all occupations in the United States, for they were flabbergasted to find women working in stores, in offices, and in schools as early as the 1870s. They were astounded, to begin with, to find so many maids and waitresses in hotels and restaurants, above all in the West, particularly since these young women had often received a solid education that contrasted with their present situation. Thus the kindly Abbé Vigneron saw nothing wrong with his innkeeper's daughter serving at table, but he was taken aback to see her wield a broom before she sat down at the piano. But women's activities went further than that, and it was not rare to see them accomplish unusual tasks, as on this train: "The engineer is a young woman who wears goggles, and this detail is very American. We are in the land of emancipation," Léo Clarétie could exclaim.

It was not too upsetting to the French that most of the schoolteachers were of the so-called weaker sex, for teaching was directly related to women's natural role in bringing up children. But there were also women doctors, women lawyers, and women factory workers, and none of this caused any trouble:

> Women are working almost everywhere in America; they preserve a natural dignity because they have great freedom, and perhaps the mores of the country cause them to be looked at with indifference, even though they often work alongside of men: at school, in the office, and on the shop floor they eventually come to be seen as just another competitor, who will be treated bluntly and without delicacy.[30]

Women's work in offices, often seen first in government departments in Washington, was one of the greatest surprises. Women employees were sometimes the only personnel in an office, a huge room without dividing walls, where all of them were busily pounding on typewriters without paying attention to the visitors, whose embarrassment was proportionate to the number of young women present. This type of work as stenographer, correspondent, or librarian seemed to suit these women so well that our gallant Frenchmen were filled with admiration. Pierre de Coubertin was fascinated by their eagerness and their punctuality – "When will we finally decide to let women enter our offices, their natural

---

30. A. Keufer, *Exposition de Boston* (Paris: Imprimerie nouvelle, association ouvrière, 1884), p. 12. This famous printshop worker was surprised to find women everywhere in the workplace.

domain?"[31] – and Urbain Gohier was pleased to see so many of them working in businesses and government offices, for this freed men for "the big jobs."

No occupation seemed to be closed to women, except in the army, and it was not out of the question that some day a women could be President of the Republic! In fact, women revealed their abilities in many areas, almost threatening the positions of men, as Ferdinand Buisson had feared as early as 1876:

> And finally, in all businesses where they are in direct contact and in competition with men, their lack of sentimentality and their selfishness, in conjunction with their cleverness and their natural subtlety, give them an acknowledged superiority.[32]

In addition to doing these unusual jobs, women were also employed in industry and in the service trades, which did not surprise the French as much, although it did raise quite a few questions. Both bourgeois and workers were used to this kind of female work, but American women did not seem to perform it in the same spirit as their French counterparts. To be sure, they were equally efficient, even outstanding, "being usually endowed with a precocious and subtle intelligence," but they did not work only to contribute to the household expenses. American women were not satisfied with a small apartment, as French women were; they wanted a big house, carpets, a piano, and all kinds of knickknacks, and they worked in order to satisfy these highly questionable needs. This kind of behavior worried the French worker-delegates, for this was a way to extend the rules of conduct dictated by "the bourgeois moralists" to the wage-earning class; a wife who insisted that her husband dress well and abstain from drinking would thus become "the often unwitting accomplice of the boss."[33]

It was also noted that most of these female factory workers, as well as most female office workers and schoolteachers, were very young, since most stopped working as soon as they were married. Men wanted to show that they were able, by themselves, to make a living for their family, while women considered marriage an "emancipation," and did not care that they would no longer earn a salary which, though of course lower than that of their husbands, was nonetheless something to consider. This truly amazed the French observers. The bourgeois among them, however, found it much better than what was going on in France, for when the

31. P. de Coubertin, *Universités transatlantiques* (Paris: Hachette, 1890), p. 214.
32. Deschamps, *A travers*, 18–19.
33. A. Métin, "Le travail aux Etats-Unis," *Exposition internationale de Saint Louis, rapports* (Paris: Cornély, 1907), p. 10.

American female worker no longer had to leave her home, she was able to take much better care of it and did not have to entrust her child to "charitable or mercenary hands."[34] For the workers, this only reinforced the fears they had about the disastrous "bourgeois tendencies" of their American colleagues, even if they acknowledged the superiority of American wages, without which such a lifestyle would be impossible.

The work of American women, then, was conceived in a very special way and produced admirable progress of the kind that could be seen in the Women's Palace at the Chicago World's Fair, which had been built entirely by women. Yet it also produced fairly surprising forms of behavior that almost seemed to invalidate such advances.

The conclusions of the French, while relatively well documented, were nonetheless extremely paradoxical.

It was, for instance, perfectly true that American women were able, not without considerable difficulties, to move into a variety of positions, but they constituted only a tiny fraction of the most prestigious occupations and they never made it to the top. However, the flexibility and the diversity of American institutions made it possible for them to advance in various fields that were even more difficult to break into in France, where until the early twentieth century no woman could plead before a higher court and where no Marie Curie was admitted to the Sorbonne. In other words, the existence of a lag between France and the United States, in terms of both time and institutions, accounts for some of the French reactions, which nonetheless considerably embellished the actual situation.

It is also true that once they were married, American women rarely worked; only 5.6 percent of married women had a job around 1900, and two thirds of the female work force consisted of poor and unmarried young women. Moreover, many more French than American women were working, namely, 37 percent of all women over the age of fifteen, as compared to less than 21 percent of Americans.

Although they were not altogether unaware of these facts, the French observers of the late nineteenth century did not seem to realize the paradoxical character of their assessments. For while they admired the accomplishments of American women, they approved of their leaving the work force very early, yet in a different context also criticized them for their idleness.

34. Comte d'Haussonville, "Le travail des femmes aux Etats-Unis et en Angleterre," *Revue des Deux Mondes* (1 July 1892). The author felt that the female American worker lived better than all her European sisters "in a regime of absolute freedom." See also Levasseur, *L'ouvrier américain*, vol. 2, p. 419, and Huret, *En Amérique*, vol. 2, p. 285.

All in all, these reactions revealed a deep ambiguity. These Frenchmen agreed that women should work in order to live, performing mean and humble tasks, and they also knew that this was often the case in France. It was therefore preferable that women stop working when they could do so. On the other hand, they made a great deal of the professional success of certain American women, depicting it as admirable in principle because it was relatively exceptional and remote and because it fit in with the extraordinary mores of the inhabitants of the United States. But then, it is not certain that everyone was looking forward to the universal spread of this situation.

### *Toward Women's Rights*

Female achievements, even when exaggerated, made it clear to the French observers that American women were not just superficial flirts interested in nothing but their clothes and drawing-room chitchat. Indeed, many of them went into raptures over the role women had played in the abolitionist movement, the energy they deployed in the struggle for the prohibition of alcohol and in various charitable organizations. They often cited Jane Addams's foundation, Hull House in Chicago, as an example of this kind of work. Such undertakings showed the strength of character and the independent spirit of American women, worthy successors to their revolutionary ancestors or to the pioneers who had opened new lands. Women as guardians of good morals and protectors of childhood deserved only praise.

The virtues of these women, their advanced education, their financial independence – which was guaranteed by law as well as by custom – and their professional achievements, all of which were touted by the French observers, constituted a set of qualities that should have led them straight to full citizenship. Indeed, this would have been the logical outcome in the country of "full-fledged feminism." Yet things were not as simple as that, and it must be said that our Frenchmen, though always ready to praise the fine qualities of the American beauties, were much more reserved when it came to this subject.

What rights did American women have? The French knew that they could have autonomy under the law, since they were granted legal competence in 1860, at least in the State of New York. What they did not know was that these advances were limited to a few Eastern states and that in many other regions, particularly in the South, American women did not enjoy many more rights than their sisters in Paris, Lille, or Marseille. However that may be, opinions were divided as to the benefits of such status to women. Female French observers, as well as a few men who looked into this matter, were all in favor of such measures, but the representative of the French carriage-makers at the Chicago World's Fair was decidedly more skeptical, wondering whether this would really make life better for the daughters, sisters, and wives of their colleagues in America.[35] All our observers, incidentally, noted that the wages of working women were decidedly lower than those of men, but this finding did not upset them and did not invalidate their appreciation of the decisive rights of American women.

The most important problem, however, concerned the right to vote, the only one that clearly indicates full citizenship. And here even the most fervent heralds of the rights of American women had to realize that even if women had the right to vote for the school board – and this was the case in only a few Western states: most famously Wyoming, then Colorado and a few others over the years, including California in 1912 – they were excluded from national elections. In other words, in this essential area the position of the American woman was equivalent to that of the French woman. Apparently it did not occur to any of these observers that under these conditions it was a paradox to speak of women's equality.

The most hostile opinions were expressed by observers who associated the struggles of the suffragists with an unbridled feminism that had, to be sure, originated in America but might well spread further in Europe, where it had already gained a foothold. Aside from Louis Simonin's perfidious remarks about these feminists who ". . . will go on asking in vain for rights that nature herself seems to have denied them," the most vigorous attack, and one that was often cited subsequently, was published in the *Correspondant* of February 1887 by Henri Destrel:

> In America . . . the newness of the institutions, the freedom of initiatives, and the love of novelty . . . all inspire women with self-confidence and a taste for bold action. That is why the gynocratic movement has its most important base of operations in that country. That is where its general staff holds its deliberations and where its assault columns against male tyranny receive their orders.[36]

He did his best to ridicule the women's movement that had grown up in the years before the Civil War around Angelina Grimké and Elizabeth Stanton, and especially the endeavors to modify women's clothes made popular by Amelia Bloomer, whose "liberating undergarments had to disappear in the face of the almost unanimous repugnance

---

35. *Délégation ouvrière . . . Mécaniciens* (Paris: Sandoz et Fishbacher, 1877), p. 159. And yet this was one of the most revolutionary workers' associations.
36. H. Destrel, "Le suffrage des femmes aux Etats-Unis," *Le Correspondant* (10 Feb. 1887): 5.

of the fair sex." Similar reactions were expressed, though in a more covert fashion, by several other authors, but they became somewhat attenuated over the years and disappeared by the early years of the twentieth century.

Yet some of the French admirers of American women stuck to their guns and declared that they should indeed be given full citizenship, precisely because of their real advance over their French sisters. This was said by Marie Dugard and the other women,[37] but also by a few men, the most determined of whom on the eve of the War was Paul Estournelles de Constant. Having had his road-to-Damascus experience in California, where he was dazzled by the simplicity and the abilities of the girls who had grown up there, he did not hesitate to give speeches in support of the local suffragists, feeling that the vote for women was bound to come in America, after it had been so successful in California.

> Not that the American woman is superior to other women, but she is freer; she has courage, as do all others, but hers is a public courage in defense of her cause, whereas the European woman is more resigned and only has courage for suffering.[38]

Such a judgment was not heard often, but it did underlie the opinion of quite a few observers, even when the issue of suffrage was not raised. What drew their attention was not so much the exact rights of American women – which in the end were not all that extraordinary and insufficient to bolster a definitive judgment – as the women's evident aptitude for obtaining and exercising them. It was in this sense, and with a certain disregard for the realities, that many Frenchmen thought that the United States was the country of women's rights, given the qualities of American women and the support provided by the respect and admiration of American men.

Such a point of view did not by any means imply that the same person would favor improving the status of women in France. Here again, distance made it possible to express opinions more firmly than one would do at home.

### The Eve of the Future

The American woman, then – beautiful, alluring, free in her manner, but a poor housekeeper – appeared to be an elite woman, sure of herself and dominating. It is not surprising that she was both attractive and disturb-

---

37. Dugard, *La société américaine*, p. 203.
38. E. de Constant, *Les Etats-Unis d'Amérique* (Paris: Colin, 1913), p. 49. For all that, the author praises the young French woman, who is discreet but all-powerful, especially in rural society.

ing, and it is therefore of interest to give a precise account of the opinions of those French observers who had the most personal reasons to think about this subject. Two groups will engage our attention, namely, French men who married Americans – the opposite almost never happened – and French women, for whom it was normal to compare their lot with that of their transatlantic sisters.

The cases of Frenchmen marrying Americans were quite spectacular, often involving wealthy heiresses and more or less impecunious aristocrats, for not much was heard of marriages of less prominent people. Such marriages were not, however, prevalent enough to yield any statistical truths, and, most important, not all of them left sufficient traces to elucidate the attitudes of the French husbands. Moreover, each one of these Franco-American couples had its own fate, shaped by the personalities of the partners, so that they cannot be reduced to a question of "races," to use this term in its nineteenth-century meaning. In the end the failed marriages of Georges Clemenceau and Mary Plummer, or of Boni de Castellane and Anna Gould, to mention only the most famous cases, were no more significant than the apparently successful unions of Charles Bigot and the woman who used the pen-name Jeanne Mairet, or of Paul Estournelles de Constant and a wife who has remained anonymous, but who may have communicated to him her enthusiasm for the emancipation of her sisters.

At most it can be shown that the attraction of the misses was due not only to their fathers' plentiful dollars but also to their charm or their lively minds. Yet it is probable that the life of such a couple was often difficult, since French men remained essentially committed to a very traditional role for the wife, which was not easily compatible with a true desire for independence. Here, as one example, is the judgment of the frequently perspicacious Marie Dugard, who was convinced that American women were imbued with egalitarian theories which, "moderate or not, . . . will always be unacceptable to men of Latin race."[39] This relative pessimism should be somewhat moderated, however, since couples in binational marriages often faced very specific problems that did not necessarily have anything to do with feminist aspirations.

These limits would seem to indicate that the admiration many French men had for the American woman remained – as far as we can judge – fairly disembodied and clung to a mythic image that might explain some of their disillusions.

The positions taken by French women addressed a different set of questions; all they did was to point out the differences between

39. Dugard, *La société américaine*, p. 175.

themselves and American women and to form a general opinion. And here one finds quasi-unanimity: French women considered the way of life and the situation of American women altogether enviable.

The views of Madame Grandin and of Thérèse deserve our special attention, for both spent a year in the United States, which put them in a better position to judge all facets of the life of American women. Without losing their critical faculties when discussing the poor housekeeping skills of American women or the overly lenient upbringing of children, these two women came to similar conclusions, despite the differences in their personalities and in the dates and places of their stays. What Madame Grandin discovered in America was a "women's paradise," for women there were given respect, freedom, and help:

> Yes, I had lived a life of freedom there, enjoying a freedom of thought and of behavior that were not permitted on our soil, where narrow prejudices, a ridiculous etiquette, and absurd conventions still flourish. I had left the country whose laws, institutions, and customs responded so well to my feelings, my aspirations, and my tastes.[40]

She could not have said it more clearly, and Thérèse only outdid her on a more general level: "No woman can be compared to the American, nor does any other occupy such a position in the world; for she walks through it triumphantly, trailing behind her the admiration of men and the envy of women."[41]

The opinions of other French women who had only visited the United States were in perfect agreement; one evoked a happy woman, "so respected, so queenly," while another also used the image of a paradise that was almost as good as what one had heard about it. Even the prim and proper Thérèse Bentzon came to think that the model of the American family would be adopted in Europe, and that women there too would come to enjoy an analogous freedom, enriched, she hoped, by "French graciousness":

> Let us hope, then, that the women of the New World will gradually raise their souls above the humble distaff, without however losing sight of that distaff, the symbol of so many sweet and touching things whose place can never be taken by more ambitious endeavors. If this were done . . . I would be delighted to see the French family of our time become a little Americanized.[42]

---

40. Mme. L. Grandin, *Impressions d'une Française à Chicago* (Paris: Flammarion, 1894), p. 312.
41. Thérèse, *Impressions d'une Française sur la côte du Pacifique* (Paris: Juven, 1901), p. 7.
42. T. Bentzon, *Choses et gens d'Amérique* (Paris: Calman-Lévy, 1898), p. 334.

For these French women, the American was thus truly a model, even if a few sharp corners would have to be rounded off; nor was this a matter of specific rights or a better position under the law. The fact that these were not the opinions of militant feminists reveals the gulf between the two countries' evolution. Yet the recriminations of so many American women at the time prove that these favorable assessments failed to go to the heart of the matter and did not capture the local reality.

Stepping back a little and summarizing the French views, one finds that a very clear and increasingly large majority was favorably disposed toward the American woman. This could go from the simple comment of a worker, who said in 1876 that women "had it better with their laws and their freedom in the United States," or that of a journalist who twenty years later found them "more respected, more pampered, and better protected," to the somewhat frightened admiration that Doctor Lannelongue expressed in 1910 for this woman who had obtained from men "submission and respect" by means of both her grace, "made of independence and strength," and "the miraculous ability to oblige a man to love her for herself instead of marrying her for a dowry she does not have and does not want to have," in the country where the dollar is king.

Such comments show how difficult it was to make comparisons with the women of France, from whom the Americans were separated by a "whole set of ideas, instincts, and traditions." The comparison more or less explicitly yielded the certainty that American women were better educated and more independent, even if they sometimes lacked the self-effacing gentleness of "our admirable Latin women, the associates, collaborators, colleagues, secretaries, or copyists of their fathers, their husbands, and their sons, to whom they give of their time and their intelligence without keeping count. . . ."[43] The superiority of the women across the Atlantic implied that their values would win out in the end:

> . . . bold, impertinent, shameless, courageous and capable, whatever the circumstance, of "taking care of herself," as she calls it, she represents a new form of humanity that may well be destined to become the woman of tomorrow.[44]

The most desirable outcome would be, of course, a moral alloy associating the qualities of the American and the European woman, "for it would perhaps bring forth the new Eve for whom thinkers have searched

43. Saint André de Lignereux, *L'Amérique au XXe siècle*, p. 213.
44. Deschamps, *A travers*, p. 23.

without finding her either here or over there," but that was impossible; and so it was the American who would "assert her royal status" by forming "the embryo of an ideal of superior womanhood."

Thus a great many misgivings were swept away, and what was left was a fascination in which a powerful attraction had a slight edge of terror.

Despite all these hesitancies, an ineluctable evolution seemed to be under way in France itself: ". . . the rapid Americanization of Europe, by which I mean the growing influence the example of the United States has exerted on our mores, our ideas about the education of girls and the ever greater freedom they enjoy."[45]

There is no question, then, that a model of the American woman was constructed at this time, even if her inadequacy with the cooking spoon almost tarnished it, and that it went beyond the traditional one, becoming more complete and more diverse. However, this model lacked real coherence, and male French observers, more than female ones, went to some lengths to avoid awkward questions. After all, it was easy to admire the freedom of young girls, even with certain reservations, and yet wish for a docile and self-effacing wife. On this point the ambivalent position of French men was best summarized by Baron de Mandat-Grancey in a fable that must be cited in full:

> Normandy, as you know, is a great region of animal husbandry. Two schools exist here side by side. In the area of Merlerault, the fillies are let out to roam freely in huge grassy meadows. . . . For several years, they happily frolic there, running in every direction, walking close to the edge of a stream, sometimes going in if it is not too deep, teasing the oxen, and having an unending wonderful time with all the other colts.
>
> The system adopted in the plain around Caen is quite different. Every morning the farmer takes his fillies to a big alfalfa field, where he ties them up in a nice green spot. One of their feet is attached to a peg by a chain that is long enough to allow them some freedom of movement, but absolutely prevents them from joining other colts that are pegged down nearby in the same manner.
>
> Like all things in this world, each of these systems has it advantages and its drawbacks. Around Merlerault there are lots of accidents. If the young animals . . . reach maturity without mishap, they are of inestimable value. . . . It is very safe to buy them, because one immediately sees their strong and weak points: but those from the plain of Caen, who almost never suffer accidents while they are growing . . . often turn out to be disappointing when one puts them into service. Many are good, but the trouble is that

45. C. de Varigny, *En Amérique* (Paris: Masson, 1895), p. 245.

they often need a bit of watching in the beginning and are liable to become restive as the devil when they get old.

As a breeder, I much prefer the system of the plain of Caen, but from the buyer's point of view, that of Merlerault has much to recommend it.[46]

In the same manner, but with less humor, it was easy to appreciate the vigor and the sense of responsibility of American children but also to reject their frankness and their somewhat rough manners. It was easy to admire the professional achievements of women but to prefer that they stay at home.

The French did not fully understand that the upbringing of children and the freedom of young women were of a piece with the life of the adults and with possibly shocking forms of behavior, and that one could not cut certain parts out of the model without breaking it and thereby making it useless.

This attitude makes it clear that, in this area as in others, adapting to a future that the French discovered in the United States was not always easy. Although the American model as they conceived it was no longer sufficient to make them accept such new realities as coeducation and freedom for girls without flinching and delay, it did reveal the complexity of French opinion on this subject. The different positions adopted by the observers, regardless of social origin or level of education, show that this was a deeply personal question, unlike others that followed more traditional dividing lines.

46. E. de Mandat-Grancey, *Chez l'Oncle Sam* (Paris: Plon, 1885), pp. 52–53.

# 10

# *From the Mormons to Americanism*

The various aspects of religion in the United States never left the French indifferent, but it is difficult to speak of a model of American religion. The proliferation of eccentric sects, among which the Mormons had definitively overtaken the gentle Quakers, appeared to the French as a kind of folklore that discredited the religious spirit of the Americans, and the manifestations of a dominant Protestantism could certainly not counterbalance this terrible impression, except in some very restricted circles. Liberal French Catholics, to be sure, were sometimes fascinated by the example and the rapid growth of the Church overseas, but their voice had little impact, particularly after the papal condemnation of liberalism in the *Syllabus of Errors* of 1864.[1]

This situation did not change drastically after 1870. The American sects continued to elicit curiosity, horror, or irony, but over the years the French were less and less interested, to the point that even the Mormons became so "normal" that after 1890 they were no longer worth a detour. Of course, the separation of Church and State as practiced in the United States became increasingly relevant as religious strife intensified in France, but what was most interesting to the French observers was the expansion of the American Catholic Church as a result of this separation. Interestingly enough, the term *Americanism*, in the precise sense of a model that can be adapted to places other than the United States, was applied to American Catholicism, whereas it was used neither for the Constitution nor for the methods that had created the success of the American economy.

The theological content of Americanism does not have to concern us here, but the very existence of this movement, however limited it

---

1. R. Rémond, *Les Etats-Unis devant l'opinion française* (Paris: Colin, 1962), vol. 2, p. 762; T. Stanton, "America in the Eyes of the French Left," Ph.D. thesis, Oxford University, 1978, pp. 215–22.

was,[2] reveals the formation of an American model of Catholicism that had been built up several years before the actual controversy broke out. In their fascination with the spectacular rise of American Catholicism, the French observers seemed to forget that the United States remained a largely Protestant-dominated country. This attitude reflects the growing weight of purely French preoccupations, to the detriment of the American reality. This explains in part why French opinions about American religion were so varied.

## MARGINAL SECTS AND THE PROTESTANT NEBULA

The strangeness of American religion was a constant theme throughout the period, even though by the 1890s the French had finally become accustomed to it and no longer paid it as much attention. What struck them most was the diversity of religions: "What a natural flowering! Once it has been leveled, cleared of all the underbrush, and cultivated, what a fertile terrain this will be."[3] Much noted as well was the peaceful coexistence of all the sects: ". . . there are never any violent doctrinal disputes, and so far all of them live in peace and fraternize in the most surprising manner. . . ."[4]

Before they could reflect more deeply on this state of things, the French observers had to satisfy their curiosity about the strangest phenomena and the most spectacular sects, which had no equivalent anywhere else. For twenty years after 1870, as before that date, that bill was filled by the Mormons, who indeed were never really replaced.

### *Mormons and More Mormons*

A great deal was written about the strange religionists of Salt Lake City, but nothing truly new could be said about them after the works published in the years 1850–60 by Jules Rémy, Prosper Mérimée, and a few others.[5] As it had been in those years, the interest in the disciples of Joseph Smith was out of proportion with their real importance in American society, but unlike in the preceding period, no book was devoted entirely to them after 1870. However, thanks to the transcontinental rail-

---

2. Cf. C. Fohlen, "Catholicisme américain et catholicisme européen; la convergence de l'Américanisme," *Revue d'Histoire Moderne et Contemporaine* 34 (April–June 1987): 215–30.
3. P. Toutain, *Un Français en Amérique* (Paris: Plon, 1876), p. 174.
4. U. Gohier, *Le peuple du XXe siècle* (Paris: Fasquelle, 1905), p. 109.
5. Rémond, *Les Etats-Unis devant l'opinion*, p. 175.

road, more visitors took the detour to the Great Salt Lake because they wanted to meet these legendary beings in the flesh. But exoticism has a way of fading, and in the wake of changes in the Mormon lifestyle, the throng of visitors and the reams of commentary began to thin out before disappearing almost entirely by the beginning of the twentieth century.

Limited though it was, the interest of the French revealed their feelings about such unusual mores. The practice of polygamy was by far the main attraction of the city founded by Brigham Young and his followers. Fantasies of lewdness and debauchery haunted the minds of the travelers, as if in some confused way this were in store for them. Added to this was their desire to probe a piece of trickery, for the odyssey of Joseph Smith and Brigham Young could be nothing else. In other words, these travelers were not filled with tolerance or understanding as they set out to walk the tree-shaded streets of this New Jerusalem, set in a landscape that at times evoked memories of Palestine.

Their opinions about polygamy were as definite as they were superficial – after a forty-eight-hour stay in the city, or even between two trains – "obscurity and pornography," said one, the breakdown of "barriers against unchastity and vice," as well as a lure for "all lovers of physical pleasure," said another. These were preconceived judgments, inspired by earlier writings and reinforced by the absolute condemnation of Catholic authors, such as Claudio Jannet, who went so far as to evoke the new Sodoms of the American West. The sexual fantasies, however, dissipated when the travelers saw the Mormon women, for they all seemed to be homely, meek, even numbed – no doubt by the orgies. Yes, these women were ". . . debased, and what one reads on their melancholy and withered faces is debasement . . . ," and moreover the children were necessarily weak and sickly, a sign of incest. Commentators liked to dwell on the legal charges brought against Brigham Young by one of his many wives and on the rare cases of women who refused to go along with polygamy and had been able to leave the community. The Mormon way of life was seen as a monstrous aberration that could not possibly last.

A very few observers did see a gentle population and peaceful women who were much more hard-working then debauched; but they too considered polygamy absolutely absurd.

After such descriptions, it is hard to see how a man like Jules Huret could still dream about Mormon polygamy; this must be attributed to his desire to hook the reader at any price. Actually, the eminent journalist found only "ice-cold virtue" in Salt Lake City.[6]

6. J. Huret, *En Amérique* (Paris: Fasquelle, 1905), vol. 2, p. 144.

The incomprehensible phenomenon of polygamy could only be explained by the constraints exercised over the people's minds and bodies by the heads of the community. All the commentaries spoke of the origins of the sect, of Joseph Smith, just another religious crank along with so many others in the United States, of the iron will Brigham Young had needed to overcome all kinds of resistance and to fight both the "Gentiles" and a harsh natural environment. His qualities as a leader of men and as an extraordinary organizer were beyond question, but that made him dangerous, and the French spread stories about murders carried out by his wholly devoted killers: "Both autocratic and popular, high priest as well as dictator, he brought divine laws to bear on the need for land. . . ."[7] The privileged few who were able to see the great man, who was suspicious of this stream of visitors, unanimously noted his air of toughness, his square jaw – an unmistakable sign of energy – his inevitably cruel glances, and his necessarily sensuous mouth – after all, he was reputed to have some thirty wives. The man, despite his rough-hewn exterior, knew how to avoid embarrassing questions and could not be pinned down. His successors, as well as all the other Saints, adopted similar attitudes, thereby confirming the visitors' hostile opinion. Clearly, the Mormons had things to hide; some of the observers evoked the existence of a veritable theocracy that enchained the faithful by a system of indebtedness and by subjecting every person's life to orders from on high, for this was the only way to maintain the coherence of the community and to recruit and keep new converts; others compared Salt Lake City to a Jesuit *reducción* in Paraguay.

The personality of Brigham Young was such that all the observers expected the sect to disappear after his death; the railroad, the influx of new settlers, and the federal government would do the rest. Yet the Mormons survived, and even the famous "Tabernacle" was finally completed in 1893, despite all the French predictions to the contrary.

It turned out that the Mormons did not depend on one man, nor on polygamy alone. These two factors would not be sufficient to explain the relative coherence of their community, yet the French were incapable of going beyond these summary explanations. Explaining the very existence of this sect by the eccentricity of the Americans, they ceased paying attention to it when polygamy seemed to disappear. In fact, this question was crucial in the accession of the territory of Utah to statehood, which was granted in 1896. The French observers thought that after that date the days of Mormonism were "numbered," and Salt Lake City hence-

7. I. Eggermont, *Voyage autour du globe* (Paris: Delagrave, 1892), p. 255. Many similar appreciations can be found.

forth attracted only a few diehards looking for clandestine cases of polygamy. The inevitable evolution of the sect, which French observers had predicted for years, was not greeted with universal enthusiasm. The Mormons had "degenerated," for they now made do with just one wife, like everyone else, and they worked like everyday Americans: They had lost all of their picturesqueness.

### Other Sects, Other Ways

The French had considerable trouble finding their way through all the sects and all the Protestant denominations, and they were not always able to distinguish clearly among the diverse forms of American religion that lacked the exceptional visibility of the Mormons:

> Any three tri-corned hats or three mob-caps have the right to form a cor-
> poration set up to teach, preach, nurse the sick, bury the dead, or just to
> eat, drink, and sleep, if they so desire – exactly as Armour, Swift, etc. are set
> up to make sausages.[8]

The French observers were at a loss to understand the changing religious fashions that caused some sects to spring up and others to disappear, so that at times all eyes were on Christian Science, and at others on the Church of Zion, or else on the Salvation Army, which was erroneously considered a sect.

During the first years of the period, some travelers made the pilgrimage to the Shaker settlement at New Lebanon or to the Free Love community at Oneida. These were the most unusual sects, whose mysterious ways and whose name – especially in the second case – stoked their curiosity. Leaving aside some a priori condemnations by the most militant Catholics and some references to the horrible orgies that were bound to take place at the famous revivals, the impressions recorded on the spot were actually rather sad. These small communities were in decline,[9] and here again the women were homely and the few ceremonies that it was possible to attend seemed ridiculous or pitiful, despite rhythmic dancing and "frightful" singing. Morality was, in fact, irreproachable, and strict rules of hygiene were observed, although some things were quite strange, for instance, that children were taken away from the

8. Laborer, "Au Texas, les femmes, les moeurs, l'Eglise catholique," *Journal des Economistes* (July 1906): 72.
9. These famous "lovers" – sometimes called "lowers" – decided to dissolve their community in 1881, whereas the Shakers continued to function. C. Allard, *Promenades au
Canada et aux Etats-Unis* (Paris: Didier, 1878), p. 60; also A. Lutaud, *Les Etats-Unis en
1900* (Paris: Editions scientifiques, 1896).

parents to be raised by the community. However, unions between young people were subject to very precise rules, and libertine behavior was out of the question. Some of these communities, incidentally, were making money, having launched successful businesses.

By the early twentieth century these sects survived only as vestiges, but it was still easy to wax ironic about the methods of the Salvation Army, which were so out of tune with the practicality of the Americans, or to marvel at the success the healer John A. Dowie had achieved in Chicago, where he attracted huge crowds with his seances, his prayer machines, and his other contraptions:

> When hearing about this fabulous exploitation of human gullibility, don't you ask yourself whether we are not living in the Middle Ages or dealing with some tribe of the Sudan, hoodwinked by some cheat at a country-fair? Surely the sociologists will have to understand, before they can generalize, ... that one can find in one population the most acute practical sense, the most ruthless and concrete realism, and material and mechanical advances at their highest point of development, coexisting with childlike credulity, illogicality, and hopeless unreason.[10]

This was one of the conclusions the French observers inevitably reached, unless, that is, they altogether condemned the sometimes exuberant flowering of religion that characterized the United States. Some thought that a society's ability to accommodate such aberrations was proof of its solid moral health. But for the most part, these observers felt called upon to present caricatures of the American sects, essentially portraying them as "... a carnivalesque variety of churches and chapels where the most unspeakable elite of rogues and ranters does its song and dance."

Beyond the inevitable exaggerations of the commentaries on marginal and truly extraordinary religious phenomena, what really baffled even the most tolerant French observers was the conduct of the American churches in general. It was difficult indeed to find one's way among so many almost identical churches and to distinguish among the different Protestant practices. Some recoiled before the "yelping" of the Baptists, while others made fun of the popularity of Methodist camp meetings in the 1880s.

The same observers who did not know the difference between the various places of worship were the first to criticize the advertising efforts made by the churches. Newspaper advertisements, posters placed on the

---

10. Huret, *En Amérique*, p. 328. Dowie also aroused the interest of such observers as U. Gohier and F. Klein, who saw him as the latest manifestation of American religious eccentricity.

church buildings, meetings organized to attract new members and funds, all these were practices that the French considered incompatible with the dignity of religion. The churches seemed to them too closely tied to ordinary social life, serving as the venue for meetings, exhibits, and discussions on themes that had nothing to do with worship. The attitude of Urbain Gohier, who was hostile to religion of any kind, is most revealing. Having heard, in Chicago, the sermon of a very young preacher who was still a newlywed, he wrote:

> After just getting out of bed, this "boy" came to dispense advice with ludicrous gravity, talking about conscience, virtue, and the meaning of life to five hundred persons who should have pulled his ears, but who meekly listened to him. Catholic priests who do this at least disguise themselves as beings of a different species; when they come to talk to us in the name of the deity, they have not spent the night with a young woman, at least as far as we know.[11]

On that day this fierce anticlerical very nearly became a Catholic! Exceptional as it was, this reaction shows that most of the French found it difficult to believe that Americans were serious about their religion, which in French eyes was discredited by the ridiculousness of the sects as much as by the vulgarity and the self-indulgence of its most visible concerns. To be sure, the few Protestant Frenchmen who observed this kind of conduct were less severe, more sensitive to the fervor one could feel in these strange churches, though equally astonished by the relaxed demeanor of their fellow Protestants.[12] But their voices were not very loud and insufficient to balance an opinion that was by and large completely unfamiliar with this American reality. How could Americans possibly fall for the foolish talk of Joseph Smith some years ago, and of John A. Dowie today? There was no answer for this question, which cast a strange light on the religious spirit of the inhabitants of the United States.

### *American Religion*

Under these circumstances, the observers had to make a special effort to adapt to so unfamiliar and complex a situation which, in fact, did not preclude genuine religious feeling. This could be seen in various manifestations, although it was perhaps "asleep, oppressed, hemmed in but

---

11. Gohier, *Le peuple*, p. 115.
12. E. Sautter, *Un coin de la vie religieuse aux Etats-Unis* (Paris: Fishbacher, 1898), p. 151; also C. Wagner, *Vers le coeur des Etats-Unis* (Paris: Fishbacher, 1908).

not exterminated by the worship of the Golden Calf, which is the official religion." Moreover, it was not difficult to find a certain consensus among the various religions concerning the major issues of patriotism, morality, and charity; and while the "religious principle" was not part of the government, it did "steer a large part of society" toward liberal laws and away from immoral or unjust acts. In this sense, the Americans were actually more religious than the French, less easily given to rationalism, and more tolerant toward the diverse forms of personal religion. This accounts for the seemingly harmonious development of so many forms of worship, so many sects.

Such an assessment, which was made by the more thoughtful authors, raised a certain number of issues. For one thing, the coexistence of different religions required a small core of values, a kind of lowest common denominator that could not attain great spiritual depth; for another, the foundations of the religious liberty that reigned in the United States would have to be elucidated in order to find out whether they could be adapted to French society, where such liberty was greatly needed.

Armed with their picturesque examples, the French do not seem to have had many illusions about the richness of American spirituality. They all agreed that theological controversies were of little interest to the inhabitants of the New World, emphasizing instead the moral and civic aspect of religion in the United States and the hazy Christianity that pervaded society. Moreover, the most thorough studies stressed the role played by Channing and the Unitarians in making rationalism part of religion and pointed out that Emerson's Transcendentalism later developed "the cult of human individuality." All of this led to a more moral than theological discourse, which came to characterize all facets of American Christianity, including Catholicism. After all, the famous Reverend Lyman Beecher maintained his prominence, despite the scandals of his private life, precisely because he refused to conform to any orthodoxy. All the churches involved themselves in national education and civilization:

> Christianity becomes a mutual aid society and is reduced to a fraternity. Parishes are institutions of solidarity, cooperatives, and clubs; the ministers are sociologists and businessmen.[13]

Indeed, the term *Protestantism* no longer suited a religion which, by its very nature, did not protest anything. The French view was that reli-

---

13. H. Bargy, *La religion dans la société aux Etats-Unis* (Paris: Colin, 1902), pp. xi–xii. The argument is developed in the main body of the book.

gious peace in the United States was founded on a transformation of the Christian faith, "rather like what happened when poetry was replaced by prose. It is a lucid, simple and sane prose that goes straight to the point, but it is a bit flat."[14]

Such an analysis led directly to the idea of a syncretism, as outlined at the famous Congress of Religions held in connection with the Chicago World's Fair. Syncretism was very controversial and had been widely condemned in France, especially by the Catholics, but it was also considered a proof of American tolerance in religious matters.

The fact is that in their tendency to systematize too much, the French attempted to press completely different phenomena, the sects and civism, into the same framework, where they would form a complete model. In doing so, they were liable to dull the fervor that could be found in the United States, even though some observers did look for it: Catholics marveled at the richness of the faith they discovered and Protestants admired the American tolerance and the work of spreading the Gospel in the West without creating a welter of denominations. Like young Emmanuel Sautter, they might exclaim: "Go and retemper your soul in the United States!"

Whatever we are to think of this view, it is true that it always rested on the principle of freedom of religion. This is what struck all the observers, regardless of the period and of their underlying convictions, and it is a fact that religious confrontations were totally absent from the American landscape. Does this mean that tolerance was really a recognized fact, or were the French sometimes carried away by an enthusiasm that made them overlook various manifestations of a quiet ostracism to which a religious group could be subjected?

Thus, at first blush, anti-Semitism did not seem to exist at all in the United States, despite the presence of large numbers of Jews. However, a closer look revealed that Jews were not received everywhere, that they had to know how to conduct themselves. Nonetheless, better relations between Jews and Christians would be easier to achieve in the United States, for what counted was that they would all be good Americans. Lazare Weiller was particularly sensitive to this question:

> I do hope that before I die, I will be able to salute the American solution to the problem between Jews and Christians. . . . My mind, which has always been thrilled by the harmony between the material and the moral world, likes to think that after the ancient rootstocks of our vineyards have been

14. E. Boutmy, *Eléments d'une psychologie politique du peuple américain* (Paris: Colin, 1911), pp. 94–95. This statement strengthened his analysis of the political system of the United States.

regenerated by young American shoots, the Lord's vineyard itself will be rejuvenated by an American vine.[15]

This is indeed the description of a certain American model of religion that seemed capable of providing a solution to fundamental problems.

It showed what religious tolerance could be. Even at this early date an American-style consensus seemed well suited to preserving public tranquillity. Many French observers noted early on that in the United States religion, even the Catholic religion, was perfectly compatible with the Republic, since Protestants worked alongside the Catholics and everyone agreed about such issues as keeping the sabbath and giving to charity. They added that the American Catholic Church seemed to benefit from the advantages given to all the different religions, for while it received no subsidies from the government, it was not hampered in any of its activities either:

> Even the Catholic Church, which cannot modify its dogmas, tries to assert its value above all by its good works, by the scope of its charities or the quality of its day- and boarding-schools; if need be, it will even work with the Protestant clergy in the common pursuit of some project for improving morality or helping the poor.[16]

The American example was used, incidentally, by French Catholics to show the harmful effects of the French laws on associations of 1881, at the time when the Freycinet government claimed to have been inspired by that very example. In the United States, they pointed out, no law was needed to guarantee the freedom of the associations, which were given real advantages, such as tax-exempt status; as a result the American clergy fervently supported the regime.[17]

For all its limitations, American religion thus set a magnificent example that should be pondered in France. Not in its eccentric and bizarre aspects, but in its general functioning, from which even Catholicism

---

15. U. Gohier did not perceive any signs of anti-Semitism, and the Marquise San Carlos and Abbé Klein made analogous remarks over a span of thirty years. See F. Klein, *Au pays de la vie intense* (Paris: Plon, 1904), p. 37; an identical comment appeared in the abbé's second book, published in 1910. See also L. Weiller, *Les grandes idées d'un grand peuple* (Paris: Juven, 1904), p. 133; over the long run, the author was not entirely wrong, but this integration was slow and relative.

16. G. Alviella, *L'évolution religieuse contemporaine* (Paris-Bruxelles: Germer-Baillière, 1884), p. 256. The author's very neutral opinion is consistent with that of many Catholics, and even of some Protestants, such as Pastor Wagner.

17. A.-L. Mothon, O.P., "La législation des Etats-Unis et les corporations religieuses," *Le Correspondant* (10 April 1882): 22–24; the author's main point was to attack the radicals in the French government: "Above all, they should not talk of liberty; above all, they should stop citing the laws of the United States, for in doing so they just continue to show their ignorance or their bad faith" (p. 41).

could benefit. It was clear that if Catholicism was able to profit from the American freedom of religion, it also had to make adjustments to that regime.

The themes underlying the controversy over Americanism were thus first sounded as early as the 1880s.

## THE ISSUE OF AMERICANISM

By the end of the 1880s, the French observers gradually turned away from the sects, even from considerations about American religion in general, and began to think more about Catholicism, as if that religion had become the main feature of religious life in the United States.

### *A Most Attractive Catholicism*

Amidst the teeming of Protestant denominations, the Catholic Church seemed to stand out by its strength and its unity, and it was only natural that the French, most of whom were Catholic, paid more attention to their Church than to the other denominations. Moreover, it was fascinating to see how American Catholicism had been able to adapt to democracy and to separation from the state, which constituted the founding principles of the United States. The observers' attention was sharpened by the realization that the Catholic Church of America had experienced real growth throughout the nineteenth century. Counting barely a few tens of thousands of members around 1800 and subjected to persecution by the Know-Nothings and antipapist sentiments, it succeeded in asserting itself, especially after the influx of the Irish provided it with vigorous new blood, so that by 1890 it had swelled to some 12 million faithful. Because the Protestant churches, despite their close similarity, were officially separate entities, Catholicism had become the largest religion in the United States. This expansion was bound to strike the French, who at home were accustomed to seeing a Church whose place and whose role were being widely questioned. The situation was thus very different from what it had been in earlier periods, when American Catholicism was in a relatively weak position.

This evolution looked even more remarkable in the commentaries of French observers who sometimes seemed to forget that the United States was still a largely Protestant country, fascinated as they were by a very beautiful tree that prevented them from seeing a whole virgin forest.

The American Church and its priests struck the French observers in different ways, and while no one raised actual theological issues, all of them were somewhat bewildered, especially those who had been to the United States. In fact, until the 1890s, the Church of the United States was known in France chiefly through the comments of travelers, including a few priests.

The first reflections concerned the contrast between the effervescence and the versatility of the Protestant churches and the apparent majestic permanence of the Catholic Church, which was attended by manifestations of an ardent faith, as it was on a Sunday in 1870 in Omaha:

> The splendor of Catholicism, which can bring such solace, especially to those whose fate condemns them to a life of prosaic drudgery, struck me more forcefully perhaps in this vulgar place, on this muddy bank of the Missouri River, than it had struck me twenty-five years earlier at Saint Peter's in Rome.[18]

But very soon the observers' attention came to focus on the special character of the American Church, beginning with its day-to-day operation. They found out that in the United States the splendor of Catholic services was much reduced in scope and took place in very different buildings than those they knew in France. The churches, both parish churches and cathedrals, were brand new and equipped with all modern comforts; they were heated in winter, the holy-water basin had a spigot, and the seats were well upholstered. As for the lights, they were of course electric. The travelers, especially the clerics, were disturbed by this intrusion of comfort into the sacred space, for they felt that it would diminish the fervor and weaken the power of prayer. Yet after they had experienced it, they had to admit that neither cold nor darkness were indispensable to the expression of faith. Moreover, they found that the crowds assembled in these large churches did not seem to be less attentive, less focused than those in Europe, who did not enjoy such conditions. It was possible, then, for Catholicism to make use of physical amenities that the French had considered fit for eccentric Protestants only. This was certainly something to think about.

These very first impressions were confirmed by encounters with the priests and bishops of these astonishing churches. These men surrounded themselves with a minimum of ceremony, were always accessible, open, and cordial. Besides, the total absence of the *soutane* and the fact that all priests had adopted the so-called *clergyman* contributed to making them much less distant from their parishioners and less gratuitously

18. E.M. Malézieux, *Souvenirs d'une mission aux Etats-Unis* (Paris: Dunod, 1874), p. 92.

conspicuous in the streets. It was not difficult at all to meet such prelates as Mgr. Gibbons in Baltimore or Mgr. Ireland in Saint Paul-Minneapolis; only a sober ring indicated their position, their lodgings were remarkably modest, and their entourage was small; but the welcome extended was always warm and direct. Some of the observers compared these men to veritable executives, who managed all aspects of their parishes and their parishioners, both in the spiritual and in the strictly material domain.

There was a powerful contrast between this and an audience with a French or Roman bishop; all the visitors were pleased to find an ambiance that would surely have shocked them in Europe. They saw it as one more proof of the favorable influence of a specifically American way of life on that country's Catholicism; after all, the Church was prospering and becoming stronger.

These, however, were appearances, and what seemed really extraordinary was the general organization of the Catholic Church of the United States and its clergy. It was clear that this Church had been able to turn the general characteristics of American religion to account and to use the separation from the state to endow itself with autonomous financial means administered by *trustees*, whom the French likened to their vestry-boards of old, only on a vastly larger scale. The American Church had also known how to stay close to the concerns of the faithful, seeking to respond to their real needs in the same manner as the Protestant churches, with whom it might even collaborate. The same behavior that called forth ironic remarks in connection with the sects was seen as both effective and praiseworthy within the reassuring framework of the Roman Apostolic Church to which the Americans seemed so particularly attached. Claudio Jannet pronounced a veritable *satisfecit:*

> The American clergy is second to none when it comes to discipline and learning. Thanks to its complete freedom from interference by the civil authorities, no unhealthy views have ever attempted to alter the great currents of its tradition. Gallicanism and liberal Catholicism have never gained a foothold in the United States.[19]

Others, by contrast, felt that the principal asset of American Catholicism was precisely its democratic character, to the point that in viewing

---

19. C. Jannet, *Les Etats-Unis contemporains* (Paris: Plon, 1876), p. 242. This precisely dated judgment was not repeated twenty years later. Nonetheless Jannet did fear the heavy influence of Freemasonry and the danger of a possible Protestant coalition modeled on the nativist movements of the 1840s. He eventually gained a better understanding of the proliferation of ethnic churches and became attuned to the faith manifested by the French Canadians. See "La race française dans l'Amérique du Nord," *Le Correspondant* (April–June 1881): 585–612 and 825–65.

its growth and that of Catholic schools, Gustave de Molinari could exclaim: "Shouldn't these free-trade Catholics take their propaganda to Europe?" Similar reactions were found in other milieux as well, and so Abbé Vigneron, a faithful reader of Jannet who can hardly be suspected of liberalism, ended his book with a veritable hymn: "I love America because it is the land of liberty: and for a man, a Christian, and a priest, this is one of the most important conditions of life."[20] Even the most reluctant observers were struck by the lofty views of the American prelates, despite the "horribly democratic" things they said, and surely the marvels accomplished by the Irish clergy in inspiring respect for Catholicism were a sign that the right way had indeed been chosen, even if there was some danger in the immersion of priests in the masses and in their participation in political demonstrations.

Thus everyone found something to admire in American Catholicism. One priest – the same one who likened a hapless Protestant minister he had met on the boat to Belial – vaunted its orthodoxy, but most observers praised its liberalism, its perfect integration into a democratic society, and its excellent relations with the Protestant churches. Beyond these general considerations, precise examples were used to express analogous opinions: One person said that the strength of the American Church was the fervor of the "Irish faith"; another thought that its vitality was symbolized by the role Mgr. Gibbons had played in making the Knights of Labor acceptable to the Holy See.

This unanimity, which did not exclude a good deal of ambiguity, necessarily led the French to investigate just what had made American Catholicism so successful. Whatever it was, could it not be made to work in France? After all, the Catholic Church was called to universality, and so, despite some inevitable differences, the experience of the American faithful might teach a great deal to their French counterparts. This would even be a just payback, considering the role of the French Church in the early stages of the Church of the United States.

However, in the late 1880s no one mentioned the existence of a veritable American model. At that time there were no specific analyses that would have made it possible to use all or part of the example of American Catholicism; there were only superficially convergent impressions. A stream of favorable opinions, even on the basis of dissimilar motivations, would eventually clarify the picture and cause the French to take note of this example.

This began to happen by the early 1890s, when the accumulation of

20. L. Vigneron, *De Montréal à Washington* (Paris: Plon, 1887), p. 284.

such remarks led to comparisons and completely new ways of looking at things, so that it became possible to speak of *Americanism*.

### A Model, Perhaps

The astonishing success of American Catholicism, however inflated it may have been by the French observers, was considered a sign of hope for the Church as a whole. Abbé Macquet was struck by the depth of religious feeling, and Georges Sauvin did not hesitate to assert: "Religion understood in this way seems to me to be the wave of the future, and before long American Catholicism might well be the most solid support of the papacy."[21] Remarks of this kind carried even more weight when they came from highly visible authors, among whom the Vicomte de Meaux, author of *L'Eglise catholique et la liberté aux Etats-Unis*, undoubtedly best represented the new awareness of the importance of American Catholicism.

Having traveled to the United States in 1889 for the celebration of the centennial of that country's Church, the vicomte, starting in early 1890, published numerous articles in the *Correspondant*; his subsequent book that brought together these articles appeared with a preface in the form of a most laudatory letter from Mgr. Gibbons.[22] This date marks the beginning of a crystallization of French interest in the American Catholic experience.

De Meaux was looking to the United States because it was there that Catholicism had found that "second wind" it had so sorely lacked since the Counter Reformation. This was to return to the project of his father-in-law, Montalembert:

> When noble souls are seized by disgust with people and things, and when they are weakened and distressed by nagging doubts about the future of humankind, it is good to find and seize reasons for hope, even if one has to look for them all the way across the Atlantic.[23]

What De Meaux appreciated above all was the liberal and popular aspect of the Church of the United States; the role played by the Irish and German clergy, though not above criticism in certain respects, solidly

---

21. G. Sauvin, *Autour de Chicago* (Paris: Plon, 1893), p. 58. This view of the future went rather too far.
22. Vicomte de Meaux, *L'Eglise catholique et la liberté aux Etats-Unis*, 2nd ed. (Paris: Lecoffre, 1893). Mgr. Gibbons's letter is dated 27 December 1892. De Meaux's book is very rich and nuanced, treating not only matters pertaining to the Church but opening other perspectives as well. It was published in *Le Correspondant* between March 1890 and February 1893.
23. De Meaux, *L'Eglise catholique*, p. 35.

anchored the Church in the working-class population and made for the circulation of "vigorous new sap" contained by deep respect for its doctrines. Not only were the priests dressed in regular clothes, they also worked harder than French priests – "their zeal is more enterprising, quicker to act, more daring" – and moreover, bishops were chosen at a very young age by the Church itself and no other authority. To be sure, there were problems connected with the Catholic schools and with the deep enmity of certain evangelical churches, but the future of American Catholicism seemed to be assured thanks to its own qualities, among them the vigor of its clergy and the solid work of its various orders, particularly the Paulists, but also thanks to extremely beneficial institutional structures.

The author was careful, of course, to keep away from any idea of imitation and to insist on the originality of the American experience and on the different manifestations of religious liberty in the two countries. Nonetheless, the American example resonated with rich significance:

> For my purpose it was enough to show that the country where in our time the Catholic religion is developing and growing more than elsewhere is precisely the one where the freest and strongest democracy on earth is flourishing.[24]

This message, which synthesized the scattered remarks of an author whose orthodoxy was guaranteed by his name and by his connection with the most influential Catholic publication, was bound to have an impact. Moreover, it came at a particularly favorable time, for this was the very moment when the embers of French liberal Catholicism were rekindled by the contributions of the "neo-Christians" and the process of "rallying" the Catholics to the Republic. The ideas of Lamennais – a free Church in a free State – returned to favor, and a lecture by Mgr. Ireland in June 1892 was a great success in these circles. It even motivated Paul Bourget to go to America for a closer look at the situation, for a voice like his could do a great deal to reinforce that of Montalembert's son-in-law.

Bourget's *Outremer* was by no means a book about religion, and much of it was devoted to worldly preoccupations, yet it is a fact that the famous member of the Académie française immediately came to admire the vitality of American Catholicism, whereas he was nauseated by the Baptist "barbarity." He was also dazzled by the "greatness of soul" of Mgr. Ireland, on whom he called in Saint Paul; this "Savonarola," he said, would play an essential role in the Church's conciliation with science and democracy. Moreover, would it not be natural for a pope to be American,

24. Ibid., p. 409.

... issued from this free nation, where the Church leaders have succeeded in returning to the ways of the first apostles; for all these men are close to the people's hearts, the hearts of these humble beings where so many irresistible ideas are fermenting.[25]

In short, it seemed to Bourget that bringing the people back to the Church was possible only in the United States.

This current of admiration never went beyond a small group of persons who, without admitting it, considered the American Church as a model that had been remarkably successful in reconciling tradition and the modern world. To be sure, these authors more or less deliberately underestimated the problems caused by the rivalry between the Irish and the German clergy or, more simply, the existence within the American clergy of a traditionalist and a conservative current; yet the influence of their analyses was far greater than their role within the French Catholic community.

This was the precise context for the quarrel over Americanism that for a few months shook the Catholic Church in both France and Italy.

### Americanism: An Ephemeral Controversy

When Comte de Chabrol presented Father Hecker to the French public in *Le Correspondant* in May of 1897, he clearly stated the question. The case of the founder of the Paulists, whose "respectful outspokenness and obedience without obsequiousness" contrasted with the cavilling ways of a Lamennais, gave him the opportunity to discuss the invaluable contribution of American Catholicism: ". . . would the freedoms that constitute the strength of the Catholic Church in the United States serve it equally well in the old European societies?"[26] The article announced a new book, the *Life of Father Hecker* by the Rev. Elliot in a translation by Abbé Félix Klein, who had been commissioned to do this work by Chabrol. When the book was published, the controversy was triggered by a campaign in the Catholic press, where Abbé Maignen, as spokesman for the conservatives, violently attacked Abbé Klein in an article entitled "Etudes sur l'américanisme, le Père Hecker est-il un saint?" ["Studies on Americanism, Is Father Hecker a Saint?"][27] In addition to such traditional Catholic

---

25. P. Bourget, *Outremer* (Paris: Lemerre, 1895), p. 191. Remarks of this kind show that progress initiated in the United States was considered ineluctable.
26. Comte de Chabrol, "Un prêtre américain: Le R.P. Hecker," *Le Correspondant* (10 June 1897): 912. The author was intent on resuming the contacts with the Church of the United States initiated before the *Syllabus*, and he chose the brilliant and open-minded F. Klein as his "light cavalry," feeling that he himself was too old.
27. This book was published in Rome (Lib. cath. inter.) with the imprimatur of the Holy See, but without that of a French bishop, which is eloquent testimony to the tendencies

publications as *La Vérité*, *Etudes religieuses*, and *La Croix*, other and more unexpected voices were heard as well. Ferdinand Brunetière, for instance, supported Klein and the Americanists in a famous article published in the *Revue des Deux Mondes* in late 1898, as well as in an exchange of letters with the Holy See[28] and with some fierce defenders of a tradition rooted in French Canada, such as Jules Tardivel and Edmond de Nevers.[29]

The partisans of Americanism denied any charges of heretical deviation, but had to back off when the sovereign pontiff intervened in *Testem benevolentiae*, his apostolic letter of 22 January 1899. Abbé Klein had to take his book off the market and for a time was afraid that he would be condemned. Quite aside from theological doctrine, diverse opinions were expressed at this point.

The Americanists had, for the most part, looked at the American example from a strictly French perspective. What they saw in the unique American situation was the dream of a decentralized Church within which each national Church would have relatively different traits without, however, deviating from the dogma.

What fascinated these observers most were the qualities they ascribed to American religion as a whole: to wit, integration into society, cohabitation with the Protestants, absence of sectarianism, acceptance and defense of the secular institutions. Agreeing that the participation of Mgr. Ireland and other Catholics in the famous Congress of Religions at the Chicago World's Fair was open to criticism, they nonetheless felt that it should not be condemned with the blind violence the conservatives had unleashed against it. Such a view had clear Gallican and liberal overtones that were part of a French tradition and could be sounded without apparent risk in connection with the American example, not to say the American model.

within the papacy. It was a reaction to the translation of F. Klein's work, which had been most successful, selling 1,200 copies in two months. Under the name of Delorme, and at the request of the editors of *Le Correspondant*, F. Klein responded to the accusations of Maignen, which had been widely circulated in the conservative Catholic press.

28. See A. Houtin, *L'Américanisme* (Paris: Nourry, 1904); Houtin was a sympathizer. For all the details, see the plea of F. Klein, "Une hérésie fantôme, l'américanisme," ch. 4 of *La Route d'un petit morvandiau* (Paris: Plon, 1949). See also F. Brunetière, "Le Catholicisme aux Etats-Unis," *Revue des Deux Mondes* (1 Nov. 1898): 140–81, as well as his letter of September 1900 to the pope, suggesting that both Mgr. Ireland and the incumbent of the see of Quebec be made cardinals as a matter of balance. Preserved in the Vatican, this letter is cited in Fohlen, "Catholicisme américain." The advice was not followed.

29. E. de Nevers, *L'âme américaine* (Paris: Jouve-Boyer, 1900), 2 vols. This is a synthesis on life in the United States, intended to tear off the overly favorable veil drawn by French observers. See also J. Tardivel, *La situation religieuse aux Etats-Unis* (Lille-Paris: Desclée et Brouver, 1900); this is a highly combative work.

The sharp reaction of an appreciable segment of the French Church showed that the seemingly unanimous view of the American Church was a fragile thing. At best, only its exotic aspects had had a certain attraction when seen on the spot, provided they were not adapted or imitated: ". . . more than a spot of mildew, more than a microbe of political phylloxera comes to us from across the sea," Mgr. Pasquier, rector of the Catholic University of Angers, could exclaim in 1896. And it is not without significance that the archbishop of Cambrai, needing an expert on the American situation, called a French Canadian to the rescue. Setting out to take apart the entire argumentation of the Americanists, Tardivel was particularly hard on Brunetière, who had promoted the image of a Catholic paradise in America, where the Church was free, fervent, and in full expansion. In Tardivel's opinion, the papal condemnation of the individualism of certain American prelates that had so impressed the French was fully justified, and democracy had nothing to do with Catholicism, whose single pole was and remained Rome. The American Church could not be different from any other, and moreover it was constantly subjected to the still vivid hostility of the Protestants, and its advances were not as noteworthy as was often said. And at any rate, such advances as had been made were brought about by priests who used the time-honored methods: "In a word, they knew and taught that today, as in the past, one goes to heaven by the Stations of the Cross and not by the stations of the railroad."[30]

The Americanist endeavor could not survive these concerted attacks, in which the papacy only slightly softened the offensive of the most conservative French-Catholic circles. Some of its leaders, who often had no first-hand knowledge of the United States, had their hopes dashed, and those who became involved in the controversy were deeply scarred by this victory of tradition and the impossibility of adapting all or part of the American examples to France. However, this virulent controversy was brief and affected only a tiny group within the French Church, which seems to have lost all memory of it.[31] At the level of public opinion, it was overshadowed by the more spectacular and far-reaching developments of the Dreyfus Affair, for which there could be no American model.

30. Tardivel, *La situation religieuse*, p. 271. The work was addressed to Mgr. Sonnois, and the preface that granted his imprimatur stressed the point that the separation of Church and State should indeed be condemned.
31. While the controversy marked the Church of the United States more deeply than the French observers of the times realized, it has left few traces in France, where it is practically never mentioned in the various histories of the Church of France, any more than in the *Revue d'histoire de l'Eglise de France*.

In this context it becomes clear that the intervention of Pope Leo XIII marked the limits beyond which the American Catholics could not go. Above all, it destroyed the notion, conceived by certain bold minds, that the American model might be applicable to other countries.

The next step is to find out whether French observers who had the opportunity to discover the Church of the United States in the early twentieth century saw it with the same eyes as their predecessors; no longer a model, was it still attractive?

### *Persistent Admiration*

It appears that by the early twentieth century unanimity reigned once again, as if it had never ceased. As France became carried away by its passions of religious politics, the American example still showed that there could be serenity, acceptance of Catholics, and successful separateness: "In the struggle over religion, it is customary to cite the United States as an example; and this is done by all of the parties."

Before turning to the new consensus, it is of interest to look into the paths taken by certain actors in the Americanist controversy who, despite their relative discomfiture, did not abandon the example of the United States. The Vicomte de Meaux had hardly modified his point of view at all when he gave two lectures at Lille in 1903; he was still persuaded of the vigor of American Catholicism, which, unlike its French counterpart, benefited from religious freedom and could therefore flourish and remain close to the people. Proof of this was the fact that Mgr. Ireland was chosen to participate in the arbitration committee set up in 1903 following the great American coal miners' strike of the preceding fall. Thus, the Church of the United States had not changed, but it was only one example of a vigorous Catholicism; there was no need to copy it or even to envy it, for all the French needed to do was to reconquer their liberty, as the Americans had done.[32] To this extent there had been a change: Admiration was still justified, but it had to remain distant and must not, under any circumstances, turn into the adoption of a model.

Even more interesting is the case of Félix Klein, who was at the very center of the Americanist tempest and one of its main protagonists. He set out to discover the United States after he had communicated for many months with American priests, excited that he would finally be able to speak with them; he went to visit churches and seminaries after he

---

32. Vicomte de Meaux, "L'Eglise catholique aux Etats-Unis," *Revue de Lille* (March–April 1904). This is the text of two lectures given at the University of Lille on 9 and 10 December 1903.

had formed a certain idea of that country, and after he had defended its example without knowing it very well. Klein experienced the clash between ideas and their implementation, between dream and reality, with unusual intensity.

At the end of his first journey, he was fully reassured and felt that he had really discovered a "free and strong land . . . [a] country that has not disappointed my expectations." In particular, he felt that the Church he was beginning to know better was indeed powerful and self-assured:

> . . . America, far from appearing, as I had expected, as a Protestant country where Catholicism is tolerated, showed itself, on the contrary, as a half-theist and half-Christian country, where Catholicism is by far the most influential religion.[33]

His opinion could not of course be neutral, but the fervor of the faithful and the mutual tolerance shown by everyone truly impressed him beyond the clichés he had brought from France. Naturally, meeting Mgr. John L. Spalding in Peoria and Mgr. James Gibbons in Baltimore made him very happy and confirmed his ideas, but it was probably his meeting with the bishop of Rochester, Mgr. MacQuaid, that made him understand fully the nature of this transatlantic Catholicism. He actually had not wanted to meet this conservative bishop who did not share his ideas, but when he could not avoid it, he was astounded that he was received warmly, without formality and ulterior motives, and that even there seminarians moved about freely without being subjected to excessive discipline. After other occasions allowed him to observe the American Church and its clergy more closely, the special character of this institution became much clearer to him. It was "the energy of the Americans combined with the mellowness of Catholicism." This conviction was confirmed on later trips, during which he came to appreciate the virtues of tolerance when he was invited to speak at secular universities, considering that France continued to struggle with its familiar demons of ideological warfare.

The perception of profound differences between the two societies made it clear that using the American Church as an actual model was not feasible, but for these somewhat chastened French Catholics it did confirm the great value of the American example.

Some of the French observers who had not been involved in the controversy considered it a false problem, for what they knew of Americanism struck them as a caricature of the real Church of the United States.

---

33. Klein, *Au pays de la vie intense*, p. 28.

Catholic clerics, of course, insisted with renewed vigor on the absence of all religious conflict in the United States, in order to show the distance between the two experiences. They could only go into raptures, as did this humble abbé in 1904: ". . . I envied that welcoming and blessed land where no one is tormented and oppressed and where everyone can live as he wishes and desires, even in accordance with the Gospel, in the invigorating sunshine of liberty."[34] Sometimes there was even a note of sadness when one of these visitors had met Mgr. Ireland, who, then as now, makes one appreciate the qualities of tolerance and energy in a prelate who had been a student in France and loved that country so much; some of his visitors felt compelled to contrast his attitude with that of some of the French clergy.

After the Americanist episode, as before it, more or less liberal clerics were still fascinated with a Church that seemed to be truly national, playing its role in the assimilation of immigrants without committing the errors illustrated in the past by Gallicanism, as well as with the seeming unity among the members of a clergy more interested in morality than in dogma. There was nothing wrong with this, but this "Church of America" simply could not be copied. Nonetheless, it continued to be a beacon of hope, for the French observers absolutely wanted to see it as the image of the Church of the future, which would be independent, strong, autonomous, and more concerned with morals than with doctrines. This went so far that, once again, it seemed natural for such a clergy to bring a breath of fresh American air to Rome: ". . . it makes me dream of a pope who would not remain immobile within the Vatican but would roam the world like an apostle and revolutionize it once again with an inspired breath."[35]

Such views were also found, albeit in different terms, among lay observers; they had not been involved in the internal conflicts of the Catholic Church and could only make comparisons with what they knew about the Church of France. Still, they also found that American Catholicism was closer to the people and bore the seal of democracy, and although they did not prejudge the future and the possible involvement of the Church in all of society's concerns, many of them felt that this attitude was more useful than continual self-examination. This general trend of the American Church was confirmed by the social role of the bishops;

---

34. Abbé Etienne, *Choses d'Amérique* (Châlons sur Marne: Imprimerie O'Toole, 1904), p. 6.
35. G. d'Avenel, *Aux Etats-Unis, les champs, les affaires, les idées* (Paris: Colin, 1908), p. 246. One recognizes P. Bourget's idea, which was also held by L. Weiller; but the pope who moved about would not be American, and the Church had to wait for him for a long time.

they were even called upon by President Theodore Roosevelt to represent the United States on certain occasions along with the diplomats, as Mgr. Ireland did at the time of the Franco-American festivities in 1900 and 1902.

The French never ceased to be surprised by these "democratic and populist" priests. As Paul Adam put it: "If in France our bishops, our parish priests, and our abbots were as tough as the American Catholic priests, everyone would shout, "down with the Free Masons!"[36] The difference was such that even as fierce an anticlerical as Urbain Gohier was shaken. He continued to think, to be sure, that "the policies of the Catholic Church are essentially opportunistic," and that its wealth and its power would soon become a genuine danger for the United States, but he was nonetheless surprised to learn that during the strikes of 1902 a part of the clergy espoused the cause of the miners, and to hear diatribes against the rich from the mouths of certain bishops. Thus, when he listened to Mgr. Spalding speaking of a larger and more intense life, ". . . it seemed to me . . . that I could be a bishop in the United States, and that that country's Catholic bishops would be headed for the stake in Europe. . . ."[37] Urbain Gohier did not realize how true this was, for in 1908 Elisée Reclus did not hesitate to push the comparison even further, as if it had not been enough to condemn Americanism:

> The Roman See wants to make very sure that the manifestations of American Catholicism remain unknown to the mass of the faithful in the Old World. The Catholic religion, in the same manner as the thousand forms of Protestantism, has had to adapt to new environments, where religious traditions and the industrial techniques of advertising form a new amalgam against an old background of animism and magic.[38]

Such comments, infrequent though they were, reveal that by the early twentieth century the relative unanimity of the 1880s had not disappeared, but had obviously been modified, as if a certain naivete were disappearing. The French still admired American Catholicism, but they no longer praised its unimpeachable orthodoxy, and most of those who expressed themselves on this subject were, more clearly than in the preceding period, part of a liberal current. The conservatives – whose

---

36. Laborer, "Au Texas," p. 74.
37. Gohier, *Le peuple du XXe siècle*, p. 136. Gohier defended himself against this worrisome attraction of the Church by stressing the hypocrisy of the Church's attitude and by predicting that it would assert a tyrannical domination over the Catholics of the United States.
38. E. Reclus, *L'homme et la terre* (Paris: Librairie universelle, 1908), p. 115.

strength had been demonstrated in the Americanist controversy – no longer seemed interested in the Church of the United States, having found that of Canada a much more reassuring example.[39]

The strangeness of the American experience and the clear end of any hope of borrowing a few prescriptions from America provided liberal Catholics with an escape from day-to-day conflicts and allowed them to evoke a kind of promised land. But this attitude caused them to underestimate the problems of the Catholic Church of the United States and to expect from it more than it could deliver.

In focusing most of their attention, first on picturesque and marginal sects and then exclusively on the Catholic Church of the United States, the French observers failed to perceive the specificity of the phenomenon of religion in that country. The multiplicity of evangelical movements and their strange behaviors showed the observers – who were looking either for exoticism or for a model – no more than the outward signs of their power, the shadow of their influence.

Thus, a great deal more time than the French would have thought around 1900 had to pass before a Catholic could become President of the United States, and for all its success, the American Church was never able to acquire the role it can play where Catholicism has a virtual monopoly. The penetration of Catholicism into the world of labor was closely tied to the Irish presence and did not portend the birth of an American brand of social Catholicism; that philosophy became a French specialty.

What accounts for this skewed perspective is the momentary conjunction of a phase of expansion in American Catholicism with a particularly grave crisis in Church-State relations in France. It should be added that what French opinion, except for a few devotees of theological questions, was looking for in the United States was not an ideological renewal; what it found fascinating was the degree to which the Catholic Church of America was imbued with typically American values, which gave it its air of liberty and its democratic tone. Perhaps this was the area

---

39. Beyond the intervention of Tardivel, the close relations between the Canadian and the French clergy, and the many communities that were warmly received [in France] after the separation crisis of 1905, one can also cite a most telling example: An article by Mgr. Baudrillart in *Le Correspondant* of 10 July 1909, "Les Universités catholiques," compared a number of cases, among them Quebec, Montreal, and Washington. On p. 9, the author states: "At the risk of surprising the convinced believers in the superiority in all things of our brethren in the United States . . ." by way of a warning before he demonstrates the inferiority of the Catholic University of Washington, D.C., compared with Laval University. In terms of numbers of professors and students, this was a fact.

where one could find some examples that might benefit the Church in France. This attitude explains why Americanism, a theological crisis that did not concern itself with French opinion as a whole, was ephemeral, whereas a superficial interest in the least directly religious facets of American Catholicism continued unabated.

# 11

# *Social Hell or Social Harmony?*

One of the components in the attraction the United States long held for French people, especially on the Left, was the apparent social equality that was said to reign in that country. Thus it was believed that all farmers worked farms of similar size, that artisans and workers were not held back from participating in politics, that there was no real poverty, and that there were multiple avenues of upward social mobility. This perception of a Promised Land of social equality culminated with the victory of the North over the South, seen as the victory of the democratic Yankee over the aristocratic Southerner, the victory of the working man, symbolized by the rail-splitter Abraham Lincoln who became President, over the rich landowner.[1] The same information made the French conservative milieux feel most uncomfortable about the reputedly uncouth and egalitarian American society.

Views of this kind did not stand up to serious examination. Social equality never actually existed, except in the form of a myth that was dispelled once and for all amidst the din of a ruthless industrialization during the years of the Gilded Age. Would the French continue to make the United States into a working man's paradise, the Promised Land of social peace? This could be done only by people who used the example of the United States to bolster their ideological presuppositions and who were not interested in the realities. By the same token, the sudden awareness of the many facts that were shattering this peaceful and egalitarian image could lead to the rejection of any American model, a rejection as absolute as the admiration of the preceding years. Between these two extremes, there was room to see the social situation of the United States as a somewhat diminished but still attractive example.

---

1. T. Sancton, "America in the Eyes of the French Left," Ph.D. thesis, Oxford University, 1987, pp. 225–28.

## THE END OF THE MYTH OF ARCADIA

Beginning with the 1870s and over the next quarter-century, the perception of the United States as the land of equality and of the working man's paradise was definitively destroyed, both by militant labor and the so-called "bourgeois." To be sure, all eyes had not yet been opened, as Elisée Reclus pointed out around 1900:

> Some backward writers still cite the United States as the example of a land of equality where all the world's disinherited find a farm and freedom; in the Union of our time, pauperism and an enormous concentration of capital are already facing each other at the two poles of society.[2]

This statement would indicate the existence of a historical time lag, which constitutes one of the essential explanations in a study of opinion, but such reactions were rare.

### *The Shock of 1876–1877*

In the first years of our period, one still finds traces of the idyllic memories of the preceding decade. Thus E. Portalis and a few others still felt that profound equality was the rule in the United States, that workers were treated splendidly, in fact on an equal footing with their employers. The earlier caveats of Cluseret clearly had not been heard. On the other hand, the very somber considerations of a Claudio Jannet, who was indeed well informed about the American situation, were freighted with a bias of systematic hostility for the world of industry, a bias that caused him to stress the inevitable conflict between workers and employers in the absence of yesterday's gentle paternalism.

As for the travelers who visited the United States on the occasion of the Philadelphia World's Fair, very few of them were interested in labor conditions, or even in social relations. This, in fact, was a constant, for the world of the workers attracted little attention. Only a few observers indicated that a social crisis was brewing in the United States, which no longer bathed in the democratic irenicism that had been so highly praised by Tocqueville and the Republicans, but their argument remained rather general, being fueled as much by the scandals of the Grant administration as by examples of social conflict.

The worker delegations who went to the United States for the same World's Fair had a different agenda. Having grown up at a time when

---

2. E. Reclus, *Nouvelle géographie universelle: La terre et les hommes, les Etats-Unis* (Paris: Hachette, 1890), p. 745.

this Promised Land was being celebrated, they came to check out the situation. They came to see the march of progress, but also to show that the French workers were not backward. Indeed, the spread of Marxism had already caused many to perceive the United States as an essentially capitalist country;[3] they were here to verify the scope of this phenomenon on the spot.

More than twenty Parisian trades, exercised in ancient guilds or as industrial jobs, were represented in this delegation. Proud of its independence, its members openly displayed a class consciousness sharpened by the recent memory of the Paris Commune as well as by their Socialist aspirations. Yet their opinions varied appreciably from one report to another, for some limited themselves to technical considerations, while others judged the conduct of their American counterparts; corporative or frankly collectivist reflexes are easy to perceive. Yet one thing was clearly and almost unanimously understood; it was expressed in the report of the mechanics, who were decidedly in the collectivist camp, in speaking of their American counterparts:

> In the United States, as in all other countries in the world, the absence of social organization makes for two totally distinct classes of citizens: the capitalists and the proletarians or, in other words, those who live on the work of others and those who produce. The latter are, in all the hideousness of that term, at the mercy of the former.[4]

This statement, which destroys any idea of an American exceptionalism, was completely confirmed by these workers' observations on various topics. The Civil War had produced astonishing fortunes, but its aftermath had not been favorable for the workers, who did not return to full employment and were increasingly pressed by very harsh competition. This was particularly true in the years 1873–77, which were extremely difficult as a result of lowered wages and ever harsher working conditions in the large companies. This reality was new and most upsetting for many of the French workers who still belonged, as is shown by the composition of the delegation, to very traditional guilds such as the silk-dyers, gunsmiths, or piano-makers, to name only a few. Working in

---

3. For this subject, see R. Laurence Moore, *European Socialists and the American Promised Land* (New York: Oxford University Press, 1970), pp. 3–52. The author examines the attitude of the French compared with that of other nationalities and finds decided differences. The French Socialists were watching the United States with less sustained attention than their German or British counterparts. These nuances are related to differences in emigration patterns.

4. *Rapports de la délégation ouvrière libre: Mécaniciens* (Paris: Sandoz, Fischbacher et Vve. Morel, 1877), p. 119. Submitted by a highly unionized trade, this is one of the richest reports.

these trades made it harder for them to grasp the conditions in large industrial plants, which were undergoing rapid development in the United States.

The difficulties of the moment did not conceal the fact that the American worker had some important advantages in terms of wages and political freedom, and some of the French workers even found that "... in America the workers have it better than in Europe," but this had to do with the special conditions of that country, its resources, and the major differences among workers, depending on whether they were "Americans" or recent immigrants. Moreover, these few advantages were ruined by widespread "layoffs," by work schedules that seemed much harsher than in France, and by utterly ruthless exploitation by the employers.[5] The conclusions of the different delegations were unanimous; no one envied the Americans for their life, except on some minor points, and in fact the Americans were chided for their failure to protect their own rights. Not one member of the delegations considered, even for a moment, emigrating to the United States. The particularly severe judgment of the men's tailors was therefore not really exceptional:

> ... far from being the Promised Land of the worker, the great American Republic has become just like Europe, a veritable social hell. The antagonism between labor and capital, which is clearly becoming more vivid and ardent every day, must dispel the last illusions of those who like to show the United States as the last refuge of human happiness.[6]

Such an indictment shows how totally the myth of a workers' paradise had disappeared, much earlier than certain observers might have thought. No need to wait for May 1886 or October 1917.

These reports of the French worker delegations, which might have passed unnoticed due to their limited circulation, actually became rather widely known, having come out just at the time when the United States was in the throes of the great railroad strike of 1877, which furnished additional proof for the deterioration of the country's social situation. More conservative circles derided both the workers' commentaries and the Americans, who were fighting two evils from which they had considered themselves immune: "... is it not curious to see the means by

---

5. *Rapport d'ensemble de la délégation ouvrière libre à Philadelphie* (Paris: Imprimerie nouvelle, 1879). Here, for instance, is the report of the shoemakers: "... the most refined schemes are used by the employers to draw the very last drop of sweat and blood from the worker" (p. 55). What so profoundly shocked the French were the highly intense methods of production.

6. *Rapport d'ensemble*, "Tailleurs d'habit," p. 125.

which the 'model Republic,' the democracy that our radicals admire so much, is planning to enforce law and order in the future?"[7]

Thus the United States was no longer considered an egalitarian country secure from social conflicts; within a few years a well-established model had almost completely disintegrated in the eyes of the Left. To some extent this happened because even the French labor unions did not approve of the way in which their American counterparts conducted their struggle, that is, without true collective action and without explicit condemnation of the existing system. During the strike of 1877, they were certainly surprised to see an American workers' association state: "Our goal is to increase our wages and to give the capitalist more security and more regular profits."[8] Under these conditions the inevitable revolution spawned by capitalism could not possibly arise on American soil.

These first indications make it clear that the American working-class experience was foreign to French workers. Conversely, the relative moderation of the American working class was bound to be appreciated by the French conservatives. A strange paradox, but this was only the beginning.

### The Flooding of the Promised Land

The years following the wrenching events of 1877 confirmed the demise of the serene image of the United States. It is hardly necessary to remind the reader of the great demonstrations in favor of the eight-hour day that culminated in the Haymarket incident in May 1886 or of the great strikes of 1892 at the Carnegie steel mills in Homestead, not to forget the strike of 1894 that started with labor disputes at Pullman.

By this time all the French who followed these events were convinced that major changes had occurred in the United States. In Socialist circles these were considered a test of analyses going back to 1876, and these looked more and more accurate as the situation hardened, especially during the events of 1886. However, French interest in American phenomena was sporadic, which is why the tone of certain analyses was less dogmatic than it might have been.[9]

---

7. A. Langlois, "La grève des ouvriers de chemin de fer aux Etats-Unis," *Le Correspondant* (25 Aug. 1877): 627.
8. E. Reclus, "La grève d'Amérique," offprint from *Le Travailleur* (Sept. 1877): 13; Reclus was deeply upset by the attitude of workers who thought that salvation could be achieved by voting.
9. A. Keufer, *Rapport sur l'imprimerie, Exposition de Boston* (Paris: Imprimerie nouvelle, Association ouvrière, 1884), p. 88. This positivist, who was to become famous later, expressed some very interesting views here.

But this relative respite did not last long; the Socialists remained abreast of the social evolution of the United States through their contacts with American colleagues, as did the workers of the delegation of 1876, who kept in touch with French militants working in the United States. What they heard was rather somber. The few columns concerning that country in the *Revue Socialiste* dwelt at length on the cruelty of American employers – they were barbaric in their treatment of women and children and made use of Pinkerton guards – and on the horrendous misery that could exist in certain regions. It is therefore not surprising that in late 1885 only one conclusion could be drawn: "How can anyone think that before long the most dreadful, but also the most liberating class war will not break out?" This last remark was meant to indicate that there might be some slight hope, that the American workers seemed to be organizing and mounting a vigorous response to the employers' attacks. Not that this could serve as a model of social struggle, but perhaps some day the United States would once again become an example to be followed.

This was the climate in which the bomb of Haymarket exploded, followed by a true travesty of justice that ended with the execution of four suspects on 11 November 1887. Just as the reactions of the more conservative milieux demonstrated a certain satisfaction with the firm attitude of the American authorities, so those of the Left were filled with indignation.

The last shred of the veil of harmony that still covered the American reality had been torn away, for the event was widely covered in the Socialist press of Europe,[10] and there is no need to remind the reader that it led to the celebration of Labor Day on 1 May. Linked to the pursuit of the eight-hour day, which had much stronger resonance in Europe, this event was appropriated by the more determined French Socialists as an example of oppression by the employer class. It was particularly symbolic because it had taken place in a country that certain bedazzled minds could still consider a Promised Land.

However, these reactions were least prevalent in France. In addition to a few editorials in a nascent Socialist press, as well as in the more generally Republican press, such as *L'Intransigeant* of Rochefort, which protested against a scandalous procedure that dishonored the United States, the *Revue Socialiste* devoted one article to the event shortly after it happened and then published the diary of one of the convicted sus-

10. Moore, *European Socialists*, pp. 33–36. See also M. Cordillot, "Les réactions européennes aux évènements de Haymarket," in *A l'ombre de la Statue de la Liberté* (Paris: Presses de l'Université de Vincennes, 1989).

pects a few years later.[11] The statement, written by Jean Longuet, in which the municipal council of Paris demanded clemency for the accused, expressed deep disappointment:

> Throughout the years it was the glory of the great Republic toward which French and European democracy was always looking that it had never known the vengeance and reprisals that have bloodied the political history of all modern nations.[12]

Decidedly, the United States no longer offered an enviable model in the political or social arena, neither to the Socialists nor to a more moderate Left. Nor was the climate much more favorable among more right-leaning observers.

One does of course detect some sneering joy that even the United States had these kinds of difficulties, but more generally one finds an awareness that American society had changed in ways that made it unfit as a model for anyone. In this sense the reflection of Baron de Mandat-Grancey, hardly a supporter of democracy, is significant. In comparing the American West with the East, he wrote:

> Among them [the Westerners], equality is so well established that one does not encounter the muted hostility that in our country the man in the workers' smock so often shows the gentleman in a fine coat. However, this observation, which is absolutely true in the West, would be subject to a few restrictions in speaking of the Eastern provinces, which are rapidly becoming Europeanized.[13]

By the end of the 1880s, then, the United States no longer had a special status in comparison with European countries. How could anyone claim that the working classes were so well off at a time when multiple strikes and conflicts showed the scope of their dissatisfaction? Not only that, but the unrest affected huge industries and paralyzed transportation, thus "taking away the wages of thousands and thousands of men," not just those of a few hundred families, as happened "on our side of the Atlantic Ocean." How could these social struggles fail to take a dire turn in the face of the staggering power of the trusts and their masters, and the obsti-

11. The *Revue Socialiste* of December 1889 printed an American article on the Chicago anarchists, accompanied by a description of the facts by Paul Buquet; the subject was continued in the January 1890 issue with the autobiography of Spies and the text of the principal speeches. It is significant that this translation appeared only two years after the events, whereas it was published almost immediately in Germany.
12. R. Vaillant, "Les condamnés de Chicago," *Revue Socialiste* (Nov. 1886): 1137. By way of comparison, the author recalls the magnanimity the North was able to show the South after the Civil War.
13. E. de Mandat-Grancey, *Dans les Montagnes Rocheuses* (Paris: Plon, 1884), p. 14.

nate resistance of the workers? "I fear that the Americans, who make fun of our revolutions, are preparing one of their own that will, to cite the words of Heinrich Heine, 'make '93 look like an idyll.' "[14]

The United States was no longer a model of social peace, no longer a Promised Land for the working man; the rich were richer there than elsewhere, and the poor probably poorer. Gustave de Molinari, moderate though he was, therefore felt in 1894 that there was ". . . no country, even aristocratic England or aristocratic Russia, where wealth is as unequally distributed as within the most democratic American union."[15]

To be sure, the followers of Jules Guesde tried to see a preponderant role for the American working class in the struggle against a particularly powerful capitalism, but by the early 1890s it became clear that not too much could be hoped for from this quarter. Besides, throughout the following years, the French still had their doubts about the organizational abilities and the requisite fighting spirit of the American workers, particularly when large numbers of studies showed that, in the end, the standard of living of American workers was appreciably higher than that of their French, even European, comrades.

This situation became even more striking when, beginning in 1896, changing economic circumstances in the United States brought the return of a certain prosperity from which the workers benefited as well.

## HOW THE AMERICAN WORKER LIVED

Even during the years when the most acerbic criticism of the social situation in the United States came into being, one finds observers, even among the French workers, who thought that American workers lived better than their French counterparts. To be sure, many of the arguments stressed the hidden side of this situation, but these remarks were so frequent that one has to analyze what may look like a contradiction.

### *Which Workers?*

Before one can speak in detail about the way of life of these American workers, who, if we are to believe a large part of the observers, were better educated, better dressed, and better paid than French workers, one must ask on which examples these findings were based.

14. M. O'Rell, *Jonathan et son continent* (Paris: Calman-Lévy, 1889), p. 76.
15. G. de Molinari, "La guerre industrielle aux Etats-Unis," *Revue de Paris* (1 Aug. 1894): 546.

The visitors, whether they were workers themselves or "bourgeois" engaged in sociological studies, had contact with only a small sample of American workers. The factories they visited were carefully selected ones, for one could not simply walk into any plant; and in any case, visitors were always most attracted by the best facilities.

Thus, in the 1880s, the textile factories of Lowell, Massachusetts, the Baldwin locomotive works in Philadelphia, the Pullman factory near Chicago, and the Carnegie steel mills in the Pittsburgh area were among the most attractive. The tour taken by the worker delegation at the Saint Louis World's Fair was quite revealing in this respect. In addition to the above sites, this group also visited the Midvale steel mills in Philadelphia, as well as Westinghouse in Pittsburgh, and above all the National Cash Register plant in Dayton and National Foods Company near Niagara. In these plants which, at the cutting edge of progress, were equipped with the latest technical improvements, the lot of the work force necessarily appeared in the most favorable light. Even Emile Levasseur, who on a more exhaustive tour of the industrial world of America visited some particularly mediocre shops, obtained most of his information from the up-to-date companies. Alexandre Seauret, a worker who had spent many years working for various American companies, was therefore not altogether wrong when he criticized these observers:

> Like a general who comes for a surprise inspection of the barracks, where he tastes the soup and assures himself of the well-being of the soldier after he has taken care to announce his visit, they too saw only what the company allowed them to see.[16]

This does not mean that all their observations were based on deception, but it is certain that, intentionally or not, they did not tell the whole story. Reports of horrendous working conditions in certain American companies thus came from American books and articles – among them Mary Van Vorst's well-known investigation of child labor in the South – that were essentially copied by French labor publications. But this kind of information did not have the same resonance as what came from sources more familiar to the French reader.

To this almost inevitable deformation must be added another that was related to the structure of American labor. For in fact – and not all observers were aware of this – there was a real distinction between

16. A.P. Seauret, "Journal d'un émigrant aux Etats-Unis," *Revue Socialiste* (July 1906): 71. The author's first trip to the United States took place around 1876, a fact that partly accounts for the dark tone of his picture.

workers recruited among recent immigrants, who often worked in the famous "sweat shops," and Americans of longer standing, who held the more skilled jobs and for the time being were the only ones who had access to certain managerial positions.

The more superficial observers, those who were simply traveling, essentially knew only the second kind of worker and considered the occupants of the tenements, which some of them had the opportunity to visit, as the dregs of the population, unable to see them as part of the working class. This attitude explains some of the precautions they took when they visited these areas in a city like New York. The French workers, particularly those of the delegation of 1876, who expressed themselves more freely, were much more aware of the problem: "First of all, we find heterogeneity. . . . This is why we should accept the expression 'American workers' only with the greatest reservations. . . ."[17] From this premise they deduced various observations about the different behaviors of workers of different backgrounds. Similarly, Emile Levasseur in his masterful study was careful to distinguish between immigrant workers who worked in the worst conditions – "the circles of Dante's Hell" – and the "American worker," on whom he essentially focused his observations. This distinction was obvious to a number of other observers as well, who in places such as the mines of Illinois could see Piedmontese side by side with Americans.

The most recent immigrants still belonged to a different world, and it remained to be seen whether they would be able to leave it to become proper Americans; that is why they could not be considered in the same way. Many of them, in fact, still showed the manners and habits of their European homeland so strongly that they were immediately recognizable.

In the end, then, the French observations were essentially concerned, whether consciously or unconsciously, with the American workers employed in the best plants, the "worker aristocracy." The set of opinions formed on the basis of such examples had little to say about the living conditions of a very large part of the work force, although these were known to be extremely harsh; differing little from those that could be found in Europe, they seemed to be less significant. Moreover, the most optimistic of the better informed observers made the point that some day even these unfortunates would become "American" workers, which was a reason to focus attention on the latter rather than on the former.

This way of looking at things remained constant throughout most of our period, since the tides of immigration constantly brought new sources

17. *Rapport d'ensemble*, "Mécaniciens," p. 118.

of labor. Over the years, however, improvements in the economy and in working conditions caused the "American workers" described by the French observers to become increasingly representative, which does not mean that the less presentable sectors of industrial activity disappeared.

### Enviable Working Conditions

In a first phase, even before they mentioned the working hours and wages, the French observers were most surprised by the favorable material conditions enjoyed by the workers across the Atlantic.

Some of the American factories seemed to be set up to make life more bearable for the worker: Attention was given to good light and sanitation on the factory floor, which might even be heated in winter, to canteens, and so forth. Thus, as early as the 1880s, a group of French workers who had participated at the Boston World's Fair were greatly surprised when they entered a factory that employed 3,000 workers:

> ... all the parquets are waxed; a spittoon is placed next to every worker, who in a room adjacent to the factory floor is given a locker where he can put his city clothes, as well as a towel and a sink. In other rooms the workers can eat their meals; all the newspapers are available there.[18]

The same effort to make the worker comfortable was noted in many other companies, particularly at Pullman, before the strike of 1894. The visitors were impressed by the existence of organized leisure for the personnel, by the quality of the industrial facilities, and by the clean and handsome plants in general. The apogee of all this was the National Cash Register Co. of Dayton. The delegates of 1904 were stunned to find there large bay windows, washable walls, green plants, rest areas, canteens where the food was "correct," and, as the height of luxury, showers where one could get clean at the end of the day. This case was not unique, and all or part of these conveniences were found at the H. J. Heinz Co. at Pittsburgh, well known for its condiments; and at Proctor and Gamble the workers were even entitled to paid vacations and could acquire shares in the company. In many of these places "idea boxes" had been set up to collect proposals for innovation from the personnel.[19] It seemed unreal.

---

18. "Au jour le jour," *Le Temps* (4 March 1884). This is the review of a presentation given by four workers in the tinsmithing trade to a small audience who had come to hear them in the Salle Graffard.
19. This initiative, which was mentioned by all the delegates who approved of it, is reminiscent of the early 1980s, when economic correspondents and the heads of American and European firms marveled at the "idea boxes" that exemplified the Japanese business spirit.

Even if such working conditions were found only in a small number of advanced companies, they were totally surprising. Excepting a few naive or self-serving remarks about the generosity of these companies' employers, it is clear, however, that most of the observers, particularly the workers, were not taken in. They noted that the aims of a Pullman or a Patterson, head of National Cash register, was to use these means to achieve greater productivity, avoid strikes, and thereby to increase his profits. Still, it would be good if the French entrepreneurs took some inspiration from these methods, which at least showed respect for the worker. It would then be up to the worker not to let himself be caught in a dependency that might lead to class cooperation while he was working in more pleasant conditions.

Agreeable working conditions did not mean that even in such factories the American worker dawdled or had extensive rights. Even as they came to appreciate this work environment, the French realized that discipline and productivity were not joking matters in American factories. Indeed, the worker delegates were dismayed to find, both at the Baldwin and the National Cash Register plants, that their American counterparts were not allowed to talk among themselves or to visitors. Moreover, advanced mechanization forced the worker to follow the rhythm of the machine; Emile Levasseur indicated that he was not believed in France when he explained that in America a single worker could operate six, even up to sixteen, looms at the same time. This development, though impressive in terms of technology and economics, was not necessarily to the advantage of the worker who, reduced to an "automaton," was made to repeat the same gesture in a state of total mindlessness.

No one thought that this was desirable. Conservatives such as Claudio Jannet saw it as a decided blow to the employer's "paternal" power over his workers, which was the only way to solve the social question, whereas the worker-delegates were not convinced that under such conditions workers could preserve their independence and their personal freedom. Moreover, everyone noted that with fewer and less detailed labor laws in America than in France, the employer had more power.

For all their misgivings, the French workers did note, throughout the period, a decrease in the number of working hours, which was one of labor's essential demands. As a result of often violent confrontations as well as of peaceful negotiations within companies, but without major legislation, the working day declined from more than ten hours around 1880 to nine, and then generally to eight by the beginning of the twentieth century. Certain firms gave not only Sundays, but even Saturday afternoons off. Such concessions showed that the American labor unions were not as inept as the French observers of the 1870s and '80s had thought, and that the situation of the American workers was not altogether horrible. Thus in 1907 Jean Jaurès, who was not particularly interested in the United States, expressed pleasure that that country's workers had achieved the eight-hour day, along with the hope that this progress would not be limited to the Americans alone.[20]

For the more determined observers, pointing out that these incontestable advantages did not benefit all the workers in the United States and that there still were sinister factories and dreadful working conditions that fostered constant strikes was a way to overcome the growing contradiction between describing a capitalist system that was as nefarious as all the others and showing the advantages it afforded some of the workers. The same dual picture emerged when it came to looking at "the worker at home."

### An Almost Bourgeois Existence

The material comforts at the factory also existed at home, and the American worker lived very well there too. All the travelers were surprised at the general demeanor of the working man:

> From the social point of view, the worker has good bearing, he dresses like everyone else and does not look very different from the petty white collar worker or the petit bourgeois. All in all, the true working man lives better than the European worker; he eats better, has cleaner clothes, and a more comfortable home.[21]

Some observers did not even see any difference between employers and workers, at least not outside the factory.

And indeed, the worker's entire existence followed a bourgeois pattern. His wife worked only rarely and the couple was anxious to acquire an individual house with all the modern conveniences. In such houses it was common to find, in addition to gas and electricity, perfectly good rugs, handsome furniture, often a sumptuous rocking chair, and frequently a harmonium or a piano. In the same manner, consumption habits were highly developed, in the areas of both food, which was often of excellent quality, and leisure activities, as well as little extras for the

---

20. *L'Humanité* (12 May 1907). The Socialist leader also praised the absence of a standing army and the education of women, which he saw as signs of major progress achieved by the Americans.
21. Vicomte d'Abzac, "Etat de New York," in Marquis de Chambrun, *Les conditions de travail aux Etats-Unis* (Rapports au Ministère des Affaires Etrangères, 1891), p. 44. This opinion of a diplomat on assignment corresponds exactly to those of travelers who simply passed through, U. Gohier or P. Dunkel, for example.

wife and the children. Since quite a few of them had received adequate schooling without encountering any true barriers, the American workers appeared to be more educated than their French counterparts. The differences were such that one of the delegates to the Saint Louis World's Fair felt that in all these areas the United States was fully a half-century ahead of France.[22]

To be sure, this situation was only the ideal, and the French observers seized upon it, just as they had seized upon the best factories; yet many workers had attained that ideal, for instance, the Alsatian working for Baldwin Pianos, who was very happy that he had been able to buy himself a house some twenty years after he had arrived in the United States, and who had no intention of returning to France. The more attentive observers were aware of the considerable contrasts between some of these "charming little villas" and the filthy back streets of New York City or Saint Louis; between the rows of neat brick houses of Pullman City and the horrible overcrowding of the tenements, although even there a minimum of sanitation could sometimes be found. However, such abominations were necessarily seen as temporary, for access to better conditions seemed possible. The workers did not feel condemned to remaining forever miserable; they aspired to living like the "bourgeois," and this was what astonished the French most of all.

The worker's way of life was directly related to his wages, and the French noted that the Americans were very well paid. The employers were perfectly willing to pay more in order to demand more, and their calculation was similar to their motivation in providing good working conditions. "We are well paid here, but we work hard."

This finding, though reported unanimously from the beginning, did not preclude controversy. Many observers found it hard to agree that the American workers were so well off, and so they sought to show that job insecurity, which was greater than in Europe, was the price one paid for these apparent advantages. They also pointed out that in the absence of cooperatives and other collective organizations, the American worker had to spend more, and that moreover the employer did not hesitate to deduct what he was owed for medical services or for strike days. That is why, especially in the 1870s and '80s, the worker-delegates went to great lengths to demonstrate that the higher wages of the Americans were a sham, and that, when all was said and done, they were paid no better than the French.

22. H. Dugué, treasurer of the metal-workers' union of Le Havre, in *Exposition de Boston*, p. 141. A generation later, the gap had not narrowed, as can be seen from the identical reactions of an author like Hyacinthe Dubreuilh in the famous *Standards*.

These discussions, as well as the complaints of the American labor unions, which claimed that wages had decreased over the last generation, prompted Emile Levasseur to demonstrate as scientifically as possible not only the superiority of American wages over those paid in Europe but also their relative but steady rise. He found that American wages, on the average and with many local and occupational differences, were about double what they were in France, England, and Germany.[23] The prices of ordinary goods needed for day-to-day living were distinctly lower than their equivalents across the Atlantic. Thus, far from being equivalent, French and American standards of living were quite different, and that of the United States was clearly superior. This accounted for the outward signs of prosperity that all observers were so eager to point out.

The conclusions of his book *L'ouvrier américain* put an end to the discussions about the respective advantages of workers in the two worlds. Repeated by all those who were interested in this subject and contested on some points of detail, these conclusions were never truly challenged. Thus all the worker-delegates of 1904 remarked on the good standard of living and the high wages of their American colleagues. At most they showed surprise that these Americans had no savings, preferring to spend everything in order to live even better. Although this attitude was considered unwise, it also brought out a certain amount of more or less repressed envy.

Some of the militant French Socialists were troubled to see that in this manner the American workers became the slaves of their employers, indebted by unnecessary purchases, especially in companies where the employer was also his employees' banker and landlord. They no longer denied that American wages were high but pointed out that the life of the French workers, less well paid and without dollars in the bank though they were, was better, more joyful and, in the end, healthier as well.[24]

To French observers, the fact that workers were able to have an almost bourgeois existence was altogether astonishing. Not that this

---

23. E. Levasseur, *L'ouvrier américain* (Paris: Larose, 1898), vol. 1, p. 212. After a long and painstaking comparison, the author made it clear that he was speaking of the "real wages." His data were used, for instance, by A. Métin for "Le travail aux Etats-Unis," *Rapports des délégués ouvriers à l'Exposition internationale de Saint Louis, 1904, recueillis, publiés et complétés par deux études sur le travail aux Etats-Unis et au Canada par A. Métin* (Paris: E. Cornély, 1907), p. 7.
24. Seauret, "Journal d'un émigrant," Sept. 1906, p. 349. Seauret considered home-ownership a form of slavery; moreover, he felt that the American workers were living beyond their means and did not even have any leisure, caught in the vise of an indebtedness that constrained them to working all the time. This opinion was marked by relatively old memories, for it contradicted most of the author's other comments.

automatically made the United States into a social paradise, but it was food for considerable thought. Praise for the absence of a gap between rich and poor was no longer heard, but was it still possible to speak of a social hell? Perhaps it took very special conditions to bring such advantages to the wage-earners. Were these created by the intelligence of the employers or by the strength of the labor organizations, by the violence of social movements or by compromise? Such questions were frequently asked; they were implied, for instance, by Emile Levasseur:

> The democratic sense of equality is nowhere . . . as widespread as it is in the United States; it gives the worker greater boldness in defending his rights, while at the same time preserving him from revolutionary excesses. It has also favored the formation of labor unions, which in turn have promoted high wages.[25]

There was a major contradiction here, for the country where social conflict was on the rise was also the one where the workers, at least some of them, were living better than elsewhere. It was clear that the labor unions had played an important role in creating this situation.

## ODD BEHAVIOR AND THE POWER OF THE LABOR MOVEMENT

The development of major social conflicts in the United States did not fail to elicit some apocalyptic predictions from French observers. One of them felt that the struggle between capital and labor was bound to harden, while another saw signs of a veritable cataclysm, and there were plenty of examples to bolster these arguments, from the Pullman strike to the miners' strikes in Pennsylvania in 1902 or in Colorado the following year. All of this was naturally magnified by foreign observers:

> The situation had become extremely serious. From abroad it looked even more serious, and our readers, who saw the facts through the prism of journalism, could believe that the very existence of the great Republic was in jeopardy.[26]

In the end, however, these great strike movements – which were hailed by certain French Socialists as fulfilling their prediction that American capitalism would eventually follow the common pattern – were resolved relatively peacefully, and there was no evidence that they escalated from

25. Levasseur, *L'ouvrier américain*, vol. 1, p. 629.    26. Ibid.

one case to the next. The confrontations could be violent, the repression bloody, but the situation always calmed down rather quickly. This led some observers to conclude that American strikes were conducted with more wisdom and common sense than those that took place in Europe.

### Knights and a Prophet

American society seemed to be permeated by all kinds of associations and a variety of organizations that not only created cohesion within these groups but also took charge of protecting their members.

The French observers were particularly struck by these forms of organization, which were very different from those to which they were accustomed. One of the first things to astonish them was the secret or mystical character of these groupings, even if they had been formed for nothing more than the defense of concrete material interests.

The conduct of the Granges, which were akin to a religious order or to an "agrarian Free-Masonry," was quite odd, but the Granges could be considered marginal, inasmuch as they were part of an agricultural world that was different and not well known to the French; but similar groups were also found among the workers. Some of the observers were still interested in the forms of a utopian "Communism" that had characterized an earlier period or stunned to discover the "Molly Maguires" and other Hibernian organizations, but the most vivid attention was attracted by the Knights of Labor.

These Knights of Labor were also akin to a Masonic organization, with their habits of secret meetings, their Grand Master, and their determination to consider themselves an order rather than a labor union. Yet they constituted, in the view of Stéphane Jousselin, "the most powerful workers' association that ever existed," and also brought together men and women on the same footing.[27] During the 1880s, the French observers were somewhat ill at ease with their apparent success. Their refusal to organize into trade groups, their claim to be concerned with more than wages, and their meddling in politics were so many incomprehensible traits for most of the French, especially the workers. Nonetheless some of the more moderate observers admired their achievements and the rapprochement with the employers, which ". . . will give birth to relations between labor and capital that before long will make strikes a historical memory, because their place will be taken by arbitration boards."

In the end, the decline of the Knights of Labor, despite the support they received from the Catholic hierarchy of the United States, was

---

27. S. Jousselin, "Les chevaliers du travail," *Revue Socialiste* (Jan. 1893): 42.

reassuring to the French. It indicated that the American workers were unwilling to make do with customs that defied analysis: ". . . they [the Knights] held out to the workers prospects of the imminent advent of a new regime." It was also clear that the decline resulted from their refusal to organize into trade groups:

> Such an organization would require incorruptible morality on the part of the leaders, along with knowledge of many fields and infallible practical judgments, all of which are impossible to find. Hence the failures, the discontent, the disaffection, and the return of workers to the old union system.[28]

Once they had returned to more familiar territory, the observers could grant the Knights a role in awakening the consciousness of American labor, which was bound to be beneficial to the development of unions that adhered to European norms.

Yet the weakening of the Knights did not spell the end of the mystical or Masonic forms of behavior that marked the social organizations of the United States. And the French never ceased to be amazed when they encountered them, whether it was in Coxey's sparse army which, during the crisis of 1893, marched to the sound of half-religious and half-Socialist songs, or in specifically anarchic manifestations. Actually, most of the anarchists in the United States had come from Europe, but there was also ". . . an autochthonous mysticism, which seems to have grown naturally out of American soil."[29]

The permanence of such traits revealed one more aspect of the social richness of the United States that simply staggered the French observers. They had a similar reaction when they discovered the original way of thinking of Henry George, the star of American Socialism.

The author of *Progress and Poverty* unquestionably drew a great deal of attention from the French, more than any other Socialist leader or writer concerned with social questions. By 1886 he was considered a typically American kind of prophet, and opinions about him were sharply divided. The French Socialists were uncomfortable. On the one hand, they could not deny his influence on the American Socialist movement or the popularity he enjoyed; on the other, they had trouble understanding his taste for glory and his increasing preoccupation with organizing an agrarian party. Benoît Malon considered him an ordinary

---

28. I. Finance, "Les syndicats ouvriers aux Etats-Unis," in *Exposition universelle de Chicago, rapports de la délégation ouvrière* (Paris: Imprimerie nationale, 1894), pp. 771–72.
29. P. Ghio, "L'anarchisme insurrectionnel aux Etats-Unis," *Journal des Economistes* (Sept. 1903): 352.

reformer, but on the people's side. "By being a talented writer, an eloquent orator, and an indefatigable militant, he has made a considerable
contribution: and this is why he has deserved a European consecration
that adds an aureole of glory to his American popularity."[30]

By contrast, observers of other tendencies sought to demonstrate the
utopian character of the solutions proposed by the Californian. Uniformly astounded by the extent of the success his theories had had in the
United States and Great Britain, they attributed it to the existence of
large landed properties, which were better suited to the "single tax"
theory he had developed. At the same time his emphasis on ownership
of the land was enormously threatening to the French, who were deeply
attached to a familial concept of landownership. Was this not to open the
way to "implacable *jacqueries*," was it not to risk overthrowing "the existing order of things"? The slow pace of the book's translation (which was
not published until 1887, that is, eight years after the first American
edition) indicate that Henry George intrigued and fascinated the French
by his personality and the quality and the vigor of his style more than
by his theories, which were both vaguely threatening and foreign to all
French traditions.

Nonetheless, this astonishing character – he also ran for mayor of New
York – and the resonance he had throughout the United States were very
much in keeping with the messianic and strangely religious tendency that
constituted an essential feature of American social organizations. The
French were unable to fathom something that was so far removed from
their own practices, and yet this surely was one of the keys to the social
vitality that characterized the United States.

However, these tendencies never received more than marginal attention, and, increasingly, all interest was monopolized by the American
Federation of Labor (AFL).

### The AFL, a Very Cautious Power

After a period of coexistence between the Knights of Labor and the
AFL, the latter more and more clearly established its position as the
major American labor organization. This achievement initially elicited
undeniable admiration from those French observers who took an
interest in social questions.

Both Isidore Finance, who wrote the report of the delegates to the

---

30. B. Malon, "Henry George," *Revue Socialiste* (Oct. 1888): 394. Henry George's visit to
Paris was planned for June 1889, and his activities were regularlay mentioned for a few
years.

Chicago World's Fair, and the agents of the Social Museum, such as Paul de Rousiers or Louis Vigouroux, were struck by the strength of this organization:

> ... in the presence of these associations, these *Unions*, which have succeeded in forming a compact body out of the majority of the workers in each trade, regardless of their language and their nationality, one is bound to be seized by the most vivid admiration for the tact and the political savvy ... that the organizers and the propagandists of these Unions had to deploy.[31]

And it is true that the social climate of the United States was not necessarily favorable to the development of a labor movement; the absolute power of the employers, the existence of legislation outlawing all concerted action, and even the attitudes of many American workers did not make it easy to pursue major campaigns to improve labor conditions. This situation, which was already deplored by the worker-delegates to the Philadelphia World's Fair, was slow to evolve, for the unions first had to establish themselves in this difficult environment and gain recognition as valid spokesmen for the workers.

This is why the AFL had made itself strong enough to become the negotiating partner of the employers by federating and organizing the unions rather than acting only as their parliament, as was the case in Great Britain. To achieve this, its leaders had not hesitated to call boycotts and strikes and to use labels to identify companies where the federation was recognized and established. Yet it also had to maintain a delicate balance among the various unions, even if the main objective was to strengthen the federation, so that it was in a better position to assert itself on behalf of the workers. This is why political or religious matters were never discussed, and why from the outset the main objective was the reduction of the work day to eight hours. The various means to achieve this goal were carefully graded and ranged from the publication of pamphlets and petitions all the way to strikes.

This kind of organization, with the extensive management it required, was the strength of the AFL, and it was this aspect which, before any ideological analysis, surprised the French worker-delegates who came in contact with it.

This was particularly clear in 1904, on the occasion of the Saint Louis World's Fair. The French delegates were dumbfounded by the luxurious offices of the federation's headquarters and stupefied to learn that its president, Samuel Gompers, received a salary of $5,000 per year.[32] But

---

31. Finance, "Les syndicats," p. 765.
32. H. Dugué, in *Rapport des délégués* ..., p. 103.

this aspect, which shocked most of them, was compensated by the demonstration of the highly effective work of the federation. Immigrants seemed to become integrated rather quickly, public education campaigns had an undeniable impact, and financial resources, kept up by high union dues, were considerable. The delegates as a group were won over by the smooth functioning of this astonishing federation, by the number of employees, and by the determination shown by the union members, who ". . . stop at nothing to keep their unions prosperous; they do not worry about liberty and are like American industrialists, practical above all."

Yet this admiration did not preclude questions, for all these extraordinary means were deployed only in the pursuit of fairly limited goals. The eight-hour day was followed by higher salary scales, and the French workers were also surprised to note that the union members had no goals beyond improving their lifestyle a little further. Here again, the French expressed doubts about the adequacy of the American workers' fighting spirit, which they certainly did not want to imitate. It is true that those observers who had the opportunity to talk to the workers in certain unions became aware of the great diversity of this labor movement and were reassured to hear some clearly anticapitalist statements, but this was rare.

The worker-delegates were thus confronted with the veritable paradox of an admirable organization serving unambitious ends. Conversely, observers of more moderate tendencies, impressed by the powerful means of the labor federation as well, feared the tyranny that the federated unions could easily exercise, given their monopoly when it came to hiring and the setting of wage scales.[33]

Some of the observers remembered only the moderation of the AFL, while others, the Socialists, vigorously denounced that same attitude, thereby illustrating their parting of the ways with the labor movement in the United States. These divisions became very clear when Samuel Gompers paid an official visit to Paris in July 1909.

While they were in the United States, the French worker-delegates, aware of the role and the effectiveness of the AFL in defending the material interests of the workers, did not really discuss the person of Samuel Gompers, who in some way, they felt, deserved his salary and his position, ". . . for he seemed . . . thoughtful, deliberate, just and honest, and very sincere in his actions. . . ." Such praise did not stand up to more careful scrutiny, reinforced by certain French assumptions.

33. G.N. Tricoche, writing in the *Journal des Economistes*, frequently mentions labor abuses related to the practice of "closed shops." An example is the article of August 1905, pp. 254–60.

The president of the AFL had come to Paris to attend the meeting of the Labor International. He was most officially received at the Confédération Générale du Travail (CGT) headquarters, where on July 16 he even gave a lecture on the American labor movement. Under these circumstances, the Socialist newspaper *L'Humanité* felt obligated to give this guest a proper welcome, but the commentaries of Jean Longuet were unusually convoluted. He did not hold back the criticism that the Socialists had raised against the practices of the AFL and was hard put to explain Gompers's membership in the Civic Federation, a group made up of businessmen and a few union leaders, as well as his high salary. Yet there was no denying that he represented both the American working class and the results that had been achieved in the pursuit of "living better": powerful unions, high wages, and shorter working days.[34] More obvious was the hostility of the *Revue Socialiste*, which objected to such moderation:

> Any progressive-minded observer who studies economic questions from a scientific perspective will find that the labor movement in the United States shows two basic characteristics: it is reactionary and it is corrupt. The sight of the head of this movement being welcomed and coddled by the official representatives of the French labor movement is strange, to say the least.[35]

The more militant American labor leaders also failed to understand why the CGT, their ideal, gave such a good reception to Gompers, whose federation "... thinks with its stomach rather than with its brain." Despite its success in certain areas, the American labor movement as a whole was rejected by the Marxists, both in France and in the other European countries, where some objected to Gompers even more virulently than the French.[36]

This attitude of the Socialists was bound to cheer the conservatives; they found this labor leader very much to their liking, for Gompers was not a rabble-rouser, talked of the fatherland, and looked like a minister. His presence at the sides of the CGT leaders was preposterous, to put it mildly. "May M. Gompers make many converts among its members. They will translate his English speeches. . . . Surely, a lot of people feel that

---

34. J. Longuet, "Le mouvement syndical américain: Ce que dit Gompers" and "La conception de Gompers," *L'Humanité* (15–17 July 1909).
35. H. Langerock, "La question syndicale aux Etats-Unis," *Revue Socialiste* (April 1910): 303. The author is very probably an American.
36. "Internationale syndicale," *L'Humanité* (15 July 1909). The Dutch syndicalists voiced harsh criticism of American-style trade unionism, but the French kept quiet about it.

this story: M. S. Gompers as guest of the C.G.T. leader Pataud, will be a joke for some time to come."[37]

The American labor movement thus gave rise to paradoxical reactions. To the Socialists it was a fascinating but disappointing power, and its moderation delighted the very people who predicted dire social catastrophies for the United States. These divergences were confirmed by the major conflicts that shook the United States.

### Strikes: The Case of 1902

The great American strikes, which brought long and hard confrontations between the powerful armies of capital and labor, seemed to contradict the attitude of a labor movement "whose habitual support of order virtually made it into an agent of social conservation. . . ." Significantly, in seeking to show that American strikes were becoming less and less violent, Albert Métin attributed the clashes of the Homestead strike of 1892 not to the Pinkerton guards alone, but also to the presence of immigrants who were still imbued with European ideas. Similarly, he blamed savage and armed miners for the Colorado strikes of 1903.

His analysis was too systematic and too debatable, but it is certain that the French had rather different ways of looking at these major conflicts. These drew considerable attention in 1877, and again in 1894, by their scope and by the use of force, and some observers came to the conclusion that the United States had inevitably been brought to the brink of an unforgiving class war. Yet in the end the French found very specific reasons for each of these strikes. The first wave seemed to occur because the Americans had no experience with labor problems; the Pullman strike, which was related primarily to the personality of the employer and his methods, did not fit easily into the usual categories and was therefore simply American, almost exotic: "The portraits of Eugene Debs and G. W. Howard, the stopped trains, and the exchange of gunfire have been made popular by photography, which never goes on strike, and by engraving, which never fails to falsify photography."[38] This did not prevent the French from making judgments about Pullman himself or from deploring the naivete of the American union leaders who asked for government arbitration, but in general there was always a certain amused condescension. It was pointed out, for example, that according to Carroll

---

37. R. Michaud, "Samuel Gompers," *L'Opinion* (24 July 1909): 112. Georges Tricoche, for his part, felt that the American authorities were right to put Gompers in prison. This showed that there was in America a strong hostility toward the labor movement, which French conservatives were bound to appreciate. No one is a prophet in his own country.
38. P. Boz, "La grève de Chicago," *Revue Socialiste* (Sept. 1895): 300.

Wright's report after this strike, Eugene Debs had never considered calling a general strike, even though the situation seemed favorable. Yes, "this was an immense moral achievement," and it could even be said that it had "legally brought Socialist elements into the governing of America," but by and large the "class consciousness" of the American workers was still not what the French Socialists thought it should be.

The miners' strike of 1902, like that of the steel workers the year before, provided a good example of a particularly powerful employer class and one of those astonishing unions that had the means to engage in a prolonged struggle. This situation should have been of particular interest to the French, considering that this strike began on 12 May and lasted until 23 October in the same autumn when the coal miners' strike in northern France received a great deal of attention.

Yet neither the daily press nor any magazine article made the slightest effort to compare these two strikes in the same economic sector or put them in perspective. The one exception was Jean Longuet, who merely evoked the need for an international organization of French and American miners which, if need be, could cooperate to ensure delivery of indispensable amounts of coal in both countries.[39] Thus, the two events were not placed on the same level, and the American conflict was not even considered comparable to its French equivalent. This not only shows that the Americanization that certain French pundits were denouncing almost at the same time was very superficial, but also that the United States still had a long way to go before becoming truly Europeanized.

Despite this lack of a comparative perspective, the American coal strike aroused a good bit of interest in French opinion. The daily papers followed it, and magazine articles called it "... one of the most extensive conflicts between capital and labor that capitalist society has experienced to date."

For the most part, the French were unanimous about the American coal miners' demands. The employers' machinations to take advantage of the ethnic heterogeneity within the ranks of the miners, the niggardliness of certain methods, such as the weighing of the coal, were excoriated by most of the observers, from the *Correspondant* by way of *Le Temps* to *La Petite République*. By contrast, the harshness and the length of the strike, the endless bargaining, the threats of violence on both sides, and the appeal to public opinion were matters that called forth different reactions.

---

39. J. Longuet, "Pour l'organisation internationale, mineurs français et mineurs américains," *La Petite République* (10 Oct. 1902).

For the Socialists – and Jean Longuet was the person who regularly commented on the United States – this was indeed an exemplary conflict. The miners simply had to refuse all compromise and show that they could make the capitalists yield: "Never have conditions been as favorable to our ideas in that industrial region. . . ." The first and initially unsuccessful endeavors of the arbitration board unleashed his irony about "these people who had naively flattered themselves that they could solve the social problem, put an end to the inherent contradiction of the capitalist system, and, in a word, do away with the class struggle."[40]

Nonetheless, the personality of John Mitchell, the flamboyant head of the United Mine Workers of America, was disquieting. Admittedly, he was a remarkable leader of men, but his membership in the Civic Federation and his penchant for negotiation did not augur well for the outcome of the conflict. Moreover, what the American workers desired above all was the right to collective bargaining, not the victory of Socialism over capitalism. Jean Longuet thus found himself in the curious position of always fearing that the miners would go along with an arbitration that would drown out their demands, that they would lose sight of their class interest and forget that final results would have to be brought about entirely by their own efforts.

By contrast, *Le Temps*, and even *Le Correspondant*, praised the relative wisdom of the union leader, his "tact and perseverance," expressing the wish that the conflict could be resolved by negotiation, particularly since the employers were using rather despicable means to manipulate public opinion.[41]

When contact was finally established – facilitated as much by J. P. Morgan as by Theodore Roosevelt – French opinions continued to be divided. Jean Longuet sympathized with the miners who faced a public opinion that supported them less and less, but he still wanted to warn them ". . . that they owe it to themselves and also to the international proletariat to safeguard the sacred interests they represent." *Le Temps*, for its part, could only congratulate the head of the miners for accepting the arbitration board proposed by Morgan: "Faithful to the spirit of peace by which he claimed to be guided from the beginning of the strike, M. Mitchell has given the signal to return to work. A great economic conflict is over."[42]

---

40. Longuet, "Grèves américaines," "Les mineurs américains," and "En Pennsylvanie, la grève des mineurs et le socialisme américain," *La Petite République* (7 and 15 June, 18 July 1902).
41. P. Ghio, "Histoire d'une grève," *Journal des Economistes* (Feb. 1903): 183.
42. "La grève de Pennsylvanie," *Le Temps* (17 Oct. 1902).

In assessing the strike, different French observers focused on different things. The Socialists, disappointed to see the end of the weak hopes they had forged, initially had to acknowledge "the colossal power of modern capitalism," but as they stepped back a little, they found renewed hope. The strike had demonstrated the power of the American labor unions; revealed admirable personalities, such as Mother Jones, the "Joan of Arc of the proletariat"; and reinforced the socialist tendencies within the AFL, despite the machinations of Samuel Gompers. Arbitration had finally led to the recognition of the union.[43] The Great Confrontation had simply been postponed.

The other observers were particularly attentive to the arbitration procedure. They considered it a "means of achieving conciliation and social peace," and the decision to set up an investigatory body for such questions aroused much interest. But then the composition of the arbitration board made it clear that France was a different society, which made comparisons difficult:

> Can anyone imagine M. Jaurès being excluded from such an investigation because no member of the Left is included? or a bishop taking his place alongside a general officer and the owner of the Creusot iron-works? Surely this is not the kind of liberalism to which the ministers of the *Action républicaine* will introduce us, for this pacification procedure would suit neither their taste nor their practices.[44]

This kind of conflict and the way to solve it provided more proof of the resources of American society and its powerful resilience. A strike lasting almost six months, attended by relatively little violence, which ended through the intervention of a President who was supported, if not pressured, by the archetypical business tycoon – this was a combination of elements the French simply could not grasp. Some saw it as no more than vaguely hopeful for the future, while others only looked at the methods used to arrive at the final conciliation.

## TOWARD A KIND OF SOCIAL HARMONY

### *The Limits of Class Struggle*

The model of American class conflict thus looked by no means enviable to the more determined French collectivists. Even the worker-delegates

---

43. J. Longuet, "La grève des mineurs," *Revue Socialiste* (Jan. 1903): 22.
44. M.F. de Witt-Guizot, "Capital et travail aux Etats-Unis," *Le Correspondant* (10 July 1905): 65–66.

to the Saint Louis World's Fair, who experienced a calmer situation, came to this conclusion, with one of them actually expressing his grief that the American Socialists were wasting their time participating in the "electoral farce" instead of "convincing the American workers that capitalism had to be abolished." Such assessments did not, however, prevent them from hoping that the American workers would suddenly spring into action, or from carefully watching those who criticized the line followed by the great federation (AFL), but this hope faded as the years passed, even if the showing of the Socialists in 1912 provided some reason for enthusiasm.

A certain disappointment with the action of the American workers, which exactly mirrored the suspicions of ineptitude voiced at the very beginning of our period, to some extent explains why many of the French Socialists put all their hopes in the further development of the trusts. This was strangely reminiscent of Marx's predictions about the capitalist concentrations that would more easily allow the proletariat to seize power:

> The capitalist trusts are at least as effective as agents of Socialism as the labor organizations. First of all because their capacities exasperate many people who would be indignant about the tyranny of labor trusts. And also because the centralization of certain plants and of all the industrial equipment will make it easier to nationalize them.[45]

The "great social laboratory" of the United States thus supplied the French Socialists with an alternative model, for they saw the outline of a new path toward Socialism in the very foundations of the capitalist system. But that Socialism remained abstract, closely related to the development of the American economy, and without immediate consequences on social relations.

In the end, the French Socialist Left did not find a social model in the United States, as many had hoped. Yet their analyses of the American situation unintentionally converged with those emanating from very different quarters. This unintended convergence made it clear that the American model of social peace was fragmented and relative.

Workers without real anticapitalist determination and employers impervious to doubt or weakness were the essential features of the analysis proposed by the French Socialists, regardless of their tendency. The same observations were made in other sectors of French opinion, although they led to entirely different conclusions. A consensus by default about the peaceful settlement of social conflicts in America thus came into being in French opinion.

45. U. Gohier, *Le peuple du XXe siècle* (Paris: Fasquelle, 1903), p. 88.

In fact, the French bourgeois were glad to find in the United States workers who were open to reason, who did not question the society in which they lived at every turn: "... a rather intelligent and educated working class milieu, which may not allow itself as easily as our workers to be hoodwinked by the rantings and the lies of rabble rousers and phrase mongers."[46] And while the Socialists deplored it, they could not help but be puzzled by gaps of this kind in the ideological training of the American workers. In the *Revue Socialiste* Adrien Veber thus described with some disappointment an attitude that pleased the partisans of law and order:

> For most of the American workers the enemy is indeed, as he is in Europe, his employer, his *boss*, but not the whole agglomerate of bosses that constitutes the capitalist class which holds all the means of production.[47]

This finding led the optimists to conclude that the American workers did not harbor any hard feelings toward the rich and that they had no real class hatred, unlike the recent immigrants from European countries. Their only goal was to make a fortune, to become a bourgeois, and Jules Siegfried was pleased to assert that the American worker had no desire to take the boss's place and that all he wanted was high wages: "He does not feel jealousy or hatred for his boss; indeed he feels himself his equal politically and even socially."[48]

Others were more disturbed by this kind of situation, which after all upset the firmly established dogma concerning the unforgiving character of the class war. The French workers did not understand why their American counterparts allowed themselves to be caught in the trap of high wages and the myth of political freedom, for both implied that they accepted the rules of the capitalist game: "What keeps the American worker from feeling the oppression that is crushing him is the hope that some day he himself will be able to oppress someone."[49]

These specifically American forms of social relations, which were eventually acknowledged by French observers of every political persuasion, were not simply a matter of working-class habits, but had to do with traits that were shared by all Americans, as Urbain Gohier pointed out:

---

46. D. Bellet, "Une curieuse organisation industrielle aux Etats-Unis," *Journal des Economistes* (Oct. 1897): 81. This was a review of an American article by M. Richard on the National Cash Register Plant of Dayton, Ohio, in the *Pratt Institute Monthly*.
47. A. Veber, "Le mouvement ouvrier et socialiste aux Etats-Unis," *Revue Socialiste* (Oct. 1896): 463.
48. J. Siegfried, "La situation économique et sociale des Etats-Unis," *Le Musée Social*, "Mémoires et documents" 1 (1902): 14.
49. Seauret, "Journal d'un émigrant," p. 340.

Employers and workers show the same characteristics of energy, willpower, self-confidence, and stubbornness; and that for a good reason, namely, that they have come from the same category of people: today's bosses were workers yesterday.[50]

The French thus had to admit, more or less willingly, that the world of the American workers was not comparable to that of the French worker, and that it did not form a nation within the nation. This reality had important consequences, for it meant that the American employers could not have the same attitudes as their confreres at Le Creusot or in Lorraine. And this completely upset their notion of a balanced society.

Conciliation between workers and employers, which was preached by people like Emile Levasseur, was not acceptable to the vehement partisans of exclusive power for the employer; they deplored that during the strike of 1904 Pullman's humanitarian efforts had not been understood by the workers. Yet there were other voices that indicated a more subtle awareness of the facts. Paul de Rousiers, for instance, who in 1890 had been a fervent admirer of the methods of the inventor of the Pullman car, felt compelled to recognize that he had been mistaken, for he had come to understand the flaws of a system in which the worker was in a two-fold position of inferiority vis-à-vis an autocratic employer and an arrogant landlord. The example of Pullman showed what should not be done, but it was also clear that for the most part American labor was treated differently and much better.

American employers, like the workers, could be harsh, but they did not refuse to discuss issues or reject compromises if they could enhance their profits. The French particularly admired cases of agreements between unions and employers to defuse conflicts. Without claiming to provide the definitive solution to social conflicts, such agreements only attempted to prevent them. The example of the mines after the serious labor conflicts of 1902 was particularly striking. Here John Mitchell's union, despite its strength, did not seek a confrontation, and the employers also agreed to work with committees representing both sides equally. These meetings took place in a completely relaxed atmosphere, and there was no perceptible difference in manner or language between the two sides:

50. Gohier, *Le peuple du XXe siècle*, p. 103. Gohier actually found the American employers more interesting than the European ones, indicating that the mine owners who invoked their "divine right" were rejected by the rest of ". . . the Americans, who are always ready for bargaining and accommodation, and who are repelled by intransigence" (p. 99).

Guided by their practical sense, the employers and the workers have simply interposed between the two conflicting forces a series of elastic buffers that postpones the collision and usually succeeds in preventing it altogether.[51]

Conduct of this kind was not unrelated to the relative impotence of the American Socialist movements; this was a specific feature of the functioning of American society. The opinion of Albert Métin, while still reserved, does show the emergence of a deeper understanding of this situation on the part of a French labor activist of the most moderate persuasion.

In America, Socialism runs into habits that the working class and the unions had acquired before it ever appeared. After this obstacle, it has to face the resistance of an employer who is richer, more free-spending, perhaps more hard-working, but in any case more aware, clever, and active than any the world has ever seen.[52]

### The Elements of Social Harmony

The outlines of an American model of social relations thus willy-nilly began to emerge. It was not particularly exciting, for it proposed no general picture and no global explanation, but it did indicate some paths that might be followed. Its basis was the realization that, despite appearances to the contrary conveyed by the daily news, antagonism between labor and capital was diminishing in the United States. Workers and employers shared certain values, and since the workers did not feel that the bosses belonged to a different world, the latter could not conduct themselves as divine-right masters. Whenever both groups sought to improve their personal positions, they were able to reach a temporary agreement about the means to achieve that goal.

Although the realities of American social relations did not completely match this pattern, there were enough examples of it to fascinate some of the French observers. This was a small group, and its extreme wings were far apart. On one side, the most doctrinaire Socialists vehemently refused to admire cases of class collaboration and could only be disappointed by the conduct of their American colleagues, but their opposition showed that the phenomenon did exist. On the other side, certain dogged conservatives blithely predicted the coming of unforgiving struggles between the rigid Socialists and all these unhappy and misunder-

51. P. Millet, "Dans les houillères de l'Illinois," *Revue de Paris* (1 March 1909): 166.
52. Métin, *Rapport des délégués* . . . , "Présentation," p. 32.

stood employers, whose only concern was the welfare of their workers. Between these two extremes, liberal thinkers and "possibilist" Socialists, from d'Estournelles de Constant to Albert Métin, from Paul de Rousiers to Urbain Gohier, to cite only a few, appreciated these consensual attempts to solve social conflicts, even partially. Imperfect attempts seemed to them much preferable to the savage confrontations that too often characterized the French situation.

They attempted to explain this very fragmentary model of relative social harmony by, among other things, the American employers' and workers' sense of belonging to the same world – hence the resemblance in dress and manner that so astonished the French. The French tourists, who knew very little about the poorest workers and the most recent immigrants, observed workers who seemed to constitute an intermediary class that sought to become similar to the employers. The latter did not have the haughtiness of an aristocracy, nor did the workers have the servile humility of the hopeless poor.

Perhaps, then, the United States furnished the model of a new social equilibrium:

> All there is is a middle class that spontaneously goes in for the industrial and commercial activities that are considered the only ones by an orthodox economy. [This middle class] is both quite disengaged from the past and freed from a sense of tradition.[53]

Penned by André Chevrillon, this was but a first outline. Not all the aspects implied were considered favorable by a Frenchman accustomed to well-established hierarchies, but it did seem to open some completely new perspectives. To be sure, these phenomena were born in Great Britain, but they truly developed only in America. By the beginning of the war the discovery of the American middle class was so recent that very few French observers were aware of it. Consequently, one cannot speak yet of a new model offered by that society across the Atlantic.

Nonetheless, this was the first appearance of a notion that would be highly successful throughout the entire twentieth century. Directly related to the observations concerning work relations in the United States, it would eventually cap a still imperfect model.

The French no longer saw the United States as a social paradise; some even thought that it was worse than Europe. Entire segments of society

---

53. A. Chevrillon, *Nouvelles études anglaises* (Paris: Hachette, 1910), p. 160. The author took his inspiration from an American work, but the notion of a middle class is not found earlier; it was to come into its own in the course of the twentieth century.

were virtually ignored. Some of the workers and recent immigrants, people who had failed to make a success of themselves, proved that this powerful society had its weaknesses. To be sure, there were charitable associations, and women were devoting themselves to combatting alcoholism and other social ills, but until the Wilson presidency, very little was done to help the down-and-out. This was enough to make some observers see the United States as ". . . the country of deified egoism, of the fierce struggle for life, the place where the harshest of all the ancient imprecations is heard more and more clearly: *Vae victis!*"[54] Others, who only saw the inexorable march of power, predicted an "inevitable cataclysm" brought about by the "maximum pressure" exerted on the "social and economic machine" that lacked "any stabilizing brake."

But no simplistic explanation was sufficient, and the French were aware that the relations between capital and labor were fraught with many paradoxes. Violent and spectacular at times, but often peaceful and serene, these relations opposed employers and workers, just as they did in Europe, but the workers were different, and so were the employers, despite certain superficial similarities.

The American workers lived better than their French counterparts and did not seem as determined to change the system; the employers, while equally unscrupulous, nonetheless showed strange weaknesses and less haughtiness. Moreover, as the federal government gradually launched a program of social legislation, a precarious balance between the "tyrannical plutocracy" and the workers may have come into being.

This preliminary model was very incomplete and fragile, but also very specific; some of the French found it quite appealing and saw it as an example to be followed. However, their approach to these subjects was deeply divided along ideological lines that had clearly changed since the preceding period. The Left, which had admired the American equality, was now in large part repelled by an increasingly complex and differentiated society. The Right, which had initially been suspicious, recognized itself in the emergence of a well-defined ruling class. Yet between these two groups there was room to accommodate new admirers of the social balance in the United States.

54. V. du Bled, "Les aliénés à l'étranger," *Revue des Deux Mondes* (15 Oct. 1886): 906.

# Part 3

# THE UNITED
# STATES AS POWER

The North American is Europe's nightmare. Statesmen, publishers, manufacturers, and workers of the Old World lose their sleep when they think about him. Their imagination gives him a colossal seize. They see themselves as mere Lilliputians, whereas their offspring across the Atlantic seems to have acquired the enormous proportions of Gulliver.

> Laborer, "Esquisses de la vie américaine," *Journal des Economistes* (June 1903): 397

The historic hour of departure has sounded. All aboard! Nothing will stop the colossal convoy as it advances toward its destiny.

> André Tardieu, *Notes sur les Etats-Unis* (Paris: Calman-Lévy, 1908), p. 273

# 12

# *Immigration:*
# *Strength or Weakness?*

American society, fascinating as it was, did not necessarily seem to be characterized by social cohesion, especially at the dawn of the twentieth century; neither equality nor social peace was its outstanding feature. Supported by the energy of its women and the ambition of its men, it was at the same time shaken by extensive social conflicts, by the persistence of the race problem and by the sad state of the Indian population. Yet at the same time the French observers frequently discerned characteristics common to all Americans, which made for a solid and coherent society.

In this ambiguous context, the immigrants who arrived in ever-increasing numbers on American soil constituted one of the most surprising facets of the capacities of such a society: Were the immigrants the constantly renewed proof of great assimilating power, or were they, as this population shift gained momentum, a source of weakness that could be cause for concern about its previously promising future?

The phenomenon of immigration to the United States peaked during our period. While a few hundred French visitors and a few tens of thousands of French immigrants landed in New York between 1870 and 1914, more than 20 million immigrants from all kinds of other places followed the same itinerary. The scope of the phenomenon was bound to disconcert the French, who at that point had never seen anything like it, even though by that time France had already become an immigration country for certain of its neighbors.

Absorbing such a large number of people called for unusual capacities on the part of the various forms of social organization, but before these could come into play, there was the problem of immigration itself, whose scope was decidedly surprising.

Immigration was indeed a decisive element in evaluating the strength, or the weakness, of this astonishing American society. The question is whether the French of the late nineteenth and early twentieth century stressed the unity and cohesion of the American nation or whether they, like many of our own contemporaries, attributed particular virtue to the capacity of ethnic survival among the immigrants to the United States.

## A REPULSIVE PHENOMENON

### *A Limited Perception*

Despite the considerable scope, the permanence, and the acceleration of immigration into the United States throughout our period, one is struck by the fact that no book by a French author, not even a complete article was devoted to this subject at the time. At most one can find, particularly in the *Journal des Economistes*, data taken directly from the American census, or a very few and thin brochures purporting to study these statistics.[1] One therefore has to make do with scattered remarks found in travel accounts, reports of workers' delegations, and a few other books.

This relative scarcity of materials reflecting French opinion on this subject indicates that the French had not really grasped its dimensions or its full significance. This confirms their pervasive lack of familiarity with a phenomenon that did not touch them directly, but it also proves that very few of these observers were really able to understand one of the major distinctive feature of American society. They considered the arrival of the immigrants secondary in comparison with other manifestations of American power, whereas in fact it was an essential explanatory factor. The French missed a chance to seize one of the essential keys to the analysis of American society.

One is also struck by the strange chronology of immigration to the United States that emerges from this scanty documentation. For the French were much more preoccupied with this phenomenon in the 1870s than in the following period and showed no particular interest during the veritable high tides that considerably swelled the flood of immigrants in the first decade of the twentieth century. This strange approach can be explained in various ways.

The French rediscovery of the United States after the Civil War, the resumption of immigration in the 1870s, along with an appreciable

---

1. M. Mandl, *Emigration aux Etats-Unis* (Paris: Imprimerie de Bière, 1879). This was in fact a pamphlet designed to attract French emigrants to Texas. See also G. Marcel, *L'immigration aux Etats-Unis* (Paris: Guillaumin, 1874), a purely technical paper reprinted from the *Journal des Economistes*; Abbé A. Villeneuve, *Les Etats-Unis et l'émigration* (Marseille: Bureaux du XXe siecle, 1891), another appeal for emigration.

increase in the number of French people going to the United States at the time of the Philadelphia World's Fair are some of the reasons for a marked interest in the immigrants. It was a time when travelers, for instance, could not help noticing the presence of these men and women in the steerage of the steamers that brought them to the United States; sometimes nostalgic songs, a sea burial, or the chatter of a lively child would draw their attention. During their stay these memories would come back and call for more elaborate reflection. In the same way the worker-delegates, rightly fascinated by the attraction the United States exerted on the working classes of many European countries, came to wonder about its reasons.

In the following period, until the beginning of the twentieth century, this attention waned, never quite to resume. This can be explained by the real decrease in the rate of immigration due to economic recession, as well as by the very permanence of the phenomenon. Visitors thus paid less attention to the immigrants on the boats and asked fewer questions about the effects of immigration on American society. The best observers often generalized on the basis of examples from the earlier period, unaware of changes that had taken place; and when they came to the Chicago World's Fair, they were struck by too many novelties to pay much attention to a phenomenon that had become quite ordinary.

Strangely enough, this hardly changed in the first years of the twentieth century. The French seem to have completely missed the great new wave of immigrants, who no longer used the same boats and no longer landed on the same docks after the opening of the facilities at Ellis Island in 1892. As this was also the period when the interest of French opinion in the United States was declining somewhat, immigration, which had never drawn very much attention, declined accordingly. Not that certain visitors did not notice the presence of Italians or Poles, but they did not make much of it, and French opinion as a whole did not realize that the influx of so many immigrants of ever more varied origin could be of major importance to the United States.

This tendency of the French to talk more about immigration when it was relatively weak than when it was strong had several consequences. Without insisting on the observers who peremptorily stated, as early as 1876, that immigration had ". . . declined so much that it looks as if the source were about to dry up,"[2] it is necessary to underline the deforma-

2. O. Reclus, *Géographie de la terre à vol d'oiseau* (Paris: Hachette, 1877), vol. 2, p. 318. The same theme was taken up fourteen years later by the author's brother Elisée, *Nouvelle géographie universelle, la terre et les hommes* (Paris: Hachette, 1892), vol. 16, p. 95: ". . . the great era of immigration is over. . . ." Predictions are obviously difficult to make.

tions that resulted from this paradoxical chronology. The French made a great deal of the Germans – "they invade everything" – throughout the period, even while the number of new arrivals was steadily declining, but this was due to the influence of purely domestic preoccupations. They were also much interested in the Chinese, and then in the Japanese, in this case following not their own prejudices but rather the attitudes conveyed by current American news.

By contrast, very few observers concerned themselves with what today's historians have rather hastily dubbed the "new immigration." There are only a few summary descriptions of the tenements that sheltered the new arrivals or the shops that employed them. Emile Levasseur, for instance, did not include the new arrivals in his category of "American worker," which he reserved for citizens of the United States.[3] Similarly, the visitors who went slumming in New York paid more attention to picturesque scenes than to the real condition of these populations who still seemed to be encamped on the margins of American society. They were not yet considered true Americans, which is why they were for the most part ignored, as if the problem of integrating them into American society were not a pressing one; but perhaps it was felt that it would sooner or later take care of itself.

### A Rather Somber View

Throughout the entire period, the immigrants to the United States were not considered favorably or optimistically by the French observers.

On the one hand, the travelers were uniformly struck by the poor appearance and the pitiful demeanor of the immigrants they might see. All of these were "déclassé, desperate, and day-dreaming characters," as one said in 1876; ". . . how wretched all of this is," another could exclaim in the same period, when he saw on the deck "many types marked by chronic vice and utter brutishness. Most of the women are disgusting. . . ." A generation later, André Chevrillon – one of the few to mention the arrival of 2,000 persons per day – spoke of the "sterile waste of Europe." Such snap judgments, which showed no effort to understand that immigrants who had just endured days of discomfort at sea could hardly be expected to be hale and hearty, had a decided influence on French opinion. One often finds them taking the place of any analysis; moreover, they were reinforced by remarks about neighborhoods where new immigrants had settled, that "terrible world," as Paul Bourget put it. This decidedly excessive vision proved to the French observers that

---

3. For the positions of E. Levasseur, see Chapter 11, above.

there was a deep gap between these unfortunate populations and the vitality of American society at large.

On the other hand, the worker-delegations to the different World's Fairs did not go along with these typically bourgeois prejudices coming from people who traveled first-class and ventured into the working-class neighborhood only with a detective, yet their views were not much more optimistic. First of all, they denounced the principle of immigration, a veritable "social trap." They pointed out that the American industrialists had not hesitated to profit from the workers' distress, both in France after the Commune and in other European countries in the aftermath of hard times: "This is organized industrial crimping. . . . Look how this favors foreign industries at the expense of ours."[4] Thirty years later, one of the delegates to the Saint Louis Fair similarly deplored that an Alsatian who had fought in the Terrible Year [1871] had to emigrate: "Is it right, in the name of patriotism, to risk one's life on the battlefield if afterward, in order to earn a living, the returning soldier is forced to leave his country?"[5]

Out of a curious sense of nationalism, the French workers thus rejected the very principle of emigration, which they considered a source of weakness for their own country, but it did not concern them that it increased the power of the United States. Still, they implicitly attached real value to the human potential that these migrants could add to a society.

In addition to their rejection of immigration on these contradictory grounds, however, the workers gave a rather pessimistic description of the conditions awaiting the immigrants as they arrived in the United States:

> . . . this nation and its deceptive material civilization that dazzles and attracts the unfortunate European who regrets too late that he has allowed himself to be carried away to that deceptive mirage called the United States of America.[6]

In particular, all the worker-delegates insisted on the difficulty of making one's way in the United States, especially if one did not have sufficient savings to get started. In that case you were in the grip of a hotel owner or a boss who cheated, robbed, and exploited you without restraint, profiting from your ignorance of the customs of the country

4. "Mécaniciens," in *Rapport d'ensemble de la délégation ouvrière à Philadelphie* (Paris: Imprimerie nouvelle, 1879), p. 119.
5. E. Martin, in *Exposition de Saint Louis, rapports de la délégation ouvrière* (Paris: Cornély, 1907), p. 286.
6. P.-A. Seauret, "Journal d'un émigrant aux Etats-Unis," *Revue Socialiste* (July 1906): 70.

and from your poor understanding of the language: "Emigration has created the material wealth of America, but also its moral poverty."[7]

Such warnings were sounded in 1876 as well as in 1898, for instance, by Emile Levasseur. He agreed with the opinion of the workers' delegation, although he defended the principle of immigration as beneficial for the United States. He also advised against emigrating without proper preparation: ". . . woe to the insufficiently armed, who will end up vegetating in that country, where the throng of the jobless is too big as it is."[8] Not that it was impossible to succeed in the United States, it was just that one had to expect "serious sacrifices."

It is not hard to understand that, given these notions, very few French workers emigrated to the United States. In addition, the political effects of immigration were not particularly fortunate, in the view of the French bourgeois or workers. The former felt that it was the immigrants who had sown within the healthy American population, such as it had been depicted by Jefferson or Tocqueville, the disastrous germs of Socialism. To the Germans "the United States owed monstrous strikes," and "the Poles and the Bohemians have brought the anarchist doctrines and the use of dynamite bombs. Southern Italy sent to New Orleans gangs with ties to the Mafia."[9] This statement of 1890 seemed to be confirmed over the following years by the great strikes of 1893–94; and, sure enough, the Germans were the basic core of the "grotesquely sinister" army of Coxey, just as they had inspired the Chicago anarchist movement.

This undeniable influence of the European Socialists on the development of social unrest in the United States by no means pleased the French workers. For they were convinced that the mix of nationalities within the American proletariat contributed to its internal divisions and prevented it from concentrating on its demands. Moreover, the leading role European immigrants had long played in the Socialist movement might well be the reason why it was so slow to take root in the working-class world of the United States. This was why the French placed great hopes in the rise of Eugene Debs at the end of this period, for it seemed to prove that "real" Americans were finally able to take over the leadership of the Socialist movement.

But there were other reasons to dislike immigration. In particular it seemed certain that a change in the immigrants' origin, which some of

---

7. "Couvreurs-plombiers-zingueurs," in *Rapport d'ensemble*, p. 122. This description even comes with the remark: "I am telling you this from experience."
8. E. Levasseur, *L'ouvrier américain* (Paris: Larose, 1898), pp. 475–76.
9. *La Grande Encyclopédie* (Paris: Librairie de la Grande Encyclopédie, 1891), vol. 16: "Eole-éthyle," p. 542. The same argument was sometimes used by right-wing observers, those writing for *Le Correspondant*, for instance, and of course Paul Bourget.

the observers did notice, would be harmful to the quality of the American population. Obviously, the new immigrants would not always remain apart, as first impressions would seem to suggest. In this connection the Duc de Noailles evoked the arrival of the Chinese, who might well supplant the Europeans:

> Deprived of that element of constant regeneration, the pure-bred Anglo-Saxon, already crossed with Germanic and Irish blood, will be lost in this promiscuity of inferior races. Could this be a design of Providence? What is this Tower of Babel that has spewed forth this confusion of skins of all shades, red, yellow, white, and black, gathering on the soil of the United States?[10]

Curiously enough, a very similar song was heard thirty years later when Emile Vandervelde, the famous Belgian collectivist, deplored the declining quality of the immigrants: ". . . considered scab-labor, Italians, Austro-Hungarians, Russians – most of them Jews. . . ." He approved of the severe controls that were beginning to be set up at the points of entry and understood the American workers who had to watch out for the legions of "Saracens," "bear-leaders," or even young Greeks or Italians sold by their parents.[11] André Chevrillon went only a step further when he wondered whether "instead of melting, amalgamating itself into this great Western country, this heterogenous matter, so full of impurities, will not in the end form a mass of confusion that will smother the old Yankee leaven."

The phenomenon of immigration in its various aspects was thus seen very negatively by the French. This position was paradoxical, to say the least, considering that beyond these often superficial judgments the French pointed out that over the years the various immigrant groups seemed to disappear into the American population as if drawn into a melting pot.

### An Effective Melting Pot

The image of the melting pot goes back to the first years of the United States. Found in Crèvecoeur already, it was often used by observers

---

10. Noailles, "Les publicistes américains et la constitution des Etats-Unis," *Le Correspondant* 106 (25 Feb. 1877): 1008.
11. E. Vandervelde, "Impressions d'Amérique," *Revue Socialiste* (March 1905): 279. Meanwhile E. Boutmy also came to deplore an increasingly depraved immigration, consisting of "the sclerotic rejects of Europe," which served only to keep up the *sweating system* and political corruption. Boutmy, *Etudes de droit constitutionel* (Paris: Plon-Nourrit, 1891), p. 63.

bewildered by the mixture of races and nationalities that characterized that country's settlers. However, it was not until 1908 that the notion of a melting pot became popular in the United States itself through the well-known article of Israel Zangwill. It was as if the Americans were wondering whether after so many transformations the melting pot could still fully play its role.

Actually, the image of the melting pot was no doubt used more by the Europeans than by the Americans, who could not always muster the distance needed to perceive it clearly. The French were not shy about formulating their vision of the mixing of peoples that was taking place on American soil. Thus Christophe Allard wrote in 1878:

> North America is like a volcanic crater in which the most dissimilar elements are bubbling. It is a crucible in which the fusion of a great variety of metals is taking place. Language, nationality, patriotism – everything is being Americanized, even proper names.[12]

Paul Bourget sounded this theme in a more anguished tone, referring to New York as

> ... the true Cosmopolis, no longer that of idlers and dilettantes, but a monstrous crucible where all the adventurers and the wretched of the whole world come to clash with one another, mix and melt in order to form a new people – but what kind of a people?[13]

### A Fusion That Has Worked

In the course of the years, certain divergences concerning the effectiveness of the famous melting pot appeared among the French observers. Was the fusion really so successful, and were there not some groups that resisted? These questions arose as the immigrants became more diverse, but they did not concern the blacks or the Indians. Marginalized once and for all, these groups were not supposed to go into the melting pot, unlike the Chinese and the Japanese.

Until the 1890s, optimism unquestionably predominated. To the visitors' astonishment, the mixing of races not only occurred but also produced a better humanity. The contrast between the wretched immigrants one saw at the beginning of the trip and the dynamic Yankees was stark; the reason had to be that the fusion had produced an alloy of superior quality:

12. C. Allard, *Promenade au Canada et aux Etats-Unis* (Paris: Didier, 1878), p. 88.
13. P. Bourget, *Outremer* (Paris: Lemerre, 1895), vol. 1, p. 272.

And here, strange to behold, all the most hostile nationalities of the old world rapidly learn to live side by side; they melt into that simmering mass of the country's population and immediately become an integral part of it, like the drop of water that disappears into the sea.[14]

Not only did the antagonism between ancestral enemies seem to disappear, it was also apparent that "the most disparate and the most enfeebled elements of Europe" were being revitalized and assimilated.

A prolonged stay within American society could do wonders. At some point French visitors remembered certain observations they might have made about the vitality of the social institutions of the United States. The American elementary school was indeed a national institution, despite the diversity of the states; its openly stated goal was to integrate the children of immigrants, to bring them in contact with the little Yankees and make them into American citizens too. Similarly, some of the French observers realized that the horrible party "machines" had only one goal, that of making the greatest possible number of the new arrivals vote, albeit without worrying too much about the means they used. To be sure, jobs in industry were not exactly the same for the immigrants as for the Yankees, but there was no lack of work, however irregular, for Germans, Italians, Serbs, and others.

American society was thus well organized to assimilate these unsociable immigrants, and the observers' initial negative impressions did not stand up to closer examination for long. It is not difficult to understand that the French, who were most interested in the cohesion of the American nation, were regularly struck by the magnitude of the task to be accomplished and by its seeming impossibility when they considered the contrast between yesterday's immigrant and today's American.

Yet pockets of resistance to this fusion could be perceived; in some places it was the Germans who preserved their national characteristics longest, in others it was the Italians. Successive observers were not fully aware that each of these ethnic groups evolved in its own way. Thus the Germans, who around 1880 seemed to constitute compact inassimilable groups, had twenty-five years later become true Americans who merely held on to some Germanic customs:

After six months the Germans who come to the United States are more American than the Yankees. This is the people that assimilates most easily. The Frenchman remains French, the Italian remains Italian, and even the

14. H. Gaullieur, *Etudes américaines* (Paris: Plon-Nourrit, 1891), p. 7.

Englishman finds it hard to forget his fatherland; but the German, I am telling you, is ready six months later to go to war against Germany.[15]

Jules Huret did not seem to realize that German immigration had dried up by the beginning of the twentieth century, whereas the Italians continued to arrive in ever greater numbers, so that they could not be assimilated right away.

The influx of a great variety of ethnic groups explains why at any time some of the observers could wonder whether the melting pot was actually working. Paul Bourget even imagined a vast race conflict between an Anglo-Saxon elite and a cosmopolitan rabble that had brought with it all the evils of Socialism and wrought havoc wherever it went: "the clash will be terrible." The author of *Outremer* was convinced that the class war was only the mask of a formidable race war that would be fought mainly in the United States. His findings were particularly welcome to Charles Maurras, who reviewed the book from a strictly French perspective.[16] But while this cataclysmic view of the situation was unusual, a more nuanced perception of American society's capacity for assimilation gradually emerged. The melting pot still played its role, but its effects were by no means immediate or uniform. This explained the Americans' occasional backlash and their refusal to accept specific groups of newcomers:

> Each of them in turn, the Irish, the Germans, the Italians, and now the Slavs and the Armenians, as long as they lived together as racial groups with their own languages, their diets, and their needs of other times, have been denounced as public dangers. But eventually one realizes that the convergence of forces such as the public schools, the ballot, the trade unions, and the churches succeeds in dissolving these compact cores.[17]

This rather perceptive view of the matter quite accurately describes the situation of the European ethnic groups at the beginning of the twentieth century. It explains why one could find typically Italian neighborhoods that were easy to spot in an earlier American environment, why there were German schools and Polish or Swedish institutions, even though the country as a whole was indeed America.

---

15. J. Huret, *En Amérique* (Paris: Fasquelle, 1903), vol. 1, p. 48.
16. Bourget, *Outremer*, pp. 285–97; C. Maurras, *Quand les Français ne s'aimaient pas* (Paris: Nouvelle librairie nationale, 1896), p. 377.
17. L. Aubert, *Américains et Japonais* (Paris: Colin, 1908), p. 219. This very pertinent observation had already been made, in slightly different form, by L. Simonin, writing as early as 1875: "The immigrants preserve the imprint of their national characteristics for a long time, and it is only in the second or third generation that they really melt into the great American family." L. Simonin, *A travers les Etats-Unis* (Paris: Charpentier, 1875), p. 332.

This nuanced and complex picture, incidentally, was the one the Americans conveyed when they tried to explain a situation that corresponded neither to the dogmatic generalizations of the fervent admirers of the great attraction of the United States nor to those of the prophets of doom who claimed that apocalypse inevitably threatened so heterogenous a people.[18]

Thus the French, once they had overcome their initial distaste, by and large came to trust the adaptive capacity of American society. This capacity proved indeed to be strong and resourceful, becoming even stronger as the society absorbed new blood that it hastened to Americanize. It broke down, however, when the protectionism that the Americans adopted in the economic arena came to encompass restrictive measures in the area of immigration, as seems to have happened in the case of the Asians.

### *Kept Out of the Melting Pot: Chinese and Japanese*

As early as the 1880s, the French observers who discovered the Chinese also discovered their systematic exclusion from the American community. Initially, most of them were shocked by these methods.

How, they asked, could the Americans, who were given to vaunting their concern for freedom and democracy, refuse all rights to a population that was famous for its hard work and its discretion? This paradox struck both the casual observer who learned about this reality from the press and some of the travelers who felt strongly about the value of Chinese civilization. They considered the attitude of the Americans utterly excessive,[19] pointing out that the federal government, in order to satisfy California, did not hesitate to outlaw the entry of the "sons of heaven" in complete disregard of the generous principles it liked to display.

But then, the teeming masses in the Chinatowns repelled many of the French visitors who, once they experienced this reality, were much less indignant about the American methods of exclusion. Emile Levasseur,

---

18. C. R. Henderson, "La rencontre des races dans la cité américaine et ses conséquences morales," *Le Correspondant* (25 March 1906): 1169–73. A professor of sociology at the University of Chicago, Henderson laid out the advantages and disadvantages of the contact betweeen "races" in a measured manner, although he completely left out the blacks. Only E. Reclus, in *Les hommes et la terre*, p. 176, indicates that "the American's blood, whatever he says about it, also contains a few drops of the blood of Negroes and Redskins."

19. C. de Varigny, *Les Etats-Unis* (Paris: E. Kolb, 1892), pp. 63–112. Also, S. Jousselin, *Yankees fin de siècle* (Paris: Ollendorf, 1892), p. 225, and, among many other books, E. Chabrand, *De Barcelonette au Mexique* (Paris: Plon-Nourrit, 1892), p. 218.

always the realist, indicated that the exclusion of the Chinese, while morally reprehensible, had to do with the American workers' fears of seeing their wages decline.

The problem of the Japanese, which became acute in California in the early years of the twentieth century, seemed to be a repeat of the Chinese one. The more attentive observers, however, remarked that the Nipponese should not be compared to the Chinese. They came from a state that was able to defend them and had very special qualities: "The Japanese has patience, endurance, and the agility of the Israelite combined with the activity and the enterprising energy of the Yankee. . . ."[20] The fact is that the American's fierce determination to limit the arrival of Asians in defiance of his own principles was, as Louis Aubert correctly pointed out, quite simply a matter of racial principles: He did not want to deal with a "yellow problem," having a "black problem" already, and moreover, "being the supreme expression of all the varieties of the white race, the white American stands as a bulwark against the black and yellow races inhabiting the same continent."

Thus the American melting pot may have functioned, but not as well as had once been believed. This was also confirmed by the problem of French immigrants to the United States.

### The French, Too Good for America

To be sure, only a few thousand French people landed in the United States with the intention of staying there, but the travelers were always glad to meet their compatriots, either in small groups in the Western plains or in more compact colonies in New York and especially San Francisco.[21]

However, these immigrants, many of whom had been successful, did not seem to adapt to American society as well as others did. The Vicomte d'Avenel was surprised that he did not find among them any great entrepreneurs or great bankers, and that they often held middling positions, "nice quiet jobs." Emile Levasseur remarked, as did the worker-delegates, that the French kept to themselves and complained about working conditions that were harder than in France, although the wages were higher; they were, he said, "morally not as happy."

These pessimistic statements tallied well with the general French judgments of immigration as a bad thing, but they still did not explain why

20. G. N. Tricoche, "Lettre, . . ." *Journal des Economistes* (May 1907): 246.
21. Cf. J. Portes, "Les voyageurs français et l'émigration française aux Etats-Unis, 1870–1914," in *L'émigration française, études de cas* (Paris: Publications de la Sorbonne, 1985), which was in part used for the following paragraphs.

these French immigrants found it particularly difficult to become assimilated. They did not seem to be made for immigration to the United States. This was the official line taken by the French consuls throughout the entire period: The French had no business coming to this country. The same impression is conveyed by various observations. The French, we hear, could not sink as low as the other immigrants, could not deal with a hard, undistinguished, and inelegant world.[22] It was therefore understandable that all they wanted was to go home, for they were too good for America, and it was most unfortunate that some, like the Alsatians, had been forced to go into exile.

The French thus did not seem to behave like other national groups. Some of the observers accounted for this with a lack of ambition, or with the fear of isolation in a strange society. This would seem to explain the extraordinary enthusiasm with which they greeted a passing compatriot, a sign that they did not want to be part of the great American whole:

> There is a rule that one has a drink together no matter what the time of day, and then one jeers at the prohibitionist Yankees who drink ice water and suffer from dyspepsia; if you want to see American life at its least favorable, go and sit down at one of these hospitable tables, and you will hear it criticized in every particular. . . .[23]

Paul de Rousiers, who met French people living in the West as farmers or market gardeners, felt that the responsibility for this situation lay above all with the French women, who were poorly prepared for life as it was lived in the United States: "Brought up with a completely different set of customs, which they have turned into a kind of inviolable code, they do not understand the conduct that goes on around them, and since they do not understand it, they decry it without reserve." This explanation is not without validity, considering the real gap that existed between the two countries in this domain, but then this was also true for Italians and some other highly patriarchal groups. Moreover, it did not apply to French men who had come as bachelors and lived in towns where some of them found a certain stability. By the second generation, these people were not particularly resistant to a certain amount of Americanization.

French opinion had a prejudice against emigration – the French don't need to emigrate! – and this prompted them to highlight difficulties and

22. Bourget, *Outremer*, p. 285, deplored the defeated look of a hapless Frenchman whom he saw in a New York prison. This made him feel better about the fact that so few French emigrated.
23. P. de Rousiers, *La vie américaine* (Paris: Didot, 1892), vol. 1, pp. 138–39.

instances of refusal to assimilate rather than success stories. Even for those who admired the melting pot there was a certain satisfaction in finding that the French balked at being absorbed. Consequently, not many observers thought longingly about the role a strong French population might have played in the Great Republic; at most a few aristocrats put forward the example of the French Canadians to show the ability of the "race" to grow and multiply. Strangely enough, they were joined by an original thinker like Urbain Gohier.[24] Even fewer called for more French immigration to the United States.[25]

The example of French immigration confirms the ambiguous feelings of the French toward the phenomenon of immigration in the United States. It was rarely a good thing, but the Americans had succeeded admirably in making the best of it; however, their desire to assimilate the newcomers subjected the French to the risk of losing their national identity, and that was intolerable for a people that took such pride in belonging to that nation.

On the one hand, the distaste with which the French viewed the immigrants, especially if they were not white, augured badly for what might be their attitude toward immigrants in their own country. On the other hand, one must ask whether this conception, which attached great importance to the cohesion of American society and emphasized the power that a properly Americanized immigrant population could represent, was peculiar to this period of transition between the nineteenth and the twentieth century or whether it had more general implications.

In view of the increasing interest of contemporary studies in showing that many ethnic minorities survived the heat of the melting pot, both in the United States and in France, one might be inclined to believe that French opinion at the beginning of this century was very optimistic indeed.

Yet it would seem that what proved pertinent in the end were the more nuanced findings of the best observers, who saw a melting pot that functioned rather slowly and Americanized but did not homogenize a wide

---

24. This was the attitude of E. de Mandat-Grancey and U. Gohier; for his part, H. Bargy, "Les Canadiens des Etats-Unis," *Le Petit Temps* (18 Nov. 1900), marveled at their energy and their domestic virtues and hoped that they would go into politics as the Irish had done.

25. H. Le Roux, *Le Wyoming* (Paris: Juven, 1904), was hoping above all that young Frenchmen would go to the United States to learn about new methods; Thérèse, *Impressions d'une Parisienne sur la côte du Pacifique* (Paris: Juven, 1902), p. 283, did not hesitate to urge young French women to come to the United States to find themselves a "handsome guy." There is no way of knowing whether her call was heard.

variety of populations. This seems indeed to be the foundation of the power of the United States during most of this century. These observers understood one of the essential pillars of American power, such as it revealed itself at the turn of the twentieth century. But most of their compatriots, as citizens of a unified and centralizing country, were hostile to immigration since they saw little need for it and were therefore unable to grasp the vital importance of this phenomenon for the United States.

# 13

# *Business*

The American naturally did business, just as Molière's *Bourgeois Gentilhomme* did prose; and it was said that

> ... business is ... the triumph of America; any history, any description of the United States is also and above all the description of a colossal and unheard-of business, an agricultural, industrial, and commercial operation such as the world has never seen or dreamt of.[1]

So pervasive was the role of economics that the French felt that the Americans conducted politics as they conducted business, that their newspapers were managed like vulgar factories for making fertilizer or shoes, that their food was produced by businesses without concern for anything but profitability. So deeply marked was American life with the seal of economic activity that the famous dollar quite naturally had become its symbol; this was indeed the "King Dollar," the almost uncontested standard for measuring the value of people and things.

Such a state of affairs was bound to surprise a French opinion that had never known the absolute reign of the laws of economics and often distrusted the world of business, which it considered necessarily shady and inevitably suspect of graft and dangerous and useless speculation. One would think, therefore, that the French would have been particularly interested in the various sectors and the functioning of the American economy as a way to help them understand this strange behavior.

But this was not the case; interest in the American economy was always rather marginal and rarely spread beyond the specialized circles of administrators, businessmen, and economic journalists. Their strictly technical approach contributed little to the formation of French opinion. Thus, disquisitions about international trade or the customs tariff were plentiful, as were those on financial matters, for these were of direct

---

1. G. D'Avenel, *Aux Etats-Unis, les champs, les affaires, les idées* (Paris: Colin, 1908), p. 82.

concern to France; by contrast, American economic activity as such was seen rather superficially, except at the special moments of the great world's fairs.

This changed by the beginning of the twentieth century, as the French became conscious of the international dimension of the American economy and discovered the power of the trusts.

## THE CRITIQUE OF PROTECTIONISM

For most of this period, France and the United States shared a pronounced taste for protectionism, but this did not imply a better understanding between the two countries.

### A Completely Wrong Policy

The 1870s brought hard times to both countries, years marked by violent efforts to restart their economies and by monetary crises. The French were therefore not surprised that trade with the United States was difficult. But very soon their interest became focused on the high American customs tariff.

This subject was not yet of widespread interest; however, in the face of mounting protectionist sentiments in France itself around 1880, certain observers thought it would be useful to point out that the imposition of a high tariff in the United States could not be more than a temporary roadblock. In particular, they showed that whereas the French wanted to use protectionism to foster their national industry, America's commercial surpluses at that time consisted essentially of agricultural products. While the tariff would no doubt be beneficial to American industry, the rapid rise of agriculture in the West was bound to bring a decrease in the American tariff. This was the opinion of observers who were still convinced that the agricultural vocation of the United States and the virtues of free trade were solely responsible for the tremendous economic boom it had experienced before the Civil War.[2] Liberal econ-

---

2. E. Masseras, "La liberté commerciale et la protection aux Etats-Unis," *Nouvelle Revue* 2 (1880): 269–85. The author was not exactly brilliant in his predictions, since he condemned the United States to an agrarian future, as did A. Ronna, *Le blé aux Etats-Unis, essais sur l'agriculture* (Paris: Berger-Levrault, 1880), p. viii. Antiprotectionist sentiments were also voiced by workers, such as this bookbinder who had come to the Philadelphia World's Fair: "A people, and especially a people that takes pride in being a democracy, does not have the right to isolate itself; isolation and egotism, whether individual, familial, or national, brings death. If the miser isolates himself, he dies on his heap of gold;

omists, incidentally, felt that it would be to the advantage of the United States to revive a liberal trade policy, even though this might be dangerous for Europe:

> We have reasoned on the basis of the present condition of the United States, but if these states, recognizing that they are rich enough, were to change their commercial system and, taking down their customs barriers, made these regions into a free market, the ensuing development would be of such proportions that Europe could not possibly stand up to it.[3]

Such reactions, very limited though they were, do show a failure to understand the American reality and, in this specific case, the primacy of preconceived ideas that reflected French ideological divergences. Moreover, when France was beginning to debate the subject of protectionism, the American example was very rarely brought up, since it had little in common with the French situation.

All of this changed considerably with the establishment in 1890 of the famous McKinley tariff. Its high level could not go unnoticed, particularly since it was authorized by Congress at the very moment when the French protectionists were about to attain their goal. Yet here again, it was mostly the supporters of free trade who spoke up, calling the McKinley bill an aberration that could not possibly last: "This is the Monroe Doctrine in the economic field, the dominant thought of the Yankee intent on defending his domain against foreign products." French observers openly spoke about the captious aspects of this legislation and the excessive designs of the industrialists, expressing their delight that the Republican defeat in the November 1890 election would quickly lead to an amendment of these measures. At most, Auguste Moireau, though by no means favorable to this tariff, did remark that the United States had a perfect right to conduct its fiscal policy as it saw fit, and that the Europeans were wrong to wax indignant about it: ". . . they made it look as if the American Union, which had not done anything but push its own principles to the limit, had committed a violation of international law, a crime against civilization."[4]

The fact is that France, which a few years earlier had not hesitated to take protectionist measures against American pork, had little reason to complain. The luxury goods that constituted the bulk of its exports were

the American will die on his heap of wheat." *Exposition internationale de Philadelphie, Délégation ouvrière libre, relieurs* (Paris, 1879), p. 98.
3. H. de Beaumont, "De l'avenir des Etats-Unis et de leur lutte future avec l'Europe," *Journal des Economistes* (15 July 1888): 83. The author went so far as to wish for a European federation that would provide protection.
4. A. Moireau, "Les Bills McKinley," *Revue des Deux Mondes* (1 July 1891): 99, 103.

not the most affected, whereas it was dependent on American wheat and petroleum; Great Britain and Germany were in a decidedly worse position. Rather, the French indignation was directed at the principles underlying the protectionist excesses of the United States, for this conduct was incompatible with the liberalism the United States liked to champion.

The same arguments were often repeated over the next few years, for the McKinley bill was not repealed until 1894. American protectionism was denounced as excessive in international trade, perverse in domestic politics because it only favored industry, and dangerous in the longer term since it fueled the discontent of farmers who would be pushed to extreme positions. By comparison, Cleveland seemed to wear a halo of great wisdom when he decided to bring down "this strange monument to international intransigence and undisguised egoism," although under the circumstances the virtues of lowering the tariff were not obvious, given the rising demands of labor, symbolized by the troops of "General" Coxey.

Actually, such wisdom was only temporary, and wrongheadedness returned as early as 1897, when the French were once again taken aback by the passage of the Dingley bill, which restored the wall of tariffs of the early years of the decade. The first real breach in this wall was not made until the Underwood bill was passed in 1913.

### We Just Have to Get Used to It

In France, the undaunted American protectionism, which the ebullient Roosevelt was very careful to leave alone, was the subject of endless debates about the duties levied on this or that product. Thus, in 1899, the Chamber of Commerce of Amiens protested against the plan of treating American manufactured goods as Favorite Nation imports, even suggesting that it would be a fair quid pro quo if France adopted an outright protectionism of its own.

> In a struggle of this kind, one must allow for different conditions in each of the opposing nations and realize that they are not fighting with equal arms. While keeping intact the cordial sentiments that now exist between the two peoples, the French nation should be permitted to benefit its industry by imposing the principles that the government of the United States, out of a well-understood sense of patriotism, has not hesitated to apply to the products of French industry as long as it felt that this was necessary.[5]

5. "Relations commerciales de la France avec les Etats-Unis," Minutes of the session of 12 July 1899 of the city council of Amiens (Amiens: Chambre de Commerce, 1899), p. 3.

In this manner, works of art like French wines were liable to be kept out of American homes and palates under the terms of the Payne-Aldrich tariff of 1909, whereas the barbaric cold cuts of Chicago could be sold all over France, along with tons and tons of steel.

Moreover, according to French liberal economists, the ferocious customs protection established by successive Republican administrations in order to keep prices and wages high bore major responsibility for the appearance of the much-feared trusts. In this manner, they claimed, the tariff further increased the inequality between the worlds of labor and agriculture, between the work force of the trusts and that of smaller enterprises. At this point the French realized that American protectionism had grown along with that country's prodigious industrial development, a phenomenon they had still considered marginal around 1880. A long way to travel in less than one generation! But it was still not clear whether protectionism had really been the driving force it was often thought to be.

The French observers who expressed their opinions on these subjects were rarely in favor of protectionism, nor could they explain it simply as an aspect of American extravagance. The question was this: "Has protectionism benefited the United States?" and it had no straightforward answer. American industries had benefited above all from foreign investments and from the existence of a large domestic market, all of this without protectionism. "Wealth would not have grown as rapidly if foreign capital had not artificially increased it; rather, it would have been distributed more fairly and more evenly."[6] This opinion of 1902 was shared by other analysts, who believed that the United States would continue to need certain European products and pointed out that the Méline and Dingley tariffs had not held back the development of Franco-American exchanges. To be sure, the price was high, but by 1905 France was able to balance its trade with the United States, so that it had no reason to protest against American imperialism. Yves Guyot, incidentally, showed the limits of the American argumentation:

> ... the Americans are too modest when they attribute their prosperity to protection. It is derived, as prosperity is in every country, from their rich agricultural, forestry, and mining resources, and also from their energy, their mechanical genius, and their organizational ability; and the day when all

6. M. Rouxel, "La protection a-t-elle profité aux Etats-Unis?," *Journal des Economistes* (Sept. 1902): 362. The author takes rather conservative positions concerning the excessive crowding of the cities and against the exaggerated development of American industry.

they will have is a revenue tariff instead of a protective tariff, they will experience a new spurt.[7]

Between 1880 and 1914 the French thus did not approve of American protectionism, not so much from self-interest, for it was not really a hardship for France, but because they felt that such a regime was harmful to the United States itself. French observers were therefore glad to hear of Woodrow Wilson's initiatives concerning the customs tariff, feeling that reason would once again prevail, but the new law had to be enacted before anything could be said about its effects.

In the end, French observers who took an interest in the United States had great reservations about that country's trade policies, even though their own government had also adopted a protectionist policy. French protectionist circles said little about the subject, as if protectionism naturally produced blinkers that made it impossible to learn anything from other countries. Supporters of free trade were slow to perceive the growth of the United States' industrial power, and it was not until the early years of the twentieth century that they seriously studied the effects of American protectionism. For years, vituperation and dogmatic statements had been a way to avoid this reality.

It seems, then, that the French, accustomed to a strictly defensive protectionism, did not quite grasp the stimulating effect of a tariff like that of the United States.

## STRANGE FINANCIAL METHODS

The undeniable prosperity of the American economy was attended by practices that startled the French.

### *Too Much Laxness in Management*

During the last years of the Second Empire the French Republicans believed that they had demonstrated that the financial system of a democracy like the United States was more cost effective than that of their own Imperial Regime. The corruption, the scandals, and the formidable monetary crisis of 1873 that plagued the Grant administration soon swept away these illusions.

---

7. Y. Guyot, "Les Etats-Unis et la protection," *Journal des Economistes* (Jan. 1905): 178. This was one of the rare "American" articles by the former minister, who had become chief editor of the review. He was to take the same positions in 1913, at the time of the Underwood tariff.

This was the moment when the French formed their opinion about American business methods, and they considered them disastrous. The visitors to the Philadelphia World's Fair found many reasons to criticize the Americans for their abuses and for relinquishing the model of frugality and rigor of earlier times. The worker-delegates, for example, and other more moderate observers as well, easily found examples of graft and fraud, among them the case of the Erie Railroad and the bankruptcy of the banker Jay Cooke, which were reminiscent of the case of the famous Tweed Ring in New York.

The effect of these commentaries, compounded by revelations in the newspapers, was such that the Americans were pigeonholed once and for all: ". . . they have not yet taught Europe to use them as a model for honesty in business, for attention to the rights of the next person, and for scrupulous financial regulation. . . ."[8] Such data, which were confirmed by current events, allowed the French build a case for the Americans' lack of seriousness in the financial field. There was general astonishment, for instance, about the treatment of bankrupts. It did not make any difference whether the bankruptcy had been fraudulent or not, or whether it involved large or small sums. The perpetrator was immediately absolved, and the banks did not hesitate for a moment to lend him money for starting a new business, even if the creditors had not been completely repaid. Moreover, no one criticized the bankrupt – we all make mistakes – and there was no social stigma; indeed, people wished him better luck next time.

Such practices flabbergasted the French observers. They seemed incompatible with common sense and the most obvious rules of honesty. They were of a piece with the kind of waste that touched the world of finance as well as the area of food or natural resources. They explained the "shameless commercialism" that so forcefully struck European shoppers, the excessive luxury of the banking houses, and the enormous role played by the omnipresent advertisements that always looked like bluff to the French. Deep down, they disapproved of any form of commercial dynamism, preferring a sometimes paralyzing discipline, criticizing incontestable abuses in the same manner as necessary flexibility, and placing wasteful spending in the same category as aggressive methods of advertising.

Emile Levasseur noted the specifically American nature of these habits, which became particularly clear in difficult times:

---

8. C. Lamarre and R. de la Blanchère, *Les Etats-Unis à l'Exposition de 1878* (Paris: Delagrave, 1878), p. 103.

... because they are very enterprising and very keen to make money, they invest absolutely everything they have and all their credit in business without the support of considerable accumulated capital reserves that their counterparts in France or England would have. These two causes compound the crisis.[9]

Such behavior, then, was not individual; it was also found in the largest companies, even in government.

As always, attention focused on the most spectacular cases; most of the observers liked to cite examples that confirmed their preconceived notions without balancing them with accounts of rigorous management in other companies.

Thus the railroad companies were still saddled with the terrible image created by the excesses of the midcentury. The memory of the savage competition and the scandals that had reverberated even in France – such things as General Fremont and the Memphis–El Paso line at the end of the 1860s, followed by other more recent misadventures – still worried the French financial milieux on the eve of the War of 1914:

> The North Americans have shown us not only the fashion of clean-shaven faces, the taste for flared-out ankle boots, and the composite art of mixing cocktails, they have also shown us a series of railroads which, when it comes to trouble, have no reason to envy – and that is to put it kindly – those of the South Americans. . . .[10]

This financial chronicler felt he should warn his readers, on the basis of recent examples, to be very careful about investing their money in these companies which did not always respect their signatures.

The intervention of the federal government in fixing the tariffs under the Hepburn law of 1906 confirmed the French distrust of these companies' modus operandi. It even led to a mini-debate between the supporters of an absolute free market and the partisans of government regulation. Georges N. Tricoche, the correspondent of the *Journal des Economistes*, was careful to point out that Pierre Leroy-Beaulieu had been mistaken when he had praised private enterprise for having generalized the use of Westinghouse air brakes on the cars of the New York Central, whereas in fact this measure was enacted by the government. For his editor, who did not disagree with the need for this measure, the

---

9. E. Levasseur, *L'ouvrier américain* (Paris: Larose, 1898), vol. 1, p. 573.
10. A. Bromberger, *Les chemins de fer exotiques* (Paris: Editions du Moniteur économique et financier, 1913), p. 16; the author cites examples of companies suspected of swindling or floating loans without security. This problem had already been evoked in J.-L. Dubois, *Les chemins de fer aux Etats-Unis* (Paris: Colin, 1896), pp. 118–53.

main question was "whether the American railroad industry, now that it has become subservient to the government, regulated and maximized [*sic*], will preserve the vigor and productiveness that it owed to free enterprise."[11]

French doubts about the management of the railroad companies also extended to banks and insurance companies. The French often admired their power and their dynamism, and American insurance companies were extremely popular in Europe. But an internal crisis that affected the Equitable Company in 1905 was sufficient to elicit criticism of the "artificial and precarious" development of these institutions and the excessive publicity in which they engaged.

Similarly, the banking system fascinated the French by its energy, but it also worried them because of its fragility, which became apparent in times of economic crisis, particularly during the recession of 1907. Profiting from their customers' taste for speculation, the bankers did not require much starting capital, thereby accentuating this tendency rather than favoring investment. It was therefore not surprising that bankruptcies happened frequently, sometimes with serious consequences for the country's financial equilibrium. In these two cases the French observers inevitably raised the question of whether government intervention or control would be able to stem these abuses.

These few examples indicate the ambivalence in the views of French observers who were attached to values that were absent in the United States. The success of American companies, undeniable though it was, always seemed fragile, the reasons being a lack of discipline in their management, little interest in stability, and the "quasi-savage" character of the banking and financial system.

The emergence of a movement calling for a greater role of government in the United States was reassuring for people accustomed to such a role in their own country, even if the American federal government did not exactly set an example of wise financial behavior.

### The Free-Silver Heresy and Other Crises

Officially, both France and the United States were still bimetallist; however, the exclusive gold standard had served the French so well that they – understandably – totally rejected the use of silver practiced in the United States.

The financial policies of the federal government during the Gilded Age

---

11. G. N. Tricoche, "Le problème du chemin de fer aux Etats-Unis," *Journal des Economistes* (Dec. 1907): 330; note of the chief editor, p. 352.

were not characterized by great discipline. The virtuous period that witnessed both the retirement of the debt incurred during the Civil War and the redemption of the mass of paper dollars brought high praise from the French, but it did not last long. Very soon the emphasis shifted to concessions Congress made to owners of silver mines in the West and to a variety of budgetary manipulations undertaken, first to absorb an extraordinary budget surplus in the 1880s and then, in the following decade, to wipe out a considerable deficit. Not surprisingly, the French looked down their noses at such unsound practices. The Duc de Noailles wrote in 1877:

> And finally, it is odd to see the poor quality of financial science in that country, which in addition to its other riches has had the good fortune of finding enough gold and silver to unleash an excessive flood of it on the world without, however, being able to maintain a normal circulation of metal in its own country.[12]

There were similar reactions to the consequences of the Bland-Allison Law of 1878 and the Sherman Law of 1890, both of which perpetuated the monetarization of silver. French observers commented very severely on what they considered an archaic proceeding whose unfortunate effects could be felt even in Europe.

The crisis of 1893, caused in part by the shift of American gold to Europe following excessive spending by the Republican Congress during the Harrison administration, did nothing to restore the financial prestige of the United States. To be sure, the French trusted Cleveland's ability to resolve the crisis, but they were quite upset by its artificial nature. If indeed the severity of these financial jolts was determined by the policies of the different administrations, this meant that the United States felt free to play dangerous games that no doubt benefited some people but also demonstrated "an unconcern that the old nations of Europe no longer permit themselves." And the most astonishing part was the country's capacity to deal with even so severe a crisis:

> ... it takes a country of prodigious vitality to survive such costly and dangerous economic experiments. It is to be hoped that the United States, having learned from this prolonged crisis, will endeavor above all to organize for the rational use of its immense resources, instead of developing them to the maximum without regard for the future and without heeding the lessons of the past. It is to be wished that it will base its national wealth

---

12. Duc de Noailles, "Les publicistes américains et la constitution des Etats-Unis," *Le Correspondant* 106 (25 Feb. 1877): 1015.

on sound financial institutions, which in times of major crises provide a nation's reserves and safeguard its credit.[13]

Discernible in these remarks is a certain condescension, which does indeed reflect the attitude of many French observers. It was only natural that they unconditionally supported the gold standard and McKinley, hoping that the Americans would return to their senses in this area. The remarkable prosperity that started in 1896 would hide problems of this kind for a time, even if American financial methods remained more or less unchanged.

The financial crisis of 1907, which was fairly brief in its most spectacular aspects, gave rise to a great deal of commentary at a time when the French had become accustomed to America's economic power, to the weight of the trusts, and to the international role of the United States. Some French observers, to be sure, saw this crisis as a consequence of industrialization, while others tried to ascertain the precise role of Roosevelt's inopportune verbal attacks on these same trusts, but most explanations had to do with the country's financial practices.

In particular, its credit policy had created an "artificial overcapitalization" that was the very basis of the crisis, according to an authoritative analyst such as R. G. Lévy: "Rashness carried to a degree unknown in the Old World, and in some cases glaring immorality, are two causes that have aggravated the situation in America to an extraordinary extent."[14] Lévy did not hesitate to vaunt, by comparison, the wisdom of the Banque de France, which would never dare touch its customers' patiently accumulated investments. The same themes were sounded by other commentators, who also condemned "the exclusive passion for money." For his part, André Tardieu deplored the absence in the United States of a national bank, which could have mitigated the disorder caused by speculation and the excessive influence of the trusts.

These explanations were not altogether unfounded, and it was indeed in the wake of the crisis of 1907 that the federal government began to study the possibilities of reforming the banking system. In 1913 this led to the creation of the Federal Reserve System, of which the French wholeheartedly approved. Between 1876 and 1913, then, despite considerable changes in the role of the federal government – of which the French were aware – they had major reservations about the American

13. A. Chabrière, *Coup d'oeil sur la situation économique des Etats-Unis en 1893* (Lyon, 1894), p. 34.
14. R.-G. Lévy, "La crise économique de 1907 et les Etats-Unis d'Amérique," *Revue des Deux Mondes* (15 Dec. 1907): 825.

financial methods, just as they had reservations about the protectionism pursued by the United States.

## AND YET IT TURNS

The extraordinary development of the economy of the Great Republic rightly compelled the recognition of all the observers. After all, by 1910 the United States had become the first industrial power and the first monetary force in the world.

### *A Power That Means What It Says*

Throughout the period, there was a plethora of observations on the wealth of the United States, both in terms of natural resources and with respect to the ways in which they were used. Great disasters were thus occasions to marvel at the speed with which the ruins were rebuilt and at the energy deployed to allow activities to resume. The great Chicago fire of 1871 was one of these occasions; no one talked about this great city without recalling the speed of its reconstruction: "You must admit that we would not do as well, and that the New World decidedly beats the old." The San Francisco earthquake of April 1906 made it clear that this economic dynamism, not even to mention the human solidarity, had by no means weakened over time and was as effective as ever.

But even the most ordinary activities and the goods produced on a regular basis were so abundant that their very mass astounded the observers before they could examine them in detail. Year by year, with a few variations caused by market fluctuations, the French found themselves swamped by American products. Louis Simonin made no bones about this in 1876:

> The United States feeds and clothes Europe; it feeds us grain and salt meat and dresses us in cotton; it gives us half of the tobacco we need, and if natural gas had not been found, we would be lit entirely by its petroleum.[15]

This development had gone quite far already, for by now agricultural products were joined not only by minerals but also by manufactured goods. Another England seemed to come into sight across the Atlantic, and its resources and its capacities were superior to those of its model.

---

15. L. Simonin, *Le monde américain* (Paris: Hachette, 1877), p. 190.

Some fifteen years later this situation had not fundamentally changed, even if the Chicago World's Fair was another opportunity to show off all the achievements of the American economy. Yet the number and the diversity of American inventions and the quantities of wheat, meat, or coal produced still elicited essentially the same reactions: "America is invading the old Europe, swamps it and will submerge it. . . ."[16] This productive power was such that it naturally became threatening: ". . . I admire the great things I have seen there but, economically speaking, I am apprehensive of the future, the near future, of our old Europe."[17]

These impressions seemed to be completely borne out when in the early years of the twentieth century the United States became more and more visible on the world markets. All of a sudden, American goods became genuine threats, competing with those of European manufacturers on their own turf. This rise in power appeared to be directly related to the flourishing of the trusts, but it was discussed in the same terms that had been used earlier. The French still spoke of invasion and submersion by products that were as abundant as they were varied, but it was only now that the full diversity of American production became clear to them:

> They are making everything in the United States, even Genevan watches, even Brie cheese. Their clock-making is not the best you can find, and their milking cow is second rate. But they have outlets. American clocks have a certain reputation.[18]

Throughout the entire period, French opinion thus perpetuated, in almost unchanged terms, the conviction that the American economy had an enormous productive capacity. This conviction preceded any analysis of the facts.

Such an abundance of products always seemed liable to lead to overproduction, and hence to the search for new markets where they could be sold. The French were convinced that the Americans produced too much without worrying about quality or outlets; it was obvious that they were constantly facing glutted markets. Indeed, it was thought that this was the greatest danger facing them, for even the conquest of colonial territories would be no more than an insufficient palliative. This was the conclusion of the economist Gustave Aubert, who was sure that the inability to find new markets would result in "the closing of a large number of factories and the ruin of hundreds of thousands of workers."

16. E. Barbier, *Voyage au pays des dollars* (Paris: Flammarion, 1893), p. 86.
17. T. Visinet, *Un mois aux Etats-Unis et au Canada* (Paris: Editions de la C.G.T., 1887), p. 132.
18. G. Moreau, *L'envers des Etats-Unis* (Paris: Plon, 1906), p. 188.

The same view was held by the worker-delegates to the Saint Louis World's Fair, who were persuaded that overproduction – necessarily compounded by the marvels of technology – was bound to bring a "capitalist social imbalance." And when President Wilson decided to lower the tariff, French observers who favored protectionism were convinced that he did so "to enable American goods to take over the world."

This type of attitude shows that the French observers, who with their rather distant view of the functioning of the American economy perceived only its major outlines, saw it as an implicit threat, considering that country's very size and a prosperity that seemed to defy reason. The spreading of American power, which looked even more daunting from afar and was exalted by the Americans themselves, seemed to be a forgone conclusion.

### *Returning from the Expo*

Philadelphia, Boston, Paris, Chicago, Saint Louis – these were places where the Americans had exhibited all the marvels they had produced and laid out the proud achievements of their economy. These fairs also allowed large numbers of French visitors to discover the United States and to become aware of its formidable power.

My purpose here is not to go into the details of what the French thought of the different pavilions or into the descriptions some of them gave, but rather to make it clear which aspects of the American economy they found most striking.

Initially the great American fairs were not appreciated by many of the French. All one heard from them were criticisms and laments about the facilities or the basic organization of these events, which were inevitably compared with those that had taken place in Paris in 1889 and 1900.

At the Philadelphia Fair the huge quantity of machines was overwhelming, the atmosphere was frenzied, and the originality of the products was not guaranteed, for large numbers of unauthorized copies could be found. For all the bright electric lights, the entryways were poorly kept, and in material terms the finishing touches often left something to be desired, since the Americans focused all their attention on celebrating the centennial.

The much more spectacular Chicago World's Fair attracted even more people than the previous one. Yet the French commentaries were rather reserved, particularly because the memory of the Paris Fair was still fresh. The Chicago Fair was disparaged when it opened, for economic difficulties had slowed down construction, so that the facilities were not ready. After a few months things improved, and thanks to a concerted effort visitors arrived in greater numbers, which improved the atmosphere and the financial rewards.[19] This evolution is reflected in the opinions of the French which, critical at first, became increasingly favorable. Many of them conceded that the fair was grandiose, even if it they found it wanting for reasons that were well analyzed by the Marquis de Chasseloup-Laubat. He showed that Paris had reflected a preexisting order thoroughly marked by symmetry, whereas Chicago was striking for its gigantism and for its absence of planning. These characteristics conveyed an impression of chaos, particularly because the buildings, which were laid out very well, had no original style and lacked a central perspective.[20] As a result, many visitors remembered only the impressive character of the organization, the powerful machines, and the variety of the pavilions, whereas others saw only the things that betrayed a lack of finish or the precariousness of the "pasteboard" installations.

More or less the same differences of opinion were present at the Saint Louis Fair. While there was definite admiration for many of the stands, there were also numerous complaints about the huge size of the half-filled installations; about the mediocrity of certain of the buildings, which did not make you feel welcome as those of Paris did in 1900; and about the lack of visitors. In this environment the French products shown seemed to be of much better quality, but they did not win many distinctions, even though they often came close.[21]

Thus the three principal world's fairs elicited rather similar commentaries. Marvelous techniques, poor finish, lack of visitors, financial difficulties, and headaches of all kinds, whether they were about customs duties or about prizes for French products which, being luxury goods or works of art, seemed almost out of place in such an environment.

Such criticism did not prevent the French from expressing great admiration for the American achievements. There is no question that seeing electricity in Philadelphia, typewriters in Paris in 1889, motors and moving sidewalks in Chicago, and machine tools in Saint Louis was in

19. E. Levasseur, "Coup d'oeil sur l'ensemble de l'Exposition," *Annales du Conservatoire des arts et métiers*, 2nd series, 55 (1894): 116–17. This was a lecture accompanied by projected images; it was the first in a series dealing with the purely technical aspects of the Columbian Fair.
20. Marquis de Chasseloup-Laubat, "Voyage en Amérique et principalement à Chicago," reprint from the *Mémoires de la société des ingénieurs civils de France* (Paris: Cité Rougemont, 1893), pp. 55–62.
21. J. Gleize, "La France et les Etats-Unis," *Nouvelle Revue* (15 Jan. 1905): 218–19. The French critics of the American buildings perfectly reveal two opposite conceptions and two different principles; the structures of Saint Louis were intended only for the fair, while those of Paris were built to last and are still here.

itself surprising and delightful to the visitors, but the impact of these fairs is reflected best in some of their overviews.

At the Paris World's Fair of 1889, America offered a confirmation of what certain visitors had already observed at Philadelphia, its prodigious industrial and technical achievements:

> ... it [the United States] appears greater, richer and more prosperous, displaying to our eyes a new conquest due to the genius of its inventors, a wealth we already knew, but which has now been doubled or tripled by ingenious machines that ease the labor of men, substituting their steel arms, which never tire and are driven by steam, for the strength of humans, which can wear out and falter.[22]

As for Emile Levasseur, he did his best to demonstrate the unfairness of the criticism that had been leveled against the Chicago Fair and to draw some lessons from it. He contended that, so shortly after Paris, its aim had not been to unveil really new products, but that it had been a highly successful educational effort to reveal to the Americans themselves the diversity of the goods produced in the world and the diversity of production styles. Moreover, the visitors were almost as numerous as they had been in Paris four years earlier, and this represented a remarkable achievement if one compared the two pools of potential visitors. The French may have complained about the lack of finish and the noisy demonstrations of certain fast-moving machines, but all of this was not primarily done for them.

The Saint Louis Fair did not have the same aims as that of Paris, with which it should not be compared. The French who traveled to it discovered, as if gathered in one place, the full power of the American economy, whose products were beginning to be adapted to the needs of the European market, whereas the French machines shown did not make much of an impression. Yes, they were refined, almost "too perfect," but nothing was done to show them to best advantage. The brochures describing them were only in French, no catalogues were distributed, samples were carefully locked up, and no demonstrations were given. It was therefore not surprising that sales were mediocre, for the competition was fierce; something could be learned from the American techniques and methods, even though they were sometimes marred by an off-hand manner of treating foreigners.

---

22. C. de Varigny, "L'Amérique à l'Exposition universelle de 1889," *Revue des Deux Mondes* (15 Oct. 1889): 844. This remark is particularly interesting because the author knew the United States very well; he was most fascinated by the typewriters and eagerly looking forward to their becoming available in Europe at a lower price.

One understands the fears of certain observers who had hitherto been convinced of their own superiority:

> If one has spent six months watching with one's own eyes as they march by, a population of solid, tall, active, intelligent, and well-fed people who do in eight hours what we do in twelve with the help of the most advanced machinery, one wonders what the near future has in store for Europe.[23]

Thus the lessons drawn from the great fairs corroborated the earlier general commentaries about the American economy. Here again, fascination and uneasiness, admiration for the whole and criticism of details were the rule.

### Agriculture and Industry

Although the economic boom of the United States in the period after the Civil War was the result of its extraordinary industrial development, this phenomenon for some reason did not attract a great deal of attention on the part of the French. This happened only when they became aware of the most spectacular form of economic organization, the famous trusts.

Given this rather limited interest, their attention was focused above all on agriculture. General studies often began with rural questions, to which they devoted considerable space. While this attitude can be explained in part by the strength of American agriculture, it was grounded above all in very French reflexes, which attached to the land virtues that were more than economic.

What struck the French about American agriculture was a far cry from the farms of equal size, run by owners imbued with agrarian values, of which Thomas Jefferson had dreamed; it was its massive productivity and its highly technical organization.

Despite variations and despite difficult times for some of the farmers, the structure of American agriculture as a whole remained strong. To be sure, a well-informed observer such as Emile Levasseur was careful to point out that conditions varied from region to region, but he also indicated that most of the farmers made a good living, thanks to their high productivity. This achievement, while related to the richness of the soils and the variety of climates, also had a great deal to do with the methods of farming, which were very different from those of France:

23. Laborer, "Les leçons de choses de l'Exposition de Saint Louis," *Journal des Economistes* (March 1905): 344.

The United States has nothing to teach France by way of agricultural doctrine, but it certainly has valuable lessons to give when it comes to the application of machinery to farming, communication and transport facilities, and the combining of agricultural and commercial pursuits.[24]

The French marveled at the routine use of machines of all kinds, such as harvesters and ploughs that were light but solidly and economically constructed; thus only their visible parts were polished and finished, the others were left "rough cast." American farmers were always ready to modernize and to adapt to new inventions, and this was to their advantage, for it allowed them to pay high wages to their farm workers. Visitors who had the opportunity to admire this array of machines were stunned, as one reported from a dairy farm at New Holland:

A multiplicity of agricultural tools, all lined up in battle order; one could set up a whole *museum*. The distance between this agricultural equipment and that of a farm in the Brie region is as great as between a Parisian department store and a little country shop.[25]

The identical reaction was reported by P. E. de Constant, who visited Brook Farm in upstate New York, owned by the former mayor of New York City, Seth Low. Every imaginable advance in dairy farming was to be found there, and this was particularly amazing to the visitor because he had not expected to find such prowess in an area where the European countries had the advantage of long and fruitful experience.

These examples do not of course summarize the conditions of American farms, and Emile Levasseur, for example, noted that these marvelous machines were not always well maintained, and that they often rusted when kept outside. Moreover, the most modern machines were not available everywhere, and when Paul de Rousiers looked for steam tractors in the Dakotas, he looked in vain. Frequently the land was not as well tended as in France or Belgium, for the main thing was to produce quickly in order to repay loans, without worrying about the waste that such practices could entail.

Thus the admiration of the French visitors was soon dampened. In particular, it became clear that these American farmers were definitely not peasants, that they did not produce much for their own consumption and bought whatever they needed, like any ordinary worker. Thanks to the Homestead Act and to the machine, any immigrant could take up farming. This new breed of farmer was not easily accepted by the French:

24. Ronna, *Le blé aux Etats-Unis*, p. viii.
25. Laborer, "Equisses . . . ," *Journal des Economistes* (Aug. 1903): 261.

Even if he was a man of the plough in his country of origin, he is now above all a speculator and has a taste for adventure. Over there they do not have a "rural class," but simply people who are ready to grow cucumbers as one would conduct a tramway or found a few newspapers.[26]

What a difference between such an agriculturalist and the peasant who, ancestrally attached to his land, saves his money penny by penny to enlarge his farm instead of mortgaging himself to the hilt, as did his counterpart across the Atlantic. This had nothing whatever to do with the poetry of the family plot. This nostalgic opinion of Comte de Keraty, who sympathized with the demands of the American farmers, was expressed in somewhat different terms fifteen years later by Georges d'Avenel. To him, rural America was ugly, looking like an "outdoor factory" which, "treated like a slave . . . obeys like a slave," without grace or joy.

American agriculture thus gave rise to mixed reactions. Admired for its great strength, its grain elevators, and its adaptation to the railroad system, it was not really analyzed in economic terms. The French, still imbued with traditional rural values, were somewhat bewildered by what they saw.

American industrial activities did not prompt commentaries of this kind. Despite their considerable size, they were not so different from their European counterparts, nor were they grounded in real traditions. A steel plant or a textile mill may have been organized differently in some details, but whether it was in Pennsylvania or in Lorraine, in New England or in the department of Nord, it was grounded in the same principles.

The French therefore simply described different factories and studied the regional distribution of various industries, remarking on the power of these organizations, the size of the facilities, and the beginnings of amalgamation, but global judgments were rare.

By contrast, the increasing use of machinery and the success of American mechanization did attract some attention. In 1876 and in 1904, the same exclamation was heard: "When it comes to machinery, the Americans have no rivals," and both workers and bourgeois admired the extraordinary improvements in American use of machinery. This evolution had decided implications, as Paul Sée indicated in evoking the *American Peril*:

Everything in the modern world is dependent on the use of machines; the nation that can produce cheap iron and coal and has a knack for machin-

26. G. d'Avenel, *Aux Etats-Unis . . .* (Paris: Colin, 1908), p. 50.

ery will dominate the world. For a long time this was the destiny of England, now it is that of America.[27]

The French were amazed by a typewriter, a telephone, or a fast-moving elevator; discovering this widespread use of machinery made it clear to them that mechanization was indeed an essential feature of American industrial development. Albert Métin, for instance, clearly showed the effects of the use of machinery on production: "In the United States, people only wear new clothes and throw away the old, and this trend is facilitated by a mechanical production that supplies the market with poor-quality but also inexpensive goods."[28] To most French observers, this attitude, along with the large sums spent to turn these mechanical advances to account and the abundant raw materials available, were the essential features of American industry.

This did not mean that all factories were modern. Both Emile Levasseur and Achille Vialatte indicated that the workshops were not all that different from those of old Europe, and that the sweatshops were even worse. Nonetheless the most commonly held view, borne out by the example of the Chicago meat-packing plants or visits to the Carnegie steel mills in Pittsburgh and a few other establishments, associated American industry with progress. Watching the rapid development of the South and the ingenious new mining techniques further confirmed this impression.

American industry was thus seen as quintessentially modern, always productive, and free of the problems of conscience posed by other economic activities. It interested the French not so much in and of itself, but rather for its inevitable social and political implications.

## THE TRUST

The trust symbolized the power of the American economy, both by the real strength it represented in its different guises and by the myth that surrounded it. The protest movement against the trust that developed in the United States and the larger-than-life personalities of certain of its tycoons were so many reasons for the French to be interested, even fascinated, by this phenomenon.

---

27. P. Sée, *Le péril américain*, offprint of the *Bulletin de la Société industrielle du Nord de la France* (Lille: Imprimerie Daneil, 1903), p. 8. The article was rather laudatory, despite the title.
28. A. Métin, "Le travail aux Etats-Unis," *Exposition universelle de Saint Louis, Rapports* (Paris: E. Cornély, 1907), p. 2. Métin felt that even the machines were not designed to last; it was indeed a different world.

### The Trust, a New Thing

It was not until the last years of the nineteenth century, 1898 or 1899, that French authors used the word *trust* in its relatively precise economic sense. These years saw the publication of an important article in the *Revue des Deux Mondes*, Paul de Rousiers's book *Les industries monopolisées aux Etats-Unis* (The Monopolized Industries in the United States), and *L'ouvrier américain* (The American Worker) by Emile Levasseur, which largely dealt with this question.[29] Thereafter, the trusts were an integral part of the American economic landscape, and the news from America ensured that they never faded from view.

French interest in these economic organizations came relatively late, considering that Standard Oil was founded in the early 1880s and that the Sherman Law, the first antitrust legislation, was passed in 1890. The French do not seem to have been altogether aware of these events, which only elicited a few scattered remarks.[30]

Thorough studies of the trusts were not undertaken until the Chicago World's Fair spawned lively French interest in the United States, as did the vicissitudes of the 1896 presidential campaign,[31] and, above all, the beginning of the economic boom that coincided spectacularly with the beginning of large-scale mergers in 1897. The French were thus prompted by current American events to study these matters.

The question soon arose whether the trust was a purely American phenomenon or whether it was the first sign of a more general trend toward industrial concentration and the creation of monopolies. French opinions were almost unanimous: There was indeed a trend toward concentration, which in Europe took the form of producers' cartels, but it was in the United States, where industrial activity was more highly developed, that the trend toward monopolies had been most fully realized. The various French commentators all insisted on the specifically American character of the trust, but none went as far as Louis Aubert: ". . . [there is] no comparison with what is happening in France, where we still do not have anything like it, fortunately."

---

29. L.-P. Dubois, "Les monopoles industriels aux Etats-Unis," *Revue des Deux Mondes* (1 Feb. 1898): 634–58. P. de Rousiers, *Les industries monopolisées aux Etats-Unis* (Paris: Colin, 1898), was the first full-length book on the subject; it was often used by subsequent authors, among them E. Levasseur.
30. For instance in the *Grande Encyclopédie* (Paris: Société anonyme de la Grande Encyclopédie, 1890), p. 577, or in E. Reclus, *Nouvelle géographie universelle* (Paris: Hachette, 1890), p. 741.
31. This argument was advanced by P. de Rousiers to explain the investigation he was asked to conduct by the Musée social in 1896.

The purpose of the trust, it was felt, was nothing very unusual; limiting production, setting and keeping prices at the most profitable level, and reducing costs were objectives that many European industrialists pursued as well. What made it specifically American was the role of the trustees and the unlimited power the French ascribed to their cartel, "the federated and therefore most solid, durable, and vital form of the trust . . . which has remained an American specialty."

The best example of this new form of concentration was the petroleum trust, the famous Standard Oil Company of the equally famous Rockefeller. This company was almost a model, and always the first to be cited. John D. Rockefeller buying up smaller companies thanks to his understanding with the railroad companies and forcing the larger ones into mergers was a showcase example for demonstrating the almost flawless mechanism of building up a trust. Here one could observe how a monopoly was achieved by the most reprehensible methods involving the domination of prices and human beings. The rebuilding of Standard Oil after its condemnation under the antitrust legislation was further proof of its dynamism. Paul de Rousiers meticulously explained the working of the system, which ranged from small and often archaic producers using rusty steam engines to the key sectors of refineries and transportation facilities, all of them tightly controlled by the directors of the trust.

In the end, however, not many other trusts fit the model so well, which made it difficult to define them. The best observers made every effort to distinguish among the different versions of the phenomenon, pointing out that some industries, like the rope manufacturers or the anthracite producers, formed only temporary cartels, while others, like the Ocean Trust of the early years of the twentieth century, were never really able to gain a foothold.[32] By contrast, detailed discussions of the formation of the steel trust particularly struck the imagination of the French. The alliance of the two giants Carnegie and Morgan, followed by the retreat of Carnegie, which resulted in the first company with a capital of $1 billion, seemed to represent a level that would not easily be superseded.

And finally, the French categorized any concentration, any merger of several enterprises as the creation of a trust. Fascinated by this quest for monopoly, most observers did not bother to ask whether it was successful or not; the word "trust" was sufficient. They were certain that they were seeing the confirmation that this was a uniquely American evolution, for it was clear to them that, at least initially, these astonishing enti-

---

32. G. Martin, *Problèmes transatlantiques* (Paris: A. Rousseau, 1903), p. 76.

ties had sprung up thanks to the apparent absence of restraints from the federal government. The very lenient character of the laws of New Jersey was another example of this situation, as was the laxness of the financial regulations; these were things that could not happen in Europe.

The French eventually came to challenge the trusts, without, however, espousing the positions of the antitrust movement as it took shape in the United States during the Progressive Era.

### *Questioning the Trusts*

Liberal observers such as Paul de Rousiers, Emile Levasseur, Pierre Leroy-Beaulieu, Germain Martin, and a few others viewed the achievements of the trusts with admiration. They were willing to acknowledge that concentration was a natural thing: "the trusts are in themselves a legitimate form of the freedom of association" and part and parcel of the apparent direction of progress. They also noted that the price of goods produced by the trusts seemed to be stable and that the workers were well paid, often better than in "non-trustified" companies.

However, increasing American criticism gave them pause. Soon some of the French said that the means employed by John D. Rockefeller to build his empire were "rather indelicate," and that "our European habits" would judge them severely. It now seemed to some that a few governmental measures could have prevented these excesses, or indeed avoided the creation of the trusts themselves, in which case the phenomenon of concentration would not be so natural after all:

> Trusts that aim to dominate the market through coalition, thereby oppressing the seller, the worker, and the buyer, are reprehensible; several have misused their strength and given American opinion reason to complain about the very principle of competition, which is a good one; in this area proper limits are hard to draw.[33]

These considerations, which were inspired by American criticism, were joined by other and more typically French ones. In particular, the various observers often distinguished between the actions of the industrialists and those of the financiers. The former were depicted as noble, aware of the problems of production and in touch with concrete reality, while the latter seemed to be soulless: ". . . many more people have become rich in the United States as speculators than as industrialists."[34] And now the

33. Levasseur, *L'ouvrier américain*, p. 92.
34. A. Raffalovich, "La compagnie d'acier aux Etats-Unis," *Nouvelle Revue* (1 July 1908): 7.

development of the trusts gave an ever greater role to such people. Over-capitalization, caused by intense speculation that was no longer related to the real needs of the economy, was now occurring: "The trust is a progressive form of industry. Only the financial methods of the trust are bad and dangerous."

The trust, then, was debated much more as a moral than as an economic issue, as a matter of principle rather than of efficiency, of which everyone approved. But this did not prevent the French from deploring the advantages it gained through high tariffs or from fearing its effect on foreign markets.

However, to observers of this ilk the main danger of the trust undoubtedly was the idea that the kind of collectivism it created would furnish "the strongest example to illustrate Karl Marx's conceptions and to show them in a powerful light."

Actually, the Marxist critique of the trust turned out to be itself rather ambiguous. Essentially argued by Marx's son-in-law, Paul Lafargue, it was structured around a few simple ideas. First:

> ... the trusts, by refusing to conform to the venerable principles of Political Economy and irreverently disproving the succinct assertions of the worthy economics experts, are doing away with competition and substituting a methodical organization for the anarchy that prevails in capitalist production.[35]

Second, the structure of the trusts gave them entirely too much power, both economically – through the creation of monopolies and the strangling of the independent producers – and politically or intellectually. J. P. Morgan could tell even Theodore Roosevelt what to do.

And last, this system oppressed the workers, stultifying them, even if they were sometimes well paid, by treating them like cattle, firing them at will, and blacklisting them. Thus: "Standard Oil, more real than the Good Lord of the Christians, is omnipresent wherever the working class is robbed." Such a situation was made to unite French bourgeois and workers in opposition.

Lafargue even argued that the class struggle in the United States was being exacerbated and might actually foster the revolution. Yet the trusts, horrible though they were, did represent a kind of progress, to the extent that under the leadership of a handful of extremely hard-working men they succeeded economically in their own domain. Hence their nationalization would be highly profitable.

---

35. P. Lafargue, *Les trusts américains* (Paris: V. Giard et E. Brière, 1903), p. v. The author uses many American studies but also relies heavily on P. de Rousiers.

Lafargue's analysis was used and expanded by most of the French Socialists who expected a great deal of these trusts and were simultaneously frightened and attracted by them, as Urbain Gohier pointed out:

> The capitalist trusts are agents of Socialism. . . . First of all because their rapacity exasperates a lot of people who would also be indignant about the tyranny of the labor unions. And second because the centralization of certain properties and of all the industrial equipment will facilitate their nationalization.[36]

Thus the flaws and the advantages of the trusts were seen in complementary ways by different French observers. Emile Levasseur deplored the same curbing of competition that Paul Lafargue was glad to see; by contrast, the system's efficiency was recognized by everyone in terms of results, though condemned in terms of morality, and everyone willy-nilly chimed in when it came to denouncing the abuses of speculation or the collusion between heads of trusts and politicians. The lack of respect for American politicians explains that almost no one expected them to resist the tempting offers of the "trustifiers," who were seen as a mere flaw in the system by some, and as an example of capitalist gangrene by others.

### The Lincoln of the Trusts

Most of the French statements on the subject of trusts date from between 1898 and 1903, a time when the unpopularity of these entities had reached a high point in the United States, though without prompting any action on the part of the federal government, least of all during the presidency of McKinley, who was known by everyone to be beholden to the powers of money. As for Bryan, he had indeed condemned the trusts, but he was not thought to have enough influence to warrant a great deal of attention.

Things changed when Theodore Roosevelt became involved in the debate, possibly impelled by nothing more than his own opinion – although he also needed to keep up his popularity, a fact that was very well understood by the French. An antitrust wind had been blowing ever since the early years of the presidency of the former colonel of the Rough Riders, and in many cases the French first became aware of the scope of the debate through the positions Roosevelt had taken as early as 1902 or 1903. It was then that many of them discovered the nature of the trusts and began to follow the struggle, keeping their eyes riveted on the President; after all, he was about to deal with this problem at the federal level,

---

36. U. Gohier, *Le peuple du XXe siècle* (Paris: Fasquelle, 1903), p. 88.

just as Lincoln had done for slavery, an initiative that by October 1902 earned him the favorable sobriquet of "the Lincoln of the trusts."[37] The campaign of 1904 was an occasion to return to these themes, but the full excitement of the raging controversy was brought home to the French in 1906–7. The vote on the Hepburn Law to regulate the railroads and especially the investigation of the meat trust that Teddy had pushed following the publication of Upton Sinclair's book *The Jungle*, as well as his dramatic declarations of 1907, clearly showed what was at stake.

The French Socialists did not believe that Teddy was sincere, nor that he had succeeded in curbing the "Morganization" of the United States; conversely, most of the other observers were glad to see that measures were finally taken to reduce the power of the trusts and restrain their abuses.

Etienne Martin Saint-Léon, who specialized in the study of concentrations and was very well informed about the abundant American literature on the subject, trusted Roosevelt's energy and willpower, even though he knew all about the capacity for resistance and the resources of the trusts. For his part, Arthur Raffalovich praised the President's "decisive, forceful, and prompt action" in this matter.[38]

Nonetheless, some of the French observers were rather surprised by the antitrust movement, for it did not seem to be in keeping with American mores: "In 1870 people in New York closed their eyes to speculations that came close to highway robbery, and in 1907 New Yorkers are scandalized by dealings that have nothing criminal about them." But the involvement of Roosevelt maintained French interest until the arrival of his successor:

> Watching the ex-colonel of the Rough Riders, with his fits of anger, his vehement speeches, and his interminable messages, one always knew what he meant; he was rather like the rooster in one of La Fontaine's fables, while M. Taft would be Raminagrobis.[39]

When Taft came to power French interest in the trusts began to fade. They were now seen as part of the decor and no longer really surprised anyone, particularly since their abuses seemed to be more or less under control. In 1912 Louis Aubert did not hesitate to evoke their "marvelous

---

37. "Lettre des Etats-Unis," *Le Temps* (23 Oct. 1902); this was the title of this rather too optimistic letter.
38. E. Martin de Saint Léon, "Le Président Roosevelt et les trusts," *Le Correspondant* (10 Sept. 1907): 894–919; A. Raffalovich, "Les horreurs de Chicago," *Nouvelle Revue* (15 Aug. 1906): 458; the author finds Upton Sinclair's book very mediocre and overly melodramatic.
39. G. Tricoche, "Lettre . . . ," *Journal des Economistes* (Aug. 1909): 246.

achievements"; after all, they had brought about a lasting drop in prices, despite many fears and passions, and moreover the mechanism of the Sherman Law had worked, restoring competition to its proper role. This did not mean that the trusts had become innocuous, for they were still protected by customs barriers and potentially dangerous at the level of international competition. Nor had the Socialists totally given up the hope of using them as vectors of revolution.

Yet the French no longer debated this issue, for the boisterous and sometimes purely symbolic initiatives of Theodore Roosevelt had contributed to masking the essence of the problem. The controversies of the campaign of 1912 did not seem to add much, now that the question of the trusts had become exclusively political. The French had mainly approached this matter from a theoretical point of view, since they themselves were not threatened by "trustification." For all their lively interest in the trusts, they failed to grasp the power of the passions they aroused in the Americans.

### The Tycoons

If American women had always fascinated and attracted the French, their male companions had not been so fortunate. With the exception of the somewhat rough picturesqueness of the cowboy, the hard-working American male did not capture much attention. His life seemed empty and completely focused on work, his manners remained brusque and his interests extremely limited. The other exception was the group of wealthy businessmen, bankers, industrialists, and the various "kings" of specific products.

Not always men of refinement, they were exemplars of energy incarnate, of success and power made flesh. The wealth of the greatest among them was such that they astounded the observer by their ostentation, if not by their cultivation. However different they were from the French ideal, they did represent the *Homo americanus economicus* in his purest form, the man who went to Europe to spend his dollars or marry off his daughters, the man who filled the scandal sheets or who, more discreetly, asserted his power over people and things. French novelists loved to write about him, for instance E. M. de Voguë in his *Maître de la mer* (Lord of the Sea).[40]

One does not have to peruse the gossip columns filled to the brim with the extravagances of rich Americans to see that these men enjoyed great prestige among all foreigners, and the French were no exception.

---

40. S. Jeune, *De F.T. Graindorge à A.O. Barnabooth* (Paris: Didier, 1963), pp. 362–88.

Thus, in the late 1880s, when Charles de Varigny compared the great fortunes in Great Britain and in the United States, he was amazed at the power of the American millionaires; Stephen Girard, J. Gordon Benett, Jay Gould, or Cornelius Vanderbilt had little reason to envy the great British families. As in the case of the British aristocrats, their growth in numbers would arouse deep social animosities.[41] Some ten years later, American millionaires had become just as numerous; this was the time when their daughters came to "re-gild the coats-of-arms" of old European families. The Princesse de Polignac and the Duchesse Decazes were daughters of the Singer family, and there were forty-four marriages between noble sons of Albion and rich Americans. During the same years, Paul Bourget, "kept prisoner" on the splendid estates of Mrs. Gardner, popularized the sumptuous comforts enjoyed by the famous "four hundred families" of New York, while Boni de Castellane allied himself with Anna Gould.

Such a situation irresistibly evoked a kind of aristocracy defined by its way of life, its contacts, and its money. Its ostentation was mind-boggling, for these wealthy Americans lived like feudal lords on their many estates, protected by bodyguards. This kinship with the aristocracy explains the popular interest of these men and their families, whose habits, carriages, and estates were discussed in great detail by the French.

However, the interest in these rich people went far beyond their present lifestyle, however fascinating it might be. For the fact was that, unlike the European aristocrats, they had come from the middle class and were therefore similar to the self-made men so typical of American society: "Many of these kings of the trusts are self-taught and have attended only the School of Life; they are poor men who have become rich." Most of the observers acknowledged, not without admiration, that those who had not gone to college had had to fight hard and work incessantly to hoist themselves to the position they occupied, although not all of them fit this legendary pattern. Germain Martin was fascinated by the amount of work accomplished by an American businessman, by the energy he deployed when he sent out ten times as many letters and cables as his French counterpart and stirred up around him a commotion which, though largely bluff, was part of what kept the country moving:

> In American society the "business man" plays a role analogous to that of the dynamo, which generates an electric current that will start up motors waiting close by or even far away.[42]

41. C. de Varigny, *Les grandes fortunes aux Etats-Unis et en Grande Bretagne* (Paris: Hachette, 1889), pp. 6, 50–51.
42. Martin, *Problèmes transatlantiques*, p. 95. Martin was struck by the ease of communi-

Their ceaseless labor in contact with others explains why these rich individuals were always ready to participate in common endeavors, as they did during the Spanish-American War, much more so than their European counterparts. It also explains why they were interested in endowing cultural and educational institutions.

This was one of the traits that most surprised the French, who could only salute Rockefeller's endowment of the University of Chicago and Carnegie's charitable foundations. Socialist critics, of course, immediately spoke of hypocrisy and were not always wrong to contrast these liberalities with the oppression of workers perpetrated by these same rich donors, but the general impression of the French was quite favorable. These patrons were able to provide help for the arts and letters from the beginning and did not wait to reward success after it was achieved, following the "vexing and warning" example of the Académie française. Nor should one turn up one's nose at what was probably not done as a public service but rather out of properly understood self-interest where "personal energy and audacity" came together, for it proved to be highly effective.

John D. Rockefeller, "the prototype of the American, thoughtful, hard working, tough, leaving nothing to chance," was admired but not particularly popular, any more than J. P. Morgan, whose taste for art was not enough to redeem him completely. Andrew Carnegie, by contrast, was quite well liked. His incomparable business abilities were complemented by those of a philanthropist who seemed more sincere than many of his colleagues. To Abbé Klein he symbolized the American businessman par excellence, just as Mgr. Spalding symbolized the religious leader and Theodore Roosevelt the civic-minded politician.[43] Henri Bargy even considered Carnegie a true philosopher, as well as a writer who was a credit to American democracy.

Even some of the lesser personalities were of interest to a French entrepreneur such as Lazare Weiller, among them the men who controlled the Chicago meat trusts – although this was before the publication of *The Jungle*: "I have had the pleasure of meeting their heads, simple, energetic, and gentle men who were completely absorbed in their work, except perhaps M. Armour and his associate, M. Meeker, both of whom are passionate about automobiles."[44] Such praise can no doubt be explained in part by a kind of corporate solidarity among entrepreneurs,

cations and, like P.E. de Constant a few years later, very excited by the fact that it took only a few minutes to establish contact with the other side of the continent.

43. F. Klein, *Au pays de la vie intense* (Paris: Plon, 1904), p. 194.
44. L. Weiller, *Les grandes idées d'un grand peuple* (Paris: Juven, 1904), p. 102.

but it is also understandable that Georges Aubert, who had met many of these men, should come to this conclusion:

> In short, there is in the United States a whole cluster of men who stand out by their intelligence, their activity, their wealth, and their commercial and industrial genius. It behooves us to pay a deserved tribute of admiration to this phalanx of eminent men who have become distinguished through a life of hard work, perseverance, and intelligence.[45]

This, then, was a true elite, not simply by dint of its external signs of wealth, but in terms of special qualities and professional skills. Implied by many French observers, this idea was made explicit by Paul de Rousiers, who evoked the "higher calling" of these exceptional men, who knew how to succeed but also to think of others, and who formed a natural aristocracy that was open to all, and not self-encapsulated like its European counterparts.[46]

This concert of praise is surprising for its scope and its relative unanimity, for even the Socialists recognized the energy and the hard work of these despised employers, who did better than their French counterparts. André Chevrillon was one of the very few French observers who frowned upon the quality of the esthetic preoccupations of these men, for whom commercial considerations were paramount, and who made fun of the extravagances of their idle sons.

The fact is that the kings of the trusts were much more highly regarded than the trusts themselves, and that the abuses for which they could be criticized were easily forgotten, redeemed as it were by their success, their luxury, and above all their patronage of the arts and the universities. These men were made in the image of America, more interested in facts than in ideas, and this was why the "overseas Jaurèses" found it so hard to bring them down; and even if it could be done, others would always spring up to follow in their footsteps.[47]

This is a curious idealization of a particular type of man, who was fascinating despite his flaws and completely lacking in refinement and measure, but impressive for his power and self-promotion. Perhaps one can also see this French attitude as respect for an elite which, despite

---

45. G. Aubert, *Le marché financier américain* (lecture of 19 Jan. 1912) (Paris: privately printed, 1912), p. 46.
46. P. de Rousiers, *La vie américaine* (Paris: F. Didot, 1892), vol. 1, p. 146, "Les nouveaux aristocrates," and p. 276: "These men are in fact magnificent specimens of the human race, they are fighters, they are obstinate and bold, and they ennoble their big profits by putting them to good use. Never feeling that they have the right to rest and enjoy the fruits of their labor, they always press on as long as they live, as if a superior vocation had assigned them to the pursuit of an ever receding goal. . . ."
47. R. Michaud, "Silhouettes transatlantiques," *L'Opinion* (30 Jan. 1909): 144–45.

major differences, seemed to bring the United States closer to European norms.

The American economy was thus seen through various prisms. It was unquestionably powerful and, hence, threatening. This was clear in 1901–2, when American products seemed about to invade Europe: "Uncle Sam became a kind of colossus, whose arms encircled the planet in the grip of his sharp claws." Certain French observers did not hesitate to envisage the "Americanization" of the world. However, many of them decried the American methods, the poor management, and the laxness of the financial system, frequently taking a self-righteous stance of wise discipline and even exaggerating the flaws that seemed to impair the performance of the American economy.

All of this more or less implicitly led to a notion of injustice. The resources of the United States were such that it could afford all kinds of economic follies; their effects would never be permanent. Nature had simply been too kind to that country. Given the same means, would not Europe, and especially France, achieve equally brilliant results? This frustration did not stand up to closer examination for very long. The trusts did not come about because of the country's wealth; they succeeded only because of human energy, deployed by both the employers and the workers without any real interference of the government. This was an explanation often advanced by French observers, both the business-minded people, who took it as inspiration, and certain Socialists, who were hoping to use this undeniable success for the benefit of the working class.

# 14

# *And Now, Imperialism*

It is only normal to expect an economically powerful and politically stable nation such as the United States to assert itself on the international scene and to bring the weight of its interests to bear on its neighbors. It is therefore not surprising that in the post–Civil War period the French, even in leftist circles, closely watched and eventually approved of the American administration's annexationist impulses in the direction of Santo Domingo, Alaska, and even Canada. Wearing the halo of victory, which was seen as the triumph of democracy and freedom, the Americans were bound to improve the fate of the populations in these territories.

Yet William Seward eventually had to cease his bluster and the Great Republic seemed to turn away from any foreign adventure. Without known foreign enemies, its army very soon returned to its skeletal proportions and its domestic tasks, and its leaders showed no desire to enhance their prestige by international posturing, with the short-lived exception of James G. Blaine, who waved the flag of a worrisome pan-Americanism.

However, certain French observers felt that this was an abnormal situation. They ranged from Claudio Jannet, who, unable to forget the annexationism he had seen before the Civil War, considered Mexico and Canada the next victims of Uncle Sam's appetite, to the author writing in the *Journal des Economistes*, who in his respect for the "natural laws of expansion" thought in 1888 that ". . . an American expedition to conquer Europe in the twentieth or twenty-first century is no more extraordinary or impossible than the European expeditions of the sixteenth, seventeenth, and eighteenth centuries."[1] Nonetheless, the era of Manifest Destiny seemed far away. At this point a dispute like the one

1. H. de Beaumont, "De l'avenir des Etats-Unis et de leur lutte future avec l'Europe," *Journal des Economistes* (15 July 1888): 81.

over seal hunting in the Bering Sea was not enough to involve the United States in a real conflict with Canada or Great Britain.[2] Yet the French could see that the Americans were not inactive in Samoa or Hawaii.

These were contradictory signals, but such a situation could not last. The ever-increasing power of the United States was bound to put an end to this reserve. The important thing was to find out when and where this would happen, and also whether this inevitable American imperialism would follow the same pattern as that of the other great powers of the day. Would they have to compete with it?

## A TREMENDOUS WAKE-UP CALL

In the space of two years, between 1896 and 1898, the French, along with the rest of the world, witnessed the molting of the North American giant. His international stature suddenly seemed to match his considerable means, and this regional power, this political dwarf, acquired the appetite and the airs of an ogre. This formidable transformation aroused a great deal of interest, and the number of "America watchers" suddenly grew larger.[3]

### *The Venezuelan Warning*

President Cleveland's differences with Great Britain over the exact delineation of parts of the frontier between the British colony of Guyana and Venezuela became the object of considerable attention, especially after the American declaration of 17 December 1895, which called for adherence to the Monroe Doctrine and did not rule out a confrontation.

The United States had already had occasion to take an interest in the way the situation in Latin America was evolving, but so far the problems had been purely American and had not directly concerned any of the European powers. Now, all of a sudden, Washington seemed intent on picking a fight with none other than her Britannic Majesty, and the affair assumed totally unexpected proportions.

Moreover, the highly charged demonstrations on the part of much of the American press and many of the politicians, about a conflict that did not even directly involve the United States, were ominous: Was this,

---

2. G. de la Sablière, "Les phoques à fourrure de la mer de Bering, le conflit anglo-américain," *Le Correspondant* (25 Aug. 1891): 628–42. The author already deplored the fate of the seals as objects of so much greed.
3. For a complete bibliography as of the year 1904, see J. Patouillet, *L'impérialisme américain* (Paris: Rousseau, 1904), pp. 3–10.

perhaps, a fit of temper that had to happen sooner or later? "The country had gotten a bit tired of its interminable debates on the abstruse and boring subjects of tariff and monetary circulation."[4] Or was it nothing more than the action of some American super-patriots?

But then again, even a judicious and moderate man like President Cleveland brandished the Monroe Doctrine like a red flag before John Bull. On this occasion the French rediscovered this somewhat forgotten text. *Le Temps*, for instance, as well as the *Revue des Deux Mondes* and the *Revue de Paris*, devoted articles to this prodigiously effective document. "Its message caused an explosion of patriotism and pride in America: political divisions faded away and all Americans formed a single party. . . ."[5]

Most French judgments were relatively nuanced. On the one hand, pointing out that this text had no legal standing, the authors limited themselves to recalling the confused conditions under which it had been written; on the other, they showed that it seemed to be a perfect reflection of the "psychology" of the American nation. The eagerness of the Americans to rally around this paper flag did not fail to impress the French.

Beyond the immediate vicissitudes of the crisis, it seemed clear that the Americans had given proof of powerful national sentiments. These had not been expressed with such vigor since the affair of the *Trent* in autumn 1861, but this time it was done solely as a display of strength. This was bound to happen, and the French observers considered it perfectly normal, particularly since France was in no way involved in this matter. American national consciousness was being forged, and it adopted the Monroe Doctrine as its flag. It had a perfect right to do so; every nation needed one. F. de Pressensé perfectly summarized this point of view when he asserted: "I fail to see why one should be so hard on the Monroe Doctrine, which at least has the advantage of being absolutely honest."

Such tolerance for the general aims pursued by the Americans did not mean, however, that the French always found it easy to accept their conduct. The brutal tone employed by the Secretary of State, Richard Olney, as well as the interference of the United States in a matter that did not directly concern it, cast a crude light both on the country's

4. F. de Pressensé, "La Doctrine de Monroe et le conflit américain," *Revue des Deux Mondes* (15 Jan. 1896): 419.
5. M.D. de Beaumarchais, *La Doctrine de Monroë; L'évolution de la politique des Etats-Unis au XIXe siècle* (Paris: Larose, 1898), p. 122. Issued from a thesis and prompted by the Venezuelan crisis, this book was first published before the Spanish-American War, but a second edition was quickly added.

intentions and on the rude vulgarity of "Jonathan," as the French some-times called "the American." But here again, such behavior was by no means unusual; at most the French could remark that the United States of the late nineteenth century seemed to have taken up the torch France had carried in 1792, when it claimed that its system was the only good one, and acted almost paternally: "Venezuela had not even asked for the protection it was given, and M. Cleveland negotiated for M. Crespo as the President of the French Republic negotiated for the Bey of Tunis."[6]

In other words, the United States had quite simply conducted itself as a great power, a status to which its strength and its wealth naturally enti-tled it. The French serenely accepted this, particularly since in this era before the Entente Cordiale a certain humiliation of Great Britain did not altogether displease them. All in all, French opinions about the Venezuelan affair were not marked by any real passion, but this would not necessarily remain so in less peaceful circumstances.

Meanwhile, the American President and parts of the Congress remained extremely reserved about international involvements. Thus Cleveland was opposed to the annexation of Hawaii, recognizing "the moral rights of other people," which was the other facet of American toughness: ". . . I believe that the great North American nation is one of the very few to whom one could speak, with some chance of success, in defense of the weak by presenting the argument of simple justice."[7]

### *The Particulars of an Unexpected War*

The war of 1898 between the United States and Spain was followed by all the major French dailies at the rate of an editorial every day or every other day during the periods of greatest tension, even though domestic concerns and new developments in the Dreyfus Affair demanded more and more attention. Articles in major magazines were not as frequent and their themes were often rather limited. The French thus showed great interest in the conflict, which for the first time pitted a European power against the United States. This interest was not always a matter of simple curiosity, and it is known that at this time parts of the popular press received subsidies from Spain,[8] which made for a general anti-

---

6. Ibid., p. 139.
7. G. de Wailly, "Hawaii libre," *Nouvelle Revue* (Jan.–Feb. 1898): 109. These illusions were short-lived; in fact, his article was already set when the author learned that the annex-ation of Hawaii was considered again. Thereupon he wrote a distressed postscript: "The public conscience can only side with Honolulu against Washington, for this annexation is a brutal step backward on the road to respect for national identity" (p. 120).
8. A. Blumenthal, *France and the United States* (Chapel Hill: University of North Carolina Press, 1970), p. 190.

American tone. This situation explains the anti-French effervescence that briefly burst forth in the United States in the summer of 1898 and also accounts for this reaction of a Cuban:

> One would be correct to say that hatred of the American is the least divisive sentiment among the French, for such unanimity has never been seen before. Some Republicans defend a retrograde monarchy, some free thinkers noisily wish for the success of a nation of fanatics, and some conservatives, guardians of family values, use the expression "pork mongers" for the maternal ancestors of noblemen who tomorrow will bear some of the most illustrious names in France.[9]

This vision of French opinion, however, is rather too summary and biased; it was, in fact, more nuanced and complex.

In the period just before the outbreak of the war, opinions were relatively concordant. Despite some observers' positive feelings for what Spain had meant in history and in the world, few approved of the way that country had treated its Cuban possession. The best the French could say was that there was hope for improvement, considering that the Cuban insurgents had received a promise of autonomy in March of 1898: "To arrive at this result," Spain would have to act "with wisdom and courage." However, the repressive Spanish policy left little room for illusion; moreover, Spain had a particularly bad reputation in all leftist French circles, which suspected it of having little aptitude for democracy. These more or less pronounced reservations explain why the Spanish government felt that it should make a special effort to shore up its image.

On the other hand, the different American initiatives were watched with the greatest suspicion by even the best French friends of the United States. In particular, everyone realized with more or less tolerance or indignation that in this case the aims pursued by the United States were by no means disinterested. The more conservative milieux did not trust the humanitarian declarations in which the American leaders laid out their concern for the fate of the Cubans, particularly since the statements in the "yellow press" demonstrated the country's pervasive and violent chauvinism at this time. Juliette Adam could thus, in all good conscience, contrast chivalric Spain with the "jingoist" United States,[10] testifying to increasing French hostility toward the United States as the situation became more tense.

9. A. Ruz (Egmont), *Les Etats-Unis, l'Espagne et la presse française* (Paris: Dupont, 1898), p. 46.
10. J. Adam, "Lettres sur la politique étrangère, *Nouvelle Revue* (March–April 1898): 705–6, "Où est le machiavélisme hypocrite ou la chevaleresque sincerité?"

More liberal, even Socialist circles, without going this far, were skeptical as well. They did not deny the sincerity of American idealism but felt that this was not sufficient to account for the relentless effort to implicate the Spanish in the explosion of the *Maine* or the perfidious publication of a private letter by the Spanish ambassador in the United States, Dupuy de Lôme. There must have been something else: "It turns out that the material desires of the Republic coincided with the conclusions based on reason and sentimentality."[11] Moreover, it seemed clear that the most virulent exponents of American chauvinism were gaining the upper hand, both in the press and in the administration and Congress. *Le Temps* was particularly indignant about the excesses of the American newspapers, which were a far cry from its own model of measure, restraint, and reflection. *Le Temps* also feared President McKinley's alignment with the most extremist positions, writing following the Spanish amnesty for the Cuban insurgents:

> Forcing a rupture in feverish haste would reveal the utter hypocrisy of the Americans' humanitarian pretexts; it would show the world, instead of a philanthropic undertaking and the generous pledge of a war of liberation, the hateful militarism of a kind of international buccaneering. In a word, it would be a mistake as well as a crime.[12]

At this point, French opinion was not fixed and had not yet clearly chosen between Spain and the United States. While the methods of Spain gave no cause for enthusiasm, the proceedings of the United States were altogether detestable, as was the demagoguery that seemed to have carried the day.

Yet those who sympathized with the Cuban cause, for all their doubts about the purity of the American intentions, came to accept an intervention of the United States as a chance to bring freedom to the inhabitants of the great Caribbean island. The American record and some of the aims that had been loudly proclaimed by important American leaders made them think that the American policy might be a little better than the intentions of certain European powers: ". . . for by serving selfish interests, this policy will accomplish the freeing of a population engaged in a just rebellion and consecrate its right to do so." Such rather balanced statements might make it seem as if the *Revue Socialiste, La Petite République,* or *L'Aurore* were favorable to the United States. It should be kept in mind, however, that this current of opinion was much more hostile toward Spain than it was pro-American, and that it was

11. P. Louis, "A propos de la guerre hispano-américaine," *Revue Socialiste* (May 1898): 608.
12. B.E., *Le Temps* (11 April 1898).

intent on seizing what it saw as a possibility of improving the fate of Cuba.

Those who did not care too much about a people's right to self-determination felt that the brutal, even hypocritical American methods completely disqualified the Americans, for all their claims to virtue and their idealistic declarations.

Thus it cannot be said that in this period of approaching war French opinion decisively sided with Spain, but this does not mean that it favored the American version of events. The high drama created by the war clarified these positions somewhat.

### The First Lessons of the War

Relatively short though it was, the Spanish-American War seemed to the French observers to be dragging on and on. The rare and mediocre ground actions carried out on Cuban soil and the much later naval victory won by Admiral Dewey at Cavite contributed to this impression. The relatively slow pace of the action seemed incompatible with the superiority that all observers, regardless of which side they favored, attributed to the Americans. While no one knew much about their soldiers, their fleet, which had been overhauled at the urging of Alfred T. Mahan, was known and seemed decidedly more modern and effective than the somewhat degenerate offspring of the Invincible Armada.

The very power of the United States, which, as everyone knew, had the energy and the resources to make up for any purely military weakness, in part explains the renewed favor Spain came to enjoy. Many French observers, sure that ineluctable defeat was in store for that country, showed it sympathy and support, which at times was akin to simple pity. This propensity for giving support to the weaker party is one of the reasons for the pro-Spanish tone of much of French opinion. This attitude was further strengthened by a sentiment of cultural community in the face of Anglo-Saxon power. The kinship of Latin origins and Catholicism suddenly seemed to be particularly important and worthy of being preserved and protected both to conservative and to liberal observers, even those who hitherto had not paid it too much attention. And then this sentiment was reinforced by certain American statements:

> Pious churchmen . . . complacently . . . proclaim that it is in God's eternal plan to banish Latin civilization from a hemisphere destined for the legitimate domination of the Anglo-Saxons.[13]

13. Ibid., (9 April 1898).

Anti-American attitudes were fostered by the more conservative French circles, who constantly glorified Spain and denounced the unfairness of the American victory when it came into view. Thus *Le Figaro* gloated over the errors committed by the American navy, while other observers highlighted the lack of moral qualities of the American troops and the poor organization that had marred the unfolding of operations "that were too costly to be enjoyed." These French commentators sought to show the unfair character of the American victory, which allowed them to cite the famous proverb, "Ill-gotten gain profiteth not."

Most of these assessments, while expressing charitable feelings for Spain, were perfectly willing to acknowledge the extent of the American victory. This does not mean that the French did not discuss the United States' right to declare war on a country with which it was not in direct conflict, nor that many of them did not deplore the Americans' refusal to try mediation before starting the hostilities, but then they had to bow to reality. Moreover, the criticism that could be leveled against the American methods did not prevent the French from acknowledging that Spain, given its carelessness in political and military matters, had deserved this defeat, just as its conduct in Cuba had explained, though perhaps not justified, the action of the United States: "I am not saying that the Americans have any right to intervene in Cuban affairs, but since the Spaniards have shown themselves incapable of governing the pearl of the Antilles, they should give it up."[14]

Such a recognition of the American success amounted not quite to a justification but, rather, to an obligation to come to grips with a new situation. Pro-Spanish sentiments must not be allowed to make the French lose sight of the interests involved here; after all, France had had no real reason to oppose the United States in this matter. The mediation efforts undertaken by Jules Cambon were made to satisfy both the supporters of Spain, who were hoping to spare that country an even greater humiliation, and those of the United States, who wanted to make sure that the Americans would not be drawn into an interminable conflict that could only harm it.

Actually, as they looked more closely, the more realistic observers admitted that the Spanish presence in Cuba had become archaic: "Spain has the misfortune that Cuba is located too close to the United States, much too close to the center of its magnetic field." This cold appraisal of Charles Benoist repeatedly appeared in the *Revue des Deux Mondes*, for which he covered the conflict. Madrid's West Indian possession would be best served if it fell "like a ripe fruit" into the basket held up by Uncle

14. H. Girard, "L'Espagne et les Etats-Unis," *Le Matin* (25 April 1898).

Sam. Some French observers now discovered the long-standing American interest in Cuba, which was no excuse but did account for this action:

> ... we would simply like to point out the following fact: that its [Cuba's] emancipation and impending annexation by the North American federation is a long-standing goal, the mainstay of American diplomacy and of the Monroe theory in the nineteenth century.[15]

Emile Ollivier, in one of the rare pieces he devoted to the United States, did not hesitate to go even further. He felt that a Cuba protected or annexed by the United States would be in better hands than in those of Spain, which had ruined all of its American possessions. He likened the American intervention to that of revolutionary France, asserting that liberty was indeed on the American side:

> It is possible that there was some admixture of selfish motives and unavowable speculation in the generous impulse that propelled it to Cuba, but this impure alloy cannot prevent us from appreciating the general nature of the enterprise itself.[16]

Thus the defeat of Spain was not considered a catastrophe, and there was no point in blaming the United States for the manner in which it had won its victory. This realism, which was fairly widespread in the most influential French papers, was rather severely shaken, however, by the American demands during the peace negotiations. In particular, the repudiation of the Cuban debt was seen as close to a sleazy proceeding, the annexation of Puerto Rico seemed to be no more than a vulgar bonus for the victor, and the demand for all of the Philippines surprised the French by its crudeness, for which they could see no justification.

What came into view, then, was quite simply an imperialist power that no longer bothered with the fig leaf into which the Monroe Doctrine had turned and no longer dissimulated a strategic and economic appetite that was as vigorous as that of the other major powers. With the exception of the Socialists – who, as in the case of Cuba, were hoping that the Filipinos would be better off once the Americans had freed them from

---

15. A. de Ganniers, "Les dessous de la diplomatie américaine," *Nouvelle Revue* (Jan.–Feb. 1899): 252.
16. E. Ollivier, "Les Etats-Unis, l'Espagne et la France," *Revue Bleue, Politique et Littéraire* (3 Sept. 1898): 293. This article, the only one Ollivier wrote on the subject of the United States, is very rich, and his position is intriguingly close to that of a Georges Clemenceau on the eve of the war. The article was written for the New York magazine *Century*, directed by the francophile Theodore Stanton.

the Spanish yoke – the French observers were shocked by the American greed.[17] Yet the Puerto Rican affair did not have the same appeal; bargaining around a negotiating table lacked the spectacular aspect of the Cuban affair; the American press had not had time to seize upon this matter, and the French knew nothing about this remote archipelago. The Americans had shown what they could do, that was enough; a minority of French observers remained hostile to them as a matter of principle, but most of them more or less eagerly resigned themselves to the new situation:

> It is useless to try to deny it, the Treaty of Paris consecrates the fall of Spain as a colonial and maritime power. May all Latin peoples meditate upon its clauses and avoid the errors that have led the unfortunate Castilian nation to the abyss. . . . Let us be watchful![18]

Beyond its international aspects, and before the problem of the new American colonies demanded attention, the Spanish-American War prompted a certain number of French observers to reflect on the evolution of the United States itself. Before long most of them expressed the conviction that these developments could not leave the country unscathed and that it was following a road long marked out by the European powers. The Great Republic would be unable to avoid the fearful weight of militarism, and it was the cost of a military establishment that drew the attention of observers like Gustave de Molinari, Paul Louis, or Achille Viallate:

> An imperialist policy will have the same consequences for this Republic as it has for other countries, and it will have to resign itself to seeing once again, as it did after the Civil War, bills that in principle are passed for the sole purpose of being prepared for extraordinary circumstances.[19]

By broaching such questions at the time of this war, the French indicated that they had become aware of a veritable "turning point in the world's evolution" in the span of these few months of 1898. This explains

---

17. Thus *La Petite République* thought the Philippines were better off with the Americans, but this did not keep Jean Jaurès from predicting, on 28 July 1898, the victory of American militarism. By contrast, L. Le Fur, in his *Etudes sur la guerre hispano-américaine de 1898* (Paris: Pédone, 1899), denounced "the right of the strongest" as exercised on this occasion. The "purchase" of the archipelago shocked the French because of its crass mercantile aspect.

18. Capitaine C. Bride, *La guerre hispano-américaine de 1898* (Paris: Chapelot, 1899), p. 267.

19. A. Viallate, "Les finances américaines et la guerre espagnole," *Le Correspondant* (25 Sept. 1898): 1191; see also G. de Molinari, "La guerre hispano-américaine," *Journal des Economistes* (May 1898): 161–69, or Louis, "A propos."

why over the next few years more and more reflections on the nature of this nascent American imperialism were focused on understanding it and on learning any lessons that might be drawn from it.

Was the United States simply becoming Europeanized, or did it bring new methods and principles to this new phase of its history?

## WHAT KIND OF IMPERIALISM FOR
## THE UNITED STATES?

The war of 1898 and its immediate aftermath had suddenly brought to light some major divergences within French opinion. A pervasive distrust of the means used by the Americans led the most conservative milieux to a real anti-Americanism, but prevented neither a relative tolerance on the part of the Socialists, who suspended judgment, nor a cold realism on the part of others. These attitudes were by no means fixed, and, once the shock of the defeat of Spain had passed, the French focused their reflection on the true nature of American imperialism.

### *Only an Economic Peril*

The formula "American peril" was used again and again by French authors in the earliest years of the twentieth century, often prompted by an essentially economic interpretation of imperialism as a parallel to the commercial thrust of the United States.

They saw the war as a logical extension of a phase of economic expansion, brought about by an excessive and perverse protectionism that had resulted in a "glut" that the Americans wanted to discharge beyond their frontiers. Such a movement might not have any real limits and could even threaten Europe, considering that the Americans no longer shied away from methods they seemed to have hitherto eschewed and that they were about to ". . . substitute for the old doctrine 'America for the Americans' the new formula 'the world for the Americans.' "[20]

Hastily formulated in the immediate aftermath of the Spanish-American War, this diagnosis was substantiated by a recapitulation – which is still impressive today – of the exact production statistics, the financial power, and the export figures of the United States. These seemed to make it obvious that the sole ambition of the United States was to prosper and to accumulate new wealth in order to increase what

---

20. F.E. Johannet, "Le monde aux Américains," *Le Correspondant* (10 Aug. 1898): 498; this
formula came to be widely used.

it already possessed. This overwhelming appetite for riches condemned the Americans to ". . . either starving to death while sitting on their treasures or extending indefinitely and at any price the radius of their influence and even their commercial domination." This was the central theme of an important article published in 1899 by Octave Noël in *Le Correspondant* under the title "The American Peril." Noël claimed that in the service of such ambitions, the American energy was necessarily dangerous: "The American is still too close to the state of nature, his overheated and artificial civilization has made him too assertive to be guided by a purely moral idea or decisively influenced by generosity."[21]

This article had a major impact. In fact, it was in the lineage both of earlier French critics of the excessive development of the American economy and of those who had been scandalized by what they considered outright aggression against Spain. Everything seemed to find a clear and logical explanation: the designs on the Panama Canal or on Nicaragua, on all of Latin America, on the Chinese market, and even on Europe.

This global analysis was more or less implicitly accepted by many French observers, even beyond those on the lunatic fringe. Nonetheless it did raise a certain number of problems, given the fact that, for all the figures Octave Noël had piled up, it was grounded in a mechanical and summary vision.

No one made the effort to discern an economic strategy of the United States on the basis of its precise expenditures to cover the needs for raw materials or the search for specific markets; what was happening was simply seen as the consequence of the inevitable American "glut" that was bound to overflow like the lava of a Hawaiian volcano. The American economy had so many resources that it did not seem to need anything from the outside; all it had to do was to sell its industrial and agricultural products. It was easy to remind readers that Europe could not do without American wheat, cotton, petroleum, and sugar, and that it had even needed grapevines from America. Moreover, since the United States was the paradise of the machine, its cotton cloth and its steam engines necessarily followed its raw materials.

American imperialism was thus naturally seen as an economic phenomenon, and there was no need to ask further questions. It was not even a clearly outlined policy. Conceptually – despite a shared diagnosis and

---

21. O. Noël, "Le péril américain," *Le Correspondant* (25 March 1899): 1081. This article marked a turning point in the Catholic review, which became violently anti-American in the area of foreign politics, although not much was said about the fate of most of Catholic Spain.

a superficial resemblance – the French were still far from the theses Lenin had expounded in *Imperialism, the Last Stage of Capitalism.*

This relative blindness explains why the famous "open door" policy was ignored by an opinion that looked only at the general picture. Discussed only in government offices, this "policy" did not appear in reviews or books. The Americans' intervention in China thus seemed to be exactly like that of the other industrial countries, devoid of any theoretical foundation.

Certain French observers made the effort to distinguish among the areas subjected to American influence or evaluated the various supports available to the United States. It appeared that its domination of the American continent was a forgone conclusion and that in order to achieve it, the United States did not need help from anyone. It could therefore take shelter behind the Monroe Doctrine in order to avoid European interference of any kind. Conversely – particularly at the time when Great Britain, involved in the Boer War, sought a rapprochement with the United States – many of the French envisaged an alliance between these two countries for the purpose of dividing up the rest of the world and its markets. This was the meaning of the "Americanization of the world" that figured prominently in certain English dreams, dreams that were reported with horror tinged with admiration by some French columnists.[22]

Yet the United States seemed to have little taste for such shared ownership of the world. All that could be said was that by taking over colonial territories, the United States might easily fall into the rut of the old colonial countries, rather than be inspired to follow the British methods:

> If the United States simply wants to enlarge the outlets for its products, all it has to do is abolish protectionism. . . . it could find ways to exchange its surpluses with highly civilized peoples, which would be safer and more profitable than dealing with the Chinese, the Filipinos, or other more or less decadent or primitive tribes who do not need anything and also do not have anything to pay with.[23]

These minor nuances did not invalidate the demonstration, which was immediately picked up by the Socialists, who were disappointed by the

---

22. For instance, A. Léger, "L'américanisation du monde," *Le Correspondant* (25 April 1902): 221–53. This is a review of the book by T.W. Stead, which envisages the Americanization of every aspect of life, and speaks of a "detestable internationalism." "Henceforth, we cannot close our borders to foreign ideas any more than to foreign goods. This form of Americanization is not the least remarkable" (p. 243).

23. Rouxel, "La politique coloniale américaine," *Journal des Economistes* (Jan. 1901): 76.

Americans' behavior in Cuba and especially in the Philippines. Thus Paul Louis, who in 1898 had shown a certain tolerance for the side effects of the American expansion, had changed his mind; barely a year later, the Great Republic looked just like any other country:

> It has demonstrated down there in Insulinde that its morality was no more exalted or sensitive than English, French, or German morality; all it has attested is that the uniform economic system of the major powers of the day has spread among them a uniform civilization marred by the same flaws everywhere.[24]

The French Socialists believed that this evolution could be stemmed only by the struggle against capitalism; but other observers felt that it was incumbent on France, indeed all of Europe, to make a stand against these inordinate American ambitions. Whether in the form of a European *Zollverein* or through a new balance among nations under the leadership of France, it seemed absolutely necessary to take quick action against the "gravest and most imminent" threat facing the Old World. On the one hand, the outlines of a united Europe, on the other, the adumbration of Gaullism.

However, these fears became attenuated after 1903, as if the danger were fading. The American commercial offensive was no longer as threatening, and the imperialism of the United States, while continuing to manifest itself, turned out to be confined to the American continent, where it did not really endanger the European positions. Moreover, the personality of Theodore Roosevelt, and his way of presenting things, paradoxically served to soften the edges of American imperialism somewhat, for he was able to package it in a more classical, not strictly economic and materialist manner.

Finally, after a few years, certain French observers came to distinguish between economic power and imperialist policy. The threat of caesarism or a "military Imperator" was no longer considered acute; expansionist goals were not to be found in that quarter but rather among the men who "ran" the trusts. This evolution might serve to diminish the American peril; in particular, it appeared that the United States would return to its usual ways in approaching international relations:

> . . . the Americans will treat them [international relations] as business or *strict business principles*; and this will be easy for them since their imperialism is essentially opportunistic, driven by circumstances, not rigid, logical, and touchy in matters of honor.[25]

24. P. Louis, "La grandeur des Etats-Unis," *Revue Socialiste* (Aug. 1899): 194.
25. P. de Rousiers, *La vie américaine* (Paris: Didot, 1899), vol. 2, p. 214.

The economic explanation for American imperialism, appealing though it was, was thus insufficient; it was seen to have different foundations.

## *Power Obliges*

The effect the Monroe Doctrine had had in 1895 and the Americans' repeated references to it forced the French to give it their attention. It furnished a key to understanding the international power of the United States, and it was not something that could be dismissed with an ironical stroke of the pen.

Various more or less obscure French studies of American imperialism and the Monroe Doctrine that seemed to sustain it discovered that this movement had started neither in 1898 nor in 1895. The stages of the United States' territorial expansion clearly showed the existence of an earlier expansionist effort that had not been merely a matter of keeping the European powers out of the American continent. That concern had been advanced after the fact as a simple and rather pretentious justification which, understandable up to a point, was insufficient to legitimize American actions in the Pacific and even in parts of the Antilles. The Monroe Doctrine, such as it was invoked, did show that the Americans had not acted haphazardly. They had had a full-fledged imperialist agenda, more or less hypocritically disguised by principles which, initially defensive, could become aggressive if necessary.[26]

It was clear to these observers that the doctrinal basis of American imperialist intentions made it a complete phenomenon which, being endowed with both means and principles, could not be reduced to economics alone.

It is not surprising that in the aftermath of the war of 1898 the rediscovery of the American ambitions should have led French observers to the conclusion that the European possessions in the Antilles would be the next targets, even before those in the southern part of the continent; but Theodore Roosevelt quickly reassured the French on this point. In return, however, the various manifestations of Roosevelt's interest in world affairs – from taking Russia to task for its pogroms and participating in actions to put down the Boxer Rebellion in China to acting as arbiter at the end of the Russo-Japanese War – were seen as signs of even grander ambitions. The Marquis de Barral de Montferrat was concerned about this evolution. "*Quo non ascendam*? That seems to have become

26. Marquis de Barral, "La Doctrine de Monroe et les évolutions successives de la politique étrangère aux Etats-Unis," *Revue d'Histoire Diplomatique* (Dec. 1903): 594–619, and (Jan. 1904): 21–52, 379–405.

the motto of the United States after the Cuban war!" Nor did Teddy's initiatives reassure him, even if they were peaceful, as in 1905, for they revealed the "same ardent desire . . . to enlarge the role of the United States every day."[27]

Such a role, supported by real power and activated by a strong will, was not necessarily immediately dangerous. But it might well be the first sign of an evolution toward American world domination throughout the twentieth century and, concurrently, of the decline of Europe, or even, as Urbain Gohier thought, its "burial." However, this fear or the apprehension about an implicit and general threat was not widespread.

In fact, realistic analyses of the kind that were published during the Venezuelan episode resurfaced as soon as the passions of the Spanish-American War had cooled down. This realism was reinforced over the following years, when it appeared that American imperialism knew how to limit its ambitions and did not constitute a direct and pressing threat to old Europe and remained circumscribed. The Monroe Doctrine was just a flag, which every country needed, and since it had been recognized by the other powers, it did not matter that the Americans used it in their own way, illogical though it might be. At most, they would have to abandon certain of their pretensions: "A region that becomes actively involved in everything that goes on from one end of the world to the other cannot very well forbid other countries to do the same."[28] Emile Boutmy wrote that the United States had simply fallen into the "psychological state" of imperialism, a phenomenon that according to him had started in England around 1860. It took a somewhat different form in every country; thus the army could play an essential role, as in France or Germany, while territorial and commercial domination were also important motives, as in the case of Great Britain. The Great Republic had obeyed its own imperatives, which were simpler but very impressive:

> It feels that power obliges. Its strength gives it a right, that right becomes a claim, and that claim turns into a duty to have a say in all questions that until recently were resolved by agreements among European powers alone. The world encourages this. In any conflict it looks toward the United States, anxiously wondering what the great nation across the seas will be tempted to do about it.[29]

27. Barral, *De Monroe à Roosevelt (1829–1905)* (Paris: Plon, 1905); this was a collection of his articles, with a preface by Vicomte d'Haussonville.

28. G.N. Tricoche, "Lettre . . . ," *Journal des Economistes* (Feb. 1907): 237.

29. E. Boutmy, "Les Etats-Unis et l'impérialisme," *Annales de Sciences Politiques* 17 (Jan. 1903): 3. A very rich article, which, under the title "L'impérialisme et la constitution," constitutes the only addition to the first edition of *Eléments d'une psychologie politique du peuple américain* (Paris: Plon, 1902).

This assessment was implicitly repeated by most of the French observers who did not limit themselves to imprecations. The fact that the United States thus joined the concert of powers, they pointed out, did not necessarily mean that it would adopt all of their methods and habits. For instance, the battle of San Diego Bay, like the exploits of Admiral Dewey, had aroused militaristic enthusiasm, which made some observers say that the Americans could no longer do without soldiers, and that they would rally to the first victorious military man with a bit of demagogical skill. Yet two or three years later it became quite clear that, except when there was trouble in the Philippines, the army remained quite small, that the fleet was essentially used for defending the American continent, and that the elections were perfectly normal. Similarly, the constitution did not need any amendments, even though the status of the new territories was not an easy problem to solve. And finally, imperialism – despite some understandable misgivings on the part of a people unaccustomed to its manifestations – was well accepted by the American population at large and by the political class. André Tardieu indicated that in Washington he had met some Democrats who spoke to him about their opposition to their government's Philippine policy, but that one of them was a candidate for governor of the archipelago.

American imperialism was thus both akin to that of the European powers and different. Its development did not necessarily confirm the dire predictions about financial cost or the perversion of the democratic system. Yet, like every other imperialism, it was destined to last and flourish, for "power obliges," and this power was growing ever stronger. Realistic French observers insisted that their compatriots had to reckon with this new fact and accommodate to it.

This powerful imperialism, they said, did not represent more of a menace than any other. One simply had to take its measure, for it followed its own interests and corresponded to specific motivations that seemed dangerous only because they were new. In reality it also grew out of a truly specific historical tradition.

### An Idealistic Imperialism

Most of the observers, whether critical or realistic, were quite naturally interested in American power, albeit without always perceiving the existence of countervailing tendencies that differentiated American imperialism even further. They only read articles about imperialist actions and for the most part met only supporters of this trend. They therefore needed to be either very well informed about the United States or extremely attentive if they were to grasp both the anti-imperialist movement itself and the signs of idealism that could be found even in the imperialist camp.

Thus, at the time when tensions about Cuba were high, Georges N. Tricoche noted that "every year private expeditions composed of clergymen, physicians, and nurses leave the United States for the purpose of founding missions combined with hospitals everywhere in the world."[30] To be sure, such initiatives could be seen as an aspect of the famous "Americanization of the world," but the fact remained that they were signs of rather unusual behavior.

Such behavior reappeared in connection with the war itself. Although the "yellow press" attracted all the attention, there was also an insistent movement opposed to this belligerent development. Having grown out of the "wisest part of the population," the circles who remained attached to George Washington's farewell address, it regained new vigor at the time of the Philippine war. Anti-imperialism was represented by a heterogenous group, in which a minority opposed all forms of foreign entanglements, while the greater number was simply against any form of territorial annexation. This distinction, of which almost no one but Paul de Rousiers was aware,[31] showed that not all Americans were ready to engage in a policy of conquest, as the more superficial observers claimed.

To be sure, anti-imperialism was powerless to change the course of things, and its decline soon became obvious; nonetheless, as Pierre Leroy-Beaulieu said, the United States had no reason to be ashamed: "Indeed, one can say to the credit of the Americans that the policy of conquest probably encountered more resistance in their country than it would have met with anywhere else."[32]

Greatly appreciating this resistance to imperialism, the French also considered it with a certain longing. It did, of course, constitute a rearguard action, which eventually succumbed to the needs of the economy and the ample means of the imperialists. However, it indirectly contributed to the American unwillingness to annex Cuba, which surprised those who had been quick to predict that the great island would become just another colony. Moreover, neither Santo Domingo nor Haiti, where the United States decided to intervene on short notice, were annexed. And the takeover of the Philippines, highly questionable though it was,

30. G.N. Tricoche, "Lettre . . . ," *Journal des Economistes* (May 1898): 230.
31. P. de Rousiers, "L'impérialisme américain," *Revue de Paris* (15 March 1899): 429.
32. P. Leroy-Beaulieu, "Les Etats-Unis, puissance coloniale," *Revue des Deux Mondes* (1 Jan. 1902): 85.

did not ipso facto make the archipelago an American colony. This situation, which at the time struck the French as odd, was paradoxical, for it was attended by brutalities and typical colonial actions. In all these circumstances, the Americans seemed to show a certain restraint and liked to stress the purity of their intentions. The claim that they were conducting a "Christian" policy based on the "law of nations" was usually considered pure hypocrisy by the French; yet they wondered whether it did not also reflect a "very high idealism" along with the undeniable manifestation of material interests.

This question was asked sometimes, especially as Theodore Roosevelt began to pursue an undeniably imperialist policy, accompanied by an idealistic discourse and carefully designed to preserve a semblance of democratic forms in places like the Philippines or Cuba. The French were particularly receptive to this attitude and reacted with a certain confusion. Joseph Patouillet, for example, reflected these conflicting views when he evoked in the same breath clear examples of unscrupulous dealings and proofs of a noble attitude:

> If their intervention really . . . resulted in the organization of new societies, they would be proof that a colonizing and civilizing role must be played by civilized nations. American imperialism will not have been the simple manifestation of a policy of force; its humanitarian role will make us forget its brutal side.[33]

This relative oddity of American behavior that a few observers had pointed out was confirmed by the staying power of the democratic values and by the fact that caesarism of any kind was most unlikely to come into being. All these were traits contrary to European habits that called for some explanation. American imperialism, despite its success and the support it enjoyed among most of the American population – men and women, whites and blacks – did not have to be as imperious as its counterparts elsewhere. "At bottom, imperialism is only a luxury here. It is an ornament for the nation, a vain and sterile glory, whereas English imperialism is quite simply a necessity." This was an interesting explanation, which took into consideration the ambiguity the observers had noticed. There could be resistance, to the point of desertion, as Thérèse reported in 1901 of some soldiers who refused to sail for the Philippines, and as André Siegfried saw in 1914 with respect to Mexico,[34] or there

---

33. Patouillet, *L'impérialisme américain*, p. 357.
34. Thérèse, *Impressions d'une Parisienne sur la côte du Pacifique* (Paris: Juven, 1902), p. 180. Also A. Siegfried, *Deux mois aux Etats-Unis à la veille de la guerre* (Paris: Colin, 1916), p. 94.

could be a relatively restrained policy toward Latin American countries, as in 1907:

> Uncle Sam has enough to do at home to get involved in the details of his neighbors' business. He is looking at things from a more general perspective and does not seek to run things as an administrator; but as a protector – and a supplier – that's a different story.[35]

This form of practical imperialism, which could easily be observed in the guise of Pan-Americanism, was one more facet of a specifically American phenomenon.

All these tendencies explain why on the eve of the war Jean Jaurès could celebrate "the pacifying force of American idealism" in these terms: "There is a third force for peace, and that is the rebirth in Anglo-Saxon America of the old Puritan ideals."[36] To be sure, at that point it was important to celebrate the virtues of arbitration, but Jaurès's statement also meant that the United States was not an imperialist power quite like the others. The same attitude was expressed by Paul Estournelles de Constant, a fervent defender of the American virtues, who saw Wilson's victory in 1912 as a chance for the retreat of imperialism in favor of this "American idealism" that would enlighten Europe.

These questions and hopes remained quite marginal and did not prevent the denunciations of American practices in the new territories. Yet some of the French observers, going beyond the facile explanation that the United States was simply becoming Europeanized, sought out or sensed the difference. Their voices were not listened to very much, for it is always easier to retain only the most evident and comparable aspects of things.

## AN IMPERIALISM IN ACTION

Most judgments about American imperialism, even if well informed, remained bookish and general. Very few of the French took the trouble to actually go to the American "colonies" to find out what was happening there. Their observations are particularly interesting in that they sometimes went beyond the more obvious political divergences and led to comparisons with the French colonial situation.

---

35. Y.M. Goblet, *Le panaméricanisme* (Tours: Imprimerie Rivière, 1907), p. 8.
36. J. Jaurès, "La force pacificatrice de l'idéalisme américain," in *Conciliation internationale*, no. 3 (1912): 47 (speech given in the Chambre des Députés on 19 and 20 Dec. 1911).

### *American Colonies*

Despite minor nuances concerning the nature of American imperialism, the French rightly felt that Cuba, the Philippines, and especially Hawaii and Puerto Rico were outright colonial territories. The United States, despite all its principles, had not escaped the common fate, and in some way this was reassuring for the citizens of a colonial power such as France.

In the years around 1900, the continuing unrest in the Philippines and the ongoing occupation of Cuba raised the question of how these territories were administered. The Americans did not seem particularly well equipped to carry out a task that called for qualified personnel and a firm hand. The abominable spoils system had not yet been eliminated, and, despite some genuine progress, the United States still did not have a true English-style civil service or a French-style colonial administration to provide proper administrative control. The French observers had seen too many examples of carelessness in federal agencies, from the customs service to the Bureau of Indian Affairs, to have much hope for rapid improvement.

Furthermore, the Americans, like the European powers, had made every effort to deny the territories under their control any economic freedom, subjecting them to the needs of their own economic interests or to the trusts and preventing some of their products from freely entering the territory of the United States.

While some observers felt that in order to deal with these problems, the United States would necessarily have to build up a considerable army and increase the number of government officials, in short, complete its seemingly ineluctable Europeanization,[37] others were more attentive to the originality of the American methods. Perhaps their strength lay elsewhere than that of France or England, as was argued by Pierre Leroy-Beaulieu, usually a very cautious observer:

> As for the administration of the Antilles and the Philippines, the Americans may not yet have proven their ability to govern peoples of different origins, but have they not, better than anyone else, proven their ability to develop new countries, and does not their economic experience largely make up for their political inexperience?[38]

37. E. Driault, "L'impérialisme aux Etats-Unis," *Revue Bleue, Politique et Littéraire* 21 (April 1900): 502–5.
38. Leroy-Beaulieu, "Les Etats-Unis," p. 11. He agreed with P. de Rousiers, who also vaunted the advantages of using economic means, although he did fear abuses.

The Cuban situation was of course very different from that of the Philippines, as the French understood. Their interest in the great island soon died down, as if it were normal for it to fall into the United States' lap. Given that country's designs on Central America and the Canal, it was obviously working on carving out for itself a good old zone of influence and obeying a logic of "natural frontiers" that was perfectly acceptable to the French. This was not the case in the Philippine archipelago, where special problems had to be faced.

It soon became clear that the United States, contrary to what many had believed in 1898, would not annex Cuba. But this restraint, which was all to its credit, obviously did not mean that it would let go of the island. All the French commentators stressed the disingenuous position of the Americans with respect to their principles, pointing out that their promises of freedom had deceived the Cubans, especially after the Platt Amendment had severely curtailed Cuban independence. So the Cuban flag might well wave in the place of the star-spangled banner, but this did not change anything: "Strictly speaking, this is called a protectorate. Cuban independence is gone. And so are the promises of the United States. . . ."[39]

Indeed, the Cubans made no mystery of their disenchantment with the American presence, which turned out to be burdensome, despite the undeniable good intentions of certain American generals. Their effects were detailed by the writer Paul Adam, one of the very few Frenchmen to go to Cuba after the war. Adam was pleased to see the infrastructure created by the Americans and the improved sanitary conditions. But he saw only the surface of things. Having accomplished so much, he said, the Americans had known when to go home, leaving behind a true democracy: "It has to be admitted that few victors have ever given such an example of historical unselfishness."[40]

One should not neglect the point of view of a man who actually visited the area, but it is nonetheless a fact that most of the French derived a certain intellectual pleasure from the United States' inability to carry out its own promises. However, this situation did not arouse any passion, for French opinion had almost completely lost interest in the fate of Cuba once it had become clear that the Americans behaved correctly there, even if they could not exactly claim a resounding success.

In the Philippines the Americans seemed to be caught in an unfortunate concatenation of circumstances. Whereas the French had quickly realized that what had brought the United States to Cuba was long-

---

39. B.E., "Cuba et les Etats-Unis," *Le Temps* (1 March 1901).
40. P. Adam, *Vues d'Amérique* (Paris: Ollendorf, 1906), pp. 297–306.

standing interest, the takeover of the archipelago struck them as brutal and unexpected. Moreover, as they followed the campaign, they learned about the demands of Aguinaldo and the insurgents in their struggle against Spain and about the promises made by Admiral Dewey. But all of this seemed to end in a bloodbath, and the American soldiers who were supposed to restore order were sucked into a difficult struggle that did not show them in their best light. The Americans thus added to a record of broken promises of democracy in the Philippines, engaging in a repression that was difficult to justify and for a time seemed ineffective as well.

In a first phase, this situation was widely denounced by the French, who used it to show the hypocrisy of the American principles. Had the United States not thwarted national aspirations which, much more than those of Cuba, were akin to its own of 1776? Instead of playing the role France had played for those insurgents, the Americans acted as if they were successors to the Spanish, which was rather ironic. They had actually felt compelled to institute press censorship in order to "cover up" the actions of their soldiers, whose atrocities came to light in the spring of 1902. From this *La Petite République* simply deduced that "here as well as there, the development of capitalism spawns imperialism; here as well as there, imperialism spawns the return to barbarism."[41] Others were more nuanced, counting on Theodore Roosevelt to break this vicious cycle, but they also remained skeptical about the Americans' chances of extricating themselves from a perilous situation: ". . . deeply convinced of the superiority of their civilization, they had not made a sufficient effort to discern just who these Filipinos are."

These various criticisms echoed and often repeated the arguments of the Anti-Imperialist League in the United States, which was also much more interested in the Philippines than in Cuba.

Yet the few observers who took their analysis a little further were struck by contradictory facts:

> . . . that the Americans were of good faith in their conquest, convinced that all that was needed to bring conciliation to the archipelago was their presence, endowed with a patrimony of democratic ideas and freedom for the people – no one will dispute that.[42]

41. E.M., "Les atrocités américaines," *La Petite République* (12 April 1902); Jean Jaurès condemned imperialism in his preface to H. Turot, *Aguinaldo et les Philippins* (Paris: Le Cerf, 1900), p. vii.
42. A. Lebon, "Un conflit de races: Américains et Philippins," *Revue des Deux Mondes* (15 Feb. 1901): 900, 917.

Thus the investigatory commission headed by William H. Taft seemed to the French awkward, incompetent, and slightly ridiculous, yet its report was admired for its fairness and thoroughness. It was also noted that while hateful repression continued in the countryside, the Americans endeavored to set up a form of local democracy. To be sure, the promise to respect the independence of the archipelago was a sham, and the statute they had enacted particularly hazy and lame; still, the Americans had tackled these problems with their "sense of practical action and vigorous common sense."

This sentiment was expressed as early as 1901 by Charles Garnier, a traveling fellowship student of the University of Paris who went to the archipelago when the American organization was being set up while the rebellion continued. He found nothing to justify the American takeover, aware that such a situation could have nefarious consequences for American democracy, but he was impressed by the activities of the Americans who were there. The military, especially General Otis, acted as if they were workers rather than conquerors, and the newly formed administration did a remarkable job. How could one fail to marvel at "the spirit and the method of this work, which is unique in the annals of colonization"?[43] Not only had the Americans been flexible in their dealings with the Catholic Church – even if the Concordat negotiated by Taft would have made Laboulaye and Toqueville turn in their graves – they had also been able to avoid the traps of the spoils system. One could criticize them for their wastefulness, for their brutality, and for their certainty of always being right, but no one could deny that they had achieved results.

A few years later, the Filipinos were still very ill at ease with a power that remained the occupier, and feelings between them and the Americans were still cool. Yet the scope of the progress accomplished was undeniable, and peace had been restored: In six years, the Americans had done more than Spain had done in three centuries.

Thus the situation of the American "colonies" did not, despite the initial impression, prompt the French to make snap judgments. The Americans, it appeared, were acting just like all other mother countries, yet also used methods that were theirs alone and could at times be disturbing.

### *Toward World Power*

The French observers soon realized that American imperialism did not aspire, at least for the time being, to dominate the entire world but

---

43. C.M. Garnier, "Les Américains aux Philippines," in *Autour du monde* (Paris: Alcan, 1904), p. 200.

remained more or less confined to the American continent and to the Pacific. Prominent among its objectives was the inter-oceanic canal, which was bound to arouse the French observers' interest.

The manner in which Ferdinand de Lesseps's undertaking had collapsed and the ensuing scandal had caused the French to distance themselves somewhat from the Panama Canal. French opinion therefore did not look too closely at the different maneuvers by which the United States attempted to gain control of the future waterway. The involved negotiations between Washington and London were an occasion to show the boundless appetite of the United States and to make ironic remarks about the weakness shown by Great Britain: "The reason is that she was dealing with a rival of her own blood, possessed to the point of exaggeration of her own qualities and her own flaws."[44] At most the French might consider it regrettable that Europe should thus allow the United States to make its way toward exclusive control of the future canal. Only Victor Bérard protested against selling to the United States shares of the new company and appealed – in vain – to the politicians and financiers of France to stop this giveaway by the French negotiators.[45] But in the end the French very calmly watched the vicissitudes of the creation of the state of Panama, which aroused little indignation.

It was only on the eve of the completion of the canal that some French commentators finally felt honor-bound to strike a highly symbolic blow. The matter of transit fees, which exclusively favored American ships, inevitably led to a comparison with the Suez Canal that showed the contrast between Taft and Lesseps:

> One is a Yankee, the other was a man. President Tafts are manufactured by the dozen in every country. But only France can bring forth Lessepses and Pasteurs, selfless benefactors and servants of humankind.[46]

The completion of the canal made it quite clear that the Americans would control the Pacific from Hawaii to the Philippines. This was not a pleasing prospect, but the rising power of the United States and its competition with Japan were of limited interest to the French, who were on their guard against any country that might become dominant. At most, they watched the crisis of 1907–8 between the Empire of the Rising Sun and the Great Republic with a certain anxiety. Taken straight from

---

44. P. Lefébure, "A la conquête d'un isthme: Espagne, Angleterre, Etats-Unis," *Annales de Science Politique* 16 (1901): 144; or B.E., "Etats-Unis et Angleterre," *Le Temps* (22 July 1901).
45. V. Bérard, "Questions extérieures: Panama," *Revue de Paris* (15 Jan. 1902): 423–44.
46. J. Bardoux, "Le conflit anglo-américain," *L'Opinion* (7 Sept. 1912): 97.

American arguments, this attitude was uncritically spread by observers such as André Tardieu and Félix Klein.

The various episodes of the Pan-American soap opera were watched by the French in a very similar manner – without passion but with a certain anxiety. There was no discussion of the American aim of controlling the entire continent, yet the reluctant attitude of the major South American countries and the highly fragmented results of the various intercontinental conferences made it difficult to foresee the intrinsic nature of its realization. Actually, French diplomats as well as journalists were perfectly willing to acknowledge that the United States was implicitly entitled to a kind of right of the eldest over Latin America, whose guardian it was destined to become.[47]

This relative tolerance, which did not preclude a few acerbic comments about the American initiatives, was severely shaken by Woodrow Wilson's intervention in Mexico. And in this case the denunciations of imperialism by the new President and his Secretary of State, William Jennings Bryan, made it even more difficult to accept their brutal meddling in a country over which the United States had long exerted an oppressive influence. It was not so much the intervention itself that shocked the French – there had been others in Nicaragua and Honduras – as the manner in which it was presented:

> But please! Kindly ... play an honest game over there, and do not use the occasion to let us have yet another sermon; for truly, this perpetual way of confusing God with the idols, of draping the Golden Calf in a clergyman's frock-coat and shamelessly placing an open Bible between its forefeet has become for us Latins the most upsetting thing in the world.[48]

Again, rather like in 1898, there were French condemnations of American hegemony, occasioned more by the "Mexican mess" than by the policies pursued throughout the preceding years. The French had become accustomed to an undeniable imperialism exerted essentially within a circumscribed area. This they had accepted as a matter of realism and out of admiration for Theodore Roosevelt, but Woodrow Wilson's initiative rekindled an anti-Americanism that had largely died down.

47. A. Viallatte, "Les Etats-Unis et le Panaméricanisme," *Revue des Deux Mondes* (15 May 1909): 438, evokes the "right of the eldest"; *Le Temps*, in its editorial of 16 December 1902, speaks of the natural role of the United States as a tutor. Similar formulations are found in J.J. Jusserand to Rouvier, Archives du Ministère des Affaires Etrangères, nouvelle série, Etats-Unis III. These diplomats saw nothing wrong with Roosevelt speaking in the name of the other American republics, particularly since they could not do anything about it.
48. R. Perraud, "Mexicains et Yankees," *L'Opinion* (20 Sept. 1913): 360.

The mounting danger in Europe soon overshadowed these manifestations of American power. Actually, André Siegfried, who was in New York when the war was declared, did not envy the Americans, who seemed to him above all concerned about their security and their petty interests, treating the French with "a kind of friendly and benevolent pity." This was a far cry from worrying about American imperialism which, as was said in 1901, was about to submerge Europe.

When it came to American imperialism, the opinion formed by the French was in fact more nuanced than a rapid overview would have indicated. They even perceived certain of the most characteristic features of the foreign policy of the United States, even if they were not always able to reconstitute all the pieces of a puzzle that was made up of highly materialistic interests along with much more idealistic preoccupations. These contrast could be quite shocking: ". . . and yet this humanitarianism did not prevent them from massacring the Redskins, lynching negroes, and shooting women and children in the Philippines."[49]

However, in general the French, as well as their government, did not fear the direct effects of American imperialism. They were convinced that the United States would play an increasing role in the world and that it would not abandon the road it had largely opened in 1898. The country had become a nation, with all the attributes that this implied, and Félix Klein made a point of this new maturity: "If the American flag were insulted anywhere in the world, we would see the nation standing tall, quivering, not to be appeased."[50]

This was seen as one more proof, despite some nuances, of a certain Europeanization of the United States. Someday, perhaps, its strength would become a threat, but it also contributed to bringing the United States closer to the other major powers. In 1913 or 1914 no one could know that the war would accelerate this development, first by dispelling the fears that certain French observers still harbored about the worldwide aspirations of the Great Republic, and then by raising new ones after 1918. The subject of American imperialism was not closed.

49. "La Doctrine de Monroe et la politique panaméricaine," *Le Correspondant* (10 Aug. 1906): 417.
50. F. Klein, *L'Amérique de demain* (Paris: Plon, 1910), p. 18.

# 15

# *Is There a Culture in the United States?*

Observing the power of the United States inevitably led the French to make comparisons. Its relative equality on the international level could be accepted; its economic supremacy was not really enviable, any more than its social heterogeneity; but what about American culture? Could it be compared to French culture, and was it strong enough to provide a noble capstone to this very material, even materialistic power?

The French, after all, felt strongly that power without culture is but the shell of a civilization.

Yet they saw little evidence that the United States had achieved distinction in arts and letters, which to Europeans of the old school were the only marks of true culture. Many attractive things could be seen in America, but its few authors and artists were not well known. French observers who took an interest in these matters spoke of a few examples that they soon considered old-fashioned – Emerson, Longfellow, Fenimore Cooper, Washington Irving, Mark Twain, and later – with some difficulty – Walt Whitman and, as always, Edgar Allan Poe, who was more acclaimed in France than in his own country.[1] Even the best works on the United States had only a meager list of a few presentable examples.

Yet a country, it was felt, that was so confidently growing in all areas could not possibly remain without a true culture. As the years passed, this became strongly evident; the United States of 1910 was not what it had been in 1870.

> We are far from the time when one could say to the Americans: "You don't know anything, you have no understanding of what is noble and beautiful. You have neither a poet nor a philosopher, neither a musician nor a sculptor. You are living, with very few exceptions, in complete

---

1. See C. Arnavon, *Les lettres américaines devant la critique française (1887–1917)* (Paris: Les Belles Lettres, 1951).

ignorance of literature and fine arts." Today this latter accusation is absolutely untrue.[2]

But this realization only began to broach the problem; the development of education and the appearance of a cultivated class was not tantamount to the emergence of a true culture. Many of the French remained convinced that in this domain they held assets and privileges they might, perhaps, be willing to share, but which would always be their special birthright.

## OBSTACLES TO CULTURE

The fascination with the United States the French had experienced during the first three quarters of the nineteenth century had had little to do with the discovery of an original culture. They therefore never ceased asking whether the Americans had their own cultural capacity beyond some mediocre imitations of Great Britain.[3]

### *Doubts about Aptitude for Culture*

The French associated their conception of culture with a favorable environment, made up of traditions, serenity, and measure and transmitted and enriched from generation to generation. And while this irenic vision did not always correspond to a reality wrought with constraints, official commands, and conflicts between the representatives of the old order and the defenders of modernism, it does explain French reactions to the American situation.

In particular, the American way of life as the French saw it was based on values diametrically opposed to those they considered indispensable to the blossoming of true culture. Indeed, that "manipulated and mechanized" social life and the primacy of economic preoccupations created a particularly pernicious environment.

This certainty was forcefully expressed by French observers when the United States was rocked by the scandals of the Grant administration and by the frenzied development of the railroads and of business in

---

2. O.M. Lannelongue, *Un tour du monde* (Paris: Larousse, 1910), p. 326. The quote is from R. Lindau, "Le chemin de fer du Pacifique I, San Francisco et l'inauguration," *Revue des Deux Mondes* (1 Nov. 1869): 13.
3. No full-length study had yet been devoted to this aspect of American civilization, aside from a few articles on specific points and a brochure on the arts by S. Bing, *La culture artistique en Amérique* (Paris: 22 rue de Provence, 1896), which probably did not circulate widely.

general. When Claudio Jannet held "the almighty dollar" and the reign of money responsible for "the inferiority of literature and the arts . . . [and] the mercantile ways adopted by the professions we call liberal," he took on an entire concept of existence; but many admirers of the United States also held this view. Louis Simonin, for instance, a rationalist thinker, thought that this was a matter of division of labor:

> It is evident that the Americans' mission is not yet to write theater plays. They are here to create fertile soil, to open roads, canals, and mines, to build factories everywhere, to put up cities in the middle of the desert, to shorten and ease manual labor through mechanical inventions. This would seem to be their principal role for the moment, and it is quite enough for them.[4]

The apparent absence of a "leisure class," while satisfying to those who appreciated the energy manifested by the people of the United States, had some totally unexpected consequences: ". . . the absorption of a whole people in business is an obstacle to the development of the arts, sciences, and literature."

Would the development of the American universities and the undeniable refinement shown by a certain category of persons at the end of the nineteenth century modify these very pessimistic judgments? How could the observers not ask this question, considering that the Americans had available to them increasingly ample means as well as a language that had "every right to call itself the universal idiom."[5] Indeed, could the dynamism the Americans exhibited in every other area not be extended to that of culture as well?

By the 1880s, there were French voices to assert just that: "Ah! the Americans are robust minds. And as soon as they decide to take a serious stab at literature, they will go all out for it."[6] And indeed it was just as logical to claim that the business mentality would prevent the development of culture as it was to assert that these very qualities could contribute to it.

By the early twentieth century, many French observers, aware of the progress achieved, predicted that the Americans would not always be content to put up some Bougereau paintings in fashionable restaurants or to slap a Corinthian cornice on a skyscraper to show the extent of their culture. Paul de Rousiers perceived this: ". . . the efforts made in all

---

4. L. Simonin, *Le monde américain* (Paris: Hachette, 1877), p. 24.
5. E. Reclus, *Nouvelle géographie universelle; La terre et les hommes* (Paris: Hachette, 1890), vol. 16, p. 772; this is a strikingly insightful remark for its time.
6. N. Ney, "Autour d'une statue, quinze jours au pays de la liberté," *Nouvelle Revue* (Jan. 1887): 352.

kinds of directions to advance artistic developments testify to general aspirations that may well surprise us."[7] Urbain Gohier agreed:

> We had better hurry to make fun of today's Americans while they are working for their sons. Tomorrow's Americans will take their revenge. They already have everything else, and they will have an art before fifty years are out. They work, they search, they strive, they desire, and so they will succeed.[8]

Now it remained to be seen whether this cultural development would have genuine value. Many doubted it, for it seemed to them that the Americans, however hard they tried and studied, would never be able to acquire "... our fine manners, our tact, and our social skills." Moreover, the practical and economic orientation of their existence remained in 1910 what it had been in 1880, and it was still not clear whether it would be compatible with a true cultural blossoming. Surely, the rise of the United States was caused essentially by its "commercial evolution," and it was futile to expect anything else. As convinced an Americanophile as Paul Estournelles de Constant came to wonder about this by way of a Tocquevillean contrast between the Empire of the Czars and the Great Republic:

> Compare their [the Americans'] feverish activity with the unconcern of the Russians, for instance, and tell me whether that apparent unconcern, with its resigned acceptance of winter and of endless nights, is not fecund, fecund in masterworks of art and of thought.[9]

All the French observers who took an interest in these matters noticed that the Americans did a great deal of copying, both in literature and in art, and that this seemed to be enough for them. This might be considered a method of learning and finding one's own direction, but it looked more like an easy solution, which allowed for more rapid commercialization and was a far cry from the disinterestedness of true creation. Saint André de Lignereux was concerned and doubtful about this, as others had been thirty years earlier:

> As long as the American ideal is the cowboy who has struck it rich, this will certainly be a powerful nation, but it will not be a nation looking for moral perfectibility, for without veneration for the mind, man regresses, and since no elite will burst forth, the arts will not burst forth either.[10]

---

7. P. de Rousiers, *La vie américaine* (Paris: Didot, 1889), vol. 2, p. 288.
8. U. Gohier, *Le peuple du XXe siècle* (Paris: Fasquelle, 1903), p. 203.
9. P.E. de Constant, *Les Etats-Unis d'Amérique* (Paris: Colin, 1913), pp. 119–20.
10. A. Saint André de Lignereux, *L'Amérique au XXe siècle* (Paris: Taillandier, 1909), p. 148.

These many questions, which were consistently asked for forty years, turned out to be paradoxical. Those who asked them made little effort to find out about the cultural achievements of Americans in the traditional fields, nor did they always perceive that in some areas the United States had developed relatively original forms of culture.

### Original Cultural Manifestations

Most of the French doubts about the cultural development of the Americans grew out of an observation of reality that constantly referred back to European values and a very French definition of culture. Thus the absence of a past was used as an essential and peremptory argument to explain the situation of the Americans and to demonstrate their inherent cultural inferiority; Félix Klein's was almost the only attempt to state the problem in somewhat different terms: "... what they lack is having lasted. But perhaps this is better than having lasted too long, perhaps the lack of a past can (over time) be repaired more easily than a lack of present vigor and future possibilities."[11]

Still, the question was whether a people that delighted in outrageous spectacles, liked to assert its power and its glory, and cultivated the most vulgar extravagances was not altogether without a sense of culture.

The French did not recognize the signs of a true culture in these different manifestations, for they simply did not conform to their notion of culture. Thus the commentaries on the Barnum and Bailey Circus, and even the Buffalo Bill Show when it came to Paris in 1889, reported nothing more than the facts and appeared only in the columns of the daily papers. Depicted as demonstrations conceived for the masses and prepared by a powerful publicity blitz, these shows were the object of contempt tinged with pity on the part of the more thoughtful observers. Yet the success of these spectacles in France – the American flag was saluted with hurrahs, and crowds in a holiday mood came to see Buffalo Bill – showed that here the Americans had brought together important assets and manipulated them with consummate skill. It was clear, even then, that they were extremely good at displaying a mass culture founded on excitement tinged with exoticism to seduce this foreign public. But for the most part these spectacles were intended for the United States; French travelers were struck by the lack of refinement of the theater pieces they saw – for example, the excessive commotion in the scenes that the local public enjoyed so much. These shows did not even have

11. F. Klein, *Au pays de la vie intense* (Paris: Plon, 1904), p. 259.

the exotic character they would have if they were performed in France with a text in French!

André Tardieu gave a good description of that typically American form of entertainment known as the musical comedy, which fascinated both the student and the shopkeeper, but which had "nothing to do with literature or art":

> Imagine that all the actors are acrobats who, whenever it fits, and even when it doesn't, turn somersaults, jump out of windows, and dance a jig. Then season this with little songs that have no connection at all with the subject. . . . Forget all notions of common sense. Take fancy to the point of folly, and folly to the point of absurdity. Let all of this take off in the wild careening of frenzied agitation: this will give you the musical comedy.[12]

The French observers were not fully aware of the importance of these phenomena; they liked to criticize American entertainers precisely for those things that the public loved, and would love throughout the entire twentieth century.

In the same manner, a great deal was said by the French from 1870 to 1914 about the Americans' general ignorance about Europe, and about their certainty that they were the *ne plus ultra* of contemporary civilization, the "best country in the world." And of course, irony, even irritation, was the only possible response to such reactions, which were out of proportion with the level of culture the country had achieved. Marie Dugard showed well how this behavior distinguished the American from the European. Here is what she said about young people:

> . . . hence their *puffism*, a kind of bragging that at first one mistakes for humbug and impudence, but which usually is no more than a lack of measure. Their tastes, marked by primitive roughness, also have something exaggerated about them . . . an absence of sobriety and delicacy. . . .[13]

Moreover, this boastful attitude prompted many Americans to show deep contempt for artists and intellectuals, which to a French person was the height of vulgarity.

All of these American "qualities" were, of course, the precise opposite of those required by the traditional culture, which is why the French were unable to understand that they underlay an original cultural trend.

12. A. Tardieu, *Notes sur les Etats-Unis* (Paris: Calman-Lévy, 1908), pp. 81–82. Tardieu noted the success of the cinematograph, which, however, did not yet have a specifically American character. "The cinematograph is an international institution, which provides the identical satisfactions in all latitudes" (p. 85).
13. M. Dugard, *La société américaine* (Paris: Hachette, 1896), p. 225.

This set of traits, along with the newness of the institutions of higher education, seemed incompatible with the remarkable flourishing of American science and the achievements of American inventors, who certainly were typical representatives of the culture of the United States. Jules Huret stated the problem very clearly:

> ... how is it that men less learned than we are and with a culture that, to say the least, is not as general and wide-ranging as ours, are able to do so much better, when it comes to inventions, than the best of our engineers and the most industrious of our workers?[14]

Such a query reveals a great deal about the attitude of the French. On the one hand, it questions the conditions of the American achievements, seeing them as anomalous because they did not rest on any of the solid and supposedly indispensable bases; on the other hand, it tends to exaggerate the American achievements, which made them even more inexplicable and extraordinary.

In fact, however, the French knew very few of the many American inventors and scientists and were not particularly interested in meeting them, a sign that science was not high on their agenda. Aside from some passing references to Graham Bell and a few other men of science, their attention was focused on the archetype of the inventor, that is to say, Thomas Edison! But he was so well known – the gossip columns had seized upon his person – that thoughtful appraisals could hardly be expected; an occasional traveler might make the pilgrimage to Menlo Park, and almost none of the writers of articles devoted a few pages to him.

If there was no lack of admiration for this hero known on two continents, it can also be said that the opinions about him perfectly revealed the ambivalent attitude of the French toward this strange American culture that he so brilliantly represented. They liked to stress his qualities, but also his weaknesses:

> ... an intrepid investigator, always pursuing several projects at once, bold in the extreme, often lucky and favored by success, but also sometimes failing where others, working less feverishly and more slowly, have had complete success.[15]

The French liked to point out that Edison, the inventor – "he is the professional inventor, the inventor as such" – had not hesitated to

---

14. J. Huret, *En Amérique* (Paris: Hachette, 1903), vol. 1, p. 68.
15. J. Bianchon, "Th. Edison et ses inventions," *Nouvelle Revue* (1880): 92; this is an essentially technical article.

become involved in spectacular financial or publicity operations. This did not detract from his prestige or from the fact that he was bound to leave a trace in the world, but he was rather far from the French ideal of the disinterested scientist incapable of concerning himself with the practical aspect of things. This was also seen as proof of the originality of the Americans in such areas, which were part of the all-inclusive French conception of culture.

To the French it seemed perfectly clear that the Americans were not destined to experience the flourishing of as rich and varied a culture as that of the major European countries. Yet more painstaking observation allowed some of them to discover the American culture whose advent, which had been long in coming, they had foreseen. The problem that now arose was that of the relations between the self-assured and dominating French culture and this sometimes rather arrogant newcomer.

## A CULTURE IN GESTATION

The culture of the United States did not belong only to the future, nor did its relative inferiority, compounded by its strangeness, mean that the Americans were truly uncultivated. This is what the French gradually came to realize.

### *History and Art*

The French might scoff at the ignorance of many Americans in matters of art or hope for a future "flourishing," yet they could not help noticing the existence of an American public of "genuine connoisseurs." In this respect the United States was not fundamentally different from France, where the masses were also quite uncultivated, although the elite was much larger than across the Atlantic. Above all, it was more concentrated, thanks to the role of the Parisian bourgeoisie, the only class to frequent theaters and concert halls.

The conductors who made the crossing, from Offenbach to Saint-Saëns, discovered attentive listeners, who by no means acted like ignorant barbarians. American theatergoers, by contrast, except for a small minority who loved French plays, seemed less refined, content to watch the vulgar shows that delighted so many Americans.

In the early years of the twentieth century, the American experts who crisscrossed Europe in order to buy French paintings or works of Greek and Egyptian antiquity and the desire of American millionaires to fill their vast mansions with works of art were not necessarily considered contemptible. This conduct revealed a true interest in art, even if it did not prove the existence of a specifically American culture, and the irony of Georges Moreau could not quite conceal a certain fascination:

> ... taken as a mass, the Americans are fundamentally ignorant. They know nothing about antiquity and detest the arts. This does not prevent them from going to Egypt, to Greece, to Italy ... and from hiring ad hoc intermediaries who can make them an art collection.[16]

This was how the Americans set up museums and filled libraries that might well bring forth an original culture, the result of a giant gestation.

Meanwhile certain French observers – and not only because they were flattered by American interest in the manifestations of European culture – discovered in that of the United States aspects that were neither excessive nor barbaric and flashy. Pierre de Coubertin was particularly impressed with the American potential for culture:

> And all of this comes from the United States, the much-maligned Republic that people take for a nation of traffickers and chasers after the dollar without thinking that it has already given the world a hero like Washington and soldiers like Lee and Sherman, and without noticing that very great ideas are already growing in its fertile soil.[17]

Yet most French observers did not pay much attention to the history of the United States. It was as if the role France had played in obtaining the independence of the colonies overshadowed the originality of the American independence or even served to keep alive certain warmed-over grievances, and the image of its great heroes seemed to be frozen in time. Although a few perfectly adequate general works by French authors did exist and could impart a good knowledge of the American past, they did not really try to explain it, and there were no special studies about the figures evoked by Coubertin, any more than about Lincoln or Jefferson. The French, largely because of the traditional Gallo-centrism of French historians, were not fully aware of the fact that the history of the United States was an essential element of its culture.

The French often commented about the youth of the United States and about its lack of references and real traditions, which were detrimental to the rise of a culture. Yet a few observers did realize the great importance history had in that country. This was more than the history with which children were inculcated in their classrooms, it was the cultivation of living memories of the Civil War as well as lectures on

---

16. G. Moreau, *L'envers des Etats-Unis* (Paris: Plon, 1906), p. 250.
17. P. de Coubertin, *Souvenirs d'Amérique et de Grèce* (Paris: Hachette, 1897), p. 98.

Washington or the origins of the Constitution that were presented frequently: "Thus in that country, which so religiously cultivates the memory of itself, one would have to close one's mind, one's ears, and one's eyes if one did not want to become willy-nilly steeped in its history."[18]

Would not the importation of European works of art, when added to this passion the Americans had for their history, result in the emergence of a specifically American art?

Aside from the spectacular achievements of American architecture, from the Brooklyn Bridge to the skyscrapers, which fascinated many of the French observers, the different facets of the art of the United States were for the most part completely ignored. However, at the Chicago World's Fair the visitors did have the opportunity to discover some examples of the artistic activity of that great country, but these did not leave any unforgettable memories; most of the French preferred to count how many French works could be seen and to vaunt their superiority.

Yet this was also the occasion when Samuel Bing produced the first and only inventory of American art to be made at this time. Looking at the different fields of art, he realized that in a great many endeavors, American energy could be seen at work in art. This elan augured well for the development of an American art and might even "sweep our ancient wisdom along to new springtimes . . . open unknown paths to our measured steps, which no longer dare go beyond the domains bequeathed by our forefathers."[19]

In Bing's view, American painting had not gone beyond European, especially British, influences, and only a few artists showed that American freshness; sculpture was much too academic, while architecture, of course, showed a "striking vigor" and the decorative arts were soaring. These two domains revealed a genuine American inventiveness. According to Bing, the skyscrapers were adapted to the landscape, as were the railroad stations of the East and the huge hotels. Functionalism dominated everywhere and gave a special stamp to every building, from the humblest to the most sumptuous. In the same manner, the decorative arts experienced an extraordinary development which combined the resources of industry with esthetic innovation, as could be seen by the example of the Tiffany Company. This was a democratic form of art, which was not crushed by "great art" as in France. The United States was even able to produce beautiful things serially, thanks to the machine. This was the very first time that a French observer discovered a phenomenon

18. L. Cons, *Les Etats-Unis de 1789 à 1912* (Paris: Nouvelle Librairie Nationale, 1912), p. ix.
19. Bing, *La culture artistique*, p. 8.

that would mark the entire twentieth century, but he had no followers, for most French people were totally incapable of envisaging this strange association of machinism and esthetics.

Bing's assessment stressed the areas that did indeed show a powerful American originality, free of European influences. He rightly perceived the emergence of an American art that was by no means inferior. "Within this pompous reign of money, an intellectual aristocracy is being formed, and it will go fast and far. The time is near when this group will consider poverty of feeling for art more embarrassing than poverty of money."[20]

These few examples showed that an original American culture was indeed coming into existence, even if some of its manifestations still made the French smile and even if most observers had no idea that this was happening. And at any rate, as far as the French were concerned, only literature could provide the label of a culture worthy of that name.

### A Still Uncertain Literature

Cyrille Arnavon stated that between 1887 and 1914 every last French literary critic had answered in the negative to the famous question "Is there an American literature?"

In fact, French interest in American authors and literary works was strictly confined to the major literary reviews; moreover, the principal works about the United States, such as those of Paul Bourget, Lazare Weiller, and Urbain Gohier, gave little space to American letters beyond an established and often outdated catalogue. To this must be added the prejudices carried over from the preceding period, particularly the dark years of the 1870s, during which one would have not been entirely wrong to assert the complete lack of a literature in the United States, aside from the great but isolated works of transcendentalism. Nor should one neglect, especially for the 1880s, the intermediary role of the British critics, who were extremely hard on the letters of their transatlantic cousins.

Yet this unfavorable context did not prevent some French critics from devoting themselves to American literature, even though the most prominent among them, Ferdinand Brunetière and René Doumic, continued to deny its existence and found that it came close to nothingness. There is no question that "literary persons immersed in a secular and well-established culture" found it difficult to deal with "a production which, unsure of itself, has not yet forced their attention by political dominance."

20. Ibid., p. 114.

In the course of the years, however, most American authors did become known in France – in limited circles, to be sure, but in an irreversible manner. This led to the recognition that there was an American literature, even if it was still unsteady, even if in a "blind test" it would be difficult to identify without hesitation an American author among various others. American literature had come a long way. The first years of the twentieth century certainly had little in common, in this area as in others, with the immediate post–Civil War period; and the French, here too with a slight delay, finally became aware of the diversity of the American contribution to literature. While the ordinary observer still harped on the glories of the past, constantly evoking Longfellow and Emerson, those two giants in the desert, the best experts no longer ignored the rich and varied poetry and fiction produced overseas; the word had spread.

This gradual and limited discovery of American literature was marked by the obsessive desire to find its typically American characteristics. In a first phase, authors like Bret Harte had considerable success when they were serialized in newspapers or reviews, for they seemed rooted in the American reality; their intense picturesqueness attracted the French more than the halftones of a Henry James. The subsequent popularity of Jack London can be explained by the same reasons and once again confirms the attraction of American exoticism. But the French also looked for this Americanness in other authors, who were not as easy to classify.

Thus the summaries of American literature to be found in the works of Paul de Rousiers or Firmin Roz, among others, always insisted that these authors were very American. Longfellow, "a truly national poet," was treated together with Poe and Twain; all of them were shown to represent either the forward momentum of the United States or the practical nature of its people.[21] Even more clearly, the discovery of Walt Whitman and his poetry, which barely became known beyond literary circles, made him the very symbol of America. Some critics did not like his irregular verses or stressed his democratic excesses, which made him "too American" – and did he not actually admire Marx and Robespierre![22] – while others were fascinated by "the most original poet of America, and in this sense one of the best representatives of his race," although his uneven works "still made for some hesitation."[23]

---

21. Rousiers, *La vie américaine*, p. 283; F. Roz, *L'énergie américaine* (Paris: Flammarion, 1910), pp. 170–78.
22. H. Cochin, "Un poète américain: Walt Whitman," *Le Correspondant* (Oct.–Dec. 1877): 634–60.
23. Reclus, *Nouvelle géographie*, p. 14. Reclus cites the poet: "I heard that you ask'd for something to prove this puzzle the New World,/ And to define America, her athletic

The American works that enjoyed the greatest success in France were precisely those that the public could identify with the United States. This was as true in the case of Mark Twain, who was much in vogue in the early years of the twentieth century, as in those of Upton Sinclair, whose *The Jungle* was immediately translated into French, and Jack London. The works of Twain were abundantly commented on by French critics, who usually disdained those of the two others as too popular and, hence, minor. Even Régis Michaud, one of the best connoisseurs of American literature, expressed his reservations about the works of the author of *Martin Eden*: "big books that are better written than those of Upton Sinclair, but still unpolished and given to exaggerated realism; books that reflect not so much art as good will, although strong pages can certainly be found."[24]

American literature was thus recognized by the French, but at two different levels. The critics' doubts about the value of these works – expressed, for instance, in the condescension of a Thérèse Bentzon – and the ignorance of many other observers account for the French judgment that there was no genuine American literature. The mediocrity of American theater and the limitations of the novel were not sufficiently improved by the few recognized poets to create the impression of a full-fledged literature. The conclusion was that there were a few American literary works, but no literature.

In somewhat more open-minded French circles, these distinctions did not hold. These people appreciated American works with a social message, whose subject and ambitions they considered more important than their form or story line; this attitude explains the success of Bellamy's *Looking Backward* and later Sinclair and London. This vogue foreshadowed that of the postwar years, when the American novelists burst upon the French scene with texts that gave an unvarnished account of their era.

In the field of literature, then, the Americans did not stand out in the most traditional disciplines, which explains the reservations of the French. Yet Americans were also beginning to assert themselves in uncharted territory that was full of promise for the future. This may not have been literature and art, but there was no denying its effectiveness and its popular success.

It was all the more tempting for the French to claim that there was no

Democracy,/ Therefore I send you my poems that you behold in them what you wanted" (*Leaves of Grass*, Inscriptions, "To Foreign Lands").
24. R. Michaud, "La jeune littérature américaine: J. London, surhomme de lettres," *L'Opinion* (19 Feb. 1910): 245.

American literature in the most noble sense because this opinion was shared by many American critics. It should be added that the most traditional among these, authors such as Henry Van Dyke, Barrett Wendell, Theodore Stanton, and Mary Van Vorst – who readily pointed out that in the United States a few small groups of cultivated people were isolated amidst a barbaric society – were also those who were most widely read in France, where their works were frequently translated and fulsomely praised.

### Advantage, France

In view of their widely shared doubts about the Americans' aptitude for culture – somewhat shaken though they were by the discovery of a few fine achievements – the French were not overly concerned about the power of the United States in this area, at least for the immediate future.

Even the most fervent Americanophiles were convinced that the United States would continue for a long time to base its culture on what was brought from Europe, as it had done all along. That was Lazare Weiller's explanation for its relative inferiority:

> ... the luster of English literature and that of French painting and sculpture have contributed to holding back artistic and literary production in America, for the Americans found their ideas and their sentiments expressed almost to perfection in English books and French works of art.[25]

The authors of the volume *France-Etats-Unis*, which was devoted to the celebration of Franco-American friendship on the eve of the war, developed the same idea. France supposedly could play the role of a kindly tutor for the young America, without forcing anything upon it, which of course would not have been accepted anyway:

> Not that in intellectual and artistic matters America intends to create out of nothing. With its methodical ways, its open-mindedness, and a marvelous power of comprehension, it assimilates all the outstanding achievements the Old World has to offer.[26]

This, then, was not a matter of imitation but an enrichment that would benefit both partners. Moreover, France was assigned a very important role, for the United States seemed to acknowledge its superiority. And that was surely the wisest thing it could do in the field of the arts.

---

25. L. Weiller, *Les grandes idées d'un grand peuple* (Paris: Juven, 1904), p. 248.
26. E. Boutroux, "La pensée américaine et la pensée française," in *France–Etats-Unis* (Paris: Alcan, 1914), p. 13.

American art, while keeping its local and personal autonomy, knows that the French school will always provide it with the surest guidance on how to preserve and extend its independence, along with the best teaching and the firmest support.[27]

This vision of a peaceful complementarity between the Old and the New World corresponded to the division of labor evoked at the very beginning of the period by the realist Paul Simon. Yet this process was not necessarily as satisfactory as the members of the Franco-American lobby liked to claim. For it was also said that France, facing American competition and domination in the strategic and economic domains, had to defend its cultural bailiwick tooth and nail and loudly assert its superiority: ". . . recently defeated and now impoverished, [France] can only win people's respect by the power of its altruism, its sciences, and its arts." This attitude accounts for the disdain certain French commentators showed for the stumbling first manifestations of American culture, which could not be anything but inferior. Saint André de Lignereux expressed this point of view succinctly and with a fretful kind of peevishness:

> The American will have to resign himself to selling cotton, locomotives, and petroleum; he will build churches or construct armored ships; these people will perhaps astonish the world, they will not seduce it. They can try all they want to throw around huge checks to found universities, academies, and museums, this will not do any good; they will have to bow to our intellectual supremacy.[28]

This self-assured superiority was reinforced by the reverence shown by a certain American elite which, convinced of the inadequacy of its own literature, cherished "this kind of [French] genius" and was determined to "welcome it." How could the French help being pleased by the attention of certain Americans, such as the young professor who delighted Ferdinand Brunetière on his tour of 1897 by knowing all about his books, or by this appeal: "We need France and Europe, their artistic and literary master-pieces, and their more polished culture . . . our effort to learn is honest and sincere and will bear fruit."[29]

Without always asking themselves just how representative these Americans were, and touched by the welcome extended to artists and

27. L. Bénédite, "La peinture française et les Etats-Unis," in ibid., p. 87.
28. A. Saint André de Lignereux in ibid., p. 148; yet the author was by no means anti-American.
29. H.P. Thieme, "Ferdinand Brunetière aux Etats-Unis," in *Mélanges de littérature, d'histoire et de philologie offerts à P. Laumonier par ses élèves et ses amis* (Geneva: Slatkine Reprints, 1912), pp. 549–54. See also C.R. Henderson, "La rencontre des races dans la cité américaine et ses conséquences morales," *Le Correspondant* (25 March 1906): 1173.

lecturers in the United States, the French were finally reassured about the considerable advance they enjoyed in the cultural domain. Optimists and pessimists agreed that America was amusing and ambitious, but that French culture was not yet threatened.

These manifestations of French pride, whether amicable or aggressive, were related to a certain blindness. This made the French forget that Americans avid for European culture were only a tiny minority and that the new forms of American culture that had already come into being pursued neither the same values nor the same goals as their own. The aptitudes of the Americans were not necessarily adverse to the flourishing of a culture, but that culture might follow paths different from that of France. Paul Adam understood this when he insisted on what made the French different from the Americans, pointing out that the French sought a "synthesis between the mind and the gesture," while the Americans did their best to dissociate them:

> Hence certainly the difficulties Yankees and Frenchmen have in understanding each other. Hence the repugnance of our intellectuals for the sudden appearance of a higher life across the seas. Our friends find it inconceivable that over there a man will devote his lyrical talent to superb commercial dreams instead of expressing it exclusively through verse, music, speeches in parliament, and lectures at the Sorbonne.[30]

It now remained to be seen whether the United States would develop its own trends and overturn the European traditions that had hitherto nourished it, or whether the Americans would continue to recognize that these traditions remained superior and beneficial.

By the eve of the war, the French had understood that the United States was no longer a barbarian country and that an American culture had unfolded, although not all of them were aware of its richness. All in all, the situation was no longer comparable to that of the 1870s. There was a cultivated class and there were intellectuals and artists, many of whom showed their admiration for Europe and above all for France.

The Americans had not seemed to have any predisposition for culture, and yet they became vigorously involved in cultural undertakings, whether they took the form of vulgar acquisitions, simple copying, or original and not always appreciated creations. All of this they pursued with such intensity and such willpower that the French were bound to feel implicitly threatened in the longer run: "The time will come when the world will be told and called upon not to withhold the full measure

---

30. P. Adam, *Vues d'Amérique, ou la nouvelle jouvence* (Paris: Ollendorf, 1906), p. 354.

of its admiration for the thinking, verse-making, novel-writing America, for the America of the decorative arts and music."[31]

Yet, given the weaknesses of American culture – in terms of European and classical canons – that were still evident, this threat did not seem imminent, and the French could reassure themselves. This was one area that was still safe from the "American peril." Nonetheless, French ignorance of and disdain for the more original aspects of a culture that had been conceived for the masses accounts for the rude and sometimes painful awakening that was in store for the French in the postwar period, when America became synonymous with the Roaring Twenties.

31. R. Bazin, *Nord-Sud* (Paris: Calman-Lévy, 1913), p. 27.

# Conclusion

French opinion concerning the United States continued to express itself after 1914, despite the importance of this break; but one must choose a crucial moment to end such a study. Otherwise, especially in as shifting and diffuse a domain as the study of opinion, one might continue all the way to the present.

It should be pointed out that in a curious way the last years of the nineteenth century seem to be winking at our own, the last of the twentieth. One has only to evoke the first centennials of the Declaration of Independence and, later, the Constitution, to see that they were echoed by the French celebrations of the corresponding bicentennials: They were proof of a continued American presence. One has only to evoke the apprehensive reactions of the French to the deployment of American power around 1900 to conjure up those of the 1950s. One has only to recall French admiration for material comforts – running water and electricity – around 1900 to bring back that of the 1960s – household appliances and automobiles for everyone.

In the study of opinion the "concordance of times"[1] can open troubling perspectives; it might make us believe that continuity carried the day and that neither the United States nor the French have changed. This, of course, is not the case; more simply, these astonishing similarities show the extent of the renewal the United States had undergone since the early nineteenth century. Having wholeheartedly embraced modernity, it had more or less explicitly become the symbol of that trend; by 1880, after all, it had already invented the skyscraper and the trust, to mention only these examples. The French clearly perceived the importance of such advances in various fields; they had now become the image of the future. No longer embodied by the institutions or by the pioneer who freely tilled his land, the future was now seen in the fast-paced

1. J.-N. Jeanneney, *Concordes des temps* (Paris: Seuil, 1987).

433

rhythm of sprawling cities, in the speed of the trams, in the apparent freedom of women, and in the charm of the comforts that coddled the lives of the privileged. These examples explain why one has the impression that certain remarks and certain reflections of observers of the *Belle Epoque* could have been made today.

Beyond these similarities between yesterday and today, it is also clear that the French who took an interest in the United States between 1870 and 1914 no longer found there a single key that would unlock the doors to the future, but, rather, a number of fragmentary and incomplete models that gave rise to contrasting reactions.

On the one hand, the rush of modernism they observed further increased their certainty that the Americans were amazing people who behaved in extraordinary, often amusing, and sometimes irritating ways. It also confirmed that the United States was always ahead, always the strongest. That is why the observers marveled at the height of the buildings in New York, which was fantastic by definition, whatever it might be – eight, ten, and eventually forty stories. That is why they were all excited about the power of the rotary presses of the major American dailies, even though those of their Parisian counterparts were just as powerful. That is why they were ecstatic in their admiration for the spirited demeanor of young American women, even before they took the time to observe them. And that is why they feared the effects of American industrial overproduction, which they considered by definition unpreventable. These hasty but repeated observations are the source of the clichés that would essentially be those of the entire twentieth century.

On the other hand, the fascination with which the French observed so many excesses spawned reactions of rejection, or at least major misgivings. The fact is that as a group the French were not ready to face a future organized according to the American pattern. Thus they feared the industrialization of daily life, as can be seen by their outbursts about American food, or the apparent coldness of married life, where the husband worked like a madman and the wife was bored. Most observers also felt that the freedom enjoyed by girls, attractive as it was over there, would hardly do in France, any more than the advent of a multiracial society, even if the excesses of American segregation shocked them. As for the Americans' lenient treatment of bankruptcies and their veneration for the dollar, they were completely contrary to French traditions and deserved to be condemned.

To the French observers the future that seemed to be in preparation across the Atlantic thus looked somewhat bumpy and singularly lacking in uniformity. Each of them found there what he or she was looking for, sometimes overlooking everything else, and without arriving at a complete understanding of American society. Thus the French, with little awareness of the scope of immigration and no points of comparison in their own country, did not grasp the importance of this phenomenon for the United States and made hasty judgments about it. It was easier to harp on subjects with which they were familiar, though always with their own slant. Some admired coeducation yet also rejected its long-term consequences; others envied the standard of living of workers yet also deplored their lack of combativeness vis-à-vis management; and certain observers vaunted the American methods that had produced such great power yet feared its consequences for France and Europe.

Beyond this reluctant fascination, which characterized French opinion as a whole for many years, nuances and differences also came to light. Some of these were related to the events of the period, which gave rise to more misgivings about the United States in the 1870s than was to be the case a quarter-century later. The country's evolution was attractive to those who favored rapid industrial development and by the same token repelled those who were nostalgic for the mythical harmony of the rural world. Over the years the former attitude became increasingly prevalent in France, while the latter declined. It should be added that by the beginning of the twentieth century a solid group of Americanists had come into being; writing for various publications, they regularly "covered" current American events. Such experts as Paul de Rousiers, Urbain Gohier, and Achille Viallate can be cited as representatives of this cohort, which contributed to a better understanding and appreciation of the United States in France.

Nevertheless, certain tendencies are recognizable at any given moment. French attitudes toward the United States were no longer directly determined by political divisions, as had been the case in the first half of the nineteenth century.[2] Most notably, the republican and democratic example across the Atlantic was no longer of much interest in France. The French Republicans, proud of their own achievements, turned away from the model they had adored during the last years of the Second Empire, and Léon Gambetta sneered at its few remaining sympathizers. The monarchists, who had never appreciated Jeffersonian democracy, now liked it rather more than the one that was developing on the banks of the Seine, though not enough to approve of it. Moreover, the American reality was especially striking in its material and social aspects, and these were not subject to political reactions. That is why, when taking in the sights of the streets, studying the spirited girls or rubbing shoulders with blacks, French visitors reacted according to

2. R. Rémond, *Les Etats-Unis devant l'opinion française* (Paris: Colin, 1960).

their personal impulses rather than in keeping with their political orientations or social origins. Similarly, the trusts could be viewed with admiration by proponents of free enterprise such as Paul de Rousiers as well as by the Socialist Paul Lafargue: One saw it as the triumph of efficiency, the other as a lever with which to overthrow capitalist society from within. As for the demonstration of American power as deployed against Spain, the royalists were as worried as many Republicans, from the Marquis de Barral to Juliette Adam.

Despite their sometimes paradoxical positions, the French observers of the United States can be placed into certain distinct groups. The conservatives, both royalist and republican, did not hide their strong dislike of the extreme forms of American democracy, condemning either the regime itself or its deplorable practices. These were also the people who often expressed their concern about the rising tide of strikes in the United States, which they saw as evidence that the New World was losing its principal strength, the absence of social strife. Their ranks included the Cassandras who after 1898 warned of the omnipresent American menace or feared the contagion of barbaric tastes that would harm a culture as refined as that of France. Although this current of opinion became somewhat less popular in the course of the years, it continued to be expressed with great vigor.

On the other side, the Socialists – except for the so-called *possibilists* – also adopted very clear-cut positions. In their view, American democracy was marred by all the flaws of its bourgeois origin; there was hardly any difference between its two parties, and corruption was ravaging the system. The open display of American imperialism spelled the end of the last illusions; the United States obviously had the worldwide ambitions that characterized capitalism. Moreover, the capitalist system was particularly ferocious in that country, as was proven by the repression that occurred in 1877, in 1886, and again in 1894. From the very beginning of our period the Socialists, faithful to their strictly ideological criteria, rejected the American example, and continued to do so at an ever-accelerating pace.

In a curious way, then, the two extremes of French politics joined together in a fierce denunciation of the United States; informed by a strictly ideological logic, their arguments actually came to resemble each other in their violence and their absence of nuances.

It is therefore not surprising that the most subtle analyses of the American reality, as well as the most positive assessments of that country – which made no secret of its shortcomings either – came from the ranks of moderate Republicans and liberals of all stripes. Gustave de Molinari, Paul de Rousiers, André Tardieu, Lazare Weiller, and Urbain Gohier were representative of this tendency. They were part of a loosely defined centrist grouping that occasionally felt challenged by the United States; not that one could already speak of transatlantic solidarity, but here was the beginning of an evolution that would mark the entire twentieth century.

The attitudes toward the United States of these various groupings did not of course add up to a dominant anti-Americanism of the kind that characterized French opinion for most of the following period. At that time American power was not yet great enough to prompt the rejection that was to occur later. Yet expressions of hostility toward the United States, while still only sporadic, were all of the same nature. Here, then, were the roots of anti-Americanism, clearly identifiable by the end of the nineteenth century.

These diverse and complex reactions of French opinion tell us a great deal about its perception of the American future. Americanization, though briefly evoked in the early years of the twentieth century, was not yet truly feared; after all, the United States was still far enough away not to endanger the gentleness of French life and the peaceful ideal to which most French people aspired, whether they were of the middle or the working class, of the Right or of the Left. The American phantasm was still vague, but it helps us understand how the stronger waves of American influence that washed over France in the 1920s and especially after 1945 could bring about, at one and the same time, the easy adoption of pleasant ways and reactions of rejection that had their roots in the French cultural tradition. Yet, as early as 1900, the rising power of the United States had prompted the French to wonder whether its imperialism or the sharp social conflicts that country was experiencing would cause it to become Europeanized, thereby losing much of its originality. Wonder they might, but every facet of American power, while showing a slight European coloration, remained typical of the New World by dint of its mass-oriented cultural choices, its unusual financial methods, and the integration of its immigrants. America and Europe clearly remained distinct, even if their ties were "as close as if the ocean did not exist," and it was not yet obvious which of the two would eventually wield the greatest influence over the other. By contrast, the real gap – which some of the observers liked to overstate – that separated France from the United States gave rise to a new reaction on the part of many French people. Having experienced the American reality first-hand, they fully realized that they were Europeans, for all the admiration and empathy they might have for the Americans. French workers felt greater solidarity for immigrant workers than for born Americans, Baron de Grancey appreciated Germanic domestic virtues while traveling in the Great

American West, and Jules Huret talked to a British waiter, glad to meet another European:

> I spontaneously had a feeling of solidarity for this English waiter. I understood him like a brother. And I said to myself that here, thousands of miles away from their countries, an Englishman and a Frenchman, who in Europe would be aware only of their antagonisms, discovered that they had affinities strong enough to make them feel friendly without knowing each other.[3]

The shock of the United States was strong enough to prompt such reactions. And these were not a matter of rapprochement among Latin peoples as they had been in the first half of the nineteenth century; they signaled the emergence of a European sentiment. To be sure, this new awareness remained fragile, and the United States was indeed part of a vast occidental community, as was frequently noted by French travelers who had come there by way of Asia.

The contradictions between these two views consistently permeated French opinion; there was an admiring fascination for that faraway and nearby, foreign and familiar country, but there were also misgivings about its brutality, its greed, and its impressive but frightening efficiency.

The United States thus became increasingly present in French opinion; its presence was not yet sufficient to cause serious rifts, but it was already enough to raise all the questions France would have to face in the twentieth century that had just begun.

3. J. Huret, *En Amérique* (Paris: Fasquelle, 1905), vol. 2, p. 209.

# Selective Bibliography

The French volume corresponding to this book was published in France in 1990. Since then, there have not been many new books on French opinion of the United States, except for a few that focus on recent time periods and use as their sources opinion surveys for which data is not available prior to the 1930s. For this reason, the sources and bibliography from the French version of this book are still relevant.

A list of all books and periodicals studied for this book would not be useful to the English-speaking reader; these references may be found in the notes. Nevertheless, it is useful to explain how this work was conceived and to provide insights on some methodological books that could still be of use. A few titles published in the 1990s on related topics of interest are also indicated.

The study of public opinion has to be done methodically, as such an approach could be limitless. Though public opinion includes the views of the entire populace, only opinions expressed in print or registered in some way can be studied. In the nineteenth century, the print media was the only way to present one's views, so I used for this study nearly all the books and booklets about the United States published in France during this time. These include travelogues as well as general surveys, ambitious syntheses, and case studies – in total, about 500 travelers' memoirs and 600 other titles. I also selected some journals – *Revue des Deux Mondes, Correspondant, Revue de Paris, Nouvelle Revue, Journal des Economistes, Revue Socialiste* – and went through all their issues of the period to evaluate and ponder what they said about the United States. These journals represent, more or less, the principal tendencies of French opinion from 1870 to 1914. It would have been difficult to study the daily press over such a long period, and content analysis would have been pointless. Instead, I selected some events that would have attracted the press: presidential elections, international visits, crises, and so forth.

Based on such a study, and without the use of scientific polls, I could assume to have an accurate picture of French public opinion about the United States. Of course, it could still be possible to discover a new book or to investigate issues of some specialized journals, but the findings would not be likely to change my conclusions; they would only provide more examples of the fundamental ambivalence of the French toward the United States.

To organize this study, it was necessary to use directories such as W. G. Leland, *Guide to Material for American History in the Libraries and Archives of Paris* (Washington, 1932); G. Barringer, *Catalogue d'histoire de l'Amérique* (Paris, 1903); and Frank Monaghan, *French Travellers in the United States, 1765–1931: A Bibliography* (New York, 1933 and 1961). Some of these books, which at the time of the original research for this book could be found only in the buildings of major libraries, are now available easily at various websites and also at the site of the Bibliothèque Nationale in Paris, www.bnf.fr.

On the theory of public opinion, *Public Opinion Quarterly* has been useful, especially volume 31, number 4, Winter 1967–1968, as has *Relations internationales*, volume 41, 1985. Some good insights came from Jean-Baptiste Duroselle, *Tout empire périra, vision théorique des relations internationales* (Paris, 1981), and from Melvin Small, ed., *Public Opinion and Historians* (Detroit, 1970). *L'image de l'autre*, Rapport's Sixteenth International Congress of Historical Sciences, Stuttgart, 1985 (Paris, 1985), emphasized, as the theme of a major conference, new approaches to an old question. More recently, Akira Iriye, *Cultural Internationalism and World Order* (Baltimore, 1997), broke new ground by linking cultural exchanges, national perceptions, and international relations.

Franco-American relations of the period have been studied by Henry Blumenthal in *France and the United States: Their Diplomatic Relations, 1789–1914* (Chapel Hill, N.C., 1970) and *American and French Culture, 1800–1900* (Baton Rouge, La., 1975). The reader might also see Clarence Brinton, *The American and the French* (Cambridge, Mass., 1968), and Jean-Baptiste Duroselle, *La France et les États-Unis des origines à nos jours* (Paris, 1976). For the gift of Miss Liberty, see Marvin Trachtenberg's account, *The Statue of Liberty* (New York, 1986).

Other European views of the United States provided especially interesting comparisons. Most of these studies are not recent, but some take interesting approaches: R. H. Heindel, *The American Impact on Great Britain, 1898–1914* (Philadelphia, 1940); Richard L. Rapson, *Britons View America: Travel Commentary, 1860–1935* (Seattle, 1971); R. Laurence Moore, *European Socialists and the American Promised Land* (New

York, 1970); and Andrew J. Torrielli, *Italian Opinions on America as Revealed by Italian Travelers* (Cambridge, Mass., 1941).

Quite a few titles are devoted to French opinion of the United States in periods before or after that covered in this study. These include Donald Allen, *French Views of America in the 1930s* (New York, 1979); Durand Echeverria, *Mirage in the West: A History of the French Image of American Society to 1815* (Princeton, N.J., 1957); Simon Jeune, *De F. T. Graindorge à A.O. Barnabooth, les Types américains dans le roman et le théâtre français, 1861–1917* (Paris, 1963); and Denis Lacorne, Jacques Rupnick, and Marie-France Toinet, *L'Amérique dans les têtes: Un siècle de fascination et d'aversion* (Paris, 1986), translated as *The Rise and Fall of Anti-Americanism: A Century of French Perception* (New York, 1990). René Rémond, *Les États-Unis devant l'opinion française, 1815–1852* (Paris, 1962), is a seminal study, though more concerned with French political opinion than with the impact of the United States on France. A very interesting dissertation, never published, is Thomas A. Sancton, "America in the Eyes of the French Left, 1848–1871," Oxford University, 1978.

It was also essential to read about the history of France between 1870 and 1914, as well as about the history of the United States in the same period. Many books proved useful in understanding how each country fared during that time and also in seeing how French observations could be linked to actual American history and life. I have accumulated this knowledge during years of teaching and from many diverse sources. Only a few surveys can be listed here: Yves Lequin, *Histoire des Français, XIX^e siècle–XX^e siècles* (Paris, 1984); Alain Plessis, *De la Fête impériale au mur des fédérés, 1852–1872* (Paris, 1975); Jean-Marie Mayeur, *Les débuts de la Troisième république, 1871–1898* (Paris, 1978); and Madeleine Rébérioux, *La République radicale, 1899–1914* (Paris, 1980). Sometimes irritating, but always stimulating, is Theodore Zeldin, *France 1848–1945*, vol. 1: *Ambition, Love and Politics*, and vol. 2: *Intellect, Taste and Anxiety* (New York, 1973 and 1977). Also see Eugen Weber, *Fin de Siècle, la France à la fin du XIX^e siècle* (Paris, 1986). For the United States, Loren P. Beth, *The Development of the American Constitution, 1877–1917* (New York, 1971); Eleann Flexner, *Century of Struggle* (New York, 1958); Wayne H. Morgan, *From Hayes to McKinley: National Party Politics, 1877–1896* (Syracuse, N.Y., 1969); and Martin J. Schiesl, *The Politics of Efficiency: Municipal Administration and Reform in America, 1880–1920* (Berkeley, Calif., 1977), have been useful, as have Kenneth Stampp, *The Era of Reconstruction, 1867–1877* (New York, 1964), and, for a better view of what America was at the time, Time-Life's *This Fabulous Century, 1870–1900* (1970). Since the 1970s, thousands of books have been published on the period covered by this book; these are noted in Eric Foner, *The New American History* (Philadelphia, 1990).

Since the publication of the French version of this book, a few studies have been published on subjects related to it but not about the same period. These could be interesting to a reader eager to work on such topics. Some of the books devoted to exchanges between France and the United States document interesting conflicts of opinion, as France may be seen as the most prominent example in Europe of a stubborn resistance against American influence. See Catherine Durandin, *La France et l'Amérique* (Paris, 1995); Pierre Guerlain, *Miroirs Transatlantiques: La France et les États-Unis entre Passions et Indifférences* (Paris, 1996); Richard Kuisel, *Seducing the French: The Dilemma of Americanization* (Berkeley, Calif., 1993); Harvey Levenstein, *Seductive Journey: American Tourists in France from Jefferson to the Jazz Age* (Chicago, 1998) (a very pleasant book that may be used as a source of comparison with the first part of this one); and Jean-Philippe Mathy, *Extrême-Occident: French Intellectuals and America* (Chicago, 1993). Eugen Weber, *My France: Politics, Culture, Myth* (Cambridge, Mass., 1991), was the last overview by a great scholar of France.

Some other works are larger in scope, dealing with all of Europe. Richard Pells, *Not Like Us: How Europeans Have Loved, Hated and Transformed American Culture since World War II* (New York, 1997), documents how each European country created its own answer to American influence. Daniel T. Rodgers, *Atlantic Crossings: Social Politics in a Progressive Age* (Cambridge, Mass., 1998), emphasizes the numerous exchanges between those who worked in intellectual and social fields in European countries and in the United States.

In all these studies, the reader will find the trend of anti-Americanism. Forgotten for some years, this topic has recently enjoyed a resurgence as American world power has again come to be viewed as hegemonic. It could be interesting to compare current opinion to the first wave of anti-Americanism, which flourished at the turn of the twentieth century. Useful works on this topic include Tom Bishop, ed., *Anti-Americanisms* (New York, 2000); Paul Hollander, *Anti-Americanism: Critiques at Home and Abroad*, 1965–1990 (New York, 1992); Rob Kroes, ed., *Anti-Americanism in Europe* (Amsterdam, 1986); Jean-Philippe Mathy, *French Resistance: The French American Culture Wars* (St. Paul, Minn., 2000); and David Strauss, *Menace in the West: The Rise of French Anti-Americanism in Modern Times* (Westport, Conn., 1978).

# Index